Descartes

Descartes is often regarded as the founder of modern philosophy and is credited with placing the question of what we know and how we know it at centre stage. *Descartes: Belief, Scepticism and Virtue* seeks to reinsert his work and thought in its contemporary ethical and theological context.

Richard Davies mobilises the recently emerging notion of intellectual virtue to understand Descartes' philosophical enterprise as a whole. He examines the textual dynamics of Descartes' most famous writings in relation to background debates about human endeavour from Plato down to Descartes' own contemporaries. Bringing these materials together in an innovative format, Davies argues for a new approach to Descartes' ideas of scepticism and the sciences. The book also offers fresh interpretations of key passages from the *Meditations*.

Descartes: Belief, Scepticism and Virtue offers an original reassessment of some of the most important bodies of work in western philosophy.

Richard Davies is Professor of the History of Philosophy at the University of Bergamo, Italy.

Routledge Studies in Seventeenth-Century Philosophy

Descartes

Belief, scepticism and virtue

Richard Davies

London and New York

First published 2001
by Routledge
11 New Fetter Lane, London EC4P 4EE

Simultaneously published in the USA and Canada
by Routledge
29 West 35th Street, New York, NY 10001

Routledge is an imprint of the Taylor & Francis Group

© 2001 Richard Davies

Typeset in Baskerville by
M Rules
Printed and bound in Great Britain by
TJ International, Padstow, Cornwall

British Library Cataloguing in Publication Data
A catalogue record for this book is available from the British
Library

Library of Congress Cataloging in Publication Data
Davies, Richard, 1959
    Descartes: belief, scepticism and virtue/Richard Davies.
        p. cm. – (Routledge studies in seventeenth-century philosophy)
    Includes bibliographical references and index.
    1. Descartes, René, 1596–1650. I. Title. II. Series.
    B1873.D38 2001
    194–dc21   00–069036

ISBN 0–415–25122–2 (hbk)

Contents

Acknowledgements

My longest-standing debts remain to my undergraduate teachers at Cambridge, especially Nick Denyer and Robert Wardy, both of whom have persisted over the years in letting me inflict pieces of my prose on them. Likewise, my graduate supervisor, the late Renford Bambrough, was almost recklessly indulgent in allowing me to pursue an absurdly ambitious project of which some of the things I suspect about Descartes are fragments of a fragment. I did, in the end, produce a doctoral thesis, which was kindly read by John Cottingham and Sue James, both of whom had commented most penetratingly on earlier versions. Others who have put up with drafts and related writings include Myles Burnyeat, Edward Craig, Chris Hookway and Geoffrey Lloyd. I also owe thanks to those who made the period I spent in Birmingham less dispiriting than I would otherwise have found it: Nick Dent, Donald Peterson and the late Barrie Falk.

Since moving to Italy, I have been warmly welcomed by many people, including Giovanni Reale and Roberto Radice of the Università Cattolica in Milan, who have given me unlooked-for opportunities for research and publication. Most of all, I am very grateful to Alberto Castoldi in Bergamo for practical kindnesses of many sorts, encouraging and enabling me to press on with my own business, and in particular for giving permission on behalf of the Bergamo University Press to repropose in a new guise material from my *Descartes' Cultivation of the Intellect* (1999).

I dedicate the book to Alessandra, aware that it will never be enough.

RD
Bergamo

Abbreviations

See also Bibliography and Index of primary texts

Descartes

Con.: *Conversation with Burman*
Des.: *Description of the Human Body*
Dis.: *Discourse* by part
LP: 'Letter-Preface' to the French edition of the *Principles*
Lum.: *Discourse on Light* by discourse
Med.: *Meditations* by day
Met.: *Meteors* by discourse
Not.: *Notes on a Certain Programme* by article
Obj.: *Objections* by group and, where sub-divided, number
Pass.: *Passions* by part and article
Pr.: *Principles* by part and article
Re.: *Search*
Reg.: *Rules* by rule
Resp.: *Replies* by group and, where sub-divided, number

Plato

Ep.: *Letters* by number and Stephanus (vol. III) page
Euth.: *Euthyphro* by Stephanus (vol. I) page
Gorg.: *Gorgias* by Stephanus (vol. I) page
Men.: *Meno* by Stephanus (vol. II) page
Parm.: *Parmenides* by Stephanus (vol. III) page
Phædr.: *Phædrus* by Stephanus (vol. III) page
Rep.: *Philebus* by Stephanus (vol. II) page
Rep.: *Republic* by book and Stephanus (vol. II) page
Soph.: *Sophist* by Stephanus (vol. I) page

Theaet: *Theaetetus* by Stephanus (vol. I) page
Tim.: *Timaeus* by Stephanus (vol. III) page

Aristotle

AnPo.: *Posterior Analytics* by book and chapter, with Bekker page
Cæl.: *De Cælo*, by book and chapter, with Bekker page
Cat.: *Categories* by chapter, with Bekker page
De An.: *De Anima* by book and chapter, with Bekker page
EE: *Eudemian Ethics* by book and chapter, with Bekker page
EN: *Nicomachean Ethics* by book and chapter, with Bekker page
MM: *Magna Moralia* by book and chapter, with Bekker page
Mem.: *On Memory and Recollection* by book and chapter, with Bekker page
Metaph.: *Metaphysics* by book and chapter, with Bekker page
PA.: *Parts of Animals* by book and chapter, with Bekker page
Phys.: *Physics* by book and chapter, with Bekker page

Stoics

SVF: *Stoicorum Veterum Fragmenta* by Von Arnim volume and fragment number

Sextus Empiricus

PH: *Outlines of Pyrrhonism* by book and section
Adv. Math.: *Against the Mathematicians* by book and section

Plutarch

Adv. Col.: *Adversus Colotem* by Xylander page

Cicero

Acad.: *Academica* (= Cicero 1885) by book and section
Div.: *On Divination* (= Cicero 1933) by book and section
Fin.: *De Finibus* (= Cicero 1876) by book and section
Tusc.: *Tusculan Disputations* (= Cicero 1996) by book and section

St Augustine of Hippo

Acad.: *Contra Academicos* by book and section

Civ.: *De Civitate Dei* by book and section
Conf.: *Confessions* by book, chapter and section
Corr.: *De Correptione et Gratia* by book and section
Imp.: *Opus imperfectum* by chapter
Lib. Arb.: *De Libero Arbitrio* by book, section and paragraph
Mag.: *De Magistro* by section and paragraph
Nat.: *De Natura et Gratia* by section
Ret.: *Retractationes* by book and section
Sol.: *Soliloquia* by book, section and paragraph

St Anselm of Aosta/Bec/Canterbury

Lib. Arb.: *De Libertate Arbitrii* by chapter

St Thomas Aquinas

ST: *Summa Theologiæ* (= Aquinas 1962) by part, question and article

Lucretius

DRN: *De Rerum Natura* by book and line

Other

PL: *Patrologia Latina* (221 vols), (1844–55) edited by
J.-P. Migne, Paris: Imprimerie Catholique

Introduction

Motivation

The account of Descartes' thought presented in this essay is an effort to answer the question: 'why should anyone bother with the sort of enquiry that Descartes describes?'

The puzzle that makes this question worth asking and answering is that quite a few people have studied, many have read, and large swathes of our culture have been influenced, both directly and indirectly, by Descartes; but I doubt that more than a very few people have ever followed the guidance Descartes repeatedly gives for the conduct of an enquiry. For instance, very few people, if any, have ever sought to impose on themselves the conditions of seclusion that Descartes thinks necessary for success in his undertaking. As few have sought really to rid themselves of all their prior opinions in order to philosophise. And probably even fewer have been prepared to seek clear and distinct ideas to the exclusion of all other. And so on; but these will do for now. That is, the overwhelming majority of people, including the people who have studied, read or been influenced by Descartes, have refused outright to adopt the most basic presuppositions of what he has to say.

Why has Descartes' theory of enquiry had so few takers? Naturally, there are many quick answers. Because it is silly. Because it is a long way round. Because it is impractical. Because it presupposes Cartesianism. Because it ends you up with Cartesianism. As with other quick answers, there is something in each of these. But there is also the fact that *Descartes* was a taker. This being so, we face two pretty clear options, on which, of course, many variations could be embroidered.

On the one hand, we might think, as some commentators do think, that all the studying, reading and influencing that has been going on for three hundred and fifty years has been a dreadful mistake. I propose no stronger reason against this than the consideration that is it uncharitable both to Descartes and to all those who, in varying degrees, have fallen under his spell.

If there has been a dreadful mistake, and Descartes' theory of enquiry is, in the end, so much silly, diversionary, impractical or merely circular stuff, then there is not a lot that further consideration of Descartes can really do about that. Indeed, a further assault on Descartes, of the sort that has been fashionable of late, would itself serve mainly to reinforce his position as a figure who must be read and studied and who, therefore, will continue to be influential. This would perpetuate rather than resolve the puzzle from which I begin.

In the alternative, we might try supposing that there is more to the theory of enquiry that makes his untoward and unadopted demands than meets the eye. Might there not be something behind his apparently grotesque antics that merits serious attention, whether or not we can, in the end, believe it? Some supposition of this sort is called for to make Descartes – or any other philosopher – worth studying at all. A readiness to find something serious would be common ground, I should hope and expect, to everyone who thinks that the history of philosophy can be fruitful, both as history and as philosophy. Indeed, it is so common a premise as to be too thin to build much on. We need to flesh it out with the particulars of the bit of history and the bit of philosophy that are at issue. At some stage, there must come into play a perception of what would help to account for the things that Descartes says about the nature of enquiry and, most urgently, for their basic presuppositions. Most of this book is meant to give textual and contextual corroboration for one elementary perception about the case in hand.

The perception that I am thinking of as elementary is that the conditions of seclusion, the riddance of prior opinions and the attention to clear and distinct ideas (and many other more specific Cartesian views) are all set to avoid or overcome factors that make the gaining of knowledge difficult or impossible. In the case in hand, the setup that Descartes recommends as a basic presupposition of what he has to say should help us steer between two particularly bad habits that have obstructed most human efforts at gaining knowledge. The bad habits are (i) accepting as true things that we cannot know to be so, which I call 'credulity' and (ii) not accepting as true things that we can know to be so, which, following precedent, is called 'scepticism'. Descartes' claim would be that, in conditions of seclusion, rid of our prior opinions and by attending exclusively to clear and distinct ideas, we can steer between these two bad habits and thus gain a good deal of knowledge that it is otherwise difficult or impossible to gain.

The model adopted to try and make this claim a bit more alluring derives from longstanding theories of the virtues. Though the elementary perception probably could be worked through without the model, the tradition of virtue theory provides shortcuts to useful terminology and well-contextualised distinctions. It also focuses on what lies between the bad habits, namely a virtue.

In looking for the virtue that is staked out by the avoidance of credulity and scepticism, we get a measure of how delicate an operation Descartes is wanting to put through and of how special the equipment is that is called for to put it through.

The operation is delicate because Descartes has a vivid sense of how easy it is to fail in gaining knowledge by falling into bad habits. This is already a strong reason for us to seclude ourselves from current influences. It is also a reason for trying to rid ourselves of our prior opinions: once we accept that we have made a mess of gaining knowledge in the past, we should not trust to precedent.

The special equipment needed to perform this delicate operation comes in two main parts. One is an *infallible guide* to what is true and what may not be. For Descartes, this is the understanding or intellect, which distinguishes between clear and distinct ideas, and others. The clear and distinct ones are true and all others may not be. So the other piece of equipment that is needed is an *ability to follow* the infallible guide. This turns out to be the absolute power of the will over the beliefs we form.

Humans may, as a matter of fact, lack the special equipment that Descartes says they need if they are going to cultivate the virtue that lies between credulity and scepticism, and thus gain knowledge that it would otherwise be difficult or impossible to gain. If so, knowledge of the sort he thinks it is worth going for may not be available at all to humans. But virtually no one seems to have tried as hard as Descartes did to isolate and use the special equipment he says we have. If, then, we are prepared to see why he is so keen to show that humans do have an intellect and a will of the sort needed for what he wants, then much that has been found hard to account for in his writings at least falls into place.

A great deal of the detail of what I have to say about Descartes is indebted to other commentators. But the overall thoughts just outlined seem to me to be novel. To work them through, I employ a structure that differs from the main patterns for books on Descartes. On the one hand, there are general or introductory books that follow the sequence of the questions raised in a given text, normally the *Meditations*; on the other, there are those that follow the chronological order of his thinking and writing over the arc of his life. Instead, we start with the vice of credulity and describe how Descartes thinks it can be tamed by the will. Then I look at how scepticism works before illustrating how the intellect keeps it at bay. Only lastly do I get round to where most books on Descartes start, and discuss what both he and many subsequent commentators call his 'method'.

This choice of structure has two immediate consequences.

One is that I bypass some of the most widely and deeply discussed topics in Descartes studies: the *cogito*, the arguments for the existence of God, the so-called 'Circle', and the relations of mind to body, to name but four. I have, and sometimes mention, my views on these and other vexed questions, but I try to keep them in the background. And perhaps these are the points on which the mass of exegetical, commentarial and plain philosophical work of others has been of greatest use to me in picking out the positions that I am not here concerned or able to defend.

The other consequence is that the reader might lose the thread. What I am presenting as novel may just seem perverse or muddled. So I have tried to give a fair amount of sign-posting. There is quite a lot of cross-referencing among parts of the text. And I have given what I hope are indicative titles and sub-titles and sub-sub-titles to chapters and sections and sub-sections. In addition, I here offer a chapter-by-chapter summary of what I am up to.

The plot

Chapter 1 homes in on the intellectual virtue that I shall be calling 'doxastic rectitude' and that will be central to my account of Descartes' epistemology. Though the words are rather alien to Descartes, and will be considered in more detail as we proceed, examination of the vices to which doxastic rectitude is opposed will give us reason for beginning our enquiry by investigating credulity as the more widespread and more deep-rooted of the two.

Chapter 2 pursues the analogy between excess in belief-formation and excess in the passions. We know that we suffer from the latter: we are all more subject to the influence of the world around us than we would like to be. Descartes offers a bit of moral theory on which, he says, the cultivation of a virtue that he calls 'generosity' can help us overcome the upsets that go with having to deal with the fact that our bodies are placed in a world in which unexpected things can happen. Doxastic rectitude is the epistemological analogue of Cartesian generosity.

Chapter 3 examines how Descartes recounts his discovery of the fact that, up to the moment when we begin to philosophise about knowledge, human beings are prey to the generalised vice of credulity. In his three best-known philosophical books, the *Discourse*, the *Meditations* and the *Principles* this discovery is made in rather different ways. The differences in the ways the discovery is made tell us something about the kind of book each is. All three tend to the conclusion that almost all the beliefs we have ever formed, being based on the deliverances of the senses, are not merely false, but of completely the wrong sort and lead to a wildly mistaken picture of the world as a whole. This raises questions about whether there is anything we can, and how much we should, do about it and when.

The next two chapters seek to elucidate Descartes' doctrine on the power we have to determine the quality of our beliefs. I suggest that the main context in which this doctrine can be explored is the theological problem of evil.

In Chapter 4, we consider Descartes' reasons for thinking that error is a condition that needs to be explained: given both the divine veracity that he argues for in *Meditations* III, and the perfection of our faculty for judging that he discusses at the beginning of *Meditations* IV, we ought to be surprised that we ever assent to ideas that are not true and dissent from ideas that are not merely true, but that are guaranteed true. This encourages him to make a very strong distinction between the operation of the intellect as a container of ideas and that of the will as the agent of assent: while man's intellect is finite, his will is like God's in being infinite. Taking into account some of the traditional positions on free choice and the motivation of action, we see that Descartes' suggested solution is a variant on views that were respectable in the seventeenth century, which helps to explain why it caused relatively little comment among his contemporaries, and may be why it has been relatively little discussed by more recent commentators.

The fifth chapter then moves to look at Descartes' doctrine of assent as an operation of the will. In the first place, I try to clarify the relations between an idea's having *ratio* and the concurrence of the two faculties that Descartes distinguishes within the process of judging. This then leads to the question of how, on his theory, we are able to decide to believe. Against an objection raised by Hobbes and since repeated, I argue that Descartes' account does justice to an important feature of enquiring as an active enterprise, in which we can regulate assent. The leading analogy here is between a human's reasons for believing and God's selection of the eternal truths. This analogy is then used to throw light on Descartes' doctrine that we can dissent even from an idea that we see to be clear and distinct; thus we appear to be wholly responsible for the beliefs we have, and nothing can compel our choices.

Chapters 6 and 7 both discuss scepticism, which is the vice of defect in belief-formation.

Chapter 6 takes on the sort of scepticism that was a common move in Descartes' day. This can be called 'Pyrrhonism' and has to do with the building up of the ability to suspend judgment. I suggest that Descartes accepts large amounts of this material, as applied both to the conduct of ordinary life and to the conduct of enquiry: he rejects on Pyrrhonist grounds the idea that we can make any use of other people's views, but allows that we do sometimes have to act even when we can get no sure beliefs. Granted the power to keep the interferences that cause credulous belief in their place, we should consider the circumstances in which we have no special need for that power. These are the ideal circumstances of enquiry properly so-called, which involve cutting oneself off from everyday activities and, indeed, from anything that depends on contingent circumstances.

Chapter 7 investigates what Descartes adds to scepticism, with a model to account for the procedure of *Meditations* I. I try to show that Descartes distinguishes the scope of the doubts arising from the possibilities that he might be dreaming and that a demon is deceiving him. What he says to resolve the former doubt is less than convincing. But what others have said about the latter is even less so. In particular, I argue that Descartes nowhere does anything to prove that there is no malicious demon. If there might, for all we know, be a malicious demon, then we have to pay attention only to the ideas that he could not interfere with. These are innate in us. Those of them that we can make clear and distinct to ourselves are those that we can use in science.

Chapter 8 recounts in some detail the four precepts of *Discourse* II with attention to the failings they are meant to put us on our guard against. This gives us all there is of the 'method'. And it is not as much as many commentators have wanted. That is why I prefer to talk about the virtue of doxastic rectitude: it does not raise unfulfillable expectations, and even if the method looks meagre, we could not reasonably ask for more.

The last three chapters seek to give the outlines of what enquiry in accordance with rectitude involves.

The first part is positive: in Chapter 9, we examine what virtue requires and the shape that a completed science should take. Taking a few instances of Descartes' scientific practice, we see that the beginning of enquiry and the various stages in its prosecution and confirmation all make essential use of the innate ideas that we can make clear and distinct to ourselves in such a way as to build up a body of knowledge that should ultimately extend to all the things that we can and need to know about.

The following chapter examines the subordinate role that experience can have in guiding and stimulating virtuous enquiry. In particular, we try to find the places that moral certainty, hypotheses, observation of effects and other empirical expedients must occupy to support the overall structure of science as an enquiry into the rationally intuitable structure of reality as a whole.

Finally, Chapter 11 considers two classes of beliefs that are not sustained by doxastic rectitude. One is a class of falsehoods that cannot be arrived at by virtuous enquiry, but that are in conflict with what can be arrived at by natural means. The other is a class of truths that are supernaturally revealed and that are at odds with what we might arrive at on our own. While the first class has to be rejected, Descartes supposes that those in the second have to be embraced, even though we may have little more than good grounds for preferring them to the natural light of reason.

References

References to Descartes appear in brackets in the text, with the abbreviated title of the work cited and (where appropriate) the part, as set out in the List of abbreviations and Index of primary texts. This is followed (where possible) by a reference to volume and page of the translations by Cottingham, Stoothoff, Murdoch and Kenny (CSM(K)). I am much indebted to this translation. The English I supply is my own, with little distinction between paraphrases and what I might wish to present as my own versions. In cases where there are cross-references to a number of Cartesian texts, some of them may be relegated wholly to an endnote. In cases where the original text may be of interest or some point of language is in play, the CSM(K) reference is followed either by the relevant excerpt or by a reference to an endnote, in which the Latin and/or French is carried; the Latin has been standardised and the French has been modernised in accordance with the practice of Alquié (Descartes 1963–73), but the reference is given to the volume, part (where appropriate) and page of the revised and expanded edition of Adam and Tannery (AT). In cases where there is a substantial point of translation, alternative English and other versions may be cited in the notes as secondary sources. In two sorts of cases the AT reference appears in brackets in the text: one is when it accompanies a word or phrase that is quoted in Latin or French; the other is when CSM(K) does not supply a translation.

References to other primary sources, where there are standard editions, are by the abbreviations as set out in the List of abbreviations and Index of primary texts. In other cases, reference must be made to the Bibliography.

References to secondary sources basically follow the Harvard name-date-page system, keyed into the Bibliography; citations are made by the date of first relevant publication, though the publishing data refer to the text actually consulted. Where secondary sources are cited in translation in the text, the original is only very rarely supplied in an endnote. In some cases, the endnote develops some point at issue in the text.[1]

Part I

Structures

1 Intellectual virtues

Some structures of virtue

Straightening a stick

The scheme I adopt for setting out Descartes' theory of knowledge embodies a range of structural and conceptual features that can be traced in Aristotle's thought about the moral virtues. This latter is well-known and relatively well-understood material which has generated a large secondary literature of its own, to some of which I refer to make some of my more unfamiliar attributions to Descartes seem less wayward.

The most general structure that is indebted to Aristotle is the doctrine that a moral virtue is opposed to two vices, which are themselves opposites. Thus, at *EN*, II vii, 1107 a 33, Aristotle alludes to a diagram of the virtues and their opposed vices that may have been hanging on the wall of his lecture room (Jackson 1920), one version of which is in the text at *EE*, II iii, 1220 b 38–1 a 12, another of which is supplied in Aristotle (1953: 104). For instance, the virtue of courage is opposed to two vices: cowardice and rashness. Both of the vices are harmful to their possessor and to others, though in differing respects and at different times. In each person, the vicious tendencies will be active in different strengths.

The resulting triad provides the organisation of the following chapters into parts: first we investigate the vice of *excess* in one department of the theory of knowledge. Thus, as rashness stands as an excess relative to courage, so credulity is an excess in belief-formation. Then we see how Descartes understands the opposed vice of *defect*. As cowardice is the defect of courage, so scepticism is the failure to acquire beliefs to which we are properly entitled. Lastly, we look at the *mean* between them and the beliefs it requires, permits and forbids. Where some recent studies of Descartes have concentrated almost exclusively on scepticism and the sceptic, I aim first to illustrate how the excess of credulity constitutes a difficulty that is in several important respects prior to the defect of scepticism. The threat posed by human credulity calls for an account of the resources we have for controlling the beliefs we have and, thus, for a theory of assent and dissent that allows us to tread between the opposed vices. With this material in place, we shall be able to locate better the virtue, namely doxastic rectitude, that lies between them and understand what its actualisation amounts to.

The hope on which my choice of this articulation rests is that, by bearing in mind the terminology, the structures and expectations of virtue theory, we can overcome some standing obscurities in the reading of Descartes. If that hope is justified, then I shall have provided the means to reduce some imbalances and distortions that have crept into Cartesian studies and into epistemology in his wake. Thus, my central claim is that by applying virtue-theoretic insights we can do better for Descartes than many other ways of building on or replying to him.

Genera of virtue

But, first, a step back to get a broader view of the structures of virtues and vices that can be used to help bring these points to the fore.

One very standard taxonomy of the virtues generally divides them into the moral, the theological and the intellectual. Each of these categories has its own more or less standardised sub-divisions. The standardisation is perhaps most entrenched in treatments of the cardinal theological or 'deiform' virtues; at least since St Augustine, there is relatively little dispute about what the virtues are: and they are set out in the Bible as faith, hope and charity (I *Corinthians*, 1: 13). Presumably this is because those who give prominence to these virtues as theological are already party to a vision with a fairly unified source, namely, the medieval syntheses of Platonic and Aristotelian theory with Judeo-Christian revelation.

There is somewhat more debate about how the cardinal theological virtues are constituted and about their mutual relations. For instance, for St Thomas, it is only accidentally (relative to God) that the theological virtues are to be considered as lying in a mean, though there are human standards that apply (*ST*, Ia IIæ, qu. 64 art. iv). For this reason, the theological virtues do not provide a particularly illuminating model for what I want to say about Cartesian epistemology. This is not to deny, what I shall, in fact, frequently assert, that Descartes' basic view of the acquisition of human knowledge is theocentric and influenced by the particular revelation of the Bible and subsequent tradition.

There is rather less agreement about the right account of the moral virtues. Indeed, in the next chapter, I shall sketch the elements of a virtue theory that is non-Aristotelian in character and derivation, and that is attributable to Descartes. This is a Stoic theory, according to which the individuation of the particular virtues is a secondary matter to hammering home the idea that everything that is not under our immediate control is harmful.

Nevertheless, thinkers who have pursued, and still pursue, lines similar to Aristotle's need to determine which virtues are to be regarded as those that contribute most to a flourishing life. For instance, Aristotle gives great prominence to the sort of courage a man needed in the sort of war that was fought in his day (*EN*, III vi–ix) and he seems to take military courage to be a paradigmatic case of the virtue (*EN*, III viii). Yet, it is far from certain that courage of that particular sort, or indeed (physical) courage in any marked degree, should have the same centrality in considering the sort of life that is lived by most people in the West today. Again, there are well-known issues to be raised and settled about whether prudence or practical reason (φρόνησις) is a properly moral or an intellectual virtue; and about whether justice is a moral virtue of a specially other-regarding kind or the whole of political virtue. In considering these virtues, he does not, of course, deny either that all virtues may have some application in all spheres of life; the point, rather, seems to be that there are virtues that are equally applicable in each, as justice is identified as the complete, global or overarching virtue in *EN*, V i, 1129 b 31, and, in VI xviii, 1145 a 1–2, practical wisdom is said to be a virtue whose presence implies the presence of all the others. Some of the ways of raising and settling these questions are at least partly a matter of terminology; but such choices can have far-reaching effects on the complexion of the resulting vision, especially concerning the interrelations of the moral virtues on which we concentrate.

There is least standardisation of all when we turn to the intellectual virtues; here the picture seems to be much hazier and the room for stipulation much greater. In part, this is because one of the templates that one might think of using to begin marking out the territory – the sixth book of *EN* – is a curiously structured review of rather heterogeneous types of operation. The same can be said of the parallel passages in *EE*, V and of the highly compressed jumble of similar material in *MM*, I xxxiv, 1196 b 4–8 b 20. Though *EN*, VI presents itself as enquiring into the right principle that determines the mean between excess and defect generally (*EN*, VI i, 1138 b 20–1), it proceeds to run through some of the modes or states that are involved in the soul's arriving at truth by affirming or denying (*EN*, VI iii, 1139 b 15ff.) offering a survey that carries on to the end of the sixth chapter (1141 b 23), and then turns (or perhaps returns) to consider prudence in relation to politics and to other mental attainments.

At the very least, Aristotle's treatment in *EN*, VI is cursory and unsystematic when compared, for instance, with the more careful discriminations he employs in II vii to differentiate the functions of the various moral virtues, as having to do with the regulation of particular emotions, such as fear and confidence (1107 b 1), to do with identifiable spheres of activity, such as giving and getting money (1107 b 9), or to do with specifiable types of goods, such as honour (1107 b 22). The differentiæ he uses there provide not merely a sort of table of contents for the second part of Book III and Books IV and V, but also an understanding of the ways that certain virtues have their characteristic reference-points. Aristotle here gives a significantly more focused sense of what is involved in the moral virtues he discusses, than he does after the transition at the beginning of VI ii that introduces his discussion of the grades and types of knowledge that he stakes out.

It is also noticeable that, in his discussion of the intellectual virtues, Aristotle makes very little reference to the triadic structure to which I have already referred and that underpins his occasional admissions that there are virtues and vices for which we have no particular name, even though the structure can lead us to see what such dispositions must be. Thus, relative to temperance (σωφροσύνη), there is the excess vice of profligacy (ἀκόλασία), but the defect of taking too little pleasure, which is a sort of insensibility (ἀναισθησία), being very rare, does not have a special name *as a vice* (*EN*, III xi, 1119 a 6–12); it is *as a vice* that this sort of insensibility has no name in the sense that the use of the name is not, on its own, a way of condemning someone. But, it is easy to think that some sorts of insensibility – for instance to the relatively sophisticated pleasures of art-appreciation – do tell us something damning (though perhaps not 'morally' damning) about the person to whom they are attributed. Similarly, Aristotle notes the lack of a name for the virtue in the mean between the excess of overweeningness and the defect of unambitiousness at *EN*, II vii, 1107 b 30–5 and IV iv, 1125 b 24–6.[1]

Genus and species

Even if *EN*, VI does not provide a very satisfactory guide to follow, we can still take a hint from Aristotle's better practice – when he is dealing with the moral virtues – to individuate intellectual virtues.

There is more than one way we might do this.

We might want to distinguish some intellectual capacities in terms of their objects in order to capture the obvious differences among and within individual people that we find, for instance, in calculating skills, in remembering names-and-faces, or in abilities at learning foreign languages. Such distinctions do seem fairly salient in that they seem to go with certain types of cast of mind; but it is hard to see how deep they cut and it is unfortunate that they smother an important distinction between virtues and capacities we shall return to shortly.

Alternatively, we might follow Bacon's 'Of Studies' (1625a: 797–8) in thinking that there correspond to different types of exercise – such as conversing, reading and writing – different kinds of excellence – in this case 'readiness', 'fullness' and 'exactness' – that can be enhanced by practice and that serve to reinforce each other.[2] A typology of this sort may well give us a sense of the relations between certain abilities and their development, though it will tend to presuppose much that deserves to be made explicit about the peculiar nature of intellectual endeavours.

Again, we might seek in the work of the mind some features that correspond very closely to moral virtues, such as honesty, courage and conscientiousness (see Montmarquet 1992b: 19–34). But we can see pretty quickly that a taxonomy of this sort will be more likely a reflection of pre-existing ethical commitments than a structure that can be used to underpin such preferences. It is also likely to overstress the obligatory seriousness of mental operations.

There are also proposals that are avowedly teleological, paying appropriate attention to 'the aims of thinking or enquiring' (Cooper 1994: 460) and dividing them into kinds according to their central sites as the inquisitive, the forensic, the judicial, the educative and the all-pervasive (ibid.: 461). While appreciating the capaciousness of this sort of effort, I am inclined, for our slightly more limited purposes, to propose a scheme that discriminates primarily in accordance with the phases of cognition. I try not to prejudice the questions of what cognition might turn out to be or of what its objects are, beyond saying that cognition is to enquiry what action is to deliberation.

Thus, the beginning of enquiry will have its specific virtue, perhaps curiosity, which will lie in a mean between the defect of dullness and an excess that might be called bafflement. The sort of curiosity at issue is a prerequisite for getting going with questioning: an unwillingness to let questions lie unanswered and a refusal to raise more questions than can be contemplated at once.

Likewise, the prosecution of an enquiry depends on tenacity, a virtue lying between, on the one hand, discouragement or a sort of accidie and, on the other, the sort of stubbornness that will not accept failure. All the same, apart from the normal lack of energy to look into things deeply, there is a sort of laziness that can be raised to the status of a principle if a person has decided that he really does not need to know any more about, say, the Bloomsbury Group, or has resigned himself to never understanding what a musical key is. In the former case, there is what one might reasonably think of as a righteous impatience with the twitter of the Sunday supplements. In the latter, though, there may a kind of of self-satisfaction related to that of Dorothea's father in George Eliot's *Middlemarch*, who claims to have gone into this and that in his youth but come away thinking that no good will come of going too far into things.[3]

Pricking on and being pricked on by pertinaciousness there will be a cluster of skills, aptitudes and discriminatory faculties that are ruled by a closely related virtue that involves being aware of the grade and type of exactitude that is possible in a given sphere. This is what Aristotle attributes to the person with a sense of perspective (πεπαιδευμένος: *EN*, I iii, 1095 a 1 and *PA*, I i, 639 a 4–6).[4] While that virtue has to do with understanding what a given enquiry can yield, the dispositions subordinated to it have to do with what some recent writers have called 'reliability' and to which we shall return. This has been cited by some thinkers to help to give an account of what knowledge is. Reliability is that set of talents whereby a belief-acquirer will only have available a given belief if it is likely to be true.

Nevertheless, from the point of view of the belief-acquirer, it is presumably not a matter of indifference how much effort she has to put in to get a belief of a given degree of reliability well fixed. In fairness to her, therefore, we should expect that a full account of the matter would have to include a multiply-relativised virtue that we might call 'efficiency', which may be related to what is tested in I.Q. tests. For, in many practical circumstances, it may be as well to prefer ease or speed of having some – even any, even a false, even a wildly false – belief against being adrift with none. The sense of perspective that has to be set against time-urgency might be placed in a mean between neurotic diffidence and tergiversation.

Again, we might feel that there ought to be some place for a preparedness to acquire beliefs that may be unflattering to us; such a preparedness might be thought of as one form of courage, and set between complacency and cynicism. And it is pretty certain that there are virtues connected not so much with the acquisition of beliefs as with coping with the effects of changes in our situation and, consequently, in our beliefs about it; among these might be a type of steadfastness in dealing with changed circumstances.[5]

Just so, the keeping, the caring for and the transmitting – both orally and in writing – of the products of enquiry each demand their own virtues, which have their corresponding vices. Do I have to index my newspaper- and novel-reading as I go? How much of a mess can I let my notes get into? Why should I keep my books in order? And which order? Should I explain the possibilities and my own ingenious solutions? Can I track down the next text I intend to cite? Should I put a footnote to this sentence? Am I getting off the point? And so on.

If these kinds of partitioning of the stages by which belief-sets come to be built up, maintained and transmitted offer a useful scheme for dividing at least one genus of intellectual virtues, then we can straight away make an observation that I think is a matter of intrinsic interest and rather alarming generality. Since at least the time of Descartes, the study that we now call epistemology has centred almost exclusively on issues that have to do with the phase of the *acquisition* of individual beliefs. But the scheme of stages just outlined gives us no strong reason to think that that phase is of correspondingly exclusive importance. Hence, we have grounds for suspecting that it is partial to pay as little attention as has been paid to the other phases of cognition, such as beginning to look for, continuing in pursuit of, holding onto and passing on the discoveries that humans can make.

I do not mean here to speculate on why the partiality in favour of belief-acquisition should have developed, or to judge what it tells us about the broader culture in which a discipline like what we recognise as epistemology should have flourished; any hypothesis aimed at giving an explanation would be pure guesswork and any opinion would be mere whistling in the wind. Still, there is reason to think that the influence of Descartes' enterprise can be regarded as a non-negligible presence either in reflecting or in reinforcing this partiality for the dispositions concerned with the moment at which we receive or create our beliefs and that, for the sake of brevity and with a gesture towards conformity to established practice, I shall call 'doxastic'.

Descartes is implicated in the partiality in favour of belief-acquisition as the crucially interesting thing about knowledge, and this is a study of Descartes' vision of a doxastic virtue. So this study is doomed not to cover many of the intellectual virtues we have just referred to. But that is just too bad; we can get on all the same.

Virtues, skills and habits[6]

In addition to taxonomising the names of some intellectual virtues, it is well to be clear about the category involved in the state I am most directly concerned to individuate in Descartes. To do this, we shall pursue a sequence of distinctions in rough order of increasing specificity, with just a few necessary doublings-back to get in focus some related material that it is better to have explicit.

Exploiting rather than endorsing a snippet of Aristotelian ontology, we may say that the highest relevant genus of virtue is that of the sort of state, potency or propensity that, early in *Metaph.*, Θ, is called a δύναμις. This sort of state is related in complicated ways with what Aristotle calls an activity (ἐνέργεια), an actuality (ἐντελέχεια) and a change (κίνησις); but, fortunately, these complications are at a higher level of abstractness than need concern us here (see Radice 1995).

But it is to our purpose to observe the distinction that he makes in Θ ii between the states that can belong to things that have no soul (ἀψύχοις, 1046 a 36) and those that are peculiar to the rational parts of animate beings. The example he gives of states of the former, non-rational (ἄλογοι:

1046 b 2), type is that of heat: heat can only produce heat. Likewise, in *EN*, fire is taken not only as a prime instance of what cannot be trained to act otherwise than its tendency upwards (II i, 1103 a 22–3), but also as a prime instance of what is immutable in nature (V vii, 1134 b 26–7). The sense is clear: fire cannot not heat whatever is cooler than it and comes near to it. Aristotle goes so far as to say that such non-rational potencies admit of one result only (1046 b 5–6). But, presumably, we would also count among states of this non-rational sort also probabilistic features, such as that of a fair die to come up six a sixth of the time: the die can, and five-sixths of the time does, come up non-six, but when it does come up six, it is not because it decides to, chooses to, determines to on its own, or can be said to have any reason for doing so on this occasion rather than any other. The respect in which such states are non-rational, then, is not that in which they are invariable, but in virtue of their not having in them their own guiding principle. This is the respect in which, as Aristotle illustrates in *EN* II i, they are incapable of voluntary action.

By contrast, the example Aristotle gives in *Metaph.*, Θ ii of a rational potency is that of medicine, which can be productive either of disease or of health (1046 b 7). Since medical knowledge is knowledge, its possessor must have a soul that has the capacity for knowledge. The capacity for knowledge is a capacity of the rational soul. Hence, the possessor of medical knowledge must have a soul with a rational part.

At Θ ii, 1046 b 7–24, Aristotle appeals to the principle that knowledge is knowledge of opposites. This is the principle that it takes a thief to catch a thief recognised by Plato (e.g. *Rep.*, I, 334 A-B) and attributed by him to Homer as the source of all wisdom. On this principle, knowledge can be used to opposite ends. This is a very different sense of there being alternative outcomes from the way in which a die may or may not come up six. Though medicine has essentially (καθ᾽ αὑτὸ: 1046 b 13) to do with health, to have the knowledge to produce that, one must also have the knowledge to produce its opposite. But, as we shall see in a moment, this knowledge of the 'also' is subordinate to what specifies the rational potential in question.

Among the states that, to be instantiated, call for a rational soul, we may distinguish between those that we may call arts and those that should be called capacities. Here the distinction can be hardly be more than rough-and-ready, not to say archaic, given that the former term suffers both from aesthetic associations and from interference by the opposition between arts and sciences. We can get a better sense of it, first, by exemplifying how Aristotle's word for it, τέχνη, is used (also Plato, *Soph.*, 265 E), and, then, by comparing it with two sub-divisions of the more generic category of capacities.

Arts (τέχναι) generally fall into the class of the productive sciences, where they are contrasted principally with the theoretical and with the practical sciences (*Metaph.*, E i, 1025 b 18–6 a 23). In some cases, such as that of medicine, the possession of the art may involve the putting to work of theoretical knowledge, e.g. in anatomy, to effect that primary aim of the art, namely, health. Productive sciences may, unsurprisingly, be identified with their product, such as the varied trades that go to make up house-building (οἰκοδομικὲ τέχνη: *Phys.*, II iii, 195 b 23–6; *EN*, VI iv, 1140 a 7ff.) and that, despite their apparent differentiation, are all focused on the finished house. Conversely, classes of product can be identified by the art that produces them: tables, ships and pulleys, despite their differences, are all results of the arts of carpentry and joinery.

The exercise of an art is a conditional good in two main respects. The production of, say, chairs is a good only if chairs are called for: the good of the exercise is conditional on the worthwhileness of the product. On the other hand, there is a distinction with whose importance we shall be much concerned in considering, in Chapter 5 below, Descartes' claim that we can, if need be, dissent from clear and distinct ideas. Here, the conditionalness lies in the fact that a possessor of an art may have aims that lead her not to exercise it to produce the best result on a given occasion. These aims may be such not merely to leave intact and unimpugned the adept's possession of the art, but even to illustrate her excellence at it. When he says that in art voluntary error is not so bad as involuntary (*EN*, VI v, 1140 b 22–3), Aristotle presumably has in mind cases like that of a joiner who makes a chair that is not fit to be sat on with a view, perhaps, of showing how *not* to construct joints by showing the ways that joint-construction can go wrong. Likewise, for instance, a circus clown needs to be a good acrobat in order successfully to mimic failed acrobatics. The educative point or the joke (if you like that sort of thing) in these cases holds the principal aim of the art in abeyance; yet that aim is still being subserved even by such apparent declinations from its usual exercise. By contrast, in the exercise of a moral virtue, such as temperance, non-performance of what is excluded is a non-conditional matter. Put positively, intemperate actions (such as eating binges) are sure signs that something is amiss, however temporarily and however locally: no ulterior aims can supervene on the demands of morality.

Relative to this latter kind of conditionalness in the arts, there are surely some that make hard cases. Medicine again: a doctor who does what she knows is contraindicated or omits what is prescribed need not be being incompetent but, in ways that have spawned huge literature, unethical. If the doctor has no right to play tricks with the health of those she has in her power, then she is not just a bad person, she is a bad doctor too. Yet the more competent Crippens and Mengeles are not shown by their malpractice to lack the medical art, presumably because their initiation into it gave appropriate prominence to health as the essential end; they ought to be distinguished from quacks (see King 1998). By contrast, someone like a Renaissance court poisoner or a writer of murder novels, whose medical knowledge (productive or theoretical) is finalised on disease and death, should be regarded as having only incidental knowledge in the field (κατὰ συμβεβηκός: *Metaph.*, Θ ii, 1046 b 13 and *An.Po.*, I ii, 71 b 10); hence, they have no real part of the medical art.

Insofar as an art involves some measure of organisation of knowledge, not least relations of means to ends, it represents a fairly advanced grade in the formation of an individual. 'Capacity', the term with which I am here contrasting arts, on the other hand, covers a wide range of degrees of elaboration (Freeland 1986). At a first approximation, we can distinguish between those that can pretty straightforwardly be called innate or natural and those that are equally straighforwardly acquired. This discrimination maps fairly neatly onto some well-understood grades of potentiality and actuality (cf. *De An.*, II v): there is a recognisable difference between being the sort of creature that can learn English and being one of the creatures that can speak English. But it is worth exploring what falls into and between these two classes of capacities to get clearer about how they differ from arts as we have described them.

There is one respect in which some of the capacities that, in Aristotelian terms, demand a rational soul, and that it makes sense to call innate are similar to non-rational dispositions, such as the heat of fire or the tendency of a fair die to come up six a sixth of the time. This is the respect in which they are operative irrespective of agent choices. For example, children and many animals have memory even without being, in the full sense, able to reason and hence to set their own objectives. It is also worth noting a matter to which we shall have to recur when we come to consider, in Chapter 4 below, Descartes' explanation of the fact that our having finite intellects does not involve a privation. This is that the absence of some faculties should be described in different ways according to the genus of the creature from which they are absent. Thus, as Aristotle says in *Metaph.*, Γ xxii, a tree that cannot see is not properly called blind, while a man who has lost his sight has undergone a privation (στέρησις).

Capacities such as that of some raw ability to remember are not, so far as we can tell, equally distributed among human beings. It would be hard to deny that some people are more retentive of some kinds of information than others are. Though it might be hard to quantify in any convincing way the extent to which such retentivenesses are correlated with other capacities, such as perceptual and other sorts of sensitivity to the types of information involved, it nevertheless makes clear sense to speak of someone who has a great ability to recall information of a given type as gifted in that sphere. This sort of gift or talent is a sort of pure potentiality. Whether the gift is large or small, the sort of potentiality in question is the sort of thing that it is almost irresistible to call natural. But that does not mean that we are merely landed with what we have. For there are at least two types of ways that the potentiality can be enhanced. Sticking with memory-ability for a moment, we may distinguish between the pursuit of information that can be committed to memory, and the development of the capacity for retaining and reproducing it. In the former case, a certain type of attention may be required. Or exposure to certain types of environment: though, by some measures, the informational content may be of similar volume, it is easier to learn a set of facts from a book than it is to download the various scenes of a simple walk down the street. Not least, because, in a book, you know what you are supposed to be focusing on. On the other hand, the development of mnemonic techniques, such as 'memory palaces' and the like, may increase one's power of recall in the same sort of way that weightlifting increases muscle-mass: it adds to the potential given by nature.

Here we encounter a further pairing, between a natural capacity that can be expanded by training and an acquired or artificial capacity whose development is a matter of learning as well as of exercise. The interrelations and overlappings between these classes is one of the points at which commentators on Aristotle and, more generally, moral philosophers will find much to disagree about. Those who want to stress the role of reason in choice and in the development of a moral sensibility will tend to downplay the extent to which learning to be good involves teaching (e.g. Allan 1953: 76–7; O'Connor 1964: 57–8; Devereux 1992: 765). On the other hand, those of a more Humean disposition are liable to put the moral virtues pretty squarely in the class of natural capacities expanded by training (e.g. Burnyeat 1980a; Smith 1996). Nevertheless, it is a distinction that Aristotle himself makes very clearly at the outset of *EN*, II, between the ways that the moral and the intellectual virtues are acquired. Intellectual virtue – which will include many of the acquisitions we have been calling arts – is transmitted by instruction (ἐκ διδασκαλίας: *EN*, II i, 1103 a 15–16). By contrast, ethical excellence is a product of habituation (ἐξ ἔθους: *EN*, II i, 1103 a 18; δία τοῦ ἔθους: a 26).

In the terms of the instance cited earlier to distinguish between a capacity to learn English and a capacity to speak English, one point of overlapping might be brought out here. A child born in an English-speaking community has a capacity to become an English speaker, but it will not acquire the ability to speak that language in the same way that a 40-year old monoglot German will. Even if at some stages, the infant and the middle-aged man may have the same capacity to speak English, the child can be described as being initiated or trained where the man should be described as simply learning. The indoctrination that the child undergoes hardly involves its reasoning about 'correct forms', whereas the man, unless he is singularly unfortunate in his teachers, should be able to explain some of the bases on which he is making his linguistic choices: even if he suffers from not being taught much by way of formal grammar, he will be self-conscious about such things as how to select verb-forms.

This is, once more, a rough-and-ready case; but its development is of use to us. For, when the child grows up, it will have English as a linguistic habit to which it has no overall alternative and it will be only on rare occasions that it notices alternatives in the ways that it might understand other English-speakers or express itself. To that extent, this sort of acquired capacity of the rational part of the soul comes out to have in large measure the characteristic feature of the non-rational propensities of fire and fair dice: that of not really being a matter of choice or the voluntary. By contrast, the German businessman will not only be painfully aware of a global alternative for him to expressing himself in English (talking German), but he will be continually on his mettle in taking in and giving out sentences in that language. His preference for slow-speaking interlocutors and his own hesitance in production testify to his having to set himself to this aberrant task, which is an intellectual challenge and calls for a determination of the will.

The sort of difference indicated between a capacity acquired by training and one acquired by learning has repercussions not only for the notion of the moral virtues, but also for that of the intellectual virtues. In the course of a brisk elimination argument in *EN*, II v, Aristotle argues that a virtue is neither an emotion (πάθος) nor a capacity (δύναμις), understood as a raw sensitivity to emotion, and infers that it is a disposition (ἕξις). In the case of the moral virtues, the dispositions in question are 'states of character' (the translation preferred in Aristotle 1915) relative to the passions (1105 b 26ff.). Such a state is an underlying characteristic that serves to produce specific occurrences (e.g. courage produces courageous acts) and to explain them (e.g. that a man is courageous explains his courageous action). But it is what we might think of as a second-order disposition: it is concerned with the way we function with the sensibilities and capacities that we have; it is what came to be rendered in Latin as a *habitus* (St Thomas: '*ideo virtutes humanæ habitus sunt*': *ST*, Ia IIæ, qu. 55; also Collegium Conimbricense 1593: cols 72–3).

There are some aspects of intellectual virtue, especially concerning honesty with oneself and others, that clearly have to do with states of character in the broad sense. We would, however, expect that these virtues should be, in the main, states of the intellect in that they are regulative of how we handle the gifts, skills and acquired capacities of the sorts we have been narrowing down on. But there are remain two important cruces.

One is the matter of how we are to locate the proper site of the intellectual virtues. In particular, we shall be concerned with the situation of the virtue of doxastic rectitude, which I begin to spell out in the next section. The perplexing to-and-fro that Descartes envisages as an answer to the question of where responsibility lies for its exercise will occupy us at some length, especially in Chapters 4 and 5.

The other, connected, matter arises from the fact that moral virtue is pictured by Aristotle as involving the internalisation of a set of standards, in such a way that they become 'second nature'.

Aristotle himself does not use any phrase that directly corresponds to the English 'second nature'. In *Mem.*, he discusses repeated recollection and says that a custom takes the place of nature (ὥσπερ γὰρ φύσις ἤδη τὸ ἔθος: II, 452 a 28) and, generalising, that frequency acts like nature (τὸ δὲ πολλάκις φύσιν ποιεῖ: 452 a 31). At *EN*, VII x, he speaks of habit as being not quite so hard to break as nature; it is, nevertheless, hard to break because it is similar to nature (ὅτι τῇ φύσει ἔοικεν: 1152 a 31). Where Ross (Aristotle 1915) offers 'like nature' and Rackham (Aristotle 1926) gives 'a sort of nature', Thomson and Barnes (Aristotle 1953: 249) translate without comment as 'a sort of second nature'. Likewise, in rendering Aristotle's observation about the effects of time on character, at *Cat.*, viii, 9 a 2–3, where Ackrill (Aristotle 1963) gives 'part of a man's nature', Cooke (Aristotle 1938) uses the phrase 'second nature'.

Even though direct support for Aristotelian usage is missing, what it corresponds to certainly has a venerable lineage, the earliest occurrences of the combination '*secunda* [or *altera*] *natura*' being found, according to Lewis and Short, in what may in turn be reports of proverbs in Octavius Augustus and Macrobius, not to mention similar usages in Juvenal and Seneca. It also seems that St Thomas had a passage of Cicero (*Rhetoric*, II, 53) in mind when he speaks of an acquired habit as being like nature (*ST*, Ia IIæ, qu. 56 art. 5: '[. . .] *nihil autem est aliud habitus consuetudinalis quam habitudo acquisita per consuetudinem quæ est in modum naturæ*'); he then goes on to say that a habit becomes like nature (*ST*, Ia IIæ, qu. 58 art. 1: '[. . .] *consuetudo quodammodo vertitur in naturam et facit inclinationem similem naturali*'), which justifies McDermott's condensing the passage to, '*mores* are customs or the *second natures* that customs breed' (Aquinas 1989: 236, emphases original). By Descartes' day, the phrase seems to have had some philosophical currency as can be seen from his Jesuit schoolteachers' observation that the acquisition of virtue is a second grade of man's nature (Collegium Conimbricense 1593: cols 80–1).[7] More recent commentators who have used or come close to using the notion of 'second nature' in this connection would include Von Wright (1963: Chapter viii), Mackie (1977: 113), MacIntyre (1981: 172) and Burnyeat (1980a: 74, and, attributing the idea to Plato, 1998: 6). And accounts of the sort of internalisation that

Aristotle would have associated with the notion of 'second nature' are to be found in Guthrie (1961–81: VI, 352–7), Nussbaum (1986: 287–9 and 305–9), Lear (1988: 169–70) and Waterlow Broadie (1991: 114–18).

The internalisation in question means not merely adopting the principles that govern the sphere with which the corresponding virtue is particularly concerned (cf. *EN*, I x, 1100 b 11–17). What is called for if a state of character is to be regarded as a matter of second nature is that one's actions in the given sphere flow unhesitatingly from those principles (e.g. *EN*, II ii, 1103 b 31–4).[8] Thus, I cannot prepare myself to be courageous, e.g. in battle simply by determining to regard that sort of death as noble (*EN*, III v, 1113 a 33–5). A favourite case of this impossibility is that of Conrad's *Lord Jim*, where the novel's protagonist discovers of himself that in emergencies, such as apparent ship-wreck, he does not live up to the ideals he has set himself for conduct (Wallace 1978: 9–11; Eldridge 1989: 75–8; McInerney 1993: 205). Rather one has to bring it about that one has the disposition by acting in accordance with the principles that govern it (e.g. *EN*, II i, 1103 a 25–b 18).[9]

Even though, for Aristotle, virtue is a very hard accomplishment, like hitting the bull's eye at archery or finding the geometrical centre of a circle (*EN*, II vi, 1107 a 7–23),[10] it is a habit like any other in respect of being the sort of thing that one can acquire. And it is one that one may perhaps lose (*EN*, II i, 1103 b 19–23), despite the doctrine, presumably of Socratic extraction and later attractive to the Stoics, that the true possessor of virtue will not be tempted away from it (cf. Diogenes Laertius 1925: VII, 127). In Chapter 5, we shall see Descartes' reasons for thinking that, at least as regards the central doxastic virtue, observance of the principle is always a pretty self-conscious matter, because we can never hope to extirpate the vicious propensities that make the cultivation of the intellect so daunting a task. Doxastic rectitude never becomes second nature in humans and can easily be missed.

To further specify and begin resolving these questions, I turn now to outlining what would be demanded of us if we were to try to acquire, however briefly and precariously, the virtue that, if I am right, determines the overall shape of Descartes' thought.

Doxastic rectitude

Capacities and virtues

I have already introduced the term 'doxastic' to mean things to do with the processes of creating or receiving beliefs. These processes involve the activation of propensities some of which should be thought of as capacities or abilities and others as virtues properly so-called. Some unofficial armchair theory of perception by way of illustration of this distinction.

Sensitivities such as colour-perception are doxastic capacities because they subserve the formation of beliefs about the colours things look. I suppose that colour-perception is a doxastic capacity of a relatively low level, like a gift in the distinctions made above. That is to say, it is a natural capacity that furnishes materials on which beliefs are formed. Unlike retentiveness of memory, colour-perception is a sensitivity that most people have in much the same degree and over much the same spectrum. Whatever their other interesting properties, colour judgments are pretty consensual. But not entirely.

A person with Daltonism may be said to lack a discriminatory power that others have: his perceptions of red and green are, as such, not to be relied on. Nevertheless, the condition may be hard to detect simply because, in everyday life, brightness cues and so on can be used to supply the informational lack of some sorts of dichromatism, which may help explain why the condition was not well described until 1794. The sensitivity to these other cues may be developed at the same time as the ability to discriminate objects generally (if the Daltonism is genetic) or may be acquired at a later stage to compensate (if it results from damage to the optic nervous system). Whether or not he is aware of his condition, a person with Daltonism is unlikely to rely solely on the appearances that lead *others* to describe objects as red or green.

There is a distinction to be made and observed between the raw sensitivity of a person with normal colour vision, which is a matter primarily of the physico-chemical setup of the retina and optic nerve, and the more sophisticated re-elaboration called for to make colour judgments on the basis of other cues. Though it would ruin the fun to try to say what the more sophisticated bit is, the way in which a Daltonian handles his perceptions of red and green objects involves a different doxastic process from the sensitivity that a trichromatic (i.e. normal) person is endowed with by nature. The difference need not be either that the Daltonian is selfconscious or that he is diffident about red–green judgments. Rather, it is that the basis on which he makes them calls for some extra process relative to normal functioning. As Matteo Ricci enhanced his memory by taking a detour through a system of associations, so a Daltonian may supplement his dichromatic vision by taking account of cues that guide him to (generally consensual) colour judgments. Of course, the ability to take such a detour, whether in the case of memory or in that or colour vision, presupposes a natural capacity to do it. This, too, may be something that most people have in pretty much the same degree. But a person with trichromatic vision does not make much use of it, because she does not need to. The application of that capacity to supply the lack of more direct information requires a stance on which consensual red–green discriminations are called for but have to be furnished by indirect means.

Where the alternative sources of information are lacking – or deliberately suppressed, as in colour-blindness tests – the Daltonian will make mistakes about the colours things look and may, after all, develop a diffidence about such circumstances. If so, this readiness to turn away from some of the deliverances of one of the senses has to be brought about by learning or training. Thus we have a third grade of doxastic involvement, which comes after seeing colour and after the more or less automatic correction for chromatic distortion. What is at issue is getting pretty close to a doxastic virtue: it is a state of the attention that deals with the perturbations of sensory input, just as a moral virtue is a state of character that deals with perturbations of the passions.

The willingness of an aware Daltonian not to rush into red–green colour judgments is a virtue of a rather narrow and pretty uncommon sort. But I have suggested its outlines to offer an instance of how the category distinctions of the preceding section map onto questions of belief-formation.

'Rectitude'

I turn now to insinuate the word 'rectitude' as the tag for what Descartes is after in his theory of enquiry and to offer some formal outlines of the virtue that it names.

Two points about the derivation of the term. First negative. I have not noticed the occurrence of the Latin noun *rectitudo* or the French noun *rectitude* in Descartes' writings; and it is absent from the listing that Gilson makes of Scholastic – specifically Thomistic – terminology (Gilson 1913b). But the cognate Latin adverb *recte* does occur at some crucial points, such as in the title of the 1644 version of the *Discourse*, and in an important passage of *Meditations* IV that we shall discuss in Chapter 4. Moreover, the moral tinge comes out when Descartes describes himself as adopting a firm and constant resolution to follow the precepts that he has adopted (*Dis.* II, CSM I: 120; AT VI: 18: '[. . .] *je pris* [. . .] *une ferme et constante résolution de ne manquer pas une seule fois à les observer*'),[11] or he claims benefits for following his rules exactly (*Reg.* IV, CSM I: 16; AT X: 372–3: '[. . .] *per methodum autem intelligo regulas certas et faciles, quas quicumque exacte serverit nihil unquam falsum pro vero supponet*').[12] What these precepts and rules are and imply will occupy us in detail in Chapter 8; but nobody doubts that, taken together, they describe what Descartes calls his '*méthode*' or '*methodus*'. What I shall be calling 'rectitude' is just that virtue which consists in observing the rules. It is not itself any part of the method, as temperance is no part of desire; rather, it is the state of the mind that deals with the perturbations of all the belief-contributing inputs to which humans are subject.

More positively, the choice of 'rectitude' is meant to echo a Latin usage that became current to expound Jesus' description of the devil.

[h]e was a murderer from the beginning, and abode not in truth, because there is no truth in him. When he speaketh a lie, he speaketh of his own, for he is a liar, and the father of it.

(*John*, 8: 44; Authorised)

In the Vulgate, St Jerome uses '*veritas*' as opposed to the devil's being '*mendax*', but '*rectitudo*' is the word adopted by St Augustine, and others in his wake, to express the positive notion of truth as much of speech as of action and the will in this context (Pouchet 1964: 29–52).

In St Anselm, the term becomes the key to the understanding of the great trilogy of dialogues *De Veritate*, *De Liberate Arbitrii* and *De Casu Diaboli*. Though he nowhere gives anything like a formal definition of *rectitudo*, it is pretty clear from the first of these works that St Anselm means by rectitude that property of a thing that constitutes its doing what it ought. Thus, in *De Veritate*, he explicates the what-it-is-for (*ad quod*) of a statement (cap. 2), of a thought (cap. 3), of the will (cap. 4), of action (cap. 5), of obligation (cap. 8), of truth (cap. 11) and of justice (cap. 12) as its *rectitudo*. Likewise, in his work on freedom of choice, the central questions concern the relations of different grades of creatures (humans before and after the Fall, angels fallen and other, and God) to separable or recuperable rectitude (Anselm 1992: Chs 4, 9, 11). This material is closely related to what we shall be considering in connection with Descartes' account of the will at the end of Chapter 5, and I note it here to defend my choice of the word 'rectitude' in preference to other words, such as 'righteousness', 'care', 'scrupulousness' or 'probity', any of which might have done duty for my suggestion.

The definition I offer of what I am calling by the slightly unusual name of 'doxastic rectitude' is that it is the virtue in belief-acquisition that lies in whatever might turn out to be the mean between the vices of scepticism and credulity.

Some strategies of rectitude

It is a simple and devastating thought that what an enquirer would like to have as the product of her efforts is a set of beliefs that contains all the true beliefs that are to be had and no false ones. If someone could enact the doxastic rectitude of believing those things that ought to be believed and not leaving unbelieved those things that ought to be believed, then that person would have as good a set of beliefs as could be wished for.

There are two idealisations built into the enactment of doxastic rectitude. One is to do with the time available. As we shall see at the end of Chapter 3, Descartes is aware that the execution of his project was up against the fact of human mortality. Nevertheless, anyone who was in possession of that virtue would have a *tendency* to omniscience. Even if we cannot realistically aim to believe all truths, that is nevertheless the ideal (*per contra* Williams 1978: 46, 165). The other idealisation is to do with the conditions of enquiry. In Chapter 6, we shall consider what Descartes takes to be the ideal conditions of seclusion. And it is worth noting for now that the realisation of those conditions places a further constraint on time: it is only rarely that we can carve out peace and quiet enough for proper enquiry.

There is also a qualification of some importance. This concerns the possibility that there may be truths that are not to be had by humans by natural means. If virtuous enquiry is the acquisition of true beliefs by natural means and some truths are not to be had by those means, then, however virtuous an enquiry, it will turn up only those that are to be had by those means. Supposing there are truths that are to be had only by supernatural means, no human can make himself privy to them by the enactment of doxastic rectitude. In Chapter 11, I suggest that Descartes holds that there is quite a large class of truths – including some of the most important – that cannot be had without special divine revelation, which is to be regarded a supernatural means of belief-acquisition. Hence, for the time being, we shall limit consideration to the operations by which humans can increase their store of true beliefs and expel false ones by their own efforts and without special divine revelation or other forms of supernatural intervention.

For Descartes, what I am calling 'doxastic rectitude' is principally concerned with the move from the presence in the mind of an idea, representation, image, deliverance or content to the formation of a belief. That move comes about by assenting, which, as we shall see in Chapters 4 and 5, is an operation of the will. And we may distinguish two types of policies that concern that operation and that, together, constitute the formal rubric of doxastic rectitude.

One policy would be to aim at assent to all true ideas. This could be achieved by, for example, assenting to all ideas whatever, since it is reasonable to expect that, among the ideas presented to the mind, at least some are true. The fault in this policy is, obviously, that it would not exclude false ideas: indeed, undiscriminating omnivorousness for ideas would ensure that there are plenty of false ones; trivially, if I take on any idea and its contrary, then at least one of them will be false; and so will be the conjunction of them, if that is an extra belief. Even if we did assent to all the true ideas, we would not have distinguished them from the false. Hence, we would be quite in the dark even about what ratio there is between the true and the false. So, what we are after is a way of excluding so far as possible the false ideas.

From one point of view, the objective of one who enquires in accordance with doxastic rectitude might be regarded as 'maximising one's truth-ratio'

(Williams 1978: 54). But even this will not quite do. For, suppose a person, A, has, on some scheme of belief-individuation, ten thousand beliefs, 90% of which are true, and B has a thousand of which 99% are true, A will have nine thousand true beliefs and, though she is more error-prone than B, one might think that A has more knowledge than B. Of course, B's advantage will be in her greater reliability, but that is not quite to our present purpose. What we want is to get as large a number of the beliefs that are to be had as possible in order to get as large a proportion of those that are to be believed as possible. With none that are false.

Granting, as we must and Descartes does (e.g. *Reg.* II, VII and VIII; *Dis.* VI (CSM I: 143);[13] *Pr.* I, 49), that the set of beliefs that are to be acquired is very large, there is an asymmetry between types of failure to fulfil the requirement to acquire all the beliefs that are to be acquired. In its full realisation, perfect doxastic rectitude would be swift and fecund to a degree that, ruefully or cannily, Descartes admits his own operation is not (*Reg.* IV, CSM I: 20; *Dis.* VI, CSM I: 147).[14]

Such admissions do not, on their own, impugn the project he has in hand; they only deprecate the contingent features of himself as a finite mortal. Even the largest sheer numbers of true beliefs that a human might ever acquire will never represent more that a minute proportion of the total number to be had. The non-acquisition of all the beliefs in that very large set is not even *prima facie* evidence that one is acting in accordance with a seriously defective doxastic disposition. Defective, because human, but not of necessity seriously so. If so, some shortfalls may be regarded as relatively minor. There are, however, individual or particular beliefs that it is obligatory to acquire as a prerequisite of acquiring others. Descartes thinks that the knowledge of God's existence is one of these, and must come very early in the order of acquisition of any other beliefs whatever: without that knowledge every other belief is shaky.

Unlike a virtue such as courage, the exercise of the virtue of doxastic rectitude is focused not so much on belief-acquiring actions, as on the results of those actions, namely the incrementation of a stable belief-set. The point here can be made in terms of the distinction between production and activity (*EN*, VI iv, 1140 b 4–6): the exercise of the productive sciences, as we saw above, aims to make something external to themselves; but activities do not, for good activity is its own end. Each occasion of belief-acquisition leaves a trace, namely, the belief. In that respect, it is a production, a making (ποίησις). But if we suppose that the number of beliefs there are to be acquired is infinite – or unending from the human point of view – then what is produced at each stage in the process of incrementation is just a stage, a part of a process that is, on independent grounds, its own end: it is a doing (πρᾶξις). The independent grounds for Descartes involve the valuableness of exercising the higher faculties in order to be pleasing to God (Epistle Dedicatory to *Pr.*, CSM I: 191).

So long as the tendency is to pile up beliefs that are true, one is going in the right direction. A serious vice to be avoided here is that of not acquiring any beliefs *at all*. And, in Chapters 6 and 7, we shall discuss at some length an enterprise, called 'scepticism', that aims at acquiring as few beliefs – both as few true and as few false beliefs – as possible.

Still, there are several less self-conscious ways in which the same result will accrue. For instance, there is a sort of laziness, which I earlier called a sort of accidie, that is a disposition not to acquire beliefs even though they are available to be acquired. This sort of idleness might be usefully contrasted with the tendency not to acquire a true belief through insufficient attention to the matter in hand, letting in a false belief though a true one was to be had. A failure, for instance following popular prejudice, to seek the true belief about whether or not *p* may result in acquiescence in the (suppose, false) belief that not-*p*, because one cannot be bothered to think about whether or not *p*.

Some of these barriers to enquiry are akin to squeamishness, which leads people not to look into matters on which true beliefs are to be had relatively easily, but about which they prefer ignorance or mystification. Standard cases here would be mortality, human motivations, sex and, more generally, matters squidgily biological: almost everyone tries to duck paying too much attention to the ugly facts in at least one of these fields. Yet, declinations from a policy of acquiring all the available true beliefs may be regarded as more or less grave according to the limits on the resources of time, energy and seclusion that any given human being has at her disposal.

Moving on from the component of doxastic rectitude that consists in acquiring *all* true beliefs to that of acquiring *only* true beliefs, we notice that here, too, there is an asymmetry. In the first case, while the acquisition of *no* beliefs would show a seriously defective disposition or policy, the acquisition of fewer than all would not. In the second, the acquisition of *no* beliefs need not be considered vicious, though the acquisition of *any* false belief would betray conclusively a less than perfectly virtuous disposition. Here, quality is more important than quantity.

Under the second part of the rubric of doxastic rectitude, there appears to be an equivalence between the acquisition of only true beliefs and the non-acquisition of any false ones: if one has reduced one's beliefs to nil, one might be regarded as having minimised one's falsity-ratio and, hence, maximised one's truth-ratio. But, just as assent to all ideas is a poor way of ensuring that one assents to all true ideas, so assent to no ideas is a poor way of ensuring that one assents to none that are false. Since the aim of doxastic rectitude is to build up a body of beliefs, if no beliefs emerge, then something is amiss. Hence, our attention ought to be focused on the belief-forming processes that are 'error-*proof*' (Williams 1978: 48). Many incidental dispositions can feed into a failure to acquire only true beliefs. Some of these, such as squeamishness, coincide with those operative to block the drive to acquire true beliefs that are there to be had. But there are two particularly interesting sorts, which might also be regarded as accelerators rather than as blocks or obstacles, because they push us too quickly to have beliefs that are credulous. One arises from laziness about paying enough attention to ensure that distractions do not induce us to form beliefs too hastily or haphazardly. The other is to do with the preconceptions that everyone carries into an enquiry and that Descartes sees as interfering with our judgment. In Chapter 3, we shall reconstruct several accounts of the discovery that we have inside ourselves these two sorts of accelerators which rush us away from the acquisition of only true beliefs.

There is a question about which of the extremes of acquiring too many or too few beliefs of the right sort should be regarded as more important relative to the other and, consequently, which of the corresponding vices (credulity and scepticism respectively) is more noxious. One relativisation here concerns the intrinsic character of the different vices. On the one hand, it might seem that, at least in some cases, believing one false thing can cause other misapprehensions, as one bad apple can spoil a whole basket (*Obj.* VII: Z, CSM: 324). Error can be contagious and the contagion can be transmitted. Hence, as already noted about the necessity to acquire knowledge of God's existence near the beginning of an enquiry, credulity is a menace especially at the beginning of the reconstruction of one's belief-set. On the other hand, the paralysing effects of scepticism would mean that nothing really gets investigated at all. Hence, it is better to allow that something is to be believed than to do violence to oneself by renouncing opinions in the face of 'the external objects that press in and the passions that solicit' (Hume 1776: 132), or to offend others by lying to them (Arnauld 1683: 39).

From a quick glance at the terminology that turns up most frequently in the literature on Descartes' theory of knowledge, it would seem that the sceptic is the real malefactor, who has to be refuted and generally given a hard time. But this surface appearance is misleading, as we shall see in considering the content of the precepts that Descartes gives himself for avoiding overhasty belief-formation. More generally, a preoccupation with the sceptic would belie the fact that the Cartesian project of refounding the sciences must have as its underlying motivation the desire to extirpate the errors into which we have fallen by removing the source of those errors, which is a readiness to assent to ideas on inadequate grounds.

I return to this in a moment.

Rectitude, reliability and responsibility

Reliability a skill

Despite its unusualness, the usefulness of the tag 'rectitude' can be brought out by comparison with two notions that have been given attention in the recent literature and that could be confused with it. One is 'reliability' and the other is 'epistemic responsibility' (Code 1987). Not denying the interest of these two concepts, I do want to keep them separate from what I aim to attribute to Descartes as an interest in doxastic rectitude.

We have already had occasion to skirt the notion of reliability. One reason for skirting it was that reliability has figured as an epistemic norm, in terms of which knowledge and, specifically, the social character of knowledge, can be accounted for. Thus, to take an early instance, Thomas Reid takes it that reliability is a feature of 'the natural faculties, by which we distinguish truth from error' (Reid 1785: I, 447) and that their not being fallacious constitutes an epistemological principle concerning matters of contingent fact (Vernier 1976). In this way, the natural faculties are to be trusted as instruments for the discovery of the way the world is. As a number of more recent theorists have argued in various ways, reliability is to be regarded as arising from the proper functioning of the organs that supply ideas, representations or content to the enquirer (e.g. Armstrong 1973: Chapter 12; Dretske 1981: Part 3; Kvanvig 1986, 1992; Sosa 1991, 1993; Greco 1993). This is a notion of reliability as a truth-conducing property of an enquirer that involves a slide towards what we have distinguished in Aristotelian terms as a raw capacity, an ability or an art.

But, we have seen, it is important to observe the distinctions and to hold onto the notion of a virtue as a class on its own, not least because they help us to assess and correct malfunctions of various sorts. As Linda Zagzebski has perceptively argued, the distinction between natural capacities (in the case we cited, trichromatism as against Daltonism) and skills (in one instance she cites, that of the ability to think up insightful analogies: Zagzebski 1996: 114) helps us to keep what is acquired and praiseworthy apart from what is merely a gift (ibid.: 102–5). After reviewing the ways in which, to merit the name, intellectual virtues ought to be reliably truth conducive, she concludes that 'they are not virtues simply *because* they are reliable (ibid.: 311, emphasis original). This conclusion can be clarified with the relatively low-level case of distance-judgment, which I distinguish from that of Daltonism because there may be no longer a way round to accommodating poor performance.

Consider why we might say that a person is a reliable judge of distances. Presumably, we say so if she is likely to come to a just opinion about such matters as whether a car is twenty metres away or forty. At least, she would say that a car at forty metres was twice as far away as a car at twenty or that one at ten was twice as close as one at twenty. She has an eye for such things if she can tell how far away the car is, or at least its relative distance, just by looking; what she sees corresponds pretty well with what the laborious process of measuring on the ground would tell us; she is reliable in that she sees the different distances as appropriately different. Her capacity is one for seeing the different distances, not one for committing herself to the truth of what she sees. Such a person would be someone who would get high marks in a distance-judging test so long as, and maybe only so long as, there were nothing at stake. We may take such risk-free tests as criterial of how reliable a person is: her reliability is her sensitivity to the truth of the matter; it is her discriminative capacity, and not her willingness to bet – especially in the life-or-death conditions of road use – on how sensitive she is (cf. Ramsey 1926: 84–5).

Here it is worth separating some of the phases.

Poor judges of distance fall into two salient classes: those who trust their judgment and those who do not. From the point of view of pure epistemic reliability, they are indistinguishable; but it is pretty clear which one would prefer to have as one's driver. A poor judge of distance who trusts his judgment is doubly unreliable: not only does he not perceive distance, he does not perceive his own unperceptiveness; so he is a menace on the roads. A person of similarly impaired distance discernment, but who is diffident about her ability to see how far away a car is, is only unreliable about how far away the car is; she may well be a cautious driver and thus display rectitude because she does not risk lives on matters on which she is, indeed, unreliable. In this sort of case, the exercise of rectitude may be self-reflective, but that is not essential to the virtue as such. Rather, self-reflectiveness may be characteristic of the exercise of the virtue in cases where the vice that poses the greatest threat is credulity, e.g. when one acquires a belief that an oncoming car is fairly distant when it is not, which is not merely false but perilous.

By contrast, a person who is good at judging distances, who would get high marks in the profit-and-loss-free test, may be considered to have the epistemic virtue of reliability in this field but to have fallen into doxastic vice if he does not acquire the beliefs that were ready and waiting to be had. As in the second case above, he may be a cautious driver, overestimating distances without need. He sees how things stand but does not believe that he is as right as he, in fact, is. Here, again, there need be nothing specifically self-reflective: the sceptical disposition may be the result of observations of the shortcomings of *other* road users.

The fourth sort of case is that of someone who can discern that a car at forty metres is twice as far away as a car at twenty and is prepared to form beliefs of the sort to be acted upon on the basis of what she sees. This person not only fulfils the epistemic norm of being reliable about distances, but has the doxastic virtue of acquiring beliefs in accordance with what she is wired up, or has learnt, to see. She would get good marks on the off-road test and also move efficiently in traffic. This combination is preferable to any of the others. But, whereas a theorist who puts the accent on reliability would have to grade the discerning sceptic – namely the one who doubts that cars are as far away as they seem to him – above both of the undiscriminating observers, from the viewpoint of doxastic rectitude, it is better to be insensitive and act accordingly – specifically by erring on the side of caution and underestimating the distances – than to be insensitive and not to take account of that insensitivity.

The preoccupation of the reliabilist is that the person be perceptive, whether or not she is willing to make much of her perceptiveness. In the Aristotelian terms offered, reliability is a skill (τέχνη) because it can be put to use or not, according to the (larger) purposes of the agent. By contrast, the avoidance of the opposed vices of scepticism and credulity does not focus so much on our means for or our ability at getting the materials for true beliefs, as on what we are to do with those materials once we have got them. For Descartes, it could not be otherwise: it is a two stage-process whose inner workings are the subject of Chapters 4 and 5.

Responsibility and regulative virtues

I also want to separate doxastic rectitude from what some recent writers have called 'doxastic responsibility' (Stevenson 1975; Kornblith 1983; Montmarquet 1992a and 1992b: 19–38). In holding onto this separation, I do not deny that some of the issues I wish to raise about rectitude have figured in philosophical debates about doxastic responsibility, nor that Descartes has been cited as a significant case in some of those debates (Kornblith 1985; Montmarquet 1992b: 113–32). But, to the best of my knowledge, there has been no systematic attempt to make a direct study of Descartes with the separation clearly maintained.

As the phrase has been used, doxastic responsibility concerns not so much the virtue of being responsible *in* the forming of beliefs, as the question of how responsible we are *for* the beliefs we form. Discussion of it has consequently focused on the extent to which it can be culpable to have a mistaken belief (Prichard 1932; Firth 1981; Heil 1983), or to have no belief at all (Smith 1983), about a given matter. One key distinction relative to doxastic responsibility is that between the virtue of conscientiousness, defined as 'the desire to attain truth and avoid error' (Montmarquet 1992b: viii), and the regulative virtues, such as impartiality, open-mindedness and tolerance of others' opinions (Montmarquet 1987: 485–8; 1992b: 23–8).

Conscientiousness is indeed closely related to rectitude, as we shall uncover the notion in Descartes' theory of knowledge. But I suggest conscientiousness differs from rectitude both in quantity and in quality. In quantity, it differs in respect of being well-suited to what philosophers jocundly call 'real life'; it is concerned not so much with 'all' and 'only', as with 'some' and 'most'; there is no built-in drive to error-free omniscience of the idealised sort we have been setting up; being truth-conducive is enough. In quality, it differs in respect of being a desire, rather than a disposition; and we have already heard Aristotle distinguishing the category of the virtues from that of desires (*EN*, II v).

Similarly, the regulative virtues that are invoked to give structure to doxastic responsibility seem to involve attitudes towards the procedures of judgment, rather than modes of executing judgment. As already noted, among such attitudes are open-mindedness and tolerance. Such regulative virtues seem not to be focused so much on the avoidance of the vices I think Descartes is most concerned with, as on others, such as prejudice, bigotry and dogmatism. Though these vices of ossification are instances or effects of credulity, the fact that it is hard to relate them directly to scepticism must mean that the relevant virtue is not in the doxastic mean Descartes is seeking. Moreover, though bigotry is a vice to which a credulous person may be given, it is not because he is now credulous about a given matter but because he has been credulous in belief-acquisition and is no longer open to novelty.

The relations of credulity to scepticism

To see which doxastic vices are the greatest obstacle to rectitude, we should look at what humans are prone to.

Scepticism is not a vice that comes easily or consistently to most people; but credulity is something we are all given to by constitution and upbringing. Because credulity is widespread, Descartes uses the argumentative resources of scepticism as the means to bring to light the credulity we are all guilty of. The use of these means is noteworthy because its converse could not be applied to creatures like humans. Credulity could not be used as a corrective to scepticism, because credulity is, generally speaking, an inarticulate habit. At different stages of the enquiry, different weights are to be given to the different pulls represented by the drives to believe everything and to believe nothing.

The earliest, and most widespread, normal, deep-rooted, and understandable doxastic habit humans have is to acquire beliefs in accordance with the promptings of the senses. In Chapters 4 and 5 we consider the respect in which, for Descartes, credulity can be said to come naturally to us because it is what our nature allows to happen to us; yet humans are to be thought of as, in a certain respect, de-natured. But the habit of acquiring beliefs in accordance with the promptings of the senses is sure to lead us to form at least one belief that is not true. We can infer that the habit is less than virtuous: it is the vice of credulity. Its contours can be summarised as follows.

It is a matter of indifference whether we account credulity as acquired or not. Because it is the first effective tendency we have in point of time, we might think of credulity as 'hard-wired' in us. Yet, it can, at least temporarily and for specific purposes, be held in abeyance, though not entirely lost. Even if we suppose that credulity is in some sense an acquired tendency, there is presumably no special training involved in its coming into operation. If so, there is no tendency antecedent to it that has to be overcome, except perhaps the riotous disorganisation of belief that accounts for most children's incompetence in dealing with the world.

Doxastic rectitude is a matter of believing only the things that are to be believed and credulity involves believing some things that are not to be believed; so credulity is an excess in belief-formation. Where there is no absolute ban on acquiring this or that belief, credulity is an excess that results in our forming beliefs on which we may act in foolhardy ways. Nevertheless, in the brutal circumstances of a child's drive to grow up, it is indispensable. A child who from an early age carefully followed the precepts Descartes sets out in *Discourse* II (see Chapter 8 below) would not respond at all to the world presented by the senses. And the child would die. In this respect, the excess is not an unconditional harm; hence, in at least this same respect, possession of the virtue is not an unconditional good. Nevertheless, credulity is a particularly vicious excess in the circumstances that favour enquiry into the truth of the way the world is.

The excess vice might seem to be an extreme further from rectitude than the defect of not forming a belief that is ready and waiting to be formed. For, at first sight at least, it might seem that not forming a belief is a kind of caution. But, one who fails to form beliefs may nevertheless act, and act in ways that are at least as dangerous as those of the person who has been credulous. Thinking of one of the cruces for the interpretation of ancient scepticism (see further Chapter 6 below), we may believe either of Diogenes Laertius reports about Pyrrho of Elis (1925: IX 61): according to Diocles, Pyrrho took no precautions (μηδὲ φιλαττόμενος) to the extent of not caring about the presence of cliffs and the like; but Ænesidemus denies that Pyrrho acted carelessly in everyday matters. A man who needs his companions to keep him from wandering over cliffs is at least as far from having a well-regulated belief-set as one who comes – one might say 'jumps' – to the wrong conclusion now and again. But someone who is so cautious as to deny that he has the beliefs on which he clearly acting may seem to be up to something rather strange, at least as regards the word 'belief'.

The sort of credulity that Descartes alleges we are all subject to is not casual. It is absolutely systematic. On his account of the matter, our reliance on the senses gives us a wholly wrong picture of the way the world is. If this is so, then extreme measures are called for.

The fact that our credulity is deep-rooted in us means that we have to attempt, albeit temporarily and for specific purposes, to put ourselves in a state in which we treat ourselves as not having any of the beliefs that we have. Even if such an elimination does not seem a real possibility, pointing in the direction of it has the merit of holding in focus what is amiss with our previous practice. This over-shoot is justified by the consideration that, if a vice that is only slightly noisome in its effects has a strong hold over our habits, then it may require more draconian measures than one that causes much trouble but is superficial. Someone who only smokes one cigarette after every meal may have more trouble giving up than someone who chain-smokes himself to nausea, but only on his rare nights out.

While Descartes is rather scornful of the attractions of any generalised form of scepticism to a healthily constituted human being, he does not underestimate the obstacles to directing our attention away from the senses. Indeed, in *Principles* I, 72, he is clear that it can be done only with the greatest difficulty (CSM I: 220); in the Latin he says that it is '*perdifficile*' (AT VIIIA: 37), and the French is more emphatic still: '[. . .] *nous ne saurions nous défaire* [of a sense-based opinion] *tant a de pouvoir sur nous une opinion déjà reçue.*' (AT IXB: 60). The fact of our having formed credulous habits at a stage at which reflection was not an option makes them seem natural; we are accustomed to following them and we find them straightforward enough (*Pr.* I, 73, CSM I: 220).[15] In consequence, redirecting our attention is a hardship and labour.[16]

Nevertheless, in the 'Synopsis' to the *Meditations*, Descartes promises that the causes or reasons for doubt that he offers in the first meditation provide a very easy route to the withdrawal of assent from the senses (CSM II: 12).[17] But this promise is not really kept in *Meditations* I, as the narrator admits when he finds that he keeps on being dragged back from his strenuous undertaking to his everyday habits by a sort of laziness (*Med.* I, CSM II: 15; AT VII: 23: '[. . .] *laboriosum est hoc institutum, et desidia quædam ad consuetudinem vitæ me reducit*'). At best, the indirection of shutting his eyes and stopping his ears with which *Meditations* III begins, provides one way of not being distracted. All Descartes offers may be the easiest route to a guarantee against credulity, though that may not be the easiest route to getting some (even fairly decent) beliefs.

The following chapters review the discovery and the treatment of credulity before discussing scepticism in order to highlight the fact that credulity has several claims to priority. We have already seen that, in the temporal order, credulity is the first doxastic disposition operative in humans. In addition, it is the discovery of credulity that gets the pursuit of a well-ordered belief-set going in the first place. Whereas there is some tendency for commentators to motivate Descartes' undertaking by reference to scepticism (e.g. Popkin 1960; Frankfurt 1970; Curley 1978), we ought to remember that scepticism is itself a response to the recognition that it is easy for humans to form false beliefs. That is to say, the deployment of sceptical arguments is motivated by the fact that we are by our biological constitution given to excess in belief-formation. We must see that excess as vicious *before* deploying the arguments. Moreover, if credulity is, for humans, the vice more opposed to doxastic rectitude, because it is more difficult to eradicate, then it has priority because it is higher on the list of public enemies. It is more trouble to overcome than scepticism is, and so requires more attention. Not merely more, but of a different type.

Scepticism is a vice that can only put down the shallow roots characteristic of intellectual posturing because it is a vice of those who are already party to reasoning about the nature of knowledge. It can be weeded out of ourselves by the use of once-off arguments, be they self-refutation arguments or appeals to things that are knowable, such as the *cogito*. If other people are not impressed by such arguments, their problems are presumably not worth further serious consideration. But, for us to be able to give up the credulous habits of a lifetime, it is not sufficient – it is not even in the right ballpark – for us merely to recognise that we have made mistakes because we have assented to the promptings of the senses. A knock-down demonstration does not have the right sort of impact. We cannot be *argued* out of credulity of this sort. Wholly different procedures are called for.

These procedures include a stage in which we have to pass through sceptical positions that are meant to alert us to the flimsiness of the supposition that our day-to-day habits of belief-formation have something to do with getting at the truth about anything. Even if scepticism is a stage of the therapy, it is not itself a cure. Scepticism is an inadequate doctrine and not a resting-place. In Aristotle's image, in order to reach the mean between two vices, it may be necessary to go to the opposite extreme just as, in order to straighten a bent stick, one has to bend it further than straight (*EN*, II ix, 1109 b 2–7; also *Resp.* V, CSM II: 242).

Part II

Excess

2 Reason and virtue in the *Passions*

Ethics and epistemology

> Ethics, or the science of right and wrong, [. . .] is the theory of self-controlled, or deliberate, conduct. Logic is the theory of self-controlled, or deliberate, thought; and as such, must appeal to ethics for its principles.
>
> (Peirce 1903: § 191)

Thus the arch-anti-Cartesian, Charles Sanders Peirce, summarises in his incomplete *Principles of Philosophy*, just the view we shall be excavating in Descartes.

In addition to the general desirability both of redressing the balance in accounting for his enterprise and of providing a synoptic terminology in which to express it, my aim in dressing Descartes' vision of enquiry in the clothes of virtue theory depends on the claim that there is a close analogy between what goes in ethics and what goes in logic and epistemology.

As we proceed, I shall highlight many cases where Descartes' vocabulary and conceptual choices demonstrate that his commitment to his notion of method in science is clearly predicated on a commitment to a structurally parallel understanding of human conduct in general. In particular, I shall do my best to bring out the importance of what Peirce calls 'self-controlled, or deliberate, thought'. Here, there are at least two contrasts to be made. One is with uncontrolled and undeliberate thought, where that means any kind of thought that is random and careless: excesses and defects of substantive kinds. The other contrast is at a different conceptual level and concerns the very possibility of our having control over, or deliberating about, what we are to think or believe. For, if Descartes is to be understood aright, we must at least see that – and why – he refuses the idea that we have to be passive in the face of our intellectual environment and of the pressures on us to form beliefs of this or that kind. The control and deliberation that many of us think can be operative in dealing with practical choices, he thinks can be made operative also in theoretical matters: theorising calls on us to be active and selective about what we accept and reject.

It is easy to think, as Peirce argued in 'Some Consequences of Four Incapacities' (Peirce 1868), that Descartes' view of our doxastic situation and of what we should do about it is arbitrary and makes for an unrealistic and unnecessarily strenuous conception of what rightly conducted enquiry is like. If we can assimilate his epistemological theory to recognisable theories about our control over the practical situations in which we find ourselves, then Descartes' conception of enquiry may seem better motivated than it is often regarded as being: at least some of the arbitariness that many find in it should dissipate. In particular, some recent supporters of virtue epistemology have argued in favour of their own approach by contrasting it with what has been called 'the Cartesian perspective' (Kvanvig 1992: the tag appears twenty-one times in the index). It may, of course, be that certain approaches to epistemology traceable to Descartes do lack sufficient motivation for enquiring; but I aim to show that this is not a problem for Descartes himself.

Though I have spoken of analogies, of structural parallels and of assimilating, it would take me too far afield, and beyond my competence, to try to show just how each of the correspondences works. Instead, I shall try to present the Cartesian theory of knowledge *as* driven by much the same forces that govern ethical theories of a relatively common kind. To begin with, I review in this chapter one aspect of Descartes' moral theory as it emerges in some of the letters to Princess Elizabeth and in the *Passions of the Soul*. This move is meant to show that the accent that falls on our active participation when it comes to getting beliefs can be found also in views that are by no means rare among moralists when it comes to choosing actions and that were, as a matter of history, common enough in Descartes' day (see James 1997 and 1998).

In the first section, I try to outline some key points in the ethical theory he subscribes to, and I give it the name 'intellectualism'. Descartes' own brand of it owes a great deal pretty directly to the Stoicism that he was discussing with Princess Elizabeth (see letters 4th and 18th August 1645, CSMK: 256–62); the thoughts in play should not strike us as particularly bizarre. Most of them, indeed, are of the nature of commonplaces in the Western tradition and were much more live options in the 1640s than perhaps they have become today (Nussbaum 1994: 4; Davies 1998b).

In the second section, I illustrate the arguments he proposes for our being able to control our responses to various stimuli; these, too, are familiar enough not only in his Stoic sources (see Alquié 1950: 319–21; D'Auger 1954; Brochard 1954; Delhez 1970; Rodis-Lewis 1975: esp. 216–20) but also in Christian thought generally about the nature of temptation. Though we are often weak in the face of such stimuli, that weakness is just a sign of how much more we have to learn. As, in morals, we have to learn that the passions are a poor guide to what is good for us, so, in epistemology, we have to learn that many of our most common sources of belief are poor guides to the way the world is. The difficult business of how we can come to discover this in epistemology will occupy us in the next chapter.

In the last two sections of the chapter, I shall consider the direct relations between having control over one's passions and having knowledge of what reason dictates. Again, these are doctrines with roots at least as far back as Socrates.

Descartes' intellectualist ethics

An outline of intellectualism

One of the enduring images of Descartes, perhaps the image that has made him more enemies than any other, is as a promoter of ratiocination as the sole or central faculty operative in the search for whatever is good in human life.

The enemies that this image has made him range from those who doubt that there is any good to be had in human life, to those who suppose that ratiocination is one of the evils in human life. In between, there would be those who are apt to doubt that ratiocination can have much to do with what good there is to be had. I have little to say directly to those who take the first or the second position. Those who occupy the middle ground are apt to attribute to Descartes the view that 'we *are* essentially disengaged reason' (Taylor 1981: 102, emphasis original) and to draw from it a direly technocratic image of what it is to be human. In response to that sort of accusation, the following sketch of Descartes' position on how we can come to take control of our lives may help illustrate some of the basic moves in evidence also in his thought about what enquiry is.

Here is a phrase from a letter to Princess Elizabeth of 1st September 1645 that encapsulates and substantiates the view enduringly attributed to Descartes with which we shall be concerned:

> On the whole, we can say, nothing can utterly take away the means for our making ourselves happy so long as it does not upset our reason (CSMK: 263; AT IV: 283: '[*e*]*nfin, on peut dire généralement qu'il n'y a aucune chose qui nous puisse entièrement ôter le moyen de nous rendre heureux, pourvu qu'elle ne trouble la raison*').

In addition to being a fairly bald expression of the view that is generally attributed to, and frequently deplored in, Descartes, this phrase raises a number of important topics, which may be articulated as follows.

First, it appears to presuppose the thesis that happiness is the target at which we do, as a matter of fact, aim so long as reason is untroubled. He is thus committed to a doctrine that we might call 'psychological eudaimonism' (Annas 1994) and that is recognisable from the Stoic positions that run through the correspondence from which this letter is taken. Though he and Princess Elizabeth are discussing Seneca's *De Beata Vita*, Descartes' claim that it is reason that ensures happiness may derive directly from one of the letters to Lucilius.[1] Indeed, a little earlier than the passage just cited, Descartes asserts the thesis that everyone wishes to make himself happy and does so as long as his will is free (CSMK: 262–3).[2]

Though it is a perfectly normal word for being happy, the word that Descartes uses for 'happy' ('*heureux*') is germane to an equally normal word for luck or fortune ('*heur*'). And some commentators have suspected that there is an opposition between the beatitude ('*béatitude*') mentioned at the beginning of the letter's second paragraph (CSMK: 262; AT IV: 281) and happiness ('*bonheur*'), inasmuch as the latter depends on chance ('*hasard* (*heur*)': Gueroult 1953: II, 229; cf. Morgan 1994: 103 and n. 24). It is perhaps unfortunate that CSMK does not mark the difference but uses the word 'happiness' without modulation, despite the superior handling of the same distinction in the letter to Elizabeth of 4th August 1645, at CSMK: 257 (AT IV: 263–4); no blame attaches to the translators, of course, given the use of 'beatitude' in English to refer to the blessings of the Sermon on the Mount (*Matthew*, 5: 3–11).

Second, though, in this letter, Descartes might be thought to be running together reason ('*raison*') and will ('*volonté*'), we shall see how, in this sort of context, the latter is a species or sub-division of the former, more generic, term. The complexities of the decomposition of the mind into faculties and the relations of them will occupy us at some length in Chapters 4 and 5 below. But 'reason' must be being used here as synonymous with the mind or soul in general; when Hume says that 'reason alone can never produce any action or give rise to any volition [but] is, and ought only to be the slave of the passions' (Hume 1739–40: 414–15), the faculty that he is degrading to passivity more closely resembles what Descartes thinks of as the intellect. Yet, the Cartesian intellect is not the mere slave of the passions, although *alone* it is indeed incapable of producing action or giving rise to volition.

Third, the quoted phrase says that the target of properly-directed human aiming is within the grasp of the reason alone, though the exercise of reason may not always seem to be within our grasp. The importance of this lies in the fact that our exercise of reason is easily obstructed. Consequently, we shall be much concerned to see both what sources, internal and external, we find ourselves allowing to obstruct reason, and to what extent and by what means we are capable of overcoming them. The epistemological analogue of these obstructions is the fact that we are continually subject to the deliverances of the senses. The thesis that no obstruction, either in morals or in knowledge-gathering, is insuperable, we can call the 'willableness of the will', and we shall find evidence for attributing a strong version of it to Descartes, first in outline in ethics, and then in detail in epistemology.

And, fourth, the views that Descartes expresses fairly informally to Princess Elizabeth were got up rather more systematically by him in the *Passions of the Soul* (1649) at her behest (see her letter, 13th September 1645; AT IV: 289–90). There is some uncertainty about the relation of the *Passions* to Descartes' other published works. While in the past some denied that it is an attempt to deal in an exact fashion with morals (Gibson 1932: 329–30; Keeling 1934: 232 n. 1), a more recent trend is to see it as honouring at least some of the promise, made in the Letter Preface to the French edition of the *Principles* (CSM I: 188), to offer a theory of how to get the best out of human life (Keefe 1972; Rodis-Lewis 1989: xv; Morgan 1994: 147–8; Kambouchner 1999). For the *Passions* expresses the view that, if humans are capable of generating happiness for themselves, then, to show that happiness is within the grasp of every human it is sufficient to show that no cause of unhappiness need be allowed to interfere with the happiness we can generate for ourselves. Descartes distinguishes two sources that might cause unhappiness and, by means of arguments woven into the closing sections of *Passions* I and *Passions* II, he tries to show how each can be surmounted. The two sources of unhappiness form the exhaustive disjunction of those that are external to us and those that are internal to us.

Controlling our responses to the external world

The potential causes of unhappiness that are external to us may be further subdivided into those that are bound up directly with the passions and those that are misfortunes unpredictable by us. *Prima facie*, this disjunction is neither obviously exhaustive nor exclusive, and Descartes offers instances in each class that, from his point of view, ought to have seemed very much on a par with each other (but see Guenancia 1998: 224–56). What importantly unites them – and qualifies them as 'external' – is that they need not be made to be as they are by the soul, but are merely received by it (*Pass.* I, 17, CSM I: 335).[3] In other words, the potential causes of unhappiness that are external to us are the causes whose arising in the soul is not in the control of the soul itself.

Among the potential causes of unhappiness that are bound up with the passions are those that arise from perceptions. Perceptions may be caused in the soul either by the mediation of the nerves, and thus be caused by the presence of external objects (*Pass.* I, 22–3), or by the mere agitation of the animal spirits, and thus be of the nature of phantasms (*Pass.* I, 21, 26). Without perceptions, we would have no apprehension, however dim, of the contingent disposition of physical objects in our environment. And without apprehending them, we would not be moved to anxiety, fear or terror (*Pass.* I, 37). While being moved to these passions is presumably an obstacle to happiness, Descartes offers a line of thought to show that it is not insurmountable.

At *Passions* I, 46, he distinguishes between those minor disturbances of the animal spirits caused, e.g. by a slight noise, from which we can turn our attention by thinking about something else, and those that we cannot stop ourselves feeling, such a fire that is burning our hand (*Pass.* I, 46, CSM I: 345).[4] Whereas the minor disturbances can, by direct act of (dis)attention, be ignored, the stronger and more violent ones can only be dealt with by controlling their effects.

> The most the will can do while this disturbance is at its full strength is not to yield to its effects and to inhibit many of the movements to which it disposes the body. For example, if anger causes the hand to rise to strike a blow, the will can usually restrain it; if fear moves the legs to flight, the will can stop them; and similarly in other cases (*Pass.* I, 46, CSM I: 345; AT XI: 364: '[*l*]e plus que la volonté puisse faire pendant que cette émotion est en sa vigueur, c'est de ne pas consentir à ses effets et de retenir plusieurs des mouvements auxquels elle dispose le corps. Par exemple, si la colère fait lever la main pour frapper, la volonté peut ordinairement la retenir; si la peur incite les jambes à fuir, la volonté les peut arrêter, et ainsi des autres').

This distinction is not fixed from person to person or from time to time in the life of a given person. Where the line between the two types of case is to be drawn depends on the current state of the person's soul or will. There is also, of course, the third, 'extraordinary', though statistically unexceptional, case, in which I am not up to staying my hand or stilling my legs. For reasons that will emerge, this is a failure on my part to will and not a failure of my will to be efficacious. But Descartes goes on from his initial distinction to say that there are very few men so weak and feeble as to want nothing but what passion dictates (*Pass.* I, 49, CSM I: 347).[5] Thus, it seems that virtually everyone has the ability to set aside some of the perceptions to which they are subject and not to act on the passions that arise from them. The stronger one is, the stronger the disturbances one will be able to set aside. Vice versa, if one's passions are healthy, then one will not need to control them much; as Descartes' teachers observe, it is only in the sick soul that passions are an illness (Collegium Conimbricense 1593: cols 69–70; cf. James 1997: 276–84).

Passions I closes with a rather astonishing claim, one that absolutises the willableness of the will. At first Descartes says that there are very few men who are utterly in thrall to the passions; he then proceeds, in *Passions* I, 50, to say that there are none whatever (CSM I: 348); indeed, instead of merely denying that there happen to be any, for which '*il n'y en a pas*' would have sufficed, he seems to be ruling out the possibility when he uses the emphatic '*il n'y a point*' (AT XI: 368). The argument he employs to support this claim is that even animals, which are quite without reason,[6] can be trained to go against their natural inclinations, which are e.g. to pursue food and to avoid loud noises (cf. *Resp.* VI, CSM II: 287–8).

This may seem a curious resort, given Descartes' notorious mechanism about animals; we would expect that nothing that holds good of animals could have much bearing on the condition of humans and especially on the interrelations of the parts of the human soul. What he is offering is an argument *a fortiori*: if even a dog can do something seeming to involve a soul, then every human can. The limits set by a dog's not having a soul are:

(a)   that it cannot perform highly complex tasks: it is incapable of language and has a necessarily limited repertoire of actions; and

(b)   that it is incapable of training itself.

The *locus classicus* for (a) is *Discourse* V, though it is not always noted that Descartes concedes that a parrot or a monkey does have a soul, though wholly different in nature from ours (CSM I: 140; AT VI: 58: '*âme* [. . .] *d'une nature du tout différente de la nôtre*'). Animals may perform very accurately the actions that fall within their repertoires (*Dis.* V, CSM I: 141). Yet they are still mere mechanisms ('*automates*': AT VI: 55; '*horloges*': AT VI: 59; likewise in the letter to Newcastle, 23rd November 1646, CSMK: 304; AT IV: 575; or '*machines*': *Dis.* V, AT VI: 56). From this Descartes infers that their repertoire is necessarily limited in range (*Dis.* V, CSM I: 139–41; likewise letter to Reneri for Pollot, April/May 1638, CSMK: 99–100; and to More, 5th February 1649, CSMK: 366). As to (b), Alquié notes in connection with *Passions* I, 50, that the limitations on an animal's repertoire are the ground of its being unable to add to the range of what it can do (Descartes 1963–73: III, 996): even a young dog cannot teach itself new tricks.

Even if a dog has no soul, properly so-called, what we learn from Descartes' argumentative appeal to their case is that the passions are malleable not only by the will of the subject in which they operate, but also from without. Thus, if a human were so short of will as to be comparable with a dog, it would still be possible for him to come to exercise control over his passions. In the first instance, control over the passions would be the direct product of the work of training and guidance (*Pass.* I, 50, CSM I: 348; AT XI: 370: '[. . .] *d'industrie à les dresser et à les conduire*'). It would be control exercised by *a* will, though not that of the subject of training. At a later stage of, or in concomitance with, the process of training, the subject would, in virtue of the fact of having his passions controlled, have a more willable will.

If it were true, as Descartes says it is in *Passions* I, 50, that even those who have the weakest souls could, by these means, acquire quite absolute mastery over all their passions, then the distinction of *Passions* I, 46 would be abolished: every cause of unhappiness arising from perception and the passions could be cancelled from our attention. Therefore, with appropriate training and guidance, everyone could build up the will-power to ignore that his hand is being burnt in a fire. The occurrence in us of passions is not under the control of the soul; but we can choose not to pay them any heed and, thus, not to be brought to unhappiness by them. We are put in a position so to choose by having been appropriately trained and guided; the training to encounter all life's eventualities with this equanimity would have to involve at least some, and probably a very large amount of, intelligent self-training.

The disjunction between the external causes of unhappiness that are bound up with the passions and those that are misfortunes unpredictable by us, is not an exclusive one. For instance, I may not be able to predict that my hand will be burnt, and yet it may happen that my hand ends up in a fire. In such a case, my line of action should be to think of something jollier while presumably, but not necessarily, removing my hand from the source of damage.

Here the Stoic elements are well to the fore. If there is no *need* for me to remove my hand from the fire, it is because health and the avoidance of pain should be regarded as having at best instrumental or conventional value. They should be regarded as 'indifferents' or ἀδιάφορα, a word Descartes uses in his letter to Mesland, 9th February 1645 (CSMK: 245; AT IV: 174). Though health and pleasure may be choiceworthy (προηγμένα, e.g. Diogenes Laertius 1925: VII, 105), they are so only when they are accompanied by virtue (*SVF*, III, 62). Quite how far Descartes goes down this road, it is hard to tell either from the correspondence with Princess Elizabeth or from the *Passions*; and there are so many difficulties with the attribution and interpretation of the source-idea (see, for instance, Kidd 1971; Nussbaum 1987; Lesses 1989; White 1990; Isnardi Parente 1993: 31ff.) that it may be more profitable to turn to consider what makes the will more willable.

Knowledge and self-control

Descartes has in mind another sort of case that links the external causes of unhappiness with those arising within our souls. We learn from the discussions in *Passions* III, 191 and 171 that regret ('*repentir*': *Pass.* I, 49, AT XI: 368) and remorse ('*remords*') are both species of unhappiness ('*tristesse*'). This is affected by the claim made in *Passions* I, 49 that a will is the stronger for being founded on true judgments, because, then, we can be sure of having no cause for regret or remorse (*Pass.* I, 49, CSM I: 347). This claim will have a role to play in Chapter 5 below in understanding the difference between God's will and knowledge and ours.

Descartes has no difficulty in allowing that it is well for us to have desires whose satisfaction depends only on our will, because we always get what we were looking forward to (*Pass.* II, 144, CSM I: 379);[7] once more, this is a pretty clearly Stoic *topos*.[8] Yet Descartes sees that a major problem of following this ethic through is that of figuring out which desires have the happy characteristic of being fulfillable by the desirer alone. And he is explicit in raising this difficulty when he say that,

> the mistake that is most ordinarily made about desires is that of not distinguishing enough the things that depend wholly on us from those that do not so depend at all (*Pass.*, II, 144, AT XI: 436: '[. . .] *l'erreur qu'on commet le plus ordinairement touchant les désirs est qu'on ne distingue pas assez les choses qui dépendent entièrement de nous de celles qui n'en dépendent point*'; in similar vein, *Dis.* III, CSM I: 124 which is recast in letter to Princess Elizabeth, 4th August 1645, CSMK: 258).

So it might seem strange that he does not give even the most programmatic clue about how to spot them. Rather, he moves ahead by distinguishing those desires whose outcomes depend entirely on external causes from those depending both on us and on other factors.

As to those depending on external causes, he says, perhaps predictably, that we ought never to desire them passionately (*Pass.*, II 145; CSM I: 379). Less predictable are his general remedies against these vain desires, which are generosity and frequent reflection on divine Providence (*Pass.* II, 145; CSM I: 380; AT XI: 437–8: '[*e*]*t il y a deux remèdes généraux contre ces vains désirs: le premier est la générosité* [. . .], *le second est que nous devons souvent faire réflexion sur la Providence divine*').

It has been noted that the generosity in question has some relation to the notion of genealogy or good breeding (Descartes 1989, Voss: 109; also Morgan 1994: 193–204); and in *Passions* III 161 Descartes himself likens *la vraie générosité* (*Pass.* III, 153, AT XI: 445) to the great-souledness (μεγαλοψυχία) of which Aristotle gives a portrait (*EN*, IV iii, 1124 a 5–b 7) and Descartes regards it as the key to all other virtues and as a general remedy to all the disturbances of the passions (*Pass.* III, 161, CSM I: 388).[9] The explanation is that the genuinely generous man believes that nothing whose acquisition does not depend wholly on himself can be worth wishing greatly for (*Pass.* III, 156, CSM I: 385).[10] Because he does not wish strongly for anything that he cannot procure for himself, such a person need never be disappointed.

But it is on divine Providence that Descartes chooses to expand.

Providence is presented as a sort of immutable necessity or fate, established by God from eternity, that we should keep separate from luck, chance, fortune or the accidental (*Pass.* II, 145; CSM I: 380). Therefore, except for the matters dependent on our free will (*Pass.* II, 146, CSM I: 380), we ought to treat everything that happens as happening providentially by the will of God (*Pr.* I, 40, CSM I: 206), and everything that does not happen as having been absolutely impossible (*Pass.* II, 145, CSM I: 380). The idea of fortune is, roughly speaking, a mere index of our ignorance of the causes that God has set at work in the world. Hence, the more we know, the less prominent, and less personified or personalised, the appearances of fortune will seem,[11] and so the more we shall know how to direct our desires away from matters over which we have no control.[12]

But even where we have no control, it may be necessary to act (see, e.g. letter to Hyperaspistes, August 1641, CSMK: 188–9). The actions we take may be aimed at fulfilling desires. In the sort of case that Descartes envisages in *Pass.* II, 146, there are in play an episodic desire (to get to a certain place) and a standing desire (not to be robbed). Though we cannot, by mere act of will, ensure the fulfilment of these desires, we are called on to act rationally so as to do the most that is within our power to fulfil them:

> Even if, for example, we have things to do in a certain place, to get to which we can take either of two routes, one of which is generally much safer than the other, even though Providence may have decreed that our taking the route that seems the safer will not save us from being robbed, while we could have taken the other unmolested, that is no grounds for being indifferent about choosing one or the other [. . .] reason requires that we take the route that is generally safer (*Pass.* II, 146, CSM I: 380–1; AT XI: 439–40: '[. . .] *par exemple, si nous avons affaire en quelque lieu où nous puissions aller par deux divers chemins, l'un desquels ait coutume d'être beaucoup plus sûr que l'autre, bien que peut-être le décret de la Providence soit tel que si nous allons par le chemin qu'on estime le plus sûr nous ne manquerons pas d'y être volés, et qu'au contraire nous pourrons passer par l'autre sans aucun danger, nous ne devons pour cela être indifférents à choisir l'un ou l'autre* [. . .] *la raison veut que nous choisissions le chemin qui a coutume d'être le plus sûr*').

Though a rather contorted sentence, with its rather inexplicit nesting of conditionals, its overall sense is clear enough: under uncertainty, we cannot always avoid harm, though we can, and ought to, use what knowledge we have to minimise the rational expectation of it.

Given the Stoic tone of the passages we have been reviewing, undergoing a bit of robbery ought not really to bother a man whose soul is in good order: 'who steals my purse steals trash' (*Othello*, III iii, 157). Nevertheless, the guiding thought is that, supposing some (real or merely conventional) harm befalls me, I can at least be satisfied that I did everything that was in my power to avoid it and, therefore, have no grounds for regret or remorse (*Pass.* I, 49 again). Thus, when what turns out was unpredictable by me, or against my best predictions, I can, by having been rational, and by reassuring myself that that is what I have been, ensure that the principal inner source of unhappiness – self-reproach – has no hold over me.

If it were possible – though Descartes seems to exclude it – that the inner emotions caused by the soul itself (*Pass.* II, 147, CSM I: 380) should fail to be a source of intellectual joy (loc. cit., AT XI: 441: *'joie intellectuelle'*), but be instead causes of unhappiness, then perhaps it would be reason's task to bring them too under control. Indeed, in the following article of the *Passions*, Descartes goes so far as to say that the suffering of outrages can itself be a source of joy, insofar as it makes one aware of one's immunity to fortune (*Pass.* II, 148, CSM I: 382; AT XI: 442: *'tous les troubles* [. . .] *servent à augmenter sa joie, en ce que, voyant qu'elle ne peut être offensée par eux, cela lui fait connaître sa perfection'*).

Reason, will and virtue

Given what we have seen, we might ask whether Descartes has a settled view on the relative priority to be accorded to the will and the intellect in overcoming the causes of unhappiness to which we are from time to time subject. For, in outlining the responses appropriate to painful perceptions (the hand in the fire) and to the passions (the urge to strike a blow), it seemed as if the will was to the fore; and, in dealing with, or pre-empting, misfortune (being robbed on the safer road), it seemed as if we are preserved from unhappiness by the exercise of reason or intellect: by the calculation that we could have done nothing more rational. To which one might suggest that there is no general objection to Descartes' regarding the will as more involved in dealing with the external causes of unhappiness, such as being burnt or robbed, and the intellect as dealing with the internal causes such as self-reproach.

But he introduces a third term to answer, or anticipate, the question about whether either the will or the intellect is to be accounted the main agent in guarding against all the types of source of unhappiness.

The third term is 'virtue' (*vertu*), and it seems to be used to cover and harmonise the rather different operations of the will and the intellect in ensuring that we always have the means for happiness. Following virtue is specified, in *Passions* II, 148, as living in such a way that one's conscience cannot reproach one for ever having failed to do all the things one has judged to be the best (CSM I: 382);[13] and, in *Passions* III, 153, as feeling within oneself a firm and constant resolution to make good use of one's freedom, that is to say, never to lack the will to undertake and carry through all the things one may judge to be the best (CSM I: 384).[14]

In addition to other similarities between these statements of what following virtue involves, there is a strong element of subjectivity. For, it is an easy objection to this sort of conception of virtue that, even if one's conscience is easy, and even if one does have the feeling of firm and constant resolution, it may nevertheless be the case that one does not live in accordance with one's conscience, perhaps because one has not yet taken enough possession of one's will to do what one has judged to be best. In addition to such a 'twixt-cup-and-lip objection, there is the problem that a person who has wholly false ideas of what is best may go resolutely about what he believes to be prompted by his conscience or to be the best use of his freedom. It is well known that such a person may be an utter menace and yet feel as virtuous as can be. Subjective assurance cannot suffice for an account of what following virtue really is.

To take the sting out of this objection, we may refer again to *Passions* I, 49, in which Descartes makes, but does not defend, the claim that, just as one who follows resolutions based on acquaintance with the truth is assured of never having grounds for regret or remorse, just so, if one follows resolutions based on false opinion, when one discovers one's error, one will always have such grounds (CSM I: 347).[15] This claim needs to be defended by showing, at least, that error is sure (if only in the long run) to be exposed and that it is possible to tell when one is acquainted with the truth. Since Descartes' attempt to make good such a defence is a key to grasping why anyone should be interested in knowing the truth, we should consider, first, how the claim of *Passions* I, 49 is meant to take the sting out of the problem of subjectivity, and, second, what overall defence Descartes has to offer for that claim.

If error is sure to be exposed, then a man whose resolutions are based on false opinions will be subject to the occasional discovery that he has left undone what he would have done, or has done what he would have left undone, if only he had known the truth. Such a discovery will lead him not to have quite so firm and constant a resolution in his subsequent acts of willing. He will, therefore, be that much more in thrall to his passions, and have that much more difficulty controlling his actions and reactions.

Equally as regards beliefs about matters of fact and as regards moral principles, there are well-recognised complexities about the contagiousness of defectiveness.[16] If, for instance, I discover that I ought, in the past, to have separated glass from plastic from paper in my refuse, to what extent does that discovery of omission undermine my firm and constant resolution not to inflict unnecessary suffering on innocents? Probably not a lot. All the same, the arising of even one irresolution is the sign of some malaise and, therefore, a cause of unhappiness (cf. *Pass.* III, 170, CSM I: 390–1). It is a cause, moreover, about which I am now powerless to do anything by means either of the will or the intellect: it is too late to do anything about it. Conversely, if one can tell that a given judgment is such that there will never be reason to modify it, because it is true, then there will be never reason to be hesitant about acting on it. Again, there are puzzles about how far a person can genuinely be in possession of moral verities if he only has a limited range of them. Ringing the changes on the last example, given that it is true, and that I know it to be so, that I ought not to inflict unnecessary suffering on innocents, I might come to feel myself entitled to my occasionally brash way with people at parties (because they are not as innocent as they are sometimes thought to be).

Nevertheless, the shape of Descartes' basic point is clear enough: the less my resolutions run into difficulties of fit, the more I can feel confident about going on as I have come to do. The more I (rightly) feel confident, the fewer obstacles I shall allow to get in the way of my undertaking and putting through what I have judged to be best. As a result of successive successes, I shall become progressively habituated to trusting my own judgment.

It seems to me that these manœuvres go to the heart of the Cartesian project and can be used to give the epistemology a point and focus that it can easily be thought to lack. Both in the care of our souls and in knowledge-gathering more generally, we have to combat the tendencies that our early upbringing imposed on us. In both fields, some of these impositions are external to us: the senses to which we pay so much attention as children and the animal reactions we have to such things as noises and fire. Likewise, in both, some impositions are internal, matters of developed habit: the deliverances of the senses lead us to believe that the world is thus and so, and we come to treat matters that are not of real concern to us as if they were.

Descartes takes it that everyone can be reminded of his own fallibility in acquiring beliefs and moral habits. Yet it is easy to persist in error; and it is an effort of the will to disencumber oneself of one's usual baggage of beliefs. We turn now to consider how we can be reminded of our fallibility and shall then proceed to consider what role the will has in keeping us from further error.

3   The vice of credulity

The discovery of credulity

I have made mistakes. Some of these have been about trivial matters, such as
the number of the bus that is still distant from the stop. Others have been
about matters where I have lost out a bit, such as in lending money to someone I thought would return it. In others again, I have realised that I had
picked up a belief, for instance about the geography of the town where I live,
that I only much later subjected to scrutiny and found wanting. In these cases
and others, the mistakes I made were put right by setting one bit of evidence
against others: the bus approaches; the money does not come back; and the
old theatre can be seen from the clocktower to take up more room than I
would have expected. In one way, I should feel pleased with myself for
having been prepared to correct my mistakes. But, in another, I might think
that there is something wrong with me, something about my makeup that
made me make the mistakes in the first place.

One popular, traditionally empiricist, diagnosis of these sorts of mistakes,
which we all make, and of how we correct them, as we sometimes do, is that
we are too ready to make inferences on the basis of inadequate perceptual
inputs. This sort of diagnosis, which can easily end up in complicated theories of what the raw inputs are like, has tended to the conclusion that the
inputs are in good order and that it is the inferences that have to be kept
under control. On this diagnosis, which is apt to be of a positivist or phe-
nomenalist bent, credulity is a matter of our unbridled 'construction of the
physical world' (Ayer 1973: Chapter 5) from the ideas, sense-data, sensibilia
or qualia that perception supplies. If we stuck to what the senses tell us
directly, we would not go astray.

In the relatively recent past, this sort of diagnosis has come under attack
from thinkers, following a tradition that might perhaps be traced at least to
Thomas Reid and including, in their (very) different ways, J.L. Austin (1962),
Gilbert Ryle (1949: esp. Chapter 7), W.v.O. Quine (1951: esp. §§ 5 and 6),

Wilfrid Sellars (1963) and Richard Rorty (1980), who think that there has been a dreadful mistake of another order. The mistake, they say, is to think that there are, in any useful sense, any raw inputs that we can, in any useful sense, separate from the inferences we make to arrive at the more or less trivial beliefs that may turn out to be mistaken. In attacking the popular empiricist diagnosis of what is going on when we make trivial mistakes about the number of a bus and the like, the neo-Reidians have been apt to think that the dreadful mistake that lies at the heart of the theory of knowledge is, in one way or another, attributable to Descartes and those influenced by him, particularly Locke (e.g. Rorty 1980: Chapter III). In their view, Descartes' and the others' dreadful mistake was to suppose that there is certainty to be had in the raw deliverances of the senses.

On the interpretation of Descartes I offer, he does indeed say that the inferences we draw from the deliverances of the senses are apt to lead to mistaken beliefs. But that is not particularly because there is anything wrong with this or that inference, as empiricists from Locke onwards would say. Rather, it is because the senses are not, for the most part, attuned to the way the world is. To give them heed – even to the extent of their saying how things *seem* – is credulity.

Because credulity is a disposition that is forced on us at a very early stage of life, and that continues to have a very powerful hold on us so long as we are conscious, we ought to consider what its scope is and whether there are any measures we can take to overcome it. If it is the normal human tendency, then it is a non-trivial achievement to recognise that it is a less than satisfactory doxastic habit. For, to regard our most ingrained doxastic habits as vicious, we must systematically fly in the face of one of our strongest propensities: to assent whenever there is a stimulus that can provide us with a belief.

Against the neo-Reidians, moreover, Descartes urges an account of belief-formation that is even more profoundly anti-empiricist than theirs. As we shall see in Chapter 5, where the traditional empiricists, from at least Hobbes, have tended to think that we can judge the adequacy of our beliefs by considering how well justified they are in terms of the sensations that give rise to them, the neo-Reidian tendency is to say that, if phenomenalism of the older sort is mistaken, then the beliefs we have about the external world cannot be judged by any standard external to our commonsensical habits of comparison and negotiation. But I suggest that Descartes' scheme undermines the position shared by these trends by arguing that, once we see what common sense is like, we are free to regard it as the principal font of credulity *and error*. This freedom is the capacity to stand aside from *any* amount of belief-inducing input and to make decisions about it.

In his published writings, Descartes has three separate runs at the discovery that he has been credulous. He begins the *Meditations* with a declaration of this discovery. Given the way that this discovery seems to pull itself up by its own bootstraps, we shall consider how the autobiographical narrative of the *Discourse* provides a context for that declaration, and, then, how the anthropological sketch that we find in the *Principles* offers a causal account of credulity.

I shall offer accounts of Descartes' manœuvres in these texts that differ from each other; so it might be asked whether one is the 'official' version or whether they represent different stages in the evolution of Descartes' thought. This is not the impression I mean to give, especially as my exposition does not follow the order of the texts' original publication. Indeed, I subscribe to what might be called a 'mild unitarianism' about Descartes' thought: at least in the period from 1637 to his death in 1650, he did not substantially change his mind on the matters in hand.[1] Rather, it is the same discovery being set out in different contexts: the discovery of credulity can be approached in a variety of ways, corresponding to the different natures of the texts in which that discovery has a role to play. For, in the period in question, he set out his philosophical views in three texts of very different kinds.

The discovery of credulity has to have some place in any recitation of the opening moves of the Cartesian project, whichever text one takes as one's starting-point. By examination of the relevant passages of the *Meditations*, the *Discourse* and the *Principles*, I hope to get a clearer grip on the ways that credulity is a doxastic vice to which humans are given in the normal run of things. In the light of this examination, it may be clearer why, as claimed at the end of Chapter 1, credulity has an important priority over *scepticism* as a source of doxastic trouble.

In conclusion of this chapter, I offer some thoughts about the repercussions of the discovery that almost all the beliefs that we had taken to be the most secure turn out, after all, to be wildly misleading about the nature of the world we inhabit. How should we react to that discovery? How seriously should we take it? What should we aim to do about it? I delay to the following two chapters my attempt to describe Descartes' account of the means he alleges are available to us for bringing *credulity* under control in the face of the difficulty that humans have in suspending judgment, doubting and dissenting.

What Descartes says he has noticed in *Meditations* I

The first two assertions of the Latin version of the *Meditations* ought to be translated as follows:

I noticed some years ago now how many false things I have, since my earliest years, admitted as true, and how doubtful those things are that I have since built on them (*Med.* I, AT VII: 17: '[*a*]*nimadverti jam ante aliquot annos quam multa, ineunte ætate, falsa pro veris admiserim, et quam dubia sunt quæcunque istis postea superextruxi*').

The narrator does not say here how many were the false things that he has admitted as true.[2] It could well be twenty, a hundred and fifty-three or seventeen million.[3] But a mere one would be enough to establish that he has been credulous in the terms I have been suggesting. Nor does he say how doubtful are the things built on the false beliefs he has.[4] It could be slightly, fairly or intolerably. Since we are not told how many are the false things admitted as true, the doubtfulness that derives from those falsehoods remains unquantified. But, just as one falsehood is sufficient to establish credulity, so any amount of doubtfulness deriving from it is sufficient to impugn the narrator's earlier doxastic habits.

Despite its prominence at the very outset of the *Meditations*, the passage just quoted has received relatively little critical attention. As Garber notes (1986: 82 and n. 2 on 108–9) the consensual approach is to explain *why* Descartes starts this way in terms of his response to scepticism: it seems to be taken for granted that the narrator is entitled to his confession of failure. Most commentators begin with the second half of the sentence, in which the narrator expresses his desire for foundations on which to build anything firm and lasting in the sciences. But this is rather to jump the gun. For, what we want to know, in examining the nature of the credulity that has to be overcome, is *how* anyone can come to notice that he has admitted any false things as true.

As *Meditations* I proceeds we are given, what we are promised in the 'Synopsis', causes ('*causæ*', AT VII: 12) or reasons ('*raisons*', AT IXA: 9) for doubting all things, particularly material things. These causes or reasons, are the arguments that one may, for all one knows to the contrary, be mad, dreaming or the dupe of a malicious demon. As we shall see in Chapter 7, the sceptical arguments are, indeed, reasons for doubting of all things, including, but not particularly, material things. But they are not what the narrator of the *Meditations* claims to have noticed when he noticed how many false things he has admitted as true. For, even if one notices that one may, for all one knows to the contrary, be the dupe of a malicious demon, that does not, *on its own*, imply that one has even one false belief. After all, the possibility that, for all I know to the contrary, there is a malicious demon who is deceiving me does not imply that I am being deceived; any more than the possibility that, for all I know to the contrary, I am on the Moon implies that I am, in fact, on the Moon.

If, at the very beginning of the *Meditations,* the narrator's ground for think-ing that some of his beliefs are, in some measure, doubtful is that some of his other beliefs are false, then that doubtfulness has nothing to do with the malicious demon nor with any of the other hypotheses that nourish the scepticisms that are taken into consideration as the meditation proceeds.

I shall attempt to show that the confession of credulity that opens the *Meditations* stands in need of outside support, support that is not provided by any sceptical arguments but, in different ways, by other strategies internal to the argumentative structures of the *Meditations,* the *Discourse* and the *Principles.* The purpose of this attempt is to try to sharpen the sense in which noticing what the narrator of the *Meditations* says he noticed is a highly sophisticated operation.

Strategies for discovering one's credulity

Indirections in the Meditations

Noticing how many false things one has admitted as true is not an uncom-mon episode in people's lives. Indeed, it is banal. But even so, there are two outstanding questions: how can it happen at all; and why should it stimulate the contortions that characterise the enquiry Descartes proposes? In partic-ular, the drive to doubt anything one can doubt calls for arguments to reinforce the desire initially stimulated by the mere act of noticing one's own (past) credulity. As Curley (1978: esp. Chapter 3) has pointed out, we have to have motivations for doubting, at least as much as we do for believing.

Whatever might be the force of the sceptical arguments reviewed in *Meditations* I, by the end of *Meditations* II, Descartes takes himself to have established, among other things, that the colour of a piece of wax is not gen-uinely 'in' the wax. The establishing of that thesis seems to him sufficient to justify the dismissal of the promptings of the senses in such a matter. But the route by which he arrives at that thesis is a consequence of his considerations about what he would do well to withdraw his assent from. It cannot, there-fore, be a direct cause or reason for such withdrawal.

Unless there is at illicit work either (a) the observation that many people as a matter of fact suppose, and rightly, that they have accepted at least one false thing as true; or (b) the substantive claim that prior reflection on the constitution of, e.g. a piece of wax will have shown that the colour that we see to be in it is not genuinely in it; it is hard to see why the narrator of the *Meditations* should expect the reader of the first assertion of that work to pass without comment over his claim to have noticed that he has accepted some false things as true. If the query arises, as I am here trying to make it arise, about *how* the narrator noticed that some of his beliefs are defective, neither

(a) nor (b) is available to him to convince us that he has really noticed anything. Since Descartes is gunning for beliefs about material things that have been acquired from or through the senses, we are not going to be satisfied by his saying, as he does say,

> whatever I have accepted as most true I have acquired from or through the senses; but I have sometimes found them wanting, and it is a matter of prudence never wholly to trust things that have even once deceived us (*Med.* I, CSM II: 12; AT VII: 18: '[*n*]*empe quidquid hactenus ut maxime verum admisi, vel a sensibus vel per sensibus accepi; hos autem interdum fallere deprehendi, ac prudentiæ est numquam illis plane confidere qui nos vel semel deceperunt').[5]

The first part of this statement describes the doxastic habit the narrator had before he became cautious. It is the sort of thing that gets called a 'Principle of Acquaintance' (Flage 1999: 116). But for a 'principle', it gets abandoned pretty casually. If the narrator really had it as a 'principle', one wonders how he found it wanting. Even if he found it wanting on one occasion, is that reason enough to give up the habit of a lifetime? Still, he suddenly withdraws his trust in it. And we still do not have an answer to the question of what he found when he found that it would be prudent to be cautious. We are not told what justifies his being so dismissive of the senses, because he does not say how he found them wanting.

Though the sceptical literature in circulation in 1641, and familiar enough to Descartes, featured arguments from the contrariety of the senses, Descartes does not develop such an argument in *Meditations* I. I suggest that it would have been illicit for him to deploy such an argument or to assume the conclusion of one.

We do not find sceptical tropes involving the alleged contrariety of the senses in *Meditations* I because such arguments presuppose a notion of consistency or coherence to which our narrator is not, at the outset, entitled to help himself. To explain why the narrator of the *Meditations* is not entitled to argue from the contrariety of the senses to their being wanting, I need to indicate the notion of consistency or coherence that such arguments presuppose. To do so, I use the trite example of the 'round square tower' that flits across *Meditations* VI (CSM II: 53 and 57) without there doing the work that we might be looking to have done at the beginning of *Meditations* I.[6]

From afar, a given tower may look round and, from close up, it may look square. The apparent roundness is what some recent writers on related matters have called its 'narrow' content: it is a feature of the *look* of the tower. Hilary Putnam specifies the notion of narrowness, which he says is 'pretty explicit' in Descartes, as not 'presupposing the existence of any individual other than the subject to whom that [content] is ascribed' (Putnam 1975: 200). Roundness may also be a feature of the tower, but there is no contradiction between the look's being round and the tower's being square: even square objects can look round. Unlike the colour that a certain sort of reflection might lead us to deny is genuinely in, e.g. a piece of wax, roundness and squareness are properties that looks of a tower can share with the tower itself: that is what makes these looks true or false.

The narrator of the *Meditations* says that he used to accept as most true (and assured) whatever he acquired from or through the senses. He may have had other beliefs, including other beliefs about material objects, but these were to be accounted as less true (and assured) than the narrowly sensory ones. That was his habit in evaluating beliefs.

Suppose a person follows the narrator's trajectory and, somehow, along the way, has entertained the thought that nothing can be both round and square.[7] This thought cannot have come from viewing the tower and paying attention only to the narrow contents of the looks it presents. For, after all, the tower presents to the senses some looks that taken narrowly are round and others that also taken narrowly are square. Hence, the thought that roundness and squareness are inconsistent must derive from some source other than the narrow presentations of the senses to which the narrator so fully trusts.[8]

Now suppose that the thought about inconsistency derives from a source that we have called 'reflection'. The thought derived from reflection we may call R. What R says is that if something looks round and looks square then one of the looks must be wrong. If the narrowly sensory beliefs S1 (that the tower is round) and S2 (that the tower is square) are brought into contact with R, the person who accepts as most true what she has acquired from or through the senses will simply reject R. Either R is acquired only indirectly from the senses or is not acquired from the senses at all; in either case, it will be accounted less true than S1 and than S2. Moreover, R is accounted less true than the conjunction of S1 and S2. It is only if our enquirer accepts R as more true (or assured) than either of them or than the conjunction, that the conjunction itself becomes problematic.

R is not the only principle of reflection that we might appeal to. Consider, for instance, R*: 'some things that look round when small, and square when big should be counted as simply square'; with R*, S1 becomes the sensory belief that the tower is square-close-to-despite-or-because-of-its-roundness-from-afar. Variants on R* may even be what most of us work with. And we must not forget that some towers that look round from afar do so close up too. Because they are round.

Still, R is a thought about material things. And if the enquirer comes to reject R on the basis of S1 and S2, that may be a cause or reason for thinking that she has accepted as true something about material things that is false. But there is no reason to suppose that R has been at any time accepted. It is a mere hypothesis that is tested against experience and found not to fit the case of the tower. Hence, the enquirer will not have accepted R. Rather, she might believe that the tower is (*sic*) round from afar and is (*sic*) square close up. Indeed, it is a jolly good thing that the tower looks different according to where we look at it from: if it did not, we would not know how we were placed relative to it. Someone who takes beliefs S1 and S2 to be most true (and assured) is refusing to ask which is *the* look that the tower presents. And this is a perfectly proper way of refusing to ask what shape the tower looks both from afar and close up.

A refusal to ask these questions is compatible with a variety of theories about towers and about the shapes they are and look. One such theory is the widespread view that towers look different from different viewpoints and that, once we have relativised to viewpoint, S1 and S2 present no contrariety. Though S1 might be regarded as in one way or another better than S2 and might be used to explain it, neither is regarded as absolutely or finally *the* look of the tower. An alternative theory would be one on which towers – and the like – change shape according to where a viewer is placed. Even if this little bit of theorising may require the enquirer to be an ego-maniac, *at this stage in the proceedings*, that is not a sufficiently principled objection to it. Given that attention is only on the narrow content of the various looks of the tower, the theorising that harmonises them is, in any case, less assured than what has to be harmonised. Any harmonisation, however, must allow that S1 and S2 are consistent with what we see because they are jointly and separately things we see. The availability of even ego-maniacal theories means that there is no inevitability that the enquirer will notice that the roundness and squareness attributed to the tower could seem to be in any sort of conflict. If so, there need be no moment at which the enquirer is given the least suspicion that he has admitted the false as true.

In short, if the senses are our most authoritative source of beliefs, they will determine the contours of what we take to be consistent with what. On the doxastic habit that the *Meditation*'s narrator enunciates, there is no criterion of consistency or coherence among the deliverances of the senses antecedent to or normative of those deliverances. The trite contrarieties of the sceptical tradition cannot be discovered by the senses alone.

If the foregoing line of thought supplies Descartes with a reason for not developing an argument from the contrariety of the senses in *Meditations* I and if we charitably suppose that he is not illicitly depending on the conclusion of such an argument to get to the claim that he has been deceived by the senses, we have to look for some alternative account of what is going on.

One suggestion can be built out of the reference to prudence immediately following on the 'Principle of Acquaintance' in the statement of doxastic habit quoted above. What we might seem to have here is a policy of modesty motivating the narrator's self-attribution of credulity. Yet even a policy of being modest about one's powers stands in need of some sort of validation. And we may distinguish between policies that are validated by being given a direct or *ex ante* justification and those are given an indirect or *ex post* vindication.

Among policies we might find a direct justification for, there is the following line of thought about prudence. What we have quoted from the *Meditations* is a version of the maxim, 'once bitten, twice shy', which we know Descartes was attracted to because we find closely similar formulations in the *Principles* (*Pr.* I, 4, CSM I: 194),[9] the *Discourse* (*Dis.* IV, CSM I: 127)[10] and the *Search* (CSM II: 407).[11]

The main trouble with using this sort of maxim to get the operations of the *Meditations* going is that we have not yet seen any cause or reason for thinking that we have been bitten even once. The policy of being shy would be arbitrary and masochistic unless we had some grounds for *beginning* to suppose that we ought not to trust the senses. If, from what we have seen so far, the narrator does not have the means, within his previous doxastic habit (specified as the maximal trust in the senses of the 'Principle of Acquaintance'), to discover even one case of deception by the senses, then the prudential maxim has no application. The maxim is also self-undermining. Suppose it led us to doubt something that is true and properly acquired, even though acquired from or through the senses. If doubting means treating the object of doubt as on a par with what is 'patently false' (*Med.* I, CSM II: 12; AT VII: 18: '*aperte falsus*'; AT IXA: 14: '*manifestement faux*'), then the maxim will have misled us and we ought not wholly to trust it: it can be imprudent to be too prudent.

A confession of credulity, however humble, is not on its own a reason for believing that one has been subject to that vice, just as a guilty feeling is not itself a sufficient ground for thinking that one really has committed some sin. Nevertheless, it might be thought that the policy arising out of first assertion of the *Meditations* could be justified to some principle such as,

(P) A guarantee against credulity requires that anything that can be doubted be brought into doubt.

Descartes does offer us something very close to (P) when he says,

But since reason now sways me to be as careful about withdrawing assent from things that are not wholly certain and undoubtful as I am about those that are patently false, it will be enough for the rejection of all of them if I can find in each some reason for doubting it (*Med.* I, CSM II: 12; AT VII: 18: '*sed quia jam ratio persuadet, non minus accurate ab iis quæ non plane certa sunt atque indubitata, quam ab aperte falsis assessionem esse cohibendam, satis erit ad omnes rejiciendas, si aliquam rationem dubitandi in unaquaque reperero*').[12]

But this is a stage subsequent to the narrator's having discovered that some things are not wholly certain and that some are patently false. The work that a principle like (P) is needed do is that of directing us to such a discovery. The work that it can do is that of raising the mere possibility that we have been credulous: we can check whether we have been so by bringing what can be doubted into doubt. Even so, this puts the cart before the horse: doubting things that we can doubt may safeguard us against credulity in matters where we need and can use such a safeguard; but it does not follow that the discovery that we are capable of doubting something is a reason for thinking that we have been credulous about it. Because we have not yet found reason for thinking that we need a safeguard.

Two other points about (P).

One is that, at this stage in the *Meditations*, our capacity for bringing things into doubt looks for all the world like a mere psychological possibility. It is only later, in *Meditations* IV, that the possibility of doubting takes on its full metaphysical significance. Until then, the relation between our capacity for doubt and a guarantee against credulity is far from obvious. All we want to guarantee in guaranteeing ourselves against credulity is that we have no beliefs that are not true. There is no reason – yet – to suppose that possible objects of doubt are more likely to be untrue than things that we happen find undoubtful.

The second point is that a principle like (P) is surely among the things that are to be brought into doubt. At least, the narrator of the *Meditations*, wedded as he is to the senses, ought to doubt a deliverance of reflection like (P) more than he might doubt that a given tower is round and square.

Thus far, we have been heading towards a negative result. The first assertion of the *Meditations* refers to an act of noticing that cannot be like noticing that a given tower is round and/or square. It is, moreover, an act of noticing that cannot have resulted from an antecedently motivated policy of trying to find fault with our belief-acquiring apparatus. If this negative result were the last word on the matter, Descartes would not have put a convincing case for the supposition that he had been credulous from his earliest years. Hence the massacre of his opinions that *Meditations* I retails would be a frivolous and pointless caprice.

We may take up the distinction noted above between giving a doxastic policy a direct justification and supplying an indirect vindication. Nothing hangs on such differences as there might be between 'justifying' and 'vindicating'; but a direct justification for a doxastic policy would be a consideration that makes such a policy seem reasonable prior to its implementation. Thus, if the narrator of the *Meditations* had shown that his senses had deceived him at least once, the 'once bitten, twice shy' maxim may indicate a rational diffidence. On the other hand, a policy may be given an indirect vindication if it is shown to have had heuristic value after it has been tried. Naturally, indirect vindications of doxastic policies can vary in the rigorousness of the policies that they would support. For instance, a policy of beginning by not trusting the senses may end by reinstating some or all of the deliverances about which judgment had been suspended. And such vindications may be of varying degrees of absoluteness: we might find *ex post facto* that a given policy was the only one that could secure the goods we were after, or we might have to admit that the policy adopted was only one among a plurality, any of which would have done the trick.

The opening assertion of the *Meditations* can be given an indirect validation not so much because the narrator has first noticed anything about the senses or any other of his former habits, as because he has tried out alternatives to those habits. He has tried the suppositions, say, that no tower can be round and square or that colour is not genuinely in a piece of wax, and found that, on such suppositions, the prospects looked good for finding secure foundations on which to base something secure and lasting in the sciences. He need not have actually found those foundations or built anything on them to be able to see that, if found, they *would* offer opportunities for research that the senses alone do not.

An analogy.

Consider the situation of a person new to a town about which she has no topographical information. If she simply wants to get to the other side of it, she might begin by taking a turning that seems to be in the right general direction. Thereafter, what with one-way systems and other obstacles, she may have to take turnings that are not direct. If, in the end, she arrives at the other side of the town, the turnings taken will be seen to have been contributory to that success even though, at the time of their being taken, there was no compelling reason for supposing that they would have that result. On a subsequent occasion, the visitor will know at least one route that gets her across town, though it may not be the best.

At a slightly higher level of complexity, there are tasks of maze-solving on which one might try out a variety of algorithms that will allow one not to need to know where one is in order to get 'home'. In a sufficiently simple maze, the adoption of, say, the right-hand rule will be indirectly vindicated by the fact that one gets in and out, though one may not have been sure in advance that there were no 'islands' in the maze, and though one may have taken a less than optimal route. If the right-hand rule turns out to have worked, one can hazard the guess that there were no 'islands'. One ought not to be very confident, since there may be 'islands' on routes taken by those who do not follow the right-hand rule or who institute the rule too late in their attempt to negotiate the maze. Yet the adoption of the policy not merely gets one one's immediate objective (the ability to negotiate the maze) but also indicates something about the maze (that it is relatively simple, because traversable by the right-hand rule).

If one's aim is not merely to get to this place or that, but to have some assurance that the route one is taking is the shortest, it is necessary to come to some understanding of the shape of the town or maze that one is negotiating. As a visitor wanders around a town unknown to her, she will see the advantage of trying out suppositions such as that this lane is parallel to that, or that the one converges on the other. She need not suppose at the outset that any of the picturesque views she gets on the ground is in any way misleading. But suppositions about parallels and convergences are attempts to systematise those views into something like a bird's eye view. An uncartographical scheme of a town has the disadvantages that it is not useful for finding new routes and that it may easily contain undetected geometrical inconsistencies which will, from time to time, lead us either astray or into longer paths than necessary. The visitor can recognise that there is a privileged point of view (the bird's) that can make sense of others (pedestrians'). Long before she has completed her map-like scheme of the shape of the town, she can see that having such a scheme has distinct advantages.

Applying these analogies to Descartes, the idea is that the enquiry rehearsed in the *Meditations* cannot be the narrator's first effort at bringing his experience into order. From what we are told, the narrator does not seem, in any obvious way, to have the means to discover directly (noticing from narrow sensory inputs) that trusting the senses is a form of credulity. Rather, he has decided to see whether he can do better. In trying out some alternatives, he has had a glimpse of the ways that some policies of directing his attention away from the senses will bring him to appreciate how many false things he has accepted as true. If, therefore, he does succeed in producing a secure and lasting foundation for his beliefs, the seemingly arbitrary move of discounting the senses will be indirectly vindicated, just as adopting the right-hand rule in a maze or trying to map a town are ways of improving our ability to negotiate unknown objects.

The negative evidence for this understanding of how the *Meditations* opens is (i) that Descartes does not develop an argument from the contrariety of the senses, because to have done so would have been illicit, given his situation;

and (ii) that the 'once bitten, twice shy' maxim lacks specific reference to what the narrator can perceive of his situation. Two more positive indications are available for the claim that the narrator is depending on the results of some earlier hazards at enquiry.

One is the concession in the 'Synopsis' that the cataclysm of doubt in *Meditations* I does not appear at first sight to be useful (CSM II: 9; AT VII: 12: '*utilitas prima fronte non appareat*'; AT IXA: 9: '*bien que l'utilité* [. . .] *ne paraisse pas d'abord*'). Only once the narrator has gone through the process, or at least seen what going through the process involves, can he see that setting his earlier beliefs aside will end up producing significant advantages. The implication is that he has had some intimations of those advantages. There is a hint of this manœuvre at the beginning of *Discourse* IV, where that narrator admits that the speculations that set him going may have been too abstract and odd to be to everyone's taste and proposes to speak of them only insofar as they will help the reader to judge of their results (CSM I: 126).[13] The hint is that the years that elapsed between his resolve to re-found his beliefs and the dramatic date of *Discourse* IV were spent in seeing what would come of the enquiries that led to the *Essays*. These enquiries relied only indirectly on the senses and built up a strongly explanatory picture of the world that downgraded sensory deliverances.

The other positive indication in the *Meditations* is in the repetition, in the first paragraph of the work, of references to times earlier than the dramatic date of the meditation. The first reference is to the time at which the narrator says that he noticed what we have found he could not, in any direct way, have noticed. The repetition occurs when he refers to his having so long delayed in the implementation of the huge enterprise that he had envisaged (*Med.* I, CSM II: 12; AT VII: 17: '*tamdiu cunctatus sum*'; cf. AT IXA: 13: '*ce qui m'a fait différer si longtemps*'). In the period between his having envisaged the huge enterprise and his actually undertaking it, he has had time to consider the possibility that he has admitted false things as true. Since his expectation is that the result of the enquiry will provide him with a different set of beliefs from those that he has accepted hitherto, he may be said to have noticed that he has admitted false things as true in that he has noticed alternative lines of enquiry from those to which he has been habituated by his reliance on the senses. The expectation that the enquiry of the *Meditations* will be revisionary of his beliefs is justified by his having seen, if only in outline, what sort of shape some alternative lines of enquiry might have, and by his having seen that some of alternatives look likely to provide superior bases for an explanatory scheme of the world.

The references to times antecedent to the *Meditations* are not filled out by that work's narrator. He is a rather sparse figure. To see one way in which someone might have direct evidence for the falsity of some of her beliefs, we may turn to the more fully-rounded quasi-autobiographical narrator of the *Discourse*, whose strategies are less gnomic that those of the *Meditations*.

Common sense in the Discourse

The first sixteen or so AT pages of the *Discourse* tell the tale of a person coming to notice the untrustworthiness of the sources from which he has acquired his beliefs. This tale is the spelling out of the thought, referred to above as (a), but not available at the outset of the *Meditations*, that, as a matter of fact, everyone does know that some of the beliefs formed in earliest youth (and those built on them) are sub-standard. In this respect, Descartes' tale is commonsensical: he can expect it to resemble the experience of his readers. He is relying not just on what he finds in himself, but also on the way that the noticing of our fallibility is part of common experience.

There are perhaps two other respects in which the operation of the *Discourse* is commonsensical. One is that in which the narrator describes his education as involving a clash of authorities, to which he responds, as we shall see in more detail in Chapter 6, by supposing that none is quite what it represents itself as being. The other – perhaps as a consequence – is that this narrator is not so entirely dependent on the senses as the narrator of the *Meditations* takes himself to have been: the *Discourse*'s narrator allows that it is common experience that the senses can throw up puzzles, and nothing in the nature of their deliverances requires us to account them as truer or more assured than any other source of potential belief; the 'Principle of Acquaintance' was never really adopted.

From the point in his quasi-autobiography at which he says that he has been fed since childhood on reading-matter (*Dis.* I, CSM I: 112), the narrator of the *Discourse* focuses on what he was given to study at school. With some mitigations, he reflects on the unreliability of main components of the curriculum – the classical languages, rhetoric, poetry, ethics, theology and philosophy – as guides in the formation of beliefs and as good examples for the cultivation of doxastic habits (or as examples for the cultivation of good doxastic habits).

In particular, he observes that there is nothing in philosophy that is not subject to dispute (*Dis.* I, CSM I: 115). From this he infers without comment or further ado that everything in it is doubtful (*Dis.* I, CSM I: 115; AT VI: 8: '*et par conséquent qui ne soit douteuse*'). Given the insouciance with which he makes this inference and his similar remarks, earlier, in the *Rules* (*Reg.* II, CSM I: 11)[14] and, perhaps later, in the *Search* (CSM II: 411),[15] it is fair to attribute to Descartes and his narrator no doubt about the thesis (which one might imagine disputing and thus throwing into doubt) that everything disputed is doubtful.

Nevertheless, to each of the disputants in a going debate, the position he occupies has all the appearance of being true. That is why the debate goes on. Hence, even things that are doubtful can appear true. In the eyes of each participant, the opinion of his interlocutor will be doubtful and the interlocutor will appear credulous for having defended an opinion that has the (mere) appearance of being true. So, a disputed opinion will be one that the narrator of the *Discourse* has reason to class with matters for whose doubtfulness he might have grounds independent of the fact of there being a dispute under way. To defend an opinion about a disputed matter is thus to expose oneself to the allegation of credulity. In order to avoid that allegation, one should try to count things that merely seem to be true as if they were close to being false (*Dis.* I, CSM I: 115; AT VI: 8: '[. . .] *je réputais presque pour faux tout ce qui n'était que vraisemblable'*).

His understanding of difference of opinion among various (other) believers leads the narrator of the *Discourse* to discover the likelihood that each of us has fallen into credulity. This discovery is not so claustrophobically first-person as the first thing the narrator of the *Meditations* says he has noticed. Nevertheless, the underlying order of the discoveries is the same in the two works: first, one establishes that one has been credulous about a certain range of matters; then, one associates credulity with the doubtfulness of the matters in that range; and only lastly does one withdraw assent from those matters on the grounds that one knows that the sources of the relevant beliefs have deceived one. This comes out in the following passage, part of which we have already referred to:

> because I then wanted to attend only to the search for the truth, I thought I ought to do the opposite [*sc.* to acting on uncertain opinions] and to reject as absolutely false everything about which I could imagine the slightest doubt so as to see whether, after that, anything would remain for me to believe that was wholly indubitable. Thus, because our senses sometimes deceive us, I sought to suppose that there was nothing of the same sort as they lead us to imagine (*Dis.* IV, CSM I: 127; AT VI: 31–2: '[. . .] *parce qu'alors je désirais vaquer seulement à la recherche de la verité, je pensai qu'il fallait que je fisse le contraire, et que je rejetasse, comme absolument faux, tout ce en quoi je pourrais imaginer le moindre doute, afin de voir s'il ne resterait point, après cela, quelque chose en ma créance, qui fût entièrement indubitable. Ainsi, à cause que nos sens nous trompent quelquefois, je voulus supposer qu'il n'y avait aucune chose qui fût telle qu'ils nous la font imaginer'*).

In the preceding parts of the *Discourse*, nothing has been said about the senses' being deceptive. At least there is no argument to show that they are deceptive. The remarks about the possibility of taking for gold and diamonds what is really copper and glass (*Dis.* I, CSM I: 112) and the reference to the generality of the (new) mathematical method (*Dis.* II, CSM I: 121) might be allusions to the view that the deceptiveness of the senses may be uncovered by reason. Hence, if the narrator is entitled to help himself to that claim, it must be because he is treating it as commonsensical in two of the senses outlined above, namely, (i) that we all know that our senses sometimes deceive us; and (ii) that we are not obliged to treat the senses as *a priori* truer and more assured than any other source of potential beliefs.

Everyone is supposed to know, in the example already cited, that at least one of the two looks of a tower, as round and as square, needs to be appropriately relativised, and that neither is guaranteed adequate. In the situation set up in the first three parts of the *Discourse*, reason and reflection both have some purchase on our belief-forming habits. But, before the institution of the characteristically Cartesian enquiry, both of them are regarded as less than wholly secure. After the passage just quoted, even the simplest geometrical reasonings are put in the same doubt that has been visited on the deliverances of the senses: because there are people who make mistakes even in the simplest bits of geometry, we must reject what have passed for demonstrations (*Dis.* IV, CSM I: 127). Before applying the even-handed doubt, the narrator of the *Discourse* could have rejected any of the beliefs in conflict: any one (or more) of beliefs such as S1, S2 and R could go down before a combination of the others. Since R is neither rejected out of hand nor regarded as immune to doubt, the genuineness of the conflict can be recognised and, with the application of doubt, be used as a marker of earlier credulity.

In short, the *Discourse* exposes our susceptibility to a far-reaching credulity on the basis of common experience. Given that the senses do not undermine themselves, the narrator proceeds by showing that to trust them is to be as credulous as one who trusts the authorities of the schoolroom. The grounds of this exposure are, therefore, external to the enquiry in accordance with doxastic rectitude that Descartes proposes for himself and recommends to us. The exposure of credulity depends neither on the aspirations that that enquiry is meant to fulfil (as it appears to do in the *Meditations*), nor on any thesis that arises from the successful prosecution of such an enquiry.

Even if what the *Discourse* reveals derives from beliefs that are common enough, the application of those beliefs is very *un*common. What their application means is that a vast swathe of our most cherished beliefs are the products of a lamentable credulity.

Doctrine in the Principles

In the *Meditations*, the fact that the senses are sensitive to qualities, such as smells and colours, that we learn are not genuinely in objects, such as pieces of wax, supplies a ground for dismissing once and for all many of the promptings of the senses. But Descartes does not establish that those qualities are deceptive until the end of the second day of meditation. To see the importance of this move, we should look at a sequence of articles towards the end of the first book of the *Principles* that clearly relates reliance on the senses to the most fundamental causes of human error.

Picking up the division of the objects of perception sketched in *Principles* I, 48, Descartes considers, in article I, 66, the fact that,

> since our earliest years, we have all judged everything that we sensed to be things existing outside our minds and closely similar to what we sensed, that is to say, to the perceptions we had of them (CSM I: 216; AT VIIIA: 32: '[. . .] *nemo nostrum est, qui non ab ineunte ætate judicavit, ea omnia quæ sentiebat, esse res quasdam extra mentem suam existentes, et sensibus suis, hoc est, perceptionibus quas de illis habebat, plane similis*').

Our habit of making these judgments not only made it hard for us to limit ourselves to what was strictly – what we have been calling 'narrowly' – contained in our perceptions, but also to avoid supposing that we were seeing something clear and distinct when we saw something as coloured.

The discrimination that Descartes develops in the subsequent articles is between, on the one hand, the things that are wholly in the mind or perception (*Pr.* I 67, CSM I: 217; AT VIIIA: 32: '*in sola mente sive perceptione*') and should therefore be regarded purely as sensations or thoughts (*Pr.* I, 68, CSM I: 217; AT VIIIA: 32: '*tantummodo ut sensus, sive cogitationes*'), and, on the other, what can be clearly known to be in bodies (*Pr.* I, 69, CSM I: 217; AT VIIIA: 32–3: '*quæ in corporibus clare percipi*'), such as shape, (local) motion, position, duration, number and the like. This discrimination is further spelt out by saying that we cannot intellectually grasp any similarity between the colour we suppose to be in objects and what we experience in sense (*Pr.* I, 70, CSM I: 218).[16]

The arising of the habit of judging that colour is in the objects that we see it as being in is explained in article I, 71. The habit is there said to be the first and main cause of all our errors. And, not for the first time in the *Principles*, reference is made to the state that humans are in in their earliest years.[17] That state is one in which the mind or soul is fastened to the body (*Pr.* I, 71, CSM I: 218; AT VIIIA: 35: '*alligatus*' AT IXB: 58: '*lié*'): it is said to be stuck to the body (*Pr.* I, 71, CSM I: 219; AT VIIIA: 35: '*adhærens*', AT IXB: 58: '*étroitement uni*', also at *Pass.* I, 30, AT XI: 351), and to be drenched in it.[18]

In the following article, the contrast is made between the early period of a human's life in which the soul is enslaved to the body (*Pr.* I, 72, CSM I: 219; AT VIIIA: 36: '*servit*'; AT IXB: 59: '*sujette*') and later times at which it is freer to attend to the reasons that are available to help us rid ourselves of the beliefs formed on the basis of the senses (*Pr.* I, 71, CSM I: 220). Of course, it is 'official' Cartesian doctrine that, throughout terrestrial life, the soul of a human is very closely connected and almost mixed in with the body (e.g. *Med.* VI, CSM II: 56); but the special defect of the child is that he cannot turn his attention away from the senses.

The disposition to go with the flow of sensory promptings is not a habit that the child can be said to have chosen. Rather, it is forced on him by pressing biological demands.[19] Unless the child focuses his attention on these demands and their satisfaction, he will be unlikely to grow up at all. If he does not grow up, he will never be able to reconsider the veracity of the senses.

Even in adulthood, the reconsideration of the senses as a source of beliefs does not require the enquirer to rid herself of them more than temporarily. At most, she may take short-term measures, like shutting the eyes and so on at the beginning of *Meditations* III (CSM II: 24), so as not to be distracted by sensory promptings. A person whose sensory apparatus is not obstructed or impaired will continue to be subject to bombardment from and through them. Even an enquirer who possesses perfect doxastic rectitude neither can nor must set them aside entirely. She cannot because, however resolutely she counts them as signifying nothing, a mere act of (dis)attention is insufficient to still their sound and fury. She must not because she remains a human being and therefore periodically subject to much the same biological demands as a child.

The anthropology that Descartes is proposing is clear enough: children believe that what they see, hear, taste, smell and feel represents the way the world is. They are what epistemologists like to call 'naïve realists'. Whether or not this is a good description of infantile development, we may ask whether saying that the doxastic habits of the naïve realist are infantile is an argument against naïve realism.

In one way what is being proposed is a slightly elaborate insult. If you believe that what you see is the way the world is, then you are like a child. And we all know what children are like: they are soft in the brain.[20] In the process of growing up, we should seek to distance ourselves as much as possible from childish tendencies (Gouhier 1962: 58; Garber 1986: 91–3; Menn 1998: 303ff.). Children need to be taken in hand by adults (*Dis.* II, CSM I: 117). They have got no self-control, no sense of proportion. They do not know what is good for them. For instance, they are excessively attracted by sweet things that an adult knows should be eaten in moderation. Descartes' insult is that relying on the senses is like giving in to the offer of a third bowl of ice-cream. The insult depends on there being knowledge of what is good for us, on our knowing that self-control and a sense of proportion are preferable in the long run. These presuppositions of the criticism of childish doxastic habits are fleshed out in the *Principles* with a distinction that can, without too much pulling and pushing, be described as a distinction between 'primary' and 'secondary' qualities.[21]

Relative to bodies, Descartes has already established the primacy of the 'primary' qualities – shape, (local) motion and the rest – by having set them up as those of which we can have clear and distinct perception (*Pr.* I, 45–7) and by having identified them as the essential *propria* of corporeal substance (*Pr.* I, 53–5).[22] We sometimes judge in a childish way on the basis of the senses that colour is in the object of sight; but, according to *Principles* I, 70, the intellect (AT VIIIA: 34: '*intellectus*') or reason (AT IXB: 58: '*raison*') gives us to appreciate that there is nothing in the object that resembles what is in our senses. Rather, we should accept that we are left wholly ignorant when we see colour in an object or feel pain in a limb because we do not know what it is that we are seeing or feeling (*Pr.* I, 68, CSM I: 217). We do not know what we are seeing or feeling because what is in our perceptions does not resemble what is in the object. At best, we may properly judge that there is something, though we may not know what, in it that causes us to sense colour or feel pain.[23]

The move we are now meant to make is that, when the intellect or reason tells us that colour is not in the objects the configurations of whose surfaces prompt us to believe that those objects are coloured, we ought to believe what the intellect or reason tells us. Intellect or reason is superior as a source of beliefs to the senses because the ideas it furnishes can be clear and distinct, whereas the senses impose obscure and confused ideas on us. To prefer obscure and confused ideas is to prefer ice-cream to crisp vegetables: those who have learned to like vegetables have overcome their childish tastes and are on their way to a healthy diet.

The discovery that Descartes takes himself to have made, that the intellect is a superior source of beliefs, is clearly part of a substantive theory, not only of the nature of representation but of the nature of what exists. That theory is itself the product of the operations essentially involving the intellect. There is, of course, a separate question to be asked about the confirmation or jus-tification of the whole of the substantive theory that Descartes wishes to substitute for the beliefs of credulous children.

As we saw for the *Meditations*, if the theory that should emerge from the operation of the intellect looks more reliable, more complete, more coherent or more likely to account for the phenomena than anything we can get by reliance on the senses, then we should seek to embrace and develop it. Even without an elaborated account of the advantages of possession of such a theory, there need be nothing vicious about the apparent circularity of Descartes' operation. If it really does show that attention to the senses leads to generalised error, then, unless we have grounds for doubting the means by which that doctrine was arrived at, we really ought to think that virtually all the beliefs children form are erroneous. Moreover, given that most people go through the whole of their lives with the habits they formed in earliest childhood, because of the immediate costs of turning their attention from the senses, virtually all the beliefs about the nature of physical objects that anyone has ever formed have been erroneous.

This is a drastic conclusion. The substantive theory of representation and of substance implies that, if we are interested in getting our understanding of the world in order, then a radical overturning of our beliefs is called for. Once we discover that we have been credulous and recognise that our credulity has led us into massive error, we ought to be ready to do almost anything to overcome our infantile ways.

Whereas, in the *Meditations,* the justification for supposing that we have been credulous was indirect, arising from no more than a glimpse of what properly conducted enquiry could yield, in the *Principles,* our credulity is explained by an account of the priorities we had as children in relation to what is actually yielded by an enquiry in accordance with reason. In neither case, is the (subjective) doubtfulness we might feel about the senses – or any other source of belief – a factor of the sort we saw at work in the *Discourse.*

Responding to the discovery of credulity

In the three texts reviewed, Descartes indicates the extent and depth of his credulity. Let us separate some of the problems that the extent and the depth face him with.

The sheer variety of cases in which we are mistaken, the huge number of false beliefs we have acquired and the generalness of the errors into which we have been led certainly mean that we cannot hope to remedy the situation by trying to remove them one by one. Descartes is quite clear that this would be an endless undertaking: '[*n*]*ec ideo etiam singulæ erunt percurrendæ, quod operis esset infiniti*' (*Med.* I, CSM II: 12; AT VII: 18).

Unlike the empiricist approach referred to at the outset of the chapter, according to which I can use my other beliefs to criticise a given opinion derived from the senses, the cataclysm that Descartes envisages is so all-encompassing that it seems that no such appeal is possible, either to confirm or to reject the opinion under scrutiny. If all the beliefs of a given type are under suspicion, then none of them can be used to vindicate any of the others; nor, as we saw in considering the *Meditations,* can they be used to impugn each other. Coherence is neither a criterion nor a tool of criticism.

When we come to consider the formal structure of the sceptical arguments that make up the body of *Meditations* I, we shall see that Descartes' approach to the problem of ridding himself of such a mass of credulous beliefs is to take them as classes. The classes he picks out are relative to the conditions under which any belief from a given source would be put in doubt. He is thus treating the beliefs in the classes obliquely or non-referentially, not taking account of their content, not examining what they tell him or how they are related to each other. The advantage of adopting this approach is that it permits him to manipulate his beliefs abstractly or formally. He is regarding them as not his.

The disadvantage is that he does not really rid himself of them. He merely brackets them for the purposes of his enquiry. What is in play is akin to the state of suspension theorised by Edmund Husserl, when he claims that he is able to produce in himself a posture that he calls 'phenomenological ἐποχή' and that he describes in the following terms:

> all sciences which relate to this natural world [. . .] I disconnect them *all*, I make absolutely no use of their standards, I do not appropriate a single one of the propositions that enter into their systems, even though their evidential value is perfect, I take none of them.
>
> (Husserl 1913: 111; cf. Laporte 1945: 478)

The hypotheses of *Meditations* I, that I am mad, dreaming or the dupe of a malicious demon, respond to the problem raised by the sheer range of the beliefs that are to be rejected: they give reasons for attempting to adopt this sort of posture. But they do not give us reason for thinking that we are really able to succeed in such a venture. For, the invocation of those hypotheses leaves out of account the fact that we are deeply attached to most of our beliefs derived from the senses and would be hard put to give up the habits that went into their formation.

The depth of our attachment to sense-based ideas might seem a purely contingent matter: just as a child can, and in due course will, be taught not to gorge on ice-cream, so sufficient training might lead us to disdain the senses in a generalised and systematic way, as a matter of habit. But saying that it is purely contingent does not show that, given the way humans are constituted and placed in the world, there is an amount of training that could, in fact, bring it about that anyone ever should acquire that habit.

We have yet to see that the willableness of the will, which was so startling a feature of the *Passions'* optimism about our being able to eliminate all causes of unhappiness, applies also in the realm of belief-formation So we should think, albeit schematically, about the choices that might lead to our pursuing diffidence towards the senses as a guiding principle of the sort of enquiry that Descartes has on hand.

Consider, first, the position of an enquirer at the outset of an enterprise that involves her overthrowing all the beliefs she has derived from the hitherto privileged source. Unless she has fair grounds for expecting that she will recoup the losses involved in the hecatomb of her beliefs, it may well be simply foolish for her to undertake such an enquiry. The promise of a superior mode of belief-acquisition that we glimpsed in considering the indirect vindication of the first move of the *Meditations*, and that was taken as established in the *Principles*, may be simply too distant for it to be worth pursuing at such a cost.

Even if what she is supposed to get out of the reform of her beliefs is as guaranteed against credulity as she could wish, the enquirer has to pass through stages of high risk both as to whether anything will fit the bill and as to whether what does fit the bill is of any real or immediate use. Again, if she is taking the massacre of beliefs to be of practical significance, the risks of finding that the body of her guaranteed beliefs grows too slowly may be too high to justify her embarking on the undertaking that Descartes proposes. Hence, if she is motivated by an aversion to risk, then it is by no means clear that it will be rational for her even to pretend to have divested herself of the sense-based beliefs that brought her to be able to survey the risks involved in the various doxastic policies among which she can choose.

This line of thought has already been answered by Descartes' claim to have found that sense-derived beliefs are almost all misleading about the nature of the world. In the terms he suggests, one ought to be prepared to go any distance to find a point from which to upset the whole body of those very beliefs (*Med.* II, CSM I: 16). But, if, to find the Archimedean fulcrum (and then the standpoint from which to operate the lever), I have to divest myself of everything I hold dear, the abstract desirability of having the results of such an operation may seem insufficient to motivate the effort involved. After all, I can find my way about well enough without taking those pains.

True enough, most humans have beliefs that are adapted for many practical purposes. That being so, it is not obvious that falsity is such a bad thing. At least, it means that there is no special urgency about overhauling my beliefs. And Descartes admits as much: soon after reporting his discovery of how many false things he had accepted, he describes himself as having laid aside his programme for reform until he was old enough and adequately undisturbed to carry it through.[24] Even if it is not urgent, we should try the overhaul some time: as he says at *Principles* I, 1, '*semel in vita*' (CSM I: 193; AT VIIIA: 5).

If the enquirer is content to get along with beliefs that are generally adequate for day-to-day purposes, some resort has to be made to higher ground.

Descartes is fully aware that the cultivation of doxastic rectitude threatens to be an arduous undertaking: 'Synopsis' of the *Meditations* (CSM II: 12);

Meditations I (CSM II: 15); *Meditations* III (CSM II: 24) and *Principles* I, 72–3 (CSM I: 220).[25] So the benefits of aiming at it must be long-term. And this is one strategy that Descartes opens up, in promising not only that his method will lead to the discovery of remedies for all the ills of mind, as in the *Passions*, and body (e.g. *Dis.* VI, CSM I: 143; also letter to Mersenne, 9th January 1639, CSMK: 131),[26] but also that the outpouring of the truths that follow from the principles of physics will bring us to such a level of wisdom, perfection of life and happiness that everyone will find it irresistible (LP, CSM I: 190). Moreover, he is not shy about upping the stakes from human life on earth to the longer-term question of what God wants (Epistle Dedicatory to *Pr.*, CSM I: 191; also letter to Mersenne, 15th April 1630, CSMK: 22).

It is an nice question how far Descartes is philosophically committed to this sort of background to the epistemological choices here. It is not arbitrary, however, to see something like the notion of a 'conversion' involved in his deprecating the deliverances of the senses. In the well-known Platonic simile of the Cave in the seventh book of the *Republic* (514 A–521 C), a man determined to discover the reasons for the sensory inputs to which he has been accustomed, has to turn his back on them (περιαγωγή: 519 D) in order to face the light that accounts for them.[27] Even if, at first, such a man will be blinded by the light (*Rep.*, VII, 515 C and 516 A), and will, on first reconsidering the objects of sensory perception, make a bit of a fool of himself (517 A and D), he will, nevertheless, be able to conduct himself rationally (517 C). Though Plato admits that this procedure is a long way round (*Rep.*, VI, 504 A 4–505 B 4), that need not be a crushing objection to it. As that objection is sometimes put, e.g. by Peirce, it is arbitrary to take a long route when a shorter one seems to be available: '[i]t is, therefore, as useless a preliminary as going to the North Pole would be in order to get to Constantinople by coming down regularly upon a meridian' (1868: V, 265). Plato's and Descartes' claim must be that the apparently shorter route does not lead to where you want to get to. It is in reality a dead end because it does not lead to what we are looking for: something solid and lasting in the sciences (*Med.* I, CSM II: 12; AT VII: 17 '[. . .] *quid aliquando firmum et mansurum cupiam in scientiis stabilire*', cf. Plato, *Ep.*, VII, 342B–4C).

Even so, there may be obstacles to the execution of the project.

Once we have discovered that trust in the senses is credulous and accepted that credulity is a vice because it leads us into massive error, we still need to show that human beings can, at least in principle, dissent from all the deliverances of the senses. For, it appears that human beings are so constituted as to tend to assent to most of the promptings of the senses. That is the way they seem to be rigged up, even if Husserl thinks that he is different and Plato wants to be different. The idea of turning away from the senses is so twisted and contrary to our natures that it can be nothing but a philosopher's parlour-game, in the same league as the White Queen's believing half a dozen impossible things before breakfast (Carroll 1871: 177) or the perversely literate Irnerio who seeks to teach himself not to read (Calvino 1979: 47–8).

In one sense, of course, it is true that I *now* have no control over the beliefs that I have, in the past, picked up higgledy-piggledy. But that is not at issue. What Descartes needs is some sense in which I can *now* do what I like with the beliefs that I now have, however and whenever I acquired them and in which I can determine what sorts I pick up in the future. That is, he needs to show that I at least *can* have pretty full control over whether I believe this or that. If such control is within my reach, then the apparent impossibility of my doing away with any sense-derived belief is a false appearance.

To show this, we have to consider how we can set ourselves against our previous habits, what sorts of resolutions we can effectively form to prevent further credulity, and what means we have at our disposal for controlling the beliefs we form. This is the issue that Descartes can be seen addressing in *Meditations* IV, where he describes the very special equipment that we have for avoiding error by mobilising what we have been calling the willableness of the will.

4 The control of credulity

Error and theodicy

The ethical discovery that the passions often lead us astray, but can be reined in by virtue, is parallel to the epistemological discovery that we have been credulous, but might be able to do better. The parallelism exemplifies an important relation between what ought to be and what is. In this chapter and the next, I shall seek to illustrate a general structural affinity between the very special equipment that Descartes thinks we have for controlling assent – and therefore our tendency to credulity – and what many moralists have thought is the controlling factor in all genuinely human action. This is the will.

Descartes' specification of the will specifies very special equipment because the will is set to a task that can easily seem impossible, namely, the extirpation of all beliefs that have been or could, in future, be derived from or through the senses or that are in any other way potential carriers of falsehood. One underlying aim is to show that the specification he gives is, indeed, the specification of equipment that could perform that task: our vicious tendencies to believe all sorts of rubbish can be overcome, if we are careful, patient and diligent. But the story is not entirely rosy. Because credulity is a habit that afflicts us as animals and, so, is ultimately incorrigible, the operation of the very special equipment of the will cannot produce a fully internalised habit (as we said earlier 'second nature') to the same extent that our vicious habits can operate without our reflecting on them.

Philosophers of a mechanistic, technocratic, empiricist bent – what William James would call 'tough-minded' (James 1907: 13) – tend to regard the acquisition of a belief as an occurrence in which we have no, or very little, say and in which we are subject to biology, environment, upbringing, society and whatnot. Without being 'tender-minded', Descartes takes belief-formation to be a form of action in many respects similar to choice about conduct, in which we can affirm or deny as we see fit. So another aim of the forthcoming discussion is to support the claim that the story that Descartes tells is no less coherent and sensitive to the phenomena than the sort of explanation of doxastic behaviour on which there is virtually no room for autonomy in examining, selecting, adopting and applying both beliefs and standards of belief-formation.

Giving more attention to *Meditations* IV than is usual in general accounts of Descartes' thought, I aim to show that he there describes the operation of the human mind so as to make the conquest of credulity a central philosophical task, one that is both possible and necessary for anything deserving the name of enquiry. The phases of my account may be staked out as follows.

First, I set out a basic analogy between the traditional problem of evil and two of its applications to human action: the problem of sin and the problem of error.

In taking this line, I am conscious of placing Descartes in the context of theological discussions that are somewhat alien to modern, Anglophone, tendentially empiricist and 'analytical' accounts that seek to abstract from his writings epistemological principles that can be assessed irrespective of cultural background. That is, I seek historical reconstruction of Descartes' thought by offering motivations both for some of his moves that today may seem bizarre or simply misguided, and for the acquiescence of many of his contemporaries in those moves. Thus, at the end of this chapter, I try to show why Descartes' doctrine that the will is of a different order from the intellect did not cause a stir among the first commentators on the *Meditations*; and, at the end of Chapter 5, I try to locate his position relative to an accusation that was very popular in his day, but that does not seem to have been made against him: the accusation of being in odour of the Pelagian heresy of believing that humans are capable of salvation (and its epistemological analogue, knowledge) without divine grace. In these cases, Descartes can be seen to be giving an adequate response to pressures on his thought that are not, generally speaking, powerful today.

Second, granting that all humans are subject to error, and supposing that that fact needs to be described, I begin the analysis of *Meditations* IV, and of parallel passages in the *Principles*, by examining Descartes' claim that God is not the cause of our errors. He argues, first, that God must have given us a perfect faculty for judging; and, second, that it is because we fail to use it rightly that we make the mistakes that we do. By way of excursus to justify what I earlier called my mild unitarianism, I then consider how the thought that Descartes' expresses in and after 1641 (i.e. in the *Meditations*, the *Principles* and some of the later letters) matches what he says in his earlier writings. Specifically, I aim to show that in the *Rules*, he does not regard the intellect as the whole of the faculty for judging.

Third, I consider how it is possible to misuse the faculty for judging that

God has given us. In this phase of the argument, the theological content of Descartes' thought is perhaps at its most pervasive, and at its least persuasive and easy to follow. He proposes that the intellect is finite and that the will is infinite; the unequal distribution of these modalities seem to be derived from considerations in a complex history of debates about the relative powers of the two parts that make up the faculty of judging. I conjecture that Descartes' balancing act here, between those who stress the role of the intellect and those who give primacy to the will, helps explain why the views he expresses elicited relatively little comment from his contemporaries, though they are among the strangest from the modern point of view.

In the next chapter, I look at what happens when the faculty for judging is rightly used. Given the criterion of clear and distinct ideas established in *Meditations* III, assent to them is divinely guaranteed. But it is still worth examining in closer detail how Descartes conceives the relation between the will and the intellect when they are working as much in harmony with each other as is possible in humans. This leads to a comparison between, on the one hand, our assent to what is guaranteed by God and, on the other, His assent to and creation of the eternal truths. After a review of the grades of freedom that are involved in these operations, the chapter closes with the question, already referred to, of Descartes' theory of assent in relation to the doctrines of the Fall and of grace, with their attendant risks of heresy.

Hardly more than twenty years ago in the Anglophone world, a discussion of these matters would easily have seemed out of place in accounts of Descartes' thought. For instance, some of the most important conspectus anthologies have tended to underrepresent the question of assent; thus Doney (ed. 1968), Hooker (ed. 1978), Cottingham (ed. 1992) and Voss (ed. 1992) all lack a contribution focused on the issue. Even notably sensitive critics, such as Anthony Kenny could write at length about Descartes (Kenny 1968) and treat the theory of assent rather cursorily, though the matter is at the centre of a slightly later article, to which the present treatment is repeatedly indebted (Kenny 1972). Much more recently, a booklength study of the *Meditations* that presents itself as 'analytical and historical' virtually omits *Meditations* IV 'in the interest of brevity' (Dicker 1993: viii).

Against this trend, there has been a growing recognition that, even if what Descartes says is somehow unsatisfactory, it must be handled with some care. Of those who do address the matter with any seriousness, some are apt to regard the theological dimension as 'superficial' (Wilson 1978: 139), while others are firm that the 'analogy with traditional theodicy is misleading' (Rosenthal 1986: 407), or that Descartes' operation, from the title of *Meditations* IV onwards, is an exercise in 'eccentricity' (Caton 1973: 90). Of those who acknowledge that the way Descartes deals with this issue is 'exactly the same as [. . .] with moral wrong doing' (Williams 1978: 169), some go on to say that this is a 'misdescription' leading to a 'vacuous' solution (ibid.: 171 and 175), that it is 'scattered' and fails to be 'sustained and systematic' (Cress 1994: 145), or that it is a 'conceptual confusion' (Curley 1975: 176). More positively, others suppose that Descartes offers a classic 'free will' solution (Beck 1965: 211–12; Tierno 1997: 71–3) or that his proposal must depend instead on an appeal to a 'principle of plenitude' (Calvert 1972: 401).

The picture has been somewhat different among French commentators: whatever their other differences of opinion, we find substantial agreement among the major figures. Thus, in his seminal work on the concept of freedom in Descartes, Gilson says, 'the problem of sin is the theological form of that of error and the problem of error is the philosophical form of that of sin' (Gilson 1913a: 226); Gouhier says that Descartes 'mixes up error and sin' (Gouhier 1924: 191); Gueroult puts the point in terms of 'sin and error being species of the same order' (Gueroult 1953: I, 229 n. 21); and Alquié, commenting on *Meditations* IV, says that 'Descartes here assimilates the problem of error and that of sin' (Descartes 1963–73: II, 463 n.). So much so that it has come to seem almost uncontroversial to treat the fourth meditation as an 'epistemological theodicy' (Devillairs 1998: 70–81). With some relatively recent publications in English, such as the studies by Tierno (1997), Menn (1998), Ariew (1999) and Janowski (2000), it may become easier to introduce this material less apologetically than I am here doing.

Given the frequent references we shall be making to relations between Descartes' narrator and his God, it is well to begin at the highest level of theological generality in order to be able to locate the various particulars with which we shall be concerned. I take it that this level is to be found in the traditional problem of evil, which is a problem of the coherence of three postures. It can, in outline, be set up as the following triad of propositions, to each of which a monotheist of a Judeo-Christian stamp is *prima facie* committed:

(1) a wholly good being eliminates evil so far as it can;
(2) God is a wholly good and omnipotent being; and
(3) there is evil.

It is hard to doubt that, as they stand, (1)–(3) are in tension; and some people have thought that the fact that many forms of monotheism, especially those of a Judeo-Christian stamp, are committed to all three is an adequate refutation of those positions. Indeed, a wholly negative argument exploiting the tension among (1)–(3) can be found attributed to Epicurus, thus pre-dating the widespread of monotheism of a specifically Judeo-Christian stamp.[1]

To avoid so destructive a use of the tension among (1)–(3) many monotheists have produced supplementations, adjustments and more or less qualified denials of one or more of the members of this outline triad. These amount to elaborations of the concepts of God, of His attributes and of His creation. Such elaborations illustrate the relative straightforwardness with which each of (1)–(3) can be accepted by different theists.[2]

The traditional problem of sin is an instance of the problem of evil, where 'evil' covers not only cataclysms such as plague, famine, earthquakes, carious teeth and laddered stockings, but also human wrongdoing and perversity. It too can be presented as a triad:

(1S)   a wholly good being prevents men from sinning so far as it can;
(2S)   God is a wholly good and omnipotent being; and
(3S)   men sin.

Though we are only handling outlines, and not, so far, the doctrine of any particular theist, it will be noted how natural it is to express the first assertion of each triad in terms of a requirement that God intervene actively ('eliminate', 'prevent'[3]). The same holds in setting up the problem of error as an instance of the problem of sin (see Menn 1998: 301–7; Janowski 2000: 23–48), which is about those forms of wrongdoing that concern the formation of false beliefs:

(1E)   a wholly good being checks men's tendency to error so far as it can.

In this formulation, we thus have the incipient idea that, if men are not stopped, then it is in some way God's fault that they err. Conjoined with:

(2E)   God is a wholly good and omnipotent being; and
(3E)   men err;

we again have the outline of a tension that must be resolved. We have seen that Descartes does not deny or wish to modify the truth expressed by (3E); that is, he does not take the line that error is in some way unreal, which would be the doxastic analogue of saying with, for instance, Leibniz, that evil is only apparent. So, the pushing and pulling to be done will centre on (1E) and (2E).

I take it that (1E) would be qualified by replacing 'checks' with 'does not encourage' and supplemented by adding to 'so far as it can' the rider 'consistent with men's natures', so as to read:

(1E*)   a wholly good being does not encourage men's tendency to error, so far as is consistent with men's natures;

and that (2E) would be qualified:

(2E*) God is a wholly good and omnipotent being that has created beings
   whose (wholly good) natures are less than fully actualised.

Now, from outline to substance.

The perfection of the faculty for judging

The opening of *Meditations* IV recapitulates the steps already taken in the preceding days' meditations. The first step, corresponding to the day of *Meditations* I, is the recognition that there is very little about corporeal things that is perceived truly (*Med.* IV, CSM II: 37).[4] The narrator says that this has produced in him the habit (AT VII: 52: '[. . .] *me his diebus assuefeci*'; AT IXA: 42: '[*j*]*e me suis accoutumé*) of withdrawing his mind from the senses. Though the habit could not be set up in just one day, nor be properly applied outside the circumstances of the controlled enquiry Descartes is conducting, the products of this 'habit' have led him to the second and third steps, corresponding to *Meditations* II and III, which are the discoveries that he knows more about the human mind and much more still about God (AT VII: 53: '[. . .] *multoque plura de mente humana, multo adhuc plura de Deo cognosci*').

The purpose of the fourth day of meditation is to provide a context for these steps by explaining what had gone awry within the narrator as a result of which he did not take them before. If he had taken them before, he would have set out on a route towards uncovering all the knowledge and wisdom that are contained in God (*Med.* IV, CSM II: 37; cf. *Colossians*, 2:3). The reference here to a route that is to be taken is (AT VII: 53: '*videor aliquam viam*'), presumably, a contrast with the path of following the senses; that the roads are alternatives can be seen from a corresponding passage in *Meditations* III (CSM II: 27; AT VII: 40: '[. . .] *alia quædam adhuc via mihi occurrit*'). But it is certain that this is not the route that he has taken, because he has run into error. Therefore, the narrator raises the possibility that he has a specific faculty for error (*Med.* IV, CSM II: 38; AT VII: 54: '*facultas errandi*'; AT IXA: 43: '*puissance pour fallir*'); this would explain what he says he experiences as the presence in himself of a certain faculty for judging ('*facultas judicandi*'; '*puissance pour juger*'). If the faculty for judging were a faculty for error, then we would have an explanation of how the narrator had ended up with false beliefs.

The answer would have to be that making mistakes is part of our nature. If that were so, then to err would be human.[5] But we must be careful to distinguish this from the sense in which the Greek and Latin writers from whom this observation descends say that there is no man who has not erred.[6]

That is a fair observation and casts no particular discredit on anyone. There is no strong impulsion for a pagan to say that human beings ought to be regarded as in any special way perfect, up to God's standards or made in His image. Things become less straightforward when, with the extra strains imposed by the *Genesis* story, human nature is attributable at least in part to God's doing. The question can then arise, as it does for instance in St Augustine towards the end of the first book of *De Libero Arbitrio*, of the extent to which God is responsible for the sins that we commit (*Lib. Arb.*, I, 16, 35).

If God created us, He is responsible for our nature. And, if our nature is responsible for our sins, then He is at least indirectly responsible for our sins. But this would be to impute to Him our sins, which cannot be correct. Thus there must be something wrong with the move from saying that humans do err to saying that it is part of their nature to do so. And this prompts the thought that there may be some respect in which what is unavoidable, inevitable, normal and par for the course for human beings may, nevertheless not be properly, truly, genuinely, really, and, above all, *naturally* human: when humans err, they are not being fully human.

Because he holds that everything that is part of our nature we have received from God (*Med.* IV, CSM II: 37), Descartes must deny that error is part of our nature. The reason is that if God had placed in us something by which we should be misled, then He would have been either weak or wicked in having the desire to deceive us (also *Pr.* I, 29, CSM I: 209). We know, from the work done in *Meditations* III, that He is neither, and that He does nothing to deceive us. Given that the faculty for judging that I have, I have received from God, it cannot be in any way less than perfect of its kind or lack anything that it ought to have (*Med.* IV, CSM II: 38; AT VII: 55: '[. . .] *non videtur fieri posse, ut ille aliquam in me posuerit quæ non sit in suo genere perfecta, sive quæ aliqua debita perfectione sit privata*'). Its being perfect of its kind and lacking nothing that it ought to have means that it is the perfect kind for humans and lacks nothing that humans ought to have. As we shall see, the relativisation to kinds is of the utmost importance in seeing how it can, nevertheless, be that humans err.

The faculty for judging is not a faculty for error in the sense of having been put in us by God with a view to our going astray; as St Augustine puts it, our souls are not made so that we should sin (*Lib. Arb.*, III, 11, 32: '*non ut peccarent*'). When we are deceived, we are not fulfilling our natures as God's creatures. This move recalls the absolutising tendency concerning the mastery of the passions in *Passions* I, 50 that we saw in Chapter 2. Indeed, it might appear that the theological argument just sketched is the true ground of the astonishing claims for the willableness of the will in, especially, *Passions* III, 153, that we never lack the will to undertake and carry through all the things we may judge to be the best.

With this defence, which is prior to any acount of how the faculty for judging works, the faculty for judging is shown not to be the cause of our having
been deceived. But there is another qualification in addition to that already
noted about the appropriateness to humans of the faculty for judging that
humans have. This is that the faculty is not the cause of our being deceived
so long as it is used rightly (*Med.* IV, CSM II: 38; AT VII: 54: '*dum ea recte
utor*'). These two qualifications are reciprocal. To use the faculty rightly is to
use it in accordance with its sort: in accordance with human nature, which
is the ground of its being of its sort. Even if the faculty for judging is not the
cause of our being deceived, it is only if we know its sort that we shall be able
to know how to use it rightly and be able to avoid error, thus avoiding being
less than human.

If error is a doxastic instance of sin, we can see that the properly human
use of the faculty for judging is an instance of the properly human use of the
freedom of choice. In this connection, it may be suggestive to bear in mind
an argument St Anselm offers in the first chapter of *De Libertate Arbitrii* to
show that the freedom of choice cannot essentially involve a capacity for sinning. The Disciple offers the definition (derived perhaps from a misreading
of Augustine *Corr.*, II, 1, 1 or *Lib. Arb.*, III, 11, 32) of freedom as the power to
sin and not to sin ('*potestas peccandi et non peccandi*'). The Master's reply is to
observe that God, the angels and men can all be said to be free so long as
there is a single definition of what it is to be free, even if God and men are
free in different degrees. Though He is free, God does not have the capacity
for sinning. Since God uses any faculty He has rightly, there cannot be a faculty for sinning that God could have and use rightly without sinning. Hence,
such a capacity cannot be part of the definition of freedom of choice.
Similarly, in Descartes' case, a faculty for error can be no part of the faculty
for judging lest God be regarded as having a faculty for judging that includes
a faculty for error.

Because he knows that he has fallen into error, Descartes begins to consider what sort of faculty for judging he must have, consistent with its being
perfect of its sort and being such that, if rightly used, it will not lead the
enquirer into error. The distinction he makes is between the faculty's being
perfect of its sort and its being finite (*Med.* IV, CSM II: 38). Being finite is
consistent with being perfect of its sort if it is the nature of the faculty to be
finite. The finitude is a matter of not containing things that are contained in
the (perfect and) infinite faculty for judging that God has (*Med.* IV, AT VII:
54: '[. . .] *non sum ipse summum ens*'). It is hardly an exaggeration to say that
much of *Meditations* III is aimed at showing, precisely, that the nature of the
Cartesian narrator is not divine.

The finitude in question needs to be spelt out, again, in terms that ensure
that God did not act either weakly or wickedly in creating the narrator with

a nature that has a finite faculty for judging. This time the distinction is between a 'negation' and a 'privation'; this is a distinction that we have already noted as deriving ultimately from Aristotle (*Metaph.*, Γ xxiii, 1023 b 25–7).

Descartes' way of expressing himself here has caused some confusion.

In part this is perhaps because Descartes does not operate the Aristotelian distinction of genus and species on which the difference ultimately depends: for Aristotle, the central cases of privation (στέρησις) involve the lack of some attribute possessed naturally, as a matter of kind-membership; thus, a man who is deprived of sight is blind because men are naturally sighted, but a given mole, in Aristotle's example, is not because all moles are said (wrongly in fact) to be without sight. A better example, which had become current by Descartes' day (see Eustace of St Paul 1609: 153; also Hobbes, *Obj.* III, qu. 12, CSM II: 133), is that of a tree: it is no harm to the tree not to be able to see, because sight is not due to it (Gilson 1913b: 215).

In part the confusion also arises because the French versions of both the *Meditations* and the *Principles* further specify what a negation is, without making fully clear how this maps onto the notion of a privation: Descartes himself muddies the waters. In both the French and the Latin of our two texts, we find the notion that error is not a mere negation:

> *Med.* IV, CSM II: 38; AT VII: 54–5: '[. . .] *non enim error est pura negatio*'; AT IXA: 43: '[. . .] *car l'erreur n'est pas une pure négation*';

> *Pr.* I, 31, CSM I: 203; AT VIIIA: 17: '[. . . *Deum*] *referentur, esse tantum negationes*'; AT IXB: 38–9: '[. . .] *elles* [sc. *nos erreurs*, 38] *ne sont à son* [sc. *de Dieu*] *égard que des négations*'.

In the French versions, there is the added (negative) specification that a negation, properly so-called, is the absence of or lack from the narrator of something that was not owing to him:

> *Med.* IV, AT IXA: 43–4: '[. . .] *c'est à dire* [leg. *l'erreur*], *n'est pas le simple défaut ou manquement de quelque perfection qui ne m'est point due*';

> *Pr.* I, 31, IX A: 39: [a *négation* is not such] *qu'il* [sc. *Dieu*] *ne nous a pas donné tout ce qu'il pouvvait nous donner*'.

From the human point of view, the non-possession of an infinite faculty for judging might seem to be a privation, where by 'privation' is meant the lack of something that is owing to us or that God's generosity would dictate that He bestow on us (cf. Aquinas 1934: III, 8–9; Gallagher 1994: 258–9). When it differs from God's, the human point of view is wrong: if a human has the sense of having been deprived of what is rightly his, then he is presumptuous. A human has no more claim to an infinite faculty for judging than a tree has a claim to be able to see.

When he is challenged by Gassendi over the question of whether the privation of an infinite faculty for judging is a ground for complaint against God (*Obj.* V, CSM II: 217), Descartes firmly replies that Gassendi has wrongly supposed that what is at issue is a 'positive imperfection' (*Resp.* V, CSM II: 259; AT VII: 377: '*positiva imperfectio*'). No good has been withdrawn, though not all goods have been given. Even if it seems, to humans, that they suffer a privation in this respect, it is important to notice that, in all four expositions of the thought we are concerned with, Descartes makes an effort to mark a difference between what is so (in *Pr.* I 31, explicitly, for God: '*ad Deum*', AT VIIIA: 17) and what seems so (likewise, to us: '*ad nos*'). Any sense of grievance we might nurse about an apparent privation is misplaced because it is our nature to be finite: God has not denied us anything to which we have a just claim. When he returns, near the end of *Meditations* IV to clear the point up, Descartes reiterates that, being a non-thing, error is not caused and is, therefore, not a privation, but a mere negation (*Med.* IV, CSM II: 42).[7]

Descartes thus hopes to have shown that the faculty for judging is as good as it should be, though it is finite and though every human makes mistakes. Since it is as good as it should be, because it was placed in him by God, the narrator's errors are not attributable to Him. If the fact of human error is to be explained consistent with the non-deceivingness of God, then the cause is not to be sought in the nature of the faculty for judging. From the second qualification we noted above ('*ut recte utor*'), that fact must be explained by our not using the faculty rightly, that is, in accordance with its nature.

It is an important point of strategy that Descartes argues for the perfection of the faculty for judging *before* he considers how it functions and what its nature is. His adoption of this strategy, appealing first to divine benevolence and power, is a significant piece of evidence in favour of a theodicidic reading of *Meditations* IV. He begins by showing that God is not the cause of our errors both because he sees that such a possibility is a real threat to his position, and because it helps him to establish the outlines of the faculty for judging in a general way before looking at its workings.

The role of the intellect in the earlier writings

Before examining more closely the composition of the faculty for judging that Descartes offers in *Meditations* IV, it is worth taking up a suspicion about a possible change in his position as between his earlier writings and the

Meditations. Kenny summarises this supposed change: 'In the *Regulae*, Descartes treats judgment as an act of the intellect; in the later works he treats it as an act of will' (Kenny 1972: 2). And, in some cases of those who have thought to find this shift in position, it is related to a general change in Descartes' view of things, from 'the optimism of 1628 [. . .] Descartes had arrived at the fundamental pessimism of 1641' (Sawday 1995: 153).

As we shall see, the view of the *Meditations* and the *Principles* is that, in all belief-acquisition, it is the proper role of the will to assent or dissent. This seems to differ from the doctrine espoused, if only by doubtful implication, in the *Rules*, that, in science, it is the intellect that determines which beliefs we should have. To see why we should not be overawed by this apparent shift in position, we should look both at why the doctrine apparently offered in the *Rules* is only 'by doubtful implication' and at the nature of the exercise that the *Rules* is proposing.

In *Rules* III, Descartes is discussing exclusively the objects that fall within the purview of the only sciences that he thinks are worth studying, because, as he has already said, they yield the same degree of certainty as do the demonstrations of arithmetic and geometry (cf. *Reg.* II, CSM I: 12–13). In the closing paragraph of this rule, he reiterates the division of the types of knowledge into things that have the (self-)evidence and certainty of intuition (*Reg.* III, CSM I: 14; AT X: 369: '*intuitus evidentia et certitudo*') and those that are the remote conclusions that we can get only through deduction (CSM I: 15; AT X: 370: '*remotas conclusiones, non nisi per deductionem*').

He then seems to be conceding something when he says,

> we are not barred from believing divinely revealed things, which are more certain than any knowledge, as the objects of faith, like anything that concerns obscure things, involve not an action of the mind, but of the will (*Reg.* III, CSM I: 15; AT X: 370: '[. . .] *non impedit quominus illa, quæ divinitus revelata sunt, omni cognitione certiora credamus, cum illorum fides, quæcumque est de obscuris non ingenii actio sit sed voluntatis*').

The grammar as much as the logic of this apparent concession is less than clear.

Yet, there is some consensus among translators to the effect that what we are not barred, prevented or precluded from believing is *that* the things that are divinely revealed are more certain than any knowledge.[8] For we can certainly believe that much without believing that anything has been divinely revealed; for we might believe that, *if* something were divinely revealed, *then* it would be very certain, while doubting or denying that God has ever revealed anything either to ourselves or to anyone. This, after all, is what any agnostic who can nevertheless imagine what Descartes' God is supposed to be able to do, *should* believe. Moreover, we can believe that revelation would be certain in this degree without believing anything that has been divinely revealed; for we might believe (let us suppose) wrongly that a given deliverance of revelation is not as certain as it in fact is. On the consensual reading, what we have is a statement about the relative certainties of two classes of beliefs. Rather, on my rendering, the object of the belief that Descartes is interested in is not something about the greater certainty of revealed things, but the revealed things themselves: that is to say, the '*illa* [. . .] *revelata*' should be taken as the grammatical object of the *cred*[*i*]*mus*.[9]

The core moral must be this: though it has as its object an object of faith and, therefore, an object that is obscure to us, a belief in revelation can be more certain than belief in things (intuition and deduction) whose proprietary virtue is that they should be clear. Hence, being clear is only one mark by which we can tell that a belief is certain; being revealed can be another. This need not mean that even though the objects of faith do not fall within the class of the ideas that are clear, the criterion of clearness 'excludes faith from the scope of method' (Menn 1998: 326) in such a way that the two sorts of truths must be 'kept in separate compartments' (ibid.: 329). For, as we shall see in Chapter 11, there must be room for conflict between method and revelation and, as we already see here in the greater certainty of revealed things, Descartes thinks that the latter trumps the former.

Rather as in the letter to Princess Elizabeth of 1645, discussed in Chapter 2 (CSMK: 263), in the *Rules*, Descartes makes the contrast between the mind ('*ingenium*'; see Petrik 1992: 27–9) and the will ('*voluntas*'); this is not exactly the contrast that we shall explore in considering the *Meditations* and the *Principles*, between the *intellect* and the will. As it stands, what the text from *Rules* III says is that, in matters of revelation, the mind does not have a role; it is invalid to try to infer from this that the will has *no* role in assent when we are concerned with the proper objects of the science in hand (Caton 1973: 88). Even if, in scientific operations, the mind is the agent of assent to things (namely intuitions and deductions) that have clearness as their proprietary virtue, we have yet to show that Descartes is excluding the will from those operations, just because there is some realm in which it is the sole agent of assent. A slightly out-of-date analogy from English law suggests itself here. Lawyers – both barristers and solicitors – were concerned with defending an accused; but only a barrister could plead in the High Court. The absence of solicitors from the High Court did not entail the absence of barristers from the conferences that set the line of the case.

The precise nature of the project that the *Rules* encompasses has caused some difference of opinion. While some commentators have thought that it pursues substantially the same objectives as the later works (e.g. Beck 1952: 198ff.; Marion 1981a: 64–9 and 179–84), there is at least one respect in which, despite its name, the '*mathesis universalis*' (*Reg.* IV, CSM I: 19) is narrower in scope than the enquiries envisaged from the *Discourse* onwards (Crapulli 1969; Schuster 1980: esp. 43ff.). The relative narrowness resides in the fact that the *Rules* does not aim at unifying all the possible objects of human knowledge, but only at rendering orderly the knowledge that is mathematical in nature: the 'phantom discipline of universal mathematics disappeared [. . . when . . .] Descartes turned to the grand style of constructive metaphysics' (Schuster 1980: 80; also Gaukroger 1995: 100–3). The broader aims of the later works, of putting the whole of human knowledge on firm foundations, were not contemplated within a single project in the years that Descartes was putting together the incomplete text we know as the *Rules*.

The *Rules* does express the doctrine that we should distinguish the faculty within the intellect by which a thing is intuited and known from that which, by affirming or denying, judges (*Reg.* XII, CSM I: 45; AT X: 420: '[. . .] *distinguamus illam facultatem intellectus per quam res intuetur et cognoscit ab ea qua judicat affirmando vel negando*'). Though Descartes makes this distinction within the intellect (*intellectus*) – not the mind (*ingenium*) – he does not fully specify what the different faculties are or how they are to be related. When, as foreseen by the other rules, we are considering simple natures, it is not surprising that the description of our activity should fit a 'rationalist' model: '*ratio*' is the most powerful factor in these acts of consideration (Kenny 1972: 31).

Given that the *Rules* describes a rule-bound activity of belief-acquisition, it is no wonder that observance of the rules should be sufficient for the acquisition of beliefs. But it is by no means clear that the *Rules* expresses a doctrine that is globally rationalist; for it does not assert that all belief-acquisition is rule-bound but, if anything, its procedures presuppose the contrary. This point can be made by observing how, in the *Study*, written about 1623 (Sirven 1930: 294ff.; Bortolotti 1983: 75ff.; Garin 1967: 57–9), it is easy to see the central concerns of the *Rules* as summarised in the fourth article and contrasted with the experimental and liberal branches of knowledge, which are, thereby, admitted to be autonomous and independent of what is covered by the rules (*Study*, AT X: 202).

While the *Rules* can, if handled carefully, yield unequivocal doctrine, there is virtually nothing to be had from the *Discourse* about our ability to control the process of belief-acquisition.

In the passage at the beginning of *Discourse* IV where we might expect Descartes to give us some account of how he disencumbered himself of his credulous beliefs, we find only the embarrassed cough that he is not sure how much to recount of his first meditations (*Dis.* IV, CSM I: 126). This is followed by a perfectly unblushing sequence of verbs presupposing that, if he wanted to, he would have no trouble in putting off childish things: 'I wanted to suppose' (AT VI: 32: '*je voulus supposer*'); 'I rejected as false' ('*je rejetai comme fausses*'); 'I undertook to pretend' ('*je me résolus de feindre*'); 'while I was wanting thus to think' ('*pendant que je voulais ainsi penser*'). It is only when he runs up against the logical difficulty of expunging his belief in the fact of his own existence that Descartes' capacity to throw off credulity encounters an obstacle that has to be taken seriously.

The *Discourse* has little to say to our present purpose, because its first three parts are given over to an account, described in the last chapter as 'commonsensical', of how widespread error is. There is no question that error is possible and no need to explain its precise anatomy, so long as we hang on to the idea, whch we have already seen from the *Passions*, that correlative with the distinction between what is within our power and what is not, there is the distinction between our thoughts and everything else. Hence, for the purposes of the *Discourse*, our thoughts – including our sense-based beliefs – are within our power: '*il n'y a rien qui [est] entièrement en notre pouvoir, que nos pensées*' (*Dis.* II, CSM I: 123; AT VI: 25).

Intellect and will

The distinction of intellect and will

Let us return to the exposition of *Meditations* IV and the *Principles*. In order to explain how he has ever fallen into error, though his faculty for judging is perfect of its sort, Descartes now has to investigate what its sort is. The investigation is a search for a further specification of the faculty's finiteness.

He proceeds by decomposing the faculty for judging into its component parts, which he then treats as the concurrent causes of judgment, including erroneous judgment (*Med.* IV, CSM II: 39). Despite the slight variations in Descartes' terminology, one of these causes we shall synoptically call 'intellect',[10] and the other 'will'.[11] The former is passive and the latter active (cf. *Pass.* I, 17–19).

In the *Meditations*, these two causes are picked out as the parts of the faculty for judging; in the *Passions* (I, 17, CSM I: 335), they are individuated as the principal varieties of thought and, going a little bit further, in the *Principles* (I, 32, CSM I: 204), they appear as the only two types whatever of human cognition. Considered as the causes constituting the faculty for judging, the intellect and the will must both be operative for the operation of that faculty; and if either is non-operative, then the composite ceases to exist. Concurrence requires that the parts be jointly sufficient and severally necessary; the two sub-faculties have to marry to constitute the faculty for judging.

Given that the faculty for judging has been found not to be a faculty for error, so long as it is used rightly, the question now to be faced is: what natures do the components of that faculty have so that we may know how to use the composite rightly, that is, in accordance with its nature?

The decomposition of the faculty for judging into intellect and will in *Meditations* IV will recall the first stage of the taxonomy of the narrator's cognitive states in *Meditations* III (CSM II: 25).[12] At that stage, there is the categorisation as between those states that satisfy three criteria and those that do not. The criteria are: (i) that the states are like pictures of things (AT VII: 37: '*tanquam rerum imagines*') and so are the sorts of thing that can be properly called ideas; (ii) that, so long as they are considered only in themselves (AT VII: 37: '*si solæ in se spectentur*'), the states cannot be strictly speaking false; and (iii) that the states are not volitions, affections or judgments.[13]

Criterion (i) is not enunciated in *Meditations* IV; indeed, Descartes abandons the quasi-theory of ideas as pictures even before he gets out of *Meditations* III.[14] Instead, he sticks with '*idea*' (used six times), which is pretty much equivalent to '*perceptio*' (used three times): he also uses '*cognitio*' and '*judicium*' five times each; but, given that *cognitio* is also used to mean much the same as 'knowledge' (especially when it is God's *cognitio*) and that a *judicium* is also the result of judging, this shift of terminology may be from the frying pan into the fire.[15] Nevertheless, what criterion (i) is meant to individuate are things that we might call contents, traces, imprints, impressions or representations: they are the what-the-cognitive-state-tells-us (cf. Buroker 1996). So, whatever version he has in hand in *Meditations* IV, we shall suppose that there is something that corresponds to (i). On the other hand, criterion (ii) returns quite clearly in *Meditations* IV, where Descartes specifies that perceiving or conceiving the state 'in itself' is distinct from judging, affirming or denying (CSM II: 39).[16] Criterion (iii) is the direct subject of our discussion, so its contours should emerge as we proceed.

Descartes gives no argument to show that anything satisfies both some version of (i) as well as the reiteration of (ii), nor that anything that does will also satisfy (iii); perhaps he sees no issue here or is only interested in classifying as the contents of the intellect those cognitive states that do satisfy (i)–(iii), if any do. Insofar as the role of the intellect is simply as a container of cognitive states that do satisfy (i)–(iii), we may regard those states as pure contents. If, therefore, the intellect were our sole cognitive faculty, or were the whole of our faculty for judging, then there would be nothing in us of which we could properly say that it was false.

Meditations III aims to show that at least two of the narrator's cognitive contents are such that they cannot be considered 'only in themselves'. Consideration of what is presupposed in my possession of the idea of my own existence leads me to see that I could not have that idea if there were nothing other than the idea: my possession of it is such that it must be the idea of something, namely me. Likewise, consideration of what is presupposed by the narrator's possession of the idea of God is meant to show that he could not possess it unless it were referred to something outside himself that fitted it, namely God. The nature of these considerations and how cogent they are or ought to seem constitute two of the most important and controversial *topoi* in Descartes studies. So it is as well that I do not have to take a detailed stand on either of them here. For now, we have to hang on to Descartes' distinction between the content of an idea, and what we then do with it.

In *Meditations* IV, the narrator affirms that, when he considers only what the idea of God is referred to, he finds no source of error or falsity (*Med.* IV, CSM II: 38).[17] This affirmation sets off a comparison between the narrator's intellect and God's. On the presupposition that all created things were first in the mind of God, it is no surprise that the narrator's intellect does not encompass them all (*Med.* IV, CSM II: 38). For, whereas God's nature is to be immense, incomprehensible and infinite, the narrator knows that his own is very weak and limited (*Med.* IV, CSM II: 39).

The weakness and limitedness are spelt out, as before, in terms that do not mean that, in creating the narrator as he is, God acted out of any weakness or malice. Instead, Descartes allows – as he is surely entitled to do – that there may be countless things in creation of which the narrator has no ideas. Thus, there are some ideas, at least in the intellect of God, that are not in the narrator's intellect (*Med.* IV, CSM II: 39). But the absence of these ideas does not need to be accounted for by any special causal story; specifically, their absence is not to be referred to God's having been less than perfectly generous in creating the narrator with the (finite) intellect that He created him with.

At this point, the terminology of 'privation' makes its return.

Descartes denies that the finite enquirer suffers any privation, for no reason can be given for supposing that God ought to have given him a greater intellect than He did (*Med.* IV, CSM II: 39).[18] A finite intellect is simply one that lacks in a negative way ideas that there are to be had; and this means, as specified in the French version, that its not containing them does not involve robbing it of things that properly belong to its nature.[19] After all, some of the apparatus that nourishes the intellect, including memory and imagination, is itself very flimsy and restricted (*Med.* IV, CSM II: 40).[20]

Thus far, we have an account of the *fact of ignorance*: the finitude of the intellect is a matter of its not containing ideas of some of the things that there are to be known. Just as the *fact of error* was, so both the *fact* and the *cause of ignorance* have been squared with God's being neither weak nor malicious. But we still do not have an account of the *cause of error*.

My intellect is finite, but it does not cause error. For error involves affirming an idea that is not so, or denying an idea that is. The intellect does not affirm or deny, but merely contains, ideas.

Because the intellect comes from God, we may be sure that, when we do understand an idea, we understand it aright or rightly (*Med.* IV, CSM II: 40; AT VII: 58: '*recte intelligo*'). Yet, such acts of understanding are not themselves genuine affirmations or denials: they are a first stage, the second being the recognition that, because the idea is understood, it may be assented to. If the intellect were taken to be genuinely active in 'proposing', it might seem to be doing the first part of the will's work; but 'proposing' here is not like the recommendation of a new member to a club, but, as we shall see in the next chapter, a mere display of what has been perceived. Likewise, the will on its own cannot lead us astray. For, just as the intellect does not affirm or deny, so, of itself, the will contains no ideas that it might affirm or deny. The will is conceived of as being nothing other than our being able to do or leave undone, our being able to affirm or deny, pursue or flee (*Med.* IV, CSM II: 40).[21] Our being able to affirm or deny requires for its actualisation that there be something for us to affirm or deny; and this is what the intellect proposes (*Med.* IV, CSM II: 40).[22] In this respect, the will is a pure potentiality relative to the contents with which it is faced.

Because the intellect and the will are concurrent causes of our affirming or denying an idea, they are concurrent causes of error when we deny a true idea or affirm a false. So long as we affirm only ideas that we do understand, then we can be sure that we shall not fall into error (or sin). As we shall see in the next chapter, to understand an idea aright is to intuit it or to perceive it clearly and distinctly, with *ratio*, as having a great light shining out of it. When we do not understand an idea, it is because it goes beyond the limits of the intellect.

We do not intuit the ideas that we derive from the senses. They are not clear and distinct for us. We perceive them without *ratio*. And no light flows out of them. So, strictly speaking, we do not understand them. Nevertheless, we have a lot of them jangling about in our intellects, as the casual or adventitious contents with which we have been landed by our infantile doxastic habit of taking notice of what we see with our eyes. If we affirm ideas that go beyond the limits of the intellect, such as ideas derived from the senses, then we are easily distracted from the good and the true, and thus fall into error and sin (*Med.* IV, CSM II: 40; AT VII: 58: '*fallor et pecco*').[23]

It is an act of the will to affirm a idea, even if the idea is not understood by the intellect. The affirmation of an idea that is not understood is a wrong use of the will. Hence, the wrong use of the will, to affirm ideas that are not understood within the intellect, is the cause of error. Since it is the narrator who makes the wrong use of the will, as the active part of the faculty for judging, error can be attributed neither to the nature of that faculty nor to God.

This, in a nutshell, is Descartes' account of the cause of error. As it stands, it leaves us without answers to the questions about the control of credulity that we were hoping to have resolved. For, we have not yet seen how, by separating the intellect from the will within the faculty for judging, Descartes can hope to discipline the vicious doxastic habit of affirming ideas that come from or through the senses. Nor does the mere separation suffice to explain the relation between an idea's being fully understood and its being such that we are permitted to affirm it. To address these questions, we turn to an important disparity in Descartes' handling of the concurrent parts of the judging faculty.

The infinitude of the will

The narrator of the *Meditations* says that he experiences his will (or freedom of choice) as so great that he could conceive of nothing greater (*Med.* IV, CSM II: 40; AT VII: 57: '*ut nullius majoris ideam apprehendam*').[24] The formulation of his experience recalls the sort of terminology that St Anselm employs in setting up the ontological argument for the existence of God, e.g. in *Proslogion*, II ('*aliquid quo nihil maius cogitari potest*'). If we are ready to hear the theological echoes in the procedure of *Meditations* IV, we may ask what the terms of comparison are: what is at least as great as what?

In one respect, the narrator recognises that the will of God is stronger and more efficacious than his; and this is because God has more knowledge and power (*Med.* IV, CSM II: 40).[25] Descartes nevertheless wants to hold onto a respect in which, viewed formally or strictly (AT VII: 57: '*in se formaliter et præcise spectata*'), the human will is no less than God's. What is meant by viewing the equality formally or strictly is that there is no difference in mode of operation as between the human and the divine wills. The formal equality is in respect of the will's being a pure capacity for affirmation and denial.[26] Considered in this way, freedom does not come in degrees.

But even this leaves us with one puzzle about what experience is being reported and how we experience the infinitude of the will under this aspect, and another about why Descartes is so anxious that his enquirer should have a will that is infinite rather than one that is just separate from the (finite) intellect. To see what these puzzles amount to, I turn to Descartes' replies to Gassendi and Burman, who raised them for his clarification.

Gassendi is the only one of the authors of the *Objections*, to think that the difference of scale, magnitude or modality that Descartes sets up between intellect and will is an unwarranted partiality (*Obj.* V, CSM II: 218–19). No doubt, this is partly a reflection of Gassendi's doggedness in pursuing

Descartes wherever he can (cf. Lennon 1993: 153–67). But it is also an indicator of the fact that the position Descartes takes is regarded by his other interlocutors as a respectable contribution to a known *topos*, to which we shall return in the next section.

As the outcome of a series of arguments based on the idea that both parts of the faculty for judging can be added to, Gassendi suggests they should be counted as equal in scope (*Obj.* V, CSM II: 219; AT VII: 315: '*æque late pateant*').[27] If the ground for regarding the intellect as finite is that it does not contain ideas it might have contained, then is it not likewise a ground for thinking the will finite that it is not disposed for or against ideas not contained by the intellect? Here, Gassendi might appeal two pretty standard principles. One is that, to become operative, the will needs to be presented with something to accept or reject. Thus, St Augustine says that only things we encounter can attract the will (*Lib. Arb.*, III, 25, 74).[28] In the sense of having a proximate cause of action, then, the will depends on the intellect. The other principle is of the nature of a metaphysical commonplace: nothing infinite can depend on what is finite. If so, and if the will needs a content to be operative, and its operation is contingent on a finite proximate cause, then it must be as finite as the intellect has been admitted to be. Gassendi does not pursue these types of argument, though the point he is making may be clarified by them. Nor does he explicitly raise the question of what Descartes says he experiences when he experiences the will as infinite.

Descartes replies to Gassendi's arguments for an even-handed treatment of the two sub-faculties of the faculty for judging by reiterating his report of his experience. His experience can serve as a marker for others that they too can have the experience, and they should not be put off by the fact that Gassendi claims not to have had the experience in question (*Resp.* V, CSM II: 259–60).[29] Descartes aims to place the burden of proof on Gassendi: if, in general, someone claims to have perceived something that another admits to not having perceived, the onus must fall on the latter if he wishes to maintain that such a thing is not there to be perceived. Never seen Blackpool lights? You do not know what you have missed.

But Descartes goes further, offering the idea that no argument is called for to persuade us of what experience testifies (*Resp.* V, CSM II: 259).[30] He spells this out in his conversation with Burman in relation to our passage of *Meditations* IV (CSM II: 40):

> But it is useless to argue in this way about these things; let each person delve into himself and experience whether or not he has a perfect and absolute will, and whether he can conceive of anything surpassing him in freedom of the will. Surely no one will find it otherwise. It is in this respect, therefore, that the will is greater than the intellect and more like

God (*Con.*, CSMK: 342; AT V: 159: '[s]*ed male de hisce ita disputatur; descendat modo unusquisque in semetipsum et experiar annon perfectam et absolutam habeat voluntatem, et an possit quicquam concipere quod voluntatis libertate antecellat. Nemo sane aliter experturus est. In eo igitur major est voluntas intellectu et Deo similior*').

It is perfectly good Cartesian doctrine that introspection is sufficient to uncover the presence in us of a faculty: though we may not always be aware of the mind's powers or faculties, we can become immediately aware that there is a given faculty by setting ourselves to use it (e.g. *Resp.* IV, CSM II: 172). But what we wanted to know was not just whether introspection can reveal that we have a will, but whether it offers an appropriate sort of experience of the will's infinitude.

The queerness of the experience Descartes reports himself as having may arise from an ambiguity in the infinitudes in question (see Gueroult 1953: I, 324–5). On the one hand, I might say that my will is infinite in that nothing can impede my willing this or that: I can be presented with the idea of anything actual or possible, and plump for it if I take a fancy to it. This would be an infinitude of the *range* of my will; and the relevant experience would be an experience of there being nothing that my will could not stretch to. On the other hand, there is some sense in which I might describe my will as infinite if it is such that nothing can resist my willing once I will this or that. This would be an infinitude of the *power* of my will: an absolute willableness of the will. The relevant experience would presumably be that I can, by willing, hold any other impulsion in abeyance.

Even if I can discover, by whatever means, that my will cannot be conquered by any other drive or faculty within me, that would not establish that its power is infinite. For my will to be able to control the tendency to credulous belief-formation, which we have seen to be very strong, all I need is that the will be stronger than that tendency. Of course, if it is infinitely strong, then it does follow that it is stronger than any tendency that is of only finite strength. This might seem like Descartes' just trying to knock out all comers by a verbal trick. It is not obvious that he needs the will to be infinite to do this. Nevertheless, it seems that he is serious in his intent and is taken seriously by most of his interlocutors in pursuing it: they do not object as Gassendi does.

The seriousness of his intent can be expressed in terms of the seriousness of the problem that he is facing. This is not just that humans sometimes make mistakes, though that is, as I have been trying to illustrate, a problem of theodicy. The really serious problem is that humans seem to be rigged up to make absolutely massive, repeated, generalised and systematic error in believing, among other things, the senses. The earliest doxastic habits we form are tremendously deep-rooted and disastrously vicious. If we are to overcome these habits, the equipment at our disposal for doing so needs to be guaranteed to be extremely potent. If that equipment is to be able to overcome the habit of the senses, it has to be very special indeed. And one way of guaranteeing its specialness is to establish that it is infinite. If he can satisfy his interlocutors that the will is the equipment by which the vicious habit of credulity must be combated, and that the will is infinite, then Descartes will have vindicated the possibility of conquering that habit, at least on a belief-by-belief basis. Indirectly, he will also have vindicated divine benevolence.

In the next chapter we shall consider further the questions (i) of what is involved in Descartes' effort to establish the infinite power of the will; and (ii) of how that connects with our potential for control over the effects of credulity as a biological habit. For now, the point is that he seems to satisfy most of his interlocutors on the infinity of the will.

We have seen that it is infinitude of range with which Descartes introduces its God-like quality. Considered as a pure potentiality, the will is not limited by the fact, to which Gassendi appeals, that, as it turns out for humans, it is only presented with a finite range of ideas. What Descartes wants, in addition, is to illustrate how the infinite range of the will supports its infinite power, consistent with the notion that God's will is greater in virtue of His knowledge and power (see again *Med.* IV, CSM II: 40). One move in this direction is a thesis, already cited as a metaphysical commonplace, but not explicitly enunciated in *Meditations* IV, that what is finite cannot determine what is infinite. If my will is infinite in range, then it is infinite in some respect and hence cannot be determined by my intellect, which I know to be finite in the only respect that I encounter it, namely, as a receptacle of perceptions. But such a move looks merely invalid. Unless Descartes has up his sleeve some other type of argument, what could make it seem acceptable to all of the commentators of 1641 with the exception we have seen of Gassendi and, as we shall see in a slightly different connection, Hobbes?

Descartes' respectability

The differential treatments that Descartes offers of the intellect and the will do not elicit much attention from the authors of the *Objections*, nor from his more occasional correspondents. One approach to explaining this could be by seeing *seriatim* why each of them should have no difficulty with its outlines. What I propose instead is to sketch why, in the context, the proposal of a finite intellect and an infinite will would have seemed a respectable solution for the problem Descartes is wrestling with in *Meditations* IV. This would hold good almost irrespective of who had been invited by Mersenne to join the debate.

The context is the context of learned debate in the first half of the seventeenth century. Though most of the objectors to the *Meditations* were in holy orders, respectability here is not quite the same as orthodoxy. For Descartes, orthodoxy would be understood as literal conformity to the announced doctrines of the Roman Catholic Church; 'announced doctrine' would be, roughly speaking, the Fathers, the Doctors, the Councils (where they can be made to converge) plus broader tradition as codified by the Council of Trent. We shall return in Chapter 11 to the question of just how authoritative orthodoxy in this sense was for Descartes.

The question I am homing in on – the means we have for giving or withholding assent – is adjacent to issues on which we can discern pretty definite doctrines and equally definite heresies concerning the doctrine of Original Sin and its relation to Pelagianism, to which we return in the next chapter. But it would be too much to say that there has ever been any clear-cut or enforceable orthodoxy on the specific matter under consideration. We find ourselves close to a line between what would be a matter of doctrine and what would be a proper matter for philosophical discussion, open as much to Catholics as to non-Catholics.

In one strong respect, Descartes and his first commentators, Catholic and other, were united in turning away from the received opinion that distinguishing faculties within the mind commits one to the presence of distinct parts or separate entities (e.g. *Med.* VI, CSM II: 59). In being thus united, they reject Thomistic doctrine regarding organic faculties,[31] which was meant to derive pretty directly from Aristotle (*De An.*, II ii, 413 b 27–8),[32] who was in turn trying to make literal sense of the various Platonic images of man as a composite creature (e.g. *Rep.*, IV, 436–40; *Rep.*, IX, 588; *Phædr.*, 248; *Tim.*, 69–71). But this degree of non-conformity with relatively longstanding teaching was by no means censurable; indeed, it was only more or less self-consciously 'conservative' (Park 1988: 480) writers who held to the 'real' distinctions involved (Copenhaver 1992: 117–23). Rather, it is not wild to see Descartes' overall soul doctrine as fitting a model that derives from the Christological uses made by St Augustine and others of Porphyry's doctrine (in turn derived from the Stoics, *SVF* II, 463–81) that body and soul remain distinct in an 'unconfused union' (ἀσύγχτος ἕνωσις or *'unio inconfusa'*): the rational soul stands to the body in humans as divinity stands to humanity in Christ (Pépin 1964).

On that supposition – which I admit is neither fully worked out here nor uncontroversial – the type of operation he is engaged in should have seemed respectable enough: the discrimination of faculties boils down a matter of distinctions of function or of phase. It might be tempting, e.g. on the basis of *Principles* I, 32, to take the discrimination of modes of thinking ('*modi cogitandi*') as more fundamental than the distinction of faculties in *Meditations* IV and to treat will and intellect as modally distinct 'aspects of a single substance' (Petrik 1992: 121). This would be charitable both in not multiplying entities and in avoiding what Petrik thinks of as an implausible voluntarism (ibid.: 145–75). But such a 'holistic theory of volitions' (ibid.: 126), on which the will should be regarded as 'the conative face of an idea' (ibid.: 107) takes insufficient account of the difference in order of magnitude between the finite intellect and the infinite will. This is a difference that must be marked; and it is one that we have already seen is correlative to the distinction between the intellect as a passive container and the will as a pure potentiality.

Though it clearly distinguishes the parts of the faculty for judging as genuine faculties, *Meditations* IV attributes to the will an ascendency over the intellect that, seen close to, runs counter to the trend of Thomistic thought about freedom of choice. In considering *liberum arbitrium*, St Thomas proposes that, because the intellect is the final cause of action, it may be regarded as determining the will (*ST*, Ia, qu. 83 art. 3 ad 3),[33] though this determination is never a matter of coercion. That there is no coercion follows from the natural superiority of the intellect (*ST*, Ia, qu. 82 art. 4 ad 1: '*intellectus est simpliciter altior et nobilior* [. . .] *et prior voluntate*'); from which it further follows that the intellect determines the will 'politically' (*ST*, Ia, qu. 81 art 3 ad 2, citing Aristotle, *Politics*, I ii, 1254 b 2; cf. Kretzmann 1993: 148 and nn.). This is also the position adopted by Descartes' teachers in their commentary on the *De Anima* (Collegium Conimbricense 1598: col. 639E).

Following Aristotle (*EN*, VI ii, 1139 b 4) St Thomas defines the will as rational appetite (*ST*, Ia IIæ, qu. 6 art. 2 ad 1: '[. . .] *voluntas nominat rationalem appetitum*'). Hence, it is the rationality of an action that shows it to have been willed (*ST*, Ia IIæ, qu. 8 arts 1–2 and qu. 10 arts 1–2). Those of Descartes' commentators who were impressed by this line of thought will have been happy to see the doctrine we have already described that, when the intellect genuinely understands an idea, it understands it aright. And they will have applied the thought pretty directly also to the case of action in general.

This, too, is what Descartes learnt at school from the authors of the Coimbra commentary on Aristotle's *Ethics*, who answer affirmatively the question of whether the intellect alone suffices for purposive action (Collegium Conimbricense 1593: col. 16). They clearly locate the root of human freedom ('*radix libertatis*') in the intellect (Collegium Conimbricense 1593: cols 37–8). Because they regard the will's action as free only so long as judgment is unclouded and free ('*tamdiu motus voluntatis liber est, quamdiu judicium integrum ac liberum manet*', Collegium Conimbricense 1593: col. 50), they deny that any action that does not arise from the will is genuinely human ('*nullus omnino erit actus humanus, qui non oriatur a voluntate*', Collegium Conimbricense 1593: col. 38).

Put positively, this is the thought, which we have already seen in considering the nature that God gives to humans, that we are most fully human when we judge and act in accordance with the faculties that we have.

It might be thought that, where, in these ways, the Jesuits converge with their rivals the Dominicans on a volatile matter such as this, we have a pretty clear indicator of what a standard view for a good Catholic ought to be. But this is overquick. Both parties are Aristotelian in inspiration, and so by no means exhaust the then live options. Indeed, from its very inception, the intellectualist line just sketched provoked controversy.

In the Paris Condemnation of 1277, there is an unequivocal rejection of the view that the soul wills nothing unless it is moved by something else (Tempier 1277a: prop. 194: '[q]uod anima nihil vult, nisi mota ab alio').[34] The gloss on this condemnation is slightly unclear;[35] but the motivation for it may derive from a regress argument, of which we find a version in St Augustine, according to which a cause of sin other than the will would nevertheless require wrongful willing, namely, a will that obeyed an unjust cause (*Lib. Arb.*, III, 17, 49). Transposing this into the doxastic terms of the present discussion, this comes out as the thesis, which is the heart of Descartes' account, that the cause of error must be an erroneous use of the will.

Furthermore, the authors of the Condemnation reject the view that the will cannot abstain from what reason dictates (Tempier 1277a and b: 163: '[q]uod voluntas necessario prosequitur, quod firmiter creditum est a ratione').[36] Here, the clarification is added that the necessitation that does operate is not compulsion ('*coactio*'), but the nature of the will (Tempier 1277a and b: 163; see Wippel 1977: 192–3 and n. 54). The implication here is that the will's concurrence with reason is a matter of their joint good functioning, which is again pretty consistent with the model that has been emerging from *Meditations* IV.

Though the Condemnation was revoked within fifty years of its promulgation, the view, which came to be associated with Franciscanism, that it encapsulates continued to be influential in the writings of John Duns Scotus, William of Ockham and, less clearly, Jean Buridan (Korolec 1982: 636–9). Likewise, within the Jesuit community of Descartes' day, luminaries such as St François de Sales treated the will as the proper site of the search for a devout life (Vieillard-Baron 1992: esp. 412–14) and Descartes' first patron, the Cardinal Pierre de Bérulle, took a similar line, so far as was consistent with his Augustinianism (Marion 1981b: 407–9).

What we have, then, is a matter on which there is no announced doctrine and two traditions each with considerable weight. From what we have seen so far, Descartes' position is rather idiosyncratic, being a strong form of voluntarism that is, nevertheless, embedded in a picture that would make even acute readers think that the dominant faculty is the intellect. But this meant that the voluntaristic aspects of *Meditations* IV satisfied those, such as Arnauld, of an Augustinian leaning, while the room allowed for the active role of the (properly) finite intellect suited the more Thomistic readers, such as Caterus and Bourdin.

In short, I offer the hypothesis that, though odd to us, the balance Descartes' theory strikes among positions well-recognised at the time did not cause the dogs (except Gassendi) to bark in the night because each of them took it for a friend.

5 Reason, assent and eternal truth

Reason and light

Intuition and truth

In the last chapter, we saw how we can come to believe falsehoods, though our faculty for judging is perfect of its kind: here, I wish to consider more closely how the infinite will and the finite intellect interact to produce beliefs, and to pay more attention to what goes on when we encounter truths. Do we need the will to understand? Are we free in assenting to what is true? Can we refuse to assent to what we understand?

The following theses add up to Descartes' theory of error:

(i)   that assent to ideas that are understood by the intellect yields only truths;
(ii) that assent is an operation of the will; and
(iii) that the will extends to ideas that are not understood.

Error occurs in humans when the will assents to an idea that goes beyond the limits of the intellect.

While we may still be puzzled about why he needs the will to be infinite to get this result, Descartes must conceive of the intellect as a faculty that, in addition to being the passive container of ideas, is capable of discriminating between the ideas that are to be subjected to the will's arbitration, and those that are to be left in store. In view of what we have seen to be the central cause of credulity, those to be left in store include all the ideas derived from or through the senses. The intellect should not offer them as temptations for assent because they give a picture of the world that we can know to be erroneous.

Given the importance of (i) above, we should be more specific about what is involved in an idea's being understood aright by the intellect; I repeat the crucial phrase from *Meditations* IV: 'what I understand, because I have it from God that I understand it, there is no doubt that I understand it aright' (CSM II: 40; AT VII: 58; '[. . .] *quidquid intelligo, cum a Deo habeam ut intelligam, proculdubio recte intelligo*'). For this corresponds to the rule of clearness and distinctness adopted and vindicated as the criterion of truth in *Meditations* III, on which a word is in order (Newman 1999). Descartes' employment of clearness and distinctness as the discriminating feature of the ideas to which we may (and ought to) assent has generated a huge and sophisticated critical literature concerned, in the main, to elucidate how such a criterion can be vindicated and whether or not we could effectively recognise an idea that satisfied it. I have very little to add to what has already been said, but the position I am presupposing can be outlined as follows.

When it is first enunciated, the rule that I may treat as true what I strongly perceive clearly and distinctly (*Med.* III, CSM II: 24),[1] is not being relied on as a criterion, in the sense of a guarantee of truth (Curley 1978: 113–14). Descartes' procedure through his argument for the existence of a benevolent God vindicates the existence of a criterion in just that sense without illicit appeal to epistemological principles (Van Cleve 1979: 110–17). The criterion that is vindicated turns out to make the same requirements as the acceptance rule proposed (Beyssade 1999). The model that is applicable is that of the *ex post* vindication of the sort that appeared to be underlying the first sentence of *Meditations* I, which we have already discussed. The hypothesis that the clearness and distinctness of ideas is the rule to follow is employed to justify the acceptance of clear and distinct ideas, and thus to establish clearness and distinctness as the criterion of truth.[2]

The terminology of the *Meditations* III returns in *Meditations* IV when the criterion itself is reaffirmed virtually *verbatim* (CSM II: 41);[3] it is referred to a further five times in the remaining discussion; and it figures centrally in the conclusion that, being a work of God, what is clear and distinct is true and, hence, is what the will should restrict itself to (CSM II: 43).[4]

What we now want to know is how clearness and distinctness is related to reason (*ratio*), where that is distinguished from the faculty or power of reasoning (*intellectus*) and considered as a motivation for assenting to an idea. For, Descartes speaks of his being pushed more this way than that by reason (*Med.* IV, CSM II: 40).[5] But it is necessary to recall that, even considered in this way, *ratio* need not be a ground of belief in the way that we typically speak of evidence or justification as being a ground or support, coming first in some order of enquiry or the reconstruction of knowledge.

In the far from casual example of the *cogito*,[6] which Descartes gives towards the end of *Meditations* IV (CSM II: 41), his belief that he exists cannot be derivative of any other belief on pain of that other belief's being prior to it and, hence, either jeopardising the status of the *cogito* as establishing Descartes' first truth, or precipitating a regress. Even if the *cogito* admits of logical presuppositions, it is not founded on them (Marion 1981b: 375). Rather, the narrator perceives his own existence evidently and clearly (*Med.* IV, AT VII: 58: '*evidenter*', '*clare*'; AT IXA: 47: '*evidemment*', '*clairement*'). That being so, he does not need anything epistemically antecedent to the perception to be relieved of doubt about the matter. After all, he has already accepted that perception as a marker of the general acceptability of clear and distinct ideas (*Med.* III, CSM II: 24). Since the *cogito* is perceived as having *ratio*, we should regard *ratio* as sometimes internal to the idea whose *ratio* it is. When considering the idea of my own existence, I can see straight off that I could never have any ground for supposing it not to be true.[7]

To heed the idea of my own existence – an idea that is lurking in my intellect in any case (cf. *Pr.* I, 49 and 50) – requires an initial act of will or effort of attention. There seems to be a plurality of acts here (Schouls 1986: 292): first I set myself to pay attention to the matter and then I assent. As Alquié neatly telescopes it, 'the *cogito* is a *volo*' (Descartes 1963–73: II, 399 n. 2). Once I have heeded it, the idea is such that a great light flows out of it and the will is greatly inclined to assent to it (*Med.* IV, CSM II: 41).[8] In this way, the idea of my own existence bears its own *ratio*. I perceive it as an intuition (*intuitus*) within the procedure of the *Rules* (e.g. *Reg.* III, CSM I: 14) in the respect that it involves liberation from indifference concerning what the idea is of or about. Such ideas are those that carry on their face, within the intellect, the distinguishing mark of their truth. But that alone does not constitute assent to them.

Thus far, I hope to have illustrated with one crucial case, that, although understanding is sufficient for knowledge, the will must have a role in focusing on what is understood. In this way, there is a further level of interplay between the intellect and the will, which calls for closer examination.

A regress of faculties

Even if a given idea is contained in my intellect in such a way that, when I attend to it, I perceive it clearly and distinctly, I perceive its clearness and distinctness, I see that it is backed by *ratio* and I see a great light flowing out of it, I still might want to find a connection between that state of my intellect and the question of whether I have to assent, considered as an act of the will. Trivially, there threatens a regress of a familiar sort.

At first sight, the roles of the intellect and the will were wholly separate. But it has been emerging that the intellect cannot be a mere container of ideas; it must in some way present them or show them to the will; the intellect must have some part in illuminating or highlighting the ideas that seem like good candidates for assent, and in keeping sense-derived and other undesirable ideas out of the reach of temptation. Likewise, the role of the will is to accept or reject what it is shown; so it must have some perceptual function in picking up the brightness of the ideas.

The regress that threatens here is like the commonplace objection to a certain type of homunculus theory. If the decomposition of the faculty for judging was motivated by the need to see its inner workings, and each of its components turns out to have inner workings (the intellect quasi-assents and the will quasi-perceives), then it seems that each of the components is performing the whole of the process of judging: '[h]omunculi are *bogeymen* only if they duplicate *entire* the talents they are rung in to explain' (Dennett 1978: 123, emphases original; cf. 1993: 259–62). We are alerted to the possibility of there being a further level, on which there is intellect-like activity in the will-like activity of the intellect and will-like activity in the intellect-like activity of the will. Since Descartes introduces the decomposition of the faculty for judging as a means to explain, consistent with the perfection of that faculty, human credulity and error, he has to find some way of blocking the regress to ensure that the explanation is, indeed, explanatory.

One way to block the move to the further level, on which we say that, in some respect, the intellect assents and the will perceives, would be to admit that the talk of 'highlighting', 'seeing' and so on, is no more than metaphorical. This is the option Hobbes offers, claiming that Descartes' reference to a 'great light in the soul' has no force in the argument, but represents only subjective certitude – which may include the certitude of those who are hanging on to prejudices (*Obj.* III, 13, CSM II: 134; cf. Petrik 1992: 145–75). If talking about the light in the soul is metaphorical then it is a metaphor for some other process, perhaps one that will discriminate cases in which we are really justified in assenting to an idea. But, in reply to Hobbes' offer, Descartes declines to defend his imagery as argumentative; he insists, however, that it is obviously explanatory (*Resp.* III, 13, CSM II: 135; AT VII: 192: '[*n*]*ihil attinet ad rem quærere an vox, magna lux, sit argumentativa, nec-ne, modo sit explicativa, ut revera est*'). The explanation he gives in terms of perspicuity of cognition piles optical Ossa on perceptual Pelion (see also *Pr.* I, 45, CSM I: 207),[9] especially when the difference in truth between evident perception and prejudice is made to depend on just how bright an idea is (*Resp.* III, 13, CSM II: 135).[10]

In the alternative, it might be suggested that the will really does perceive a sort of light that is produced in the intellect. The adoption of a fully perceptual model of this sort might involve our imagining ray-diagrams on which *ratio* illuminates ideas that the will then perceives and, in a second moment, assents to. Of course, Descartes was not himself averse to drawing ray-diagrams for suspiciously similar purposes; but such a diagram would raise more questions than it answers. If an idea is a picture – as suggested by

Meditations III (CSM II: 25) – does assent to it mean that something fits it or that there is some specified bit of the world that fits it? If an idea is propositional, what has light got to do with all this? Does *ratio* illuminate from within in some cases (as in the case of the *cogito*) and from without in others (e.g. geometrical or otherwise deductive)? How is the 'eye of the will' related to assent?

Despite these imponderables, let us concentrate on whether there has to be a further explanation of how the intellect draws the will's attention to the ideas that it lights up or that light themselves up. For we may be launched on a fresh search for will-like capacities in the intellect and intellect-like capacities in the will. If successful, such a search would presumably turn up an interaction that is not ultimately explained by a (non-metaphorical) reference to light. The failure of such a search would be to continue to infinity. But Descartes has said that he does not envisage any interrelation other than the light of the intellect.

Let us suppose that, while the intellect's understanding of an idea can be partly discriminative and the will's assent is partly observational, the division of labour stops there. This model seems to have the advantages that it is relatively simple, that it looks capable of being explanatory, and that it goes some way to giving fair shares to the intellect and the will in producing assent, as we saw at the end of the last chapter. In the fully perceptual expression of the model, the light of the soul is the medium of communication between the parts of the faculty for judging; in the first stage of the regress, they may be thought of as in direct contact with each other, and not dependent on any information-carrier.

But, while these suggestions are meant to explain how the intellect selects and how the will discerns, it might easily seem that a second stage is called for to explain them. Thus, both within the eye of the will and within the light of the intellect, we would have to reproduce the whole of the perceptual model: the intellect first contains ideas, then selects them on the basis of their brightness and finally proposes them to the will, which, in its turn, first perceives the light, then is favourably inclined (or not) and only lastly assents (or dissents). This potential *mise en abîme* is a reason for avoiding even rudimentary line-drawings. Instead of the two-stage process with which we began, we have generated six phases from perception proper to full-blown assent. If six instead of two, why should we not contemplate any arbitrarily large number of stages?

A short answer is that the discrimination of phases would become excessively fine-grained. Beyond those already envisaged, there do not seem to be (m)any more that it would be worth separating out. Further elaborations will also be progressively evacuated of explanatory power. On such a scheme, the regress is well under way and the parts of the faculty for judging that are definitely intellect (container) and definitely will (assenter/dissenter) are constricted. If carried to infinity, such a process blocks the possibility of any assent whatever in a mind that cannot pass instantaneously through all of a potentially finite number of steps.

Perhaps a more principled reason for not wishing to foist such a picture on Descartes is that, in thus merging the roles of the sub-faculties, he would have to be backtracking on his commitment to a difference of order between the finite intellect and the infinite will. However we envisage the means for contact between the intellect and the will, the difference of order between them presumably implies that the former cannot usurp the latter beyond a definite limit, namely, the limitations of its particular finitude. Still, consistent with the difference of order, we have a scheme that renders explicit what Descartes has in mind in talking about the concurrence of the components of the faculty for judging (*Med.* IV, CSM II: 39). Such a mutuality of the roles of the intellect and the will does not involve the former's determining the latter, while it does attribute both activeness and passiveness to both, at different stages and in different regards.

If this is as charitable a reading as we can get of how a clear and distinct idea comes to be assented to, we can again see why it would have presented itself as respectable enough both to those of Descartes' contemporaries who gave pride of place to reason in settling what beliefs we should have as well as to those who privileged free choice in the acquisition of beliefs. As with the doctrine of the infinite will and the finite intellect, there is no cause for the dogs to bark at the story told in *Meditations* IV.

We turn now to see how the interaction between the parts of the faculty for judging enables us to take control of the process by which beliefs are formed and, so, to hold our credulous habits at bay.

Grades of assent

Deciding to believe

In the normal run of our doxastic practice, we are interested in getting beliefs. Specifically, we are interested in getting as many beliefs of the best available sorts as we can with the minimum effort relative to their quality and availability. Though we have these interests, in general we do not take much notice of them. We just get beliefs. When we discover that the normal run of our doxastic practice has led us into near-total error, then we should be very wary even of the beliefs that seemed the best available. Instead of getting beliefs, we should begin to pay attention to our ways of assessing them. This requires us to take a step back from our antecedent doxastic practice and, until further notice, not to regard our previous habits as likely to yield beliefs that it is proper for us to assent to.

In the model of assent I am building up as attributable to Descartes, this stepping back from earlier habits is the cardinal presupposition of enquiry. But it runs counter to a strong trend in empiricist thought, to the effect that the beliefs we have and the habits by which we get them are not, strictly speaking, under our control. This trend of thought stems from the idea that the getting of beliefs is a natural or naturalisable feature of our interactions with the external world. It is a process that is at bottom a matter of efficient causation, with the external world (including our perceptual apparatus) as agent and us as patient.

One outgrowth of this scheme allows that we can, indeed, reflect on how the external world imposes perceptions on us. That sort of reflection can, to some degree, help us to assess the beliefs we acquire in terms of the evidence of the senses for and against them, and it can make explicit some canons of belief-assessment. But processes of self-conscious belief-assessment are not really very different from those of belief-getting in the normal run of things.

Perhaps it is worth citing a case of the way this empiricist trend of thought can get applied. Take Hume's discussion of miracles in section X of the first *Enquiry* (Hume 1748). There is much room for debate about what Hume's arguments show and aim to show about miracles and about whether we should ever believe in reports of them (Fogelin 1990). But what I wish to bring to notice is the way that Hume seems to take the clash between the evidences for miracles and those in favour of the laws of nature to be an impersonal matter, a process in which the belief-former is effectively a spectator. He speaks as if, as each piece of evidence in favour of special divine intervention is presented, it is overwhelmed by the mass of our background beliefs that it represents 'a violation of the laws of nature' (Hume 1748: 114). What we then have is a 'mutual destruction of arguments' (ibid.: 116). Once it has been overwhelmed, each evidence of a miracle must be counted as nul, perhaps taking with it an infinitesimal part of our confidence in natural regularity; it therefore no longer counts as evidence at all. Thus, once we have decided that miracles violate the laws we happen to believe in and feel we have massive evidence for, there is no way we can change our minds (also Mackie 1982: 16–17).

In this trend of thought, there is a strong element of doxastic conservatism: every new belief grows out of our previous beliefs and the habits they embody. We acquire the beliefs we acquire in accordance with the habits we happen to have. We are caused by the way the world is, and by the way we are, to come to have the beliefs we end up with. We can often explain how we came to have this or that belief on the basis of that interaction, but it is almost only when there is something aberrant about the interaction – aberrant either in the way the world is or in the doxastic habits that a given person has – that an explanation is called for. The rest of the time, normal functioning is allowed to be as good as we can get; this is not to say that explanations of normal functioning are easy to supply; they are not, and are, on the whole, boringly inept when offered presumably because what is normal does not focus our questioning.

There is, moreover, a pragmatic paradox in saying both that this or that is the proper standard for belief-assessment and yet that the formation of beliefs comes about independently of any intervention by a controlling subject. But the fact that this paradox is in ambush is no reason for saying that many thinkers of an empiricist bent have not fallen into the double-standard in question. If we think of Locke, Mill or Russell as preaching toleration, respect for others' opinions and rationality to persons whom they held to be incorrigibly bigoted, stupid and unreasonable, we get a measure of the problem. Despite the other unkind things I have to say about Hume, this is a point on which he was consistent: an empiricist has, alas, few means to be a troublingly interesting radical.

A further way that the empiricist bias comes out is in the thesis, closer to our present concerns, that, 'it is not a contingent fact that I cannot bring it about, just like that, that I believe something' (Williams 1970: 148). If it is a fact, and a non-contingent one at that, that 'I cannot present my own belief as an achievement, because, by so presenting it, I would disqualify it as a belief' (Hampshire 1959: 157), then it might seem that the model I have been building up as attributable to Descartes ignores it. If so, we ought to find Descartes guilty of error because 'he should not have regarded assent quite so simply as a mode of the will' (Williams 1978: 178).

The argument for the alleged fact's being a fact is also an argument for its being non-contingent, that is to say, for its being of the nature of a conceptual truth. In outline, the argument is that we cannot bring it about, just like that, that we believe something because this would involve our deciding to believe; if belief could depend on our deciding, then the relation between belief and 'aiming at truth' (Williams 1970: 137 &c.) would be broken; hence, what we would have decided would not be a genuine belief because, lacking a 'truth-centred motive' (Williams 1970: 149–50), it would be a desire, a wish or somesuch: 'thought cannot be thought unless it is directed towards a conclusion' (Hampshire 1959: 159).

If Descartes' model of belief-formation does take account of the truth-centredness of assent, then we should consider whether or not he really does ignore the fact, if it is one, that I cannot bring it about, just like that, that I believe something. If he does not ignore it, we have grounds for supposing that Descartes denies that it is quite the fact that it can seem to be: he is not regarding assent as *simply* a mode of the will.

Supposing I cannot bring it about, just like that, that I believe something, then, by contraposition, when I do come to believe something, this is not a state of me that I have brought about, just like that. For instance, my coming to believe, as once I did, that the *Discourse* was published in 1637, was a product of the presence of this information in various books working on the doxastic habits that I had at the time of my coming to believe it; I had some mild curiosity about the matter and considerable readiness to believe what various books agreed upon. That was what was in the books and the way I was rigged up.

My habit was not something I could change, just like that, nor, in such a matter, should I have done anything much to prevent its operation. If I had found that my habit persistently or dangerously led me into error, or that the books did not agree sufficiently for any of them to seem adequately credible, then I could have decided that the simple credulity in what each says was something I would have to work on. When one works on one's doxastic habits one is, indeed, doing something with a 'truth-centred motive' even if one is not, at the time, getting many beliefs about what one wants the truth of. One way I could have worked on the habit that brought me to my belief about the publication date of the *Discourse* would have been a refusal to expose myself to the contamination of my intellect by what is to be found in books and to the temptations of the written word.

An alternative way of bringing it about that I am not driven to believe what I read is offered by what we all do: set up some sort of canonic of (less un-) critical reading. We more or less self-consciously accept some rough and ready rules, e.g. that an accredited specialist writing about her specialism is more believable than a person of no standing, or that a university press publication is more likely to have been vetted than a privately printed pamphlet. Such rules of thumb are, of course, just crude examples and by nature hit-and-miss. If there had been more books like M. Callinescu's *Five Faces of Modernity*, which gives the date 1634 (Callinescu 1987: 23), I might have been more sceptical of those who get it right. But I have learnt how to regard books with titles of that sort. Still, I could undermine my rule of thumb with the fact that Stephen Gaukroger, a highly respected authority on Descartes, publishing a book on him with a highly respected university press, let it slip that the *Discourse* was published in 1638 (Gaukroger 1995: 7 and 11). A critical reader knows better and he believes that Gaukroger knows better, he believes that Gaukroger believes the correct date given in the 'Chronological Table', p. xvi, on pp. 102, 222, by implication, on p. 323, and on p. 332.

The adoption and application of canons of this sort can bring about in me habits in accordance with which I am brought, passively and just like that, to believe the things that, actively and at one remove, I aim at believing, namely whatever a critical reader in search of elementary publication data would believe.

Had I confidence that my doxastic habits are well-adapted to uncovering what a skilled enquirer would believe, then I would have no reason to go against the flow of what they present to me for assent. Not only are many good empiricists, such as those I have cited, presupposing that their own habits are well-adapted in this way, but they may well be right in their confidence. Lucky them. But the situation that Descartes is envisaging is one in which this confidence is seriously, near-globally and for reasons given, undermined. He therefore has a motivation for wanting to change not just his beliefs, but also his belief-forming habits.

Descartes does not himself offer an account of the type just outlined. Yet we can use it to understand what must be going on in an exchange with Hobbes on a closely related point, and to see why the exchange presents a disappointing spectacle of cross-purposes. Hobbes occupies a position clearly anticipating the line that has become empiricist orthodoxy.

Commenting on Descartes' assertion in *Meditations* IV that assent to the idea of his own existence is an act of the will (CSM II: 41), Hobbes claims that, just as knowing something to be true, so believing it or giving assent to it, have nothing to do with the will (*Obj.* III, 13, CSM II: 134). His reason is that we do believe what is proved to us by good arguments or by credible testimony (*Obj.* III, 13, CSM II: 134; AT VII: 192: '[. . .] *nam quæ validis argumentis probantur, vel ut credibilia narrantur,* [. . .] *credimus*'). If this were the whole and simple truth of the matter, we would always be passive in belief-acquisition; we would also be stuck with whatever standards of argument and testimony we happen to have. Likewise, the acquisition of new standards would be a process in which we are always passive. Hobbes allows, however, that assertion and denial, defence and rebuttal of propositions are all acts of the will (*Obj.* III, 13, CSM II: 134; AT VII: 192: '[*v*]*erum est, quod affirmare et negare, propugnare et refellere propositiones, sunt actus voluntatis*'). His ground for this seems to be that these involve the marshalling of the arguments with which one is acquainted and the deployment of the testimony one has received. What he refuses is Descartes' likening of inner assent to these quasi-forensic activities: inner assent is not a matter of the will because we do not argue with ourselves.

If we distinguish the sorts of cases in which an enquirer is simply operating in accordance with the doxastic habits she happens to have; from those in which she is aiming at self-conscious assessment of beliefs (perhaps with a view to refining those very habits); then Hobbes gives a fair description of the former. But Descartes has the latter in mind. Indeed, it would not be excessive to hear in Descartes' stance a strong echo of the Platonic account of reasoning as a sort of shadow conversation. Exploiting the fact that the Greek word λόγος covers both the use of reason and the use of words, Socrates effectively defines reflective thought (διάνοια) as the soul's conversation with itself about a given matter, and the getting of opinions (δοξάζειν) as arising from talk that has been conducted not with someone else nor aloud, but in silence with oneself (*Theaet.*, 190 A 4–6).[11] If so, we can indeed bring it about, just like that, that we believe something, because we can deliberately bring the inner debate to a close with a judgment (cf. Montmarquet 1992b: 117–20). If Descartes is presupposing the psychological and metaphysical possibility of our exercising this sort of control, it is not hard to account for his not having seen the point of Hobbes' objection.

When we are going with the flow of our doxastic habits and assenting to ideas acquired, among other ways, through the senses, the operation of the will is like that of an idle customs official: everything gets waved through. In these cases, Hobbes and Descartes agree on the natural history of human beings: we are such that argument and testimony, as well as other influences and conditioning factors, do produce beliefs. I think everyone can agree on this much. It is a matter of everyday experience that there is considerable artificiality involved in blocking one's own tendencies to believe or disbelieve. The process of blocking here might be called 'thinking' which, taken in this rarefied sense, is an uncommon occurrence, whose uncommonness explains why most generally we do not notice having formed such princely things as beliefs. But, agreeing on this natural history, Hobbes may have missed Descartes' aim, which was to claim not that every belief we form we form by act of will, but that our will can be active in determining which beliefs we are to have.

For the purposes in hand in the *Meditations*, the customs officer is at his most strenuously vigilant and pestilential. The discovery of our credulity is a tipoff, and every idea is being counted as a potential falsity-smuggler. Only those that have been thoroughly scrutinised are allowed to pass. For this reason, in his reply to Hobbes, Descartes restricts himself to considering only the beliefs that arise out of things that we clearly perceive (*Resp.* III, 13, CSM II: 135; AT VII: 192: '*rebus clare perspectis*'). This restriction is beside the point of Hobbes' objection, which is about beliefs in general.

Descartes likens our assent to what we clearly perceive to our desire for goods that we clearly know to be such (*Resp.* III, 13, CSM II: 135; AT VII: 192: '[. . .] *idem est ac si diceretur nos bonum clare cognitum* [. . .] *appetere*'). The point he is making in making this assimilation explicit, is not merely that the ideas illuminated by the natural light are, like diplomats immune to further inspection, to be welcomed, but that Hobbes is wrong to say that we assent to them 'willy nilly' (restoring with added emphasis the words excised from *Obj.* III, 13, CSM II: 135; AT VII: 192 just cited: '*nam quæ validis argumentis probantur, vel ut credibilia narrantur*, volentes nolentes *credimus*'). But, in disagreeing with Hobbes, Descartes offers a curious mixture of touchiness and misconstrual. The touchiness is prompted by the fear lest the will be subject to any compulsion in assenting and, in particular, subject to compulsion in assenting against better judgment. That is, the infinite will cannot be suborned even by good arguments and credible testimony if there is some other good that we know to be such.

The misconstrual is that he reads Hobbes' 'willy nilly' as if it were a conjunction: when we assent to a clearly perceived idea we are both willing and unwilling. The expected way of glossing 'willy nilly' (*'volens nolens'*) would be as a disjunction: whether we want to or not.[12] Moreover, given that Latin clearly distinguishes between inclusive and exclusive disjunction, we would expect the reading of 'willy nilly' to be exclusive (using *'aut . . . aut'* or *'sive . . . sive'*),[13] not the inclusive *'vel'*, and most certainly not the *'&'* that is printed, corresponding to *'et'* ('and': CSM II: 135).[14]

This misconstrual is at first glance shocking: we should think anything rather than think that Descartes has blundered into mistaking an 'or' for an 'and'. A blunder of this sort must be concealing some more interesting reason for overhastiness which is the cause for touchiness just referred to. The cause is that Descartes is struggling to keep a balance between the doctrine that Hobbes rather flailingly contests (namely, the doctrine that the will is never necessitated by the intellect); and a doctrine, to which we shall return in the next section, that, if we are enquiring dutifully, there are truths that we encounter in such a way that we do not, as a matter of fact, refuse them (though we could if we saw a higher good in doing so).

Even if he does miss Hobbes' point, there are two issues that Descartes is wishing to exclude from his and Hobbes' consideration.

One is the sort of case in which assent to a clearly perceived idea should be accounted a bit of mixed willing when the truth I am admitting is one that is distasteful to me (cf. Descartes 1963–73: II, 626, Alquié's note ad loc.). If I am, e.g. squeamish or vain about admitting something unpleasant about myself or my better friends, such an obstacle to my assent is not a matter of my will, but is a matter of a wish or a desire (*'appetitus'*), and so should be considered as a species of passion. Here we have one use for an infinite power of the will as the agent of assent: I can recognise even the most repellent and depressing truths, insofar as my habitual self-image is not a matter of my will but is a finite propensity and, so, subject to it.

The other sort of issue that Descartes' refusal of Hobbes' 'willy nilly' brings to the surface is this. Grant, first, that the will can overcome any other tendency, whether active or passive, in the soul that might tend to obstruct assent to a clearly perceived idea. Then add the notion that, once the will is inclined to assent to such an idea, there is no contrary willing to impede assent. That the will is, in this way, unitary comes out in Descartes' likening of such an idea to a clearly perceived good, as we have just seen in *Third Replies* (CSM II: 135).

It is worth reporting two ways of coming at this thought. One, with classical antecedents, is expressed in Descartes' conversation with Burman in connection with the passage of *Meditations* IV where Descartes is saying that he can remember to withhold assent to matters that are not clear (CSM II: 43). To Burman's query about the scope of the indifference – a notion to which we shall return – that we are thus left in, Descartes cites the maxim that sins flow entirely from ignorance (*Con.*, CSMK: 342; AT V: 159: '*peccata enim fluunt fere ex ignorantia*').[15] That is to say, it is impossible to choose the lesser of two perceived goods, while perceiving them as such (see also letter to Mersenne, May 1637, CSMK: 56; AT I: 366). This commits Descartes to the thesis that, once I have determined to assent to a given idea, that determination is the unique set of my will.

The other line is more directly concerned with assent, though it is couched in a rather outlandish way. In discussing Aristotle's remarks on judgment in *De Interpretatione*, iv, the Coimbra commentators seek to exclude 'subordinate operations' ('*operationes subordinatæ*') within the intellect: if there were subordinate parts of assent, then they would each have to have their own principle; but, such principles would be related to the superordinate principle as inferior angels of a given species would be to superior angels; hence, they are identical with it (Collegium Conimbricense 1606: 491, cols 1–2). The Coimbrans appeal to what they take to be understood about hierarchies of angels in a way that we might easily find queer; but that fact should not put us off the point of principle being made. It makes no sense to speak of both willing and not willing because the will is indivisible, just as the calculation of perceived goods produces exactly one answer. Though I may have some smutty motivation for wanting some truth not to be true, once I clearly perceive that the corresponding belief is true, then that motivation ceases to be any part of the operation of the will.

Thus, Descartes requires the thought that assent is an operation in which the will is genuinely and fully active, because it is like a participant in a debate. This offers a model on which we can bring it about, just like that, that we believe something: by seeing that it is true. The capacity is one we exercise *especially* in the savagely 'truth-centred' activity of enquiring because that activity is the exercise of the highest doxastic rectitude, namely the pursuit of all and only those ideas that have the stamp of truth on them.

To see how this exercise is also an exercise in freedom, we turn to see how it is related to a sequence of grades of compulsion, beginning with cases in which we acquire beliefs though they are not properly the results of enquiry because the will either is inoperative or has been distracted.

Indifference and spontaneity

The normal run of our doxastic practice does not deserve the name of enquiry, because we are not thinking, in the rarefied sense suggested earlier, in which we suspend our usual lax acceptance of sense-derived ideas. We just jog along doing what we have always done.

If the view that I have attributed to the empiricist tradition were the whole story, then we could never do anything that deserves the name of enquiry. The sort of determinism involved in its conservative doxastic stance would mean that we are never in control of our standards of belief-assessment (cf. Keeling 1934: 203). If the causes most generally at work in our belief-acquisition were irresistible by anything within our power, the theodicidic thrust of *Meditations* IV would be lost. God would be the ultimate cause of our having the false beliefs we have acquired, e.g. from or through the senses. Since God is not the cause of our errors, the deliverances of the senses must be resistible by something within our power. They are resistible both because we can discover that they have led us into error and because they do not supply us with reasons for assenting to them: at best, they are 'teachings of nature' (*Med.* VI, CSM II: 56). Even given the givens both about the way the world is and the habits I have, Descartes seeks a gap into which to insert reasons for belief-acquisition, insisting that reasons liberate.

Because the beliefs that arise from our credulous habits are not backed by *ratio*, Descartes says that we are in a state of indifference with respect to them. It is the indifference he experiences when no reason is pushing him one way rather than the other (*Med.* IV, CSM II: 40). In the Latin, the verb he uses for what reason can do is '*impellere*', to impel (AT VII: 58); in the French, the image is of himself as passively (not) being carried by the weight of reason (AT IXA: 46: '*emporté* [. . .] *par le poid d'aucune raison*'). This indifference is thus a lack. But it does not mean that, in the normal run of things, he does not assent. Rather, it means that, when he thinks about whether to assent, either he does not see that he has to or he sees that he does not have to.

Let us distinguish two cases.

In one, assessment is simultaneous with the arising of the sensory prompting. I am considering some sensory presentation in the intellect and trying to decide on the basis of it whether, e.g. this piece of wax is white or yellow.[16] Suppose that my former habits would have led me to think that, in the state it is now, it is white. I know, however, that presentations of this sort may lead me into error. I may recall that what now looks white may turn some other colour or that what looks white may turn out to have been some other colour all along (cf. *Med.* IV, CSM II: 41). Here I am operating at the empirical level. Offered a choice about what colour to judge a piece of wax is, I can select the purposes that such a choice might subserve. For I may have some practical purposes in judging or continuing to judge that the wax is white, such as to predict how it will look on a piece of paper. But those purposes form no part of an enquiry in accordance with reason.

In the other case, where I am operating at the doctrinal level, I have arrived at the conclusion that colour does not belong to material substances. This is closer to my predicament in overhauling the body of my standing beliefs. I have, in the past, acquired beliefs in accordance with the promptings of the senses, but these will not stand subsequent scrutiny by reason. So I induce a state of indifference in myself by thinking about the genealogy of such promptings: following a tradition that goes back at least to Democritus (e.g. DK, 68A49, 68B9, 11, 125) and comes down to the present in the shape of the 'scientific' world view, I recall that objects are not coloured. Apparent colours and their contraries become equally unappealing to me. I dissociate myself from them and they cease to be my beliefs for the purposes of enquiry. The techniques for inducing this sort of state of dissociation will be the main subject-matter of the first part of our discussion of scepticism in the next chapter.

My capacity, when I think about the matter, to be indifferent to any given prompting means that I am not compelled to assent to it. This does not deny that what produced assent, when I first acquired the belief, was the compulsion of habit. But that compulsion can be overcome by my now thinking about the matter. If I break the habit sufficiently, then I am free of one sort of compulsion and find myself able to plump.

This freedom to plump is explicated as a 'two-way [. . .] power to select x or not-x' (Cottingham 1993: 65). It has been called a 'counter-causal' (Campbell 1957: 167–78; and, with specific reference to Descartes, Petrik 1992: 55) or 'contra-causal' (Cottingham 1986: 151) capacity, to emphasise the way that it is meant to stand outside the nexus of mechanical constraint. It is the capacity to go against the flow of what we would be caused to believe. Even if we do assent to what we are caused to assent to, we may be doing so as the result *also* of selection; so it might be at least as appropriate to call this freedom 'super-causal' (or 'supra-causal').

Descartes says that this is an exercise of the lowest grade of freedom (*Med.* IV, CSM II: 40; AT VII: 58: '*infimus gradus libertatis*'). As he explains to Mesland, occasions for the exercise of this power involve a lack. What is lacking is any perception of truth or goodness that impels one in one direction rather than another (letter to Mesland, 9th February 1645, CSMK: 245; AT IV: 173: '[. . .] *a nulla veri vel boni perceptione in unam magis quam in alteram partem impellitur*'). The lack of such a perception amounts to the same as the lack of a reason. All the same, it is a grade of freedom, below which are the grades of compulsion, which are the unreasoning habits of belief-acquisition and -assessment. Within this lowest grade of freedom we can distinguish the indifference that we exercise in a situation of balanced evidences, from the indifference of perversion, in which our plumping is contrary to the dictates of reason.[17]

Where I have balanced evidences, none of which convinces, and I choose one rather than another, this selecting is hardly more free than is the selecting of some purpose relative to which I might prefer to say that a given piece of wax is white. These purposes are conditional or hypothetical, and do not commit me to believing much about what the wax is *really* like. In the absence of a reason, I might plump for an option rather than do without a belief altogether.

On the other hand, in cases where I plump for a belief in spite of the considerations, short of such as would justify certainty, that run against it, I am exercising no more freedom than I do when I select some purpose for deciding that the wax is white. For I still lack a reason. If I decide to believe, to take some rather tame instances, in the miracle of Saragossa that Hume admits as strong a case as one could hope for (Hume 1748: 123–4), or in the presence of aliens on Earth as a hypothesis that fits a wide range of wayward goings-on, these determinations do at least free me from the constraints of habit. And they may be at least partly for fun. Though I might say that they have some evidential weight, the arguments I adduce for them are mostly play. I can enjoy believing such things simply because they are far-fetched or bizarre – to amuse or annoy.

Here, of course, the activity is not 'truth-centred' in the solemn empiricist sense we have referred to. But I do not see that it is proper to deny that they are beliefs, any more than it is to simply exclude, as empiricists are apt to (e.g. Williams 1955), the allegedly more serious motivations that are thought to underlie the determination, variously attributed to St Augustine and Tertullian (*De Carne Christi*, 5) to believe doctrines precisely because they are absurd or illogical. In some cases, this sort of plumping is thought to be the most proper approach; as Sir Thomas Browne complains against Anglicanism, '[m]ethinks there be not impossibilities enough in Religion for an active faith [. . .] I desire to exercise my faith in the difficultest point; for to credit ordinary and visible objects is not faith, but perswasion' (Browne 1642/3: 10–11). Such preferences for impossibilities may be exercises of liberty, but they had better not be the best uses of it.

If indifference is the lowest grade of liberty, our next job is to see what grades there are above and we are already provided with the thought that *ratio* is a key. Also, we can draw on the fairly traditional distinction between liberty of indifference, just reviewed, and liberty of spontaneity. Aristotle's account of when an action is spontaneous or voluntary (ἑκούσιος) specifies that the cause of action is internal to the agent (*EN*, III i, 1110 a 17: ἡ ἀρχὴ τοῦ κινεῖν [. . .] ἐν αὐτῷ ἐστίν). What we want to know is how Descartes characterises spontaneity and what grades he envisages of it.

In *Meditations* IV, he observes that if he always clearly saw what was true and good, he would never need to deliberate about how to judge or what to choose; if so, though he would be utterly free, he would never be in a state of indifference (*Med.* IV, CSM II: 40).[18] Seeing no alternative to a given judgment, because one sees that it is true and good, is a condition in which one escapes from indifference and, so, to a higher grade of freedom.

The absence of alternatives amounts to a *ratio* in favour of the given judgment. Descartes has in mind two ways in which he can come to have such a reason and thus be so much the freer. One is that in which he clearly understands *why* it is true and good (*Med.* IV, CSM II: 40; AT VII: 57–8: '*rationem veri et boni in ea evidenter intelligo*'); the other is that in which God has set his innermost thoughts up that way (*Med.* IV, CSM II: 40; AT VII: 58: '*intima cogitationis meæ disponit*'). Though Descartes couples these two ways with a swift 'or', their interrelations are rather more complicated.

The case in which I see for myself the *ratio* of what I judge clearly represents one grade of spontaneous assent. The ideas to whose truth I assent in this way are the truths that can be discovered by natural means; I arrive at them by following where reason leads.

We have already seen that there is at least one idea that carries its own *ratio* with it. For me, this is the idea of my own existence; for you, of yours. The *cogito*'s self-evidence requires only the usual divine concurrence in all creation. The use of reason, beginning with this foundational truth and passing through the existence and veracity of God with the aid of the common notions, will lead me to other, derived, truths. If the steps I take to arrive at them are clear and distinct, then the results will be such that I assent to them spontaneously: I see their clearness and distinctness too, why they too are true and good. In these cases, Descartes takes it to be a hallmark of our freedom that we assent to such ideas easily, for, when we are presented with them, to be free, and to act spontaneously and voluntarily are the very same thing.[19] It is easy because there is no room for dither; but it is free because I am not being acted on from without (*Med.* IV, CSM II: 41; AT VII: 58–9: '[. . .] *non quod ab aliqua vi extra me fuerim ad id coactus*').

The other sort of case of spontaneous assent – in which God has set my thoughts up in a certain way – seems to answer a call on Descartes' theory of how we get beyond the one truth that, for us, carries its own *ratio* within it.

I slid over the fact that, in moving from the establishment of his own existence by the manœuvre of the *cogito* to other truths discoverable by natural means, Descartes needs to call upon the much-puzzled-over principles of *Meditations* III, such as that there must be as much efficiently and totally in a cause as in its effect, that he says are manifest by the natural light (*Med.* III, CSM II: 28; AT VII: 40: '*lumine naturali manifestum*'). For reasons that we shall go into in Chapter 9, these principles can be treated as identical with the common notions of the *Rules* and the eternal verities of the *Principles*. But it is unclear where we get them from, how, if at all, they can be justified, and how they can be used to justifiy other discoveries.

On one persuasive reading of Descartes' doctrine about the nature of inference, we cannot be assured by 'mechanical' means that deductive procedures will lead us from truths to truths (Hacking 1973: 14). We need to see for ourselves the relations in order to be able to intuit the relata, in particular the relata further down the line from the *cogito*. That is to say, when we get into the physico-mathematical enquiries that make up the later books of the *Principles,* one respect in which they depend on the foundations of metaphysics is that in which the truths we can uncover are instances of the basic principles.

If, nevertheless, we are going to be able to use demonstration, we need the transmission of truth to be underwritten by what is in us and what God has ordained (Gaukroger 1987: 66–70; Craig 1987: 24–6). The solution to this problem that is offered by the spontaneous assent we give to what we are wired up to see as clear, may help to explain why, in the *Rules,* Descartes regards the common notions as like links in a chain by which we connect simple natures in all rational inference (*Reg.* XII, CSM I: 45; AT X: 419: '[. . .] *sunt communes illæ notiones, quæ sunt veluti vincula quædam ad alias naturas simplices inter se conjugendas, et quarum evidentia nititur quidquid ratiocinando concludiamus*'). He therefore implicitly denies that we assent to them in intuitions as we do to the simple natures themselves. Likewise, in the *Principles,* he explicitly denies that the eternal verities have any existence outside our thought (*Pr.* I, 48, CSM I: 208; AT VIIIA: 22: '[. . .] *æternas veritates, nullam existentiam extra cognitionem nostram habentes*').[20] In both cases, the justification for an inferential move is not like the major premise of a syllogism, but like an inference-rule whose rightness we just see.

It might be objected that this sort of 'just seeing' is not an exercise of liberty. For, just as our being subject to the influence of the senses is a form of compulsion, it might seem that our assent here involves our being compelled or acted on from without: God is the agent and we are patients. To this Descartes would reply, first, that these notions are true, where the deliverances of the senses are not. This makes us free. And, second, that God is not acting on us from without. Though He is, indeed, outside us, He is acting on us from within ('*intima*' at AT VII: 58, already cited), on our natures. For this reason, our assent has its source within us and, so, is spontaneous. If the spontaneous assent we give to ideas uncoverable in the course of, e.g. a physico-mathematical enquiry is, in this way, natural, then we might wonder whether there are other cases, which might be said to be supernatural.

Sensitive to the helpfulness of understanding *Meditations* IV in theological terms, some commentators have sought to explain the spontaneity of assent to what has *ratio*, or is a means of reasoning, in terms of grace and enlightenment. Thus, we have the idea that 'the disposition produced by grace is symmetrical with the evident knowledge of the understanding' (Laporte 1945: 318) and that there is thus a 'rigorous parallelism between intellectual life and the life of grace' (Gouhier 1924: 191), which means that spontaneity is 'the most enlightened (*'éclairé'*) sort of choice' (Gueroult 1953: I, 327).

This vocabulary is a useful reminder of two other features of Descartes' scheme of assent. In adopting the vocabulary of enlightenment, however, I do not wish to use it to account for what spontaneity consists in. Rather, it can be used to mark two special cases of free assent.

One is to do with belief in the dogmas of religion. These do need some backing, for it is agreed that they concern obscure matters (*Reg.* III discussed in the last chapter, also). And the solution that appeal to God's getting inside my thoughts offers is that this divine grace provides a formal reason for my assent, which Descartes says is more certain than the natural light (*Resp.* II, ad 5, CSM II: 105).[21]

This does not help us to know which of the purported revelations are actually divinely backed nor why it should be that Turks, and some Englishmen, do not assent to what Descartes regards as the truths of the Christian faith (Gouhier 1924: 189–96; Menn 1998: 326–8). But it does go some way to giving an explanation that is not merely prudential of why, as is well known, Descartes was unwilling to enter theological disputes: either the truth has been revealed to me or it has not; if it has, my trying to argue you into what may not have been revealed to you is futile; if it has not, then my obstinate opinions may simply corrupt you (Gouhier 1924: 218–19).

The other case concerns angels. Perhaps in his anxiety to avoid overt theological commitments, Descartes has frustratingly little that is positive to say about angels, even though it has been suggested that his image of what it is to be human derives from Thomistic doctrine about them.[22]

As Anthony Kenny notes in reading the letter to Mesland of 2nd May 1645 (CSMK: 231–6), we must distinguish between the positions, on the one hand, of ordinary mortals engaging in enquiry and, on the other, of angels, the blessed in Heaven and Christ on Earth (Kenny 1972: 24 and diagram 30). The latter have the advantage in always assenting spontaneously to truths. Presumably, the model here is one on which angels perceive all the truths there are in much the way that we perceive the truth each of us can establish by the *cogito*: their 'understanding functions intuitively rather than deductively' (Schouls 1989: 98). Since it would be odd to say that this is a result of the natural processes of intuition *followed by* deduction that make up the slog of human enquiry, angels may be regarded as being supernaturally enlightened on these matters.

To summarise the foregoing, we may set out the relations that Descartes sees between an ascending order of clearness of the ideas we encounter and the freedom we can exercise in assenting to them.

Sensory inputs are always obscure. If we assent to them as a matter of habit, then we are wholly unfree. If we assent to them either as the outcome of a situation of balanced evidences or where our choice is a mere plumping, then we are exercising the lowest grade of freedom, which is not really a case of enquiry. It would be literally a miracle if we were to perceive an idea derived from the senses in such a way as to assent to it spontaneously. In such a case, the distinction between naturally spontaneous assent and supernatural enlightenment would be effaced. It may be that mysterious points of doctrine, or the credibility of a miracle, require miracles of this sort. In this case, Descartes would know how to respond to the challenge Hume issues at the end of his attack on belief in the supernatural, asking about the Pentateuch:

> I desire any one to lay his hand upon his heart, and after a serious consideration declare, whether he thinks that the falsehood of such a book, [. . .] would be more extraordinary and miraculous than all the miracles it relates.
>
> (Hume 1748: 130)

The answer is: about the same.

The truths arrived at by natural enquiry are obscure unless derived from the proper sources, whose nature will occupy us in Chapter 9. When their *ratio* is perceived, then we assent to them spontaneously. But if we meet the thesis, say, from *Principles* II, 56, that the smallest force is able to set a hard body in a fluid in motion, without the chain of argument on which it depends, then it will seem like the sort of obscure thing that could have been derived from the senses. If so, assent to the thesis would be either a matter of compulsion (e.g. by what a physics teacher told us at school), a result of habit or a plumping.

When perceived at all, the common notions are perceived clearly and our assent to them is an exercise of liberty. Of course, it is possible that someone might learn to recite the formula in, for instance, *Rules* XII, that two things equal to a third are equal to each other; but, in such a case, the person would be attending to the words and not to the notion. Because there does not seem to be anything that could be said to balance or oppose it, such a truth cannot properly leave us indifferent. The same goes for the *cogito*, with the only difference that, where the common notions are set up in us by God, the truth of the *cogito* establishes itself for us.

As for the truths of faith, it seems that, for Descartes, a human being might freely assent to them if they are directly illuminated by God. In such a case, they would be clear and the object of enlightened and supernaturally spontaneous free assent. There may be no way to get to them by natural means, and assent to them in the absence of special divine intervention will be either a matter of indoctrination or arduous.

In short, when we see the clearness of clear ideas, we are free in assenting and we assent to truths. This is the positive side of Descartes' explanation of error, which centres on the failure of concurrence between the intellect and the will. The negative side is that we err when we assent to ideas that we do not see by the natural or supernatural light. Though error is an operation of the will, it is not an exercise of liberty because it lacks a perception of truth and goodness, because the will is not being used aright.

The unconditioned will and conditional assent

Reason's push and pull

When we are seeking to assent to ideas that are backed by *ratio*, what is afoot is an enquiry; when we are engaged in enquiry, the intellect does not compel or coerce the will; in all others, we must picture ourselves as potentially the victims of the ideas we happen to have.

In the terms we have seen from *Meditations* IV, a great light in the intellect is followed by a great propensity in the will (*Med.* IV, CSM II: 41; AT VII: 58–9: '[. . .] *ex magna luce in intellectu magna consequuta est propensio in voluntate*'); or, as the *Principles* says, we do spontaneously assent to what we clearly perceive (*Pr.* I, 43). This spontaneous following means that the will assents to ideas that have *ratio* as to a good. In this respect, the *ratio* is not the efficient, but the final cause of the assent. Yet, we have also seen uses of verbs of pushing for what reason does,[23] and even the necessitating notion that clear and distinct perception leaves us no alternative.[24]

Unless this is a muddle at the heart of Descartes' theory, we need some distinction or relativisation to see how he can balance the elements of efficient causation and those of final causation. A distinction that seems to be worth making is as between the human plight and what Descartes takes to be God's state; and a relativisation that helps is as between what we are doing when we enquire and what we can do absolutely.

Divine indifference and the eternal truths

The distinction between the positions of humans and of God emerges from Descartes' responses to the sixth and eighth scruples raised in the *Sixth Objections*.

Commenting on the passage, on which we too commented in the last chapter, of *Meditations* IV where Descartes asserts that his will is formally no less than God's (*Med.* IV, CSM II: 40), Mersenne's friends' sixth scruple is about the theological implications of saying that indifference in judgment is not a perfection of the power of choice, but an imperfection of it (*Obj.* VI, 6, CSM II: 280; AT VII: 416: '[. . .] *indifferentia judicii, seu libertatis, quam negas ad arbitrii perfectionem attinere, sed solam imperfectionem*'). For, if indifference is an imperfection then, since God is indifferent but always perceives by wholly clear intuitions (AT VII: 417: '[. . .] *semper clarissimo intuito perspexisse*'), it would seem to follow either that God is imperfect or that a wholly clear vision of things does not remove indifference. Each of which is intolerable.

Descartes' response is to allow that God is, indeed, indifferent to, e.g. the creation of the world in time (*Resp.* VI, 6, CSM II: 291), but that this does not mean that His will is imperfect. He asserts twice that there is a huge difference between human freedom and divine.[25] The explanation is that, in humans, indifference arises out of ignorance; for God, it is a consequence of there being no priority in order of time, nature or reason (*Resp.* VI, 6, CSM II: 291; AT VII: 432: '[*n*]*eque hic loquor de prioritate temporis, sed ne quidam prius fuit orinae, vel natura, vel ratione ratiocinata*'). For, God's willing, indifferent as it is, is the *cause* of things' being good and true; in making them so, His total indifference is the highest mark of His omnipotence (*Resp.* VI, 6, CSM II: 292; AT VII: 432: '*summa indifferentia in Deo summum est eius omnipotentiæ argumentum*').

If He wills a given thing, then that thing is *eo ipso* an object of His knowledge. As Descartes puts it in the *Principles*,

> while intellection and volition are in some way distinct operations for us, for Him they are a single unvarying and utterly simple action by which He at once understands, wills and acts (*Pr.* I, 23, CSM I: 201; AT VIIIA: 14: '[*intelligere et velle*] *ut nos, per operationes quodammodo distinctas, sed ita ut, per unicam, semperque eandem et simplicissimam actionem, omnia simul intelligat, velit et operetur*').

The harmony between the divine will and the divine intellect means that God can never be moved by His knowledge. Hence, His liberty is never the spontaneity of a human who assents to an idea that, being clear and distinct, he understands to be true antecedent to, and independent of, his assent to it.

The denial that God could be moved to act by any goodness or truth outside Himself is part and parcel of the much-discussed doctrine of the creation of the eternal verities.[26] For Him to be caused to will this or that, the object of His willing would have to be prior or external to His willing it: everything that is, is created by God, and, hence, the eternal truths are so too (letter probably to Mersenne, 27th May 1630, CSMK: 25; AT I: 152: '[. . .]

je sais que Dieu est auteur de toutes choses, et que ces vérités sont quelque chose, et par conséquent qu'il en est auteur').

The thesis that God creates all truths, including the truths of logic and mathematics, was formulated by Descartes as early as 1630 (letter to Mersenne, 15th April 1630, CSMK: 23; AT I: 145: '[. . .] *les vérités mathématiques, lesquelles que vous nommez éternelles, ont été établies de Dieu et en dépendent entièrement, aussi bien que le reste des créatures*'). We do not know precisely what Descartes was responding to in offering this formulation because Mersenne's side of the correspondence has mostly gone missing (Mersenne 1932–72: II 422, 479). And we can be sure that he still held it near the end of his life: the latest full statement of it seems to be in the letter for Arnauld, 29th July 1648 (CSMK: 358–9; AT V: 224: '*cum enim omnis ratio veri et boni ab eius* [sc. *Dei*] *omnipotentia dependeat, nequidem dicere ausim, Deum non facere posse ut mons sit sine valle, vel ut unium et duo non sint tria*'). Hence, it must be regarded as forming a constant part of the background to what he says about the relation of the human to the divine mind.

As is well known, Descartes gives few signs of it in the works prepared for publication. On one account of the matter, he felt that his view was at odds with a received or orthodox doctrine; as Gilson puts it, 'Descartes was cautious about putting it on show and seems to have hidden it, such assertions being unheard-of and untoward for the theologians he was addressing' (Gilson 1913a: 157; likewise, Bréhier 1937: 193–7). But this may underestimate the degree to which it can be read as an extension of elements implicit in St Thomas' view. Indeed, some of the commentators who are apt to stress Descartes' heterodoxy nevertheless cite passages of St Thomas in which those elements are present (e.g. Gilson (1913a: 158 n. 2) giving *De æternitate mundi;* Bréhier (1937: 194): *Summa contra Gentiles*, I, 54; Kenny (1968: 37): *ST*, Ia, qu. 25 art. 3; Funkenstein (1980: nn. 6 and 31): *De Potentia Dei*, 99, i ad xii; and Osler (1994: 134 n. 72): *Summa contra Gentiles*, II, 30, i–iv).

But an 'element' and an 'extension' are not the same thing. By suggesting that Descartes offers an extension, I mean that he is applying to logic and mathematics a structure that was a widespread position in moral theory, according to which God is the cause of the goodness of things. This is just the application that, for Gilson, was at the root of heterodoxy (1913a: 130–49; also Marion 1999). On the other hand, it is not so very far from a view pretty near the surface in St Augustine, according to which knowledge is itself God's child (e.g. *Lib. Arb.*, II, 15, 39: '[. . .] *memento* [. . .] *quod æterno Patri sit æqualis quæ ab ipso genita est Sapientia*'; see also Janowski 2000: 86–97). This, in turn, can be seen breaking through in some medieval treatments of what is true for all time, in virtue of God's (fore)knowledge of it (Normore 1982). Thus, Menn cites Bradwardine as agreeing with the thesis that the eternal truths are created and as pushing 'it to more paradoxical lengths than Descartes will do' (Menn 1998: 340 n. 3) And, in discussing future contingents, William of Ockham (1957: 148–50) takes the line that, since the future cannot determine the will of God, He must know the facts even before they have come about and is thus, in some manner, their cause.

Whatever Descartes' reason for unwillingness to set out his doctrine in full and in public,[27] he does express it in reply to Mersenne's friends' eighth question, about how the truths of geometry and metaphysics depend on God (*Obj.* VI, 8; CSM II: 281). The reply is that God's will is the efficient cause of the eternal verities (*Resp.* VI, 8, CSM II: 293–4; AT VII: 435: '*potest enim vocari efficiens*'). This answer also appears in one of the earliest letters on the matter: to Mersenne, 27th May 1630 (CSMK: 25; AT I: 151–2: '[. . .] *c'est* in eodem genere causæ *qu'il a crée toutes choses, c'est à dire* ut efficiens et totalis causa'). God counts as indifferent because there is nothing for Him to know antecedent to His willing it. His indifference is not a result of ignorance, as it is in humans; for ignorance would be an imperfection.

Curiously, then, the lowest grade of freedom for humans is the only type of freedom for God, because He cannot be swayed by reasons, insofar as He *is* what it is for something to count as a reason. When humans are pushed or swayed by reasons or given no alternative by clear and distinct ideas, they are exercising a type of freedom that has no place in Descartes' scheme of divine activity. The respect in which the human will is caused to assent in such cases is not efficient causation, but a matter of our seeing the good in it; it is teleological, a final causation. Of course, there is efficient causation when we admit ideas that are not clear and distinct; but we have seen that in those cases assent is not free.

We can now refine what we have already seen in connection with Gassendi's allegation of partiality in favour of an infinite will about Descartes'concession in *Meditations* IV that, though formally equal to God's will, his own is incomparably smaller than it. Descartes' will, being attached to a finite intellect, does not have so many objects present to it. The explanation we saw in the last chapter was that this difference is due to the knowledge and power that are attached to God's will and that make it more fixed and efficacious (cf. *Med.* IV, CSM II: 40; AT VII: 57: '*major absque comparatione in Deo quam in me* [*est*] *ratione cognitionis et potentiæ quæ illi adjunctæ sunt, redduntque ipsam magis firmam et efficacem*').

But the explanation might seem like a case of Descartes' misspeaking himself if it means that God's knowledge and power in some way reinforce His will. For this would be the most obvious reading of the 'due to' (*ratione*) and the 'make' (*reddunt*). If he is misspeaking himself in this way, it might be because he is keeping his doctrine of God's creation of the eternal verities under his hat for the purposes of the *Meditations*. It may, instead, be that he is presupposing the interdependence of the divine attributes in such a way as to move from omniscience to immutability to fixity of will (cf. Rovane 1994: 106–7). If such an interdependence is reversible, then the fixity of the divine will is as much (and as little) cause as effect of God's knowledge and power.

The appropriate sort of reversibility is just what is in play when Descartes responds to the eighth scruple of the *Sixth Objections*. The scruple refers to Descartes' partial exposition of the creation of the eternal verities in *Fifth Replies* (CSM II: 261) and arises from the apparent impossibility of God's making mathematical essences and truths other than they have been from eternity (*Obj.* VI, 8, CSM II: 281; AT VII: 418: '*Deus non videatur efficere potuisse ut ulla ex istis* [sc. *Geometricis aut Metaphysicis*, AT VII: 417] *essentiis seu veritatibus non fuerit ab æterno*'). Descartes admits that we humans cannot understand how such things could have been (*Resp.* VI, 8, CSM II: 294; cf. Rodis-Lewis (1982); LaCroix (1984)). Unless He had been the creator of every reason for truth and goodness, He would not have been indifferent in the creation of what He did create (*Resp.* VI, 8, CSM II: 293–4; AT VII: 435: '[. . .] *nihil omnino esse posse, quod ab ipso non pendeat* [. . .]; *alioqui* [. . .] *non fuisset plane indifferens ad ea creanda quæ creavit*'). But it is accepted that He is never determined in His actions; hence, the reason for the goodness of created things depends on God (*Resp.* VI, 8, CSM II: 294; AT VII: 436: '[. . .] *ratio eorum bonitatis ex eo pendet*').

But, when we consider humans, we do not find the reversibility that is applicable to God. Since I am not omniscient nor immutable, my will does not have the divine fixity of assenting simultaneously to all and only truths. Hence, when I am presented with an idea that is clear and distinct, the assent I give to it is a matter of my being moved by it as a good previously unperceived (by me). The intellect is a concurrent efficient cause of the assent, providing the material for it; but the idea itself operates as a final cause prior to my willing of it.

The hypotheticalness of enquiry

Bearing in mind the distinction between the human and the divine, we can further refine the problem about whether we are necessitated to assent to clear and distinct ideas by relativising the operations of the will to the type of project in hand. We have already seen that, unless we are engaged in enquiry, our subjection to the bombardment of the senses means that we are not free when we assent to what we see.

After the débâcle of *Meditations* I, from which it emerges that our credulity is vastly more wide-ranging than we might have imagined, the rest of the book is taken up with the things to which we may securely assent. This operation divides possible objects of assent into those we are permitted to assent to (starting with the idea of my own existence) and those we are forbidden to assent to (prominently, the deliverances of the senses about virtually everything).

If the infinity of the will guarantees that we are able to assent to the permitted things and to dissent from the forbidden, it might also enable us to dissent from the permitted. Though we may have no immediate reason for dissenting from what is permitted, inasmuch as it is underwritten by the veracious God of *Meditations* III, there is nothing in the book that serves to show that what is permitted is also obligatory.

The wobble that this thought introduces into Descartes' undertaking has a potentially disastrous consequence. For, he describes one phase of his project as that of setting his will against all the things he had previously believed, there being no excess in this sort of diffidence (*Med.* I, CSM II: 15; AT VII: 22: '[. . . *scio nihil*] *me plus æquo diffidentiæ indulgere non posse*'; recapitulated at *Med.* IV, CSM II: 39). The disastrous consequence would be that he is able to dissent from his own existence and from all the things he finds thereafter to be immune from motivated doubt. Since doubt is only genuinely such when there is some motivation, and the possibility of doubting seems to be one type of motivation, this would be disastrous if it really meant that, within the activity of enquiring, we can refuse to believe anything we can set ourselves to doubt.

If a person is pursuing the purposes of the enquiry Descartes describes in the *Meditations*, he will assent to all the ideas he perceives clearly and distinctly, and refuse assent to all others. But we need to explore what, if anything, makes it obligatory to have those purposes; for we may be simply uninterested in retracing the moves made in, or in emulating the heroes of, Descartes' books, including the *Discourse*, where the narrator says he is just offering himself as example as in a tale or fable (CSM I: 112). Nevertheless, we are all, as a matter of fact, interested in guiding ourselves out of the ignorance and perplexity that is the lot of humans. If so, then we have a general reason to adopt the measures Descartes rehearses. So long as that is our dominant aim, the infinite power of the will is bent on excluding all ideas about which we have reasons for doubt and on including all and only those that are perceived clearly and distinctly.

Guiding ourselves out of our common ignorance and perplexity can be our dominant aim only when we are engaged in the self-conscious business of enquiring. That is a fairly rare or sporadic occurrence: the six episodes of the *Meditations* are interspersed with the casual and unself-conscious affairs that are not enquiry – eating, sleeping, going for a walk. The six meditations aim at the acquisition of beliefs that are not products of credulity; but this doxastic good is not the only possible doxastic good. Nor, moreover, are doxastic goods the only sorts of goods. Understood in this way, enquiring has only a tenuous, hypothetical hold on us.

But there is also a respect in which guiding ourselves out of ignorance and perplexity is the proper fulfilment of an overarching human good. So far as the attainment of knowledge and a coherent world-view is a primary objective of intellectual activity, only so far will it be a categorical obligation to cultivate doxastic rectitude, even if only on opportune occasions. For, even this is not wholly categorical because Descartes allows not only that attempts to enquire in accordance with doxastic rectitude ought to be insulated from everyday life (Burnyeat 1984: 225), but also that, even when we have insulated ourselves from everyday life in a way appropriate to enquiry, we may have a purpose other than that of doxastic rectitude. With such a purpose, we might be prepared to withhold assent from a clearly perceived idea even while we are perceiving it to be such.

At this point we run into a doctrine about a temporarily supervening purpose relative to guiding ourselves out of ignorance and perplexity. This is a matter of freely dissenting from ideas that we are permitted to assent to. The doctrine is that the human will is such that it can withdraw assent from ideas that are evident, even while recognising that they are such.

This doctrine makes just one fleeting appearance in Descartes' late published writings. In the *Notes*, of 1647–8, he responds to Regius' claim that intellect is perception and judgment (*Explicatio*, 17, CSM I: 296; AT VIIIB: 345: '*intellectus est perceptio et judicium*'; cf. Regius 1646: II, 252), by saying that we are often free to withhold our judgment even to something that we perceive (*Not.* 17, CSM I: 307; AT VIIIB: 363: '[*viderem . . .*] *nobisque sæpe esse liberum ut cohibeamus assensionem, etamsi rem percipiamus*'); and there is no reason to exclude from such things the things that we perceive clearly and distinctly. But Descartes is not entirely clear on the point. For this reason, there is some dispute about the time of the doctrine's emergence and its coherence with what Descartes had earlier said. For we have seen that the procedure of both the *Meditations* and the *Principles* seems to depend on the claim that there is no alternative to assenting to clear and distinct ideas: our assent to them is an exercise of the liberty of spontaneity precisely because nothing could count as evidence against such ideas.

The only place where Descartes makes the new claim explicitly is in a letter that comes in three versions. In the first edition of Descartes' letters (Descartes 1657–67: I, 506–9), Claude Clerselier put out what may be his own French translation (AT III: 704) of a Latin manuscript of a letter that is clearly a composite of materials, some written as early as 1630 (dated 6th May 1630 and reproduced by AT at I: 147–50),[28] or by 1637 (AT I: 347–51), but whose date and addressee were regarded as unknown by the first editor (AT III: 378). AT describe the middle section as being possibly to Mersenne and possibly written 27th May 1641; at AT III: 378, they direct us to the letter of 6th May (AT I: 147–50). A Latin version of Descartes' minute for this was found and is reproduced in the 'Additions' to AT III (703–6). Another Latin text was recovered from the Bibliothèque Mazarine corresponding to the letter that had been thought to be addressed to Mersenne, and was classified as the continuation of a letter, in French, to Mesland and dated 9th February 1645; the two parts are reproduced in AT IV: 161–75 (the French text running pp. 162–70, the Latin pp. 173–5), which makes Kenny wonder 'why should a letter begun in French end in Latin?' (Kenny 1972: 26). To which the answer may be that this is a further case in which Descartes was less than attentive about his correspondence and his correspondents (Davies forthcoming: IV).

In the text in question, however, the doctrine that we can refuse an evident idea occurs only in the passage that cannot with any certainty be dated before 1641, and along with material that has to be later than the composition (and probably publication) of the *Meditations*.[29] Unless there were reason for further sub-dividing the texts, we have here a novelty relative to the doctrine of *Meditations* IV. Some commentators have thought that this doctrine marks a significant shift in Descartes' doctrine on the will's real and positive power of determination (Laporte 1945: 48; likewise Alquié 1950: 289–90, taken to task by Kenny 1972: 25–6). Nevertheless, while resisting the urge to regard Descartes' thought as strongly unitary, I suggest that what we have here is an outcrop of his overall theory of the enterprise of knowledge-gathering. Even if Descartes did not think of it before 1641, but did so probably after the *Principles* was completed, we do not have to think that every addition is a change to the substance of what is added to: he is responding to questions he had not anticipated in the earlier expositions.

Writing to Mesland in May 1644, Descartes says that,

> if we see very clearly that something is right for us, it is very hard, even impossible so I believe, so long as one holds onto the thought, to stop the course of our desire (2nd May 1644, CSMK: 233; AT IV: 116: '[. . .] *voyant très-clairement qu'une chose nous est propre, il est très mal-aisé, et même, comme je crois impossible, pendant qu'on demeure en cette pensée, d'arrêter le cours de notre désir*').

At that stage, Descartes tells Mesland that diversion of the attention from the clearly perceived idea allows us to conjure up reasons for doubting it (AT IV: 116: '[. . .] *sitôt que notre attention se détourne des raisons qui nous font connaître que cette chose nous est propre* [. . .] *nous pouvons représenter à notre ésprit quelqu'autre raison qui nous en fasse douter*'). In this way, the apparent impossibility of dissenting from what one is currently perceiving clearly can be circumvented. And this much is what we find in the *Principles* (*Pr.* I, 43, CSM I: 207).[30] But circumvention is not the mastery we would expect of a will of infinite power.

By February 1645, Descartes has concluded that something more robust is in order. Though he continues to think that it is very hard to go against the drives of reason (letter to Mesland, 9th February 1645, CSMK: 245; AT IV: 173: '[. . .] *vix possimus in contrariam ferri*'), the impossibility is relativised. It is only morally speaking that it is impossible (AT IV: 173: *'moraliter loquendo'*; cf. *Pr.* IV, 205, CSM I: 289–90); absolutely speaking, we can do it (AT IV: 173: '[. . .] *absolute tamen possimus*'). For there is a good that we can propose to ourselves and that can be served by our doing so: proving to ourselves our freedom of choice (AT IV: 173: '[. . .] *modo tantum cogitemus bonum libertatem arbitrii nostri per hoc testari*').[31]

This doctrine is a clear affirmation of the infinite power of the will to resist ideas that, in the rest of the theory, are regarded as irresistibly attractive. Even if, as we have seen several times, Descartes does not have great need for the will's capacity to refuse ideas to be absolutely unlimited, his extending it to some ideas that he thinks *could not* be deceptive means that it covers all the ideas that we know *could* be deceptive. Just as someone who can jump three feet can jump two,[32] so someone who can dissent from what is illuminated by the light of reason can dissent from what is illuminated by mere sunlight. Hence, we have here an absolute guarantee that we need never be subject to the deliverances of the senses, which are so much less attractive than the truths of reason. The guarantee is that we can do something even more strenuous.

There is a correlation between how radical Descartes' doxastic voluntarism is meant to be and the limits he might envisage to the hypotheticalness of the demands of enquiry. The more voluntaristic we think him, the larger the range of perspicuous truths he must allow to be deniable.

Prima facie, there ought to be some significant difference between, on the one hand, someone's withdrawing her assent to the idea of her own existence and, on the other, her having read, in the instance cited earlier, up to *Principles* II, 56, and then deciding to prove to herself her freedom of choice by suspending judgment about whether or not the smallest force is able to set a hard body in a fluid in motion. If she has been following Descartes' orderly exposition and meditating along with him, the truth of the matter should have been made evident to her. But not as evident as her own existence. If this is a difference only in degree of difficulty, then Descartes' voluntarism is not only radical, it is universal. And this seems to be the position expressed when he says that we are *always* able to hold assent at bay (letter to Mesland, 9th February 1645, CSMK: 245; AT IV: 173: '[*s*]*emper enim nobis licet*').

Contrariwise, it also seems that there must be some ideas from which I cannot withhold my assent, even for the purpose of proving my freedom of choice. The most obvious of these would be, on pain of incoherence, my idea of my own freedom of choice, which, as we have seen, Descartes takes to be directly perceptible. Moreover, this idea is certainly posterior to my idea of my own existence, because it can only be clearly and distinctly perceived by me if I can equally clearly and distinctly perceive that I exist. There might seem, then, to be a difference not only in degree of difficulty, but in *kind*, between those clearly and distinctly perceived ideas that I can dissent from and those that I cannot, even for the purpose Descartes suggests to Mesland. And it might be attractive to hypothesise that the class of ideas from which I cannot dissent so long as I am attending to them as clear and distinct would include all the ideas that are prior to (or of equal standing with) my idea of my freedom of choice. This would include all the first principles and starting-points of metaphysics – roughly, all the ideas directly defended in *Discourse* IV, in the first five parts of the *Meditations* and in Book I of the *Principles*. All the other ideas that make up the potential objects of human knowledge may be apprehended clearly and distinctly, but they may also be used in proofs of my freedom of choice by suspension of my assent to them.

There is not sufficiently direct evidence in Descartes' writings to give any decisive account of exactly how wideranging the voluntarism of the post-*Meditations* years was meant to be. But the idea of proving one's freedom of choice as an exercise of doxastic liberty reminds us that enquiry has only a hypothetical call on us because there are lots of other things that demand our attention other than the refounding of science in accordance with reason. In most of these, we assent to ideas that reason prohibits because they are obscure. When we assent to them, we are acting in ignorance and under the compulsion of biology, habit and worse. Up to a certain point, therefore, we are not really responsible for most of the beliefs we form, though we may be responsible for letting them be formed.

When enquiring in accordance with doxastic rectitude, we put ourselves in control of the situation: our dissent from prohibited ideas and assent to per-mitted (or enjoined) ideas is an exercise of freedom. Even when we dissent from a permitted idea, as in the letters to Mesland, we must have another good in hand. Nevertheless, proving our freedom of choice is an end diver-gent from the overall ends of enquiry in accordance with doxastic rectitude. This indicates a further respect in which following the dictates of doxastic rectitude is not categorically enjoined, even granting that we are engaged in precisely the undertaking that embodies the following of those dictates: enquiry properly so-called. Within enquiry, we may distinguish the overall end, which is leading us out of ignorance and perplexity, and a divergent end, which still has to do with establishing a truth, such as proving of the freedom of the will.

Let us recall a distinction between virtues and skills derived from Aristotle (*EN*, VI v, 1140 b 22–3). On the one hand, virtues have the characteristic that failure to act in accordance with them is a sure sign of incomplete possession of them. In the case of a person who betrays his friend, this means, immediately and straight off, that he is disloyal and untrustworthy. There is something, however temporarily and however locally, wrong with him. There is no higher appeal that he can make. In particular, he cannot justify himself by saying that he betrayed his friend to make a point about breach of trust or to show that he was able to. By contrast, it is a feature of skills that one who makes a mistake voluntarily is rated more highly than if she makes it involuntarily: only one who has the skill can choose. Someone who possesses the art of joinery, for instance, can choose not to make a chair as well as she can. She can explain that she wanted to illustrate some feature of what it is *not* to possess that art.

Now the question is: should we think of doxastic rectitude as a virtue or as a skill? If enquiry were categorically enjoined, then one who withdraws assent from an evident truth while knowing it to be such thereby undermines his claim to doxastic virtue. If we can subserve a good relative to enquiry by stepping back from pursuing the overall end of enquiring, then what is in play is not, after all a virtue, but a skill.

One distinction that helps resolve this is that between the properly moral or unconditional virtues and the 'executive virtues' (Dent 1981). Where, for instance, courage properly so-called, requires an ability to act in certain types of ways, and absolutely to avoid others, in circumstances of hardship and danger, and temperance, properly so-called, requires a disposition absolutely to resist certain types and degrees of temptation, there is a quality of character that we might call intrepidity, hardihood or endurance that is a general stiffener of resolve irrespective of the circumstances or ends of action. In this sense, a person who does not get distracted in his purposes, whatever they might be, might be regarded as having a trait that is of value: in the absence of the relevant character-trait, a person would have to work harder to attain an overall higher level of moral worth (Zagzebski 1996: 93). Even if the value of such a trait is primarily instrumental, it is closely related to habits that are clearly virtues because it is a 'potential for contributing to the overall moral worth of the life of its possessor' (Trianosky 1987: 133).

Using this analogy, I suggest that the doxastic virtue of rectitude is closer to an executive virtue in action than it is to the central cases of moral virtue. This has two consequences. One is that the cultivation of rectitude within the privileged (or impoverished) enterprise of enquiry in accordance with reason may have knock-on effects for one's belief-gathering practices elsewhere. An intrepid person may be a good burglar; it is at best doubtful that her resourcefulness or toughness is the same as courage (Davies 1998b). The other is that, only someone who is party to enquiry and is on her guard against credulity (and against scepticism) can be said to be genuinely choosing in adopting a purpose that runs counter to the overall dictates of doxastic rectitude. What she is doing is in the right field, even if the overarching purpose of the exercise has been temporarily suspended for reasons given, namely, the proving of the freedom of the will.

Recapitulation

A snapshot of Descartes' thinking about the perplexing matters we have reviewed in the last two chapters:

> When humans assent to an idea that is not clear and distinct, they are being credulous. Credulous assent is forced because it comes about by efficient causation. It is not a free operation of the will. Sometimes humans may fail to assent to clear and distinct ideas because they do not see them as such, as a result of inattention or confusion.
>
> When humans assent to a clear and distinct idea in the light of its clearness and distinctness, they see no reason, within the project of enquiring, for dissenting from it. The clearness and distinctness of an idea in the intellect is a guarantee that it is true. Assent to it is permissible because, in such a case, the will does not extend beyond what is understood. The intellect does not cause the will to assent, but the will spontaneously assents in view of the perceived good of the aims of enquiry.
>
> Humans may be disposed by aims other than those of enquiry to dissent from an idea that they perceive clearly and distinctly. One such purpose is the proving of their freedom of choice. Such a purpose is not an overarching human good like that of escaping from perplexity and ignorance; but it may be allowed temporarily to supervene on the aims of enquiry.

If these are the outlines of Descartes' account of assent and, consequently, of credulous assent, then that account provides an explanation of the means at our disposal to combat our tendency to believe what the senses cause us to believe and a justification of why we ought to combat that tendency. Credulous assent to the senses has nothing to do with the pursuit of the good and the true. Enquiry is the business of putting ourselves in control of the situation in such a way that its apparent arbitrariness and its apparently insuperable difficulty are surpassed by a claim to a higher purpose and by an absolute possibility respectively.

Doxastic Pelagianism

A missing accusation

By way of appendix, I wish to consider a feature of the image of the human condition that lies behind Descartes' doctrine of error and the will. I propose to do this by examining the relations between what we have seen and the view known as Pelagianism, which was (and is) a heresy concerning the efficacy of the will in salvation.

In discussing the details of Descartes' theory I have several times noted that it attracted relatively little comment at the time of publication. Specifically, his account did not draw attention to itself *as objectionable*: the dogs-not-barking-in-the-night principle, that doctrines commentators take to be respectable elicit little discussion. The question then arises of what sorts of objectionableness would have attracted comment. Given the stress that Descartes puts on the efficacy of the will in enquiry and regarding enquiry as the doxastic analogue of salvation, we might have expected the accusation of Pelagianism to have been more of a pest and an obstruction than was in fact the case. There are two sorts of grounds for this expectation: one to do with the rhetorical status of the accusation; the other to do with what Pelagianism was or was supposed to be.

Quaint as it may seem, in the seventeenth century, the accusation of Pelagianism was a stock way of bringing a view into disrepute, as much a polemical trope as an attempt at serious refutation. As one commentator on disputes slightly later in the century puts it, 'the accusation of virtual Pelagianism was made so often because no one wanted to be a Pelagian' (Kilcullen 1988: 8 n. 4). Any novelty was exposed to the accusation of heresy; Cartesianism involved at least one novelty concerning the will; and Pelagianism was equally clearly a heresy concerning the will, and so would have been a good stick with which to beat anything that presented itself as a novelty concerning the will. Though this is shabby as argument, it might be surprising that the association of ideas did not crop up more often.

This is not the place to attempt a reconstruction of the views of Pelagius or of his most direct followers on the complex matters of liberty and grace, and there is even reason for uncertainty about who, as a matter of historical fact, could be regarded as a card-carrying Pelagian. Thus, in the *Patrologia Latina*, Migne lists only four Pelagian authors (Anianus, Cœlestius, Julianus and Pelagius himself (*PL*, CCXIX, col. 835)); among the twenty authors guilty of *loca redolentia* of Pelagianism or Semipelagianism, we find also St Augustine and Zosimus; and, among the sixty-eight authors cited as Antipelagians, we find all four cited Pelagians.

But there are very strong grounds for thinking that, whatever it might turn out to have been, it was, indeed, a heresy; indeed, Arnauld describes it as 'the most subtle and dangerous of all heresies' (1775–83: XIX 486). In its day, it was opposed by two of the most inexorable Fathers of the Church: St Augustine and St Jerome, each of whom is responsible for handing down *testimonia* of Pelagius' views that might otherwise not have survived.[33] The heresy was condemned by a series of Church Councils (Vossius 1618: 585a–95b) and by two successive Popes: by Innocent I in 417 and, after a moment's reprieve caused an outcry among the African bishops, by Zosimus in 418. Throughout the fifth century, it was the object of continual repression (De Plinval 1943: 333–84). Subsequently, Pelagianism was a clear-cut case of a position, however unclear in itself, that had to be avoided (Stewart, in Pascal 1656: xv–xxiv). As we can see, for instance, from St Thomas' relatively cursory dismissals of it (e.g. *ST*, Ia, qu. 23 art. 5; Ia IIæ, qu. 109 art. 7; IIIa, qu. 87 art. 2 ad 3), he did not think that much argument was called for.

Even in the public controversies over the teaching of Cartesianism both at the University of Utrecht in 1642–3 (Verbeek 1988) and at the University of Leiden in 1647 (Verbeek 1992), where we might expect passions to have run high, the accusation of Pelagianism was made less frequently than those of atheism, of scepticism and of materialism (especially with respect to the Eucharist). All of these accusations, like that of Pelagianism, were stock accusations made not only against Descartes but against virtually anyone who ventured opinions of virtually any sort in philosophy or theology. Also, the frequency of resort to the trope, especially in the Netherlands, can be explained in part by the association between Pelagianism and the anti-Calvinist views of Arminius (Verbeek 1992: 3–5; Gaukroger 1995: 386). The effect of this association was a perception of Jesuit-inspired thought as tending to the doctrine that the human will can be efficacious in salvation.[34] Despite Descartes' education in a Jesuit college, the accusation seems, all the same, not to have been a favoured tool with which to resist his influence during his lifetime. Nevertheless, as M.E. Scribano has noted, in some of the debates in Holland after his death, the accusation of Pelagianism was a 'standard *topos* in the antiCartesian literature' (Scribano 1998: 16) and would have been justified by any theory of the human will that associated it with God's.

The other ground for thinking that Descartes should have appeared to be in odour of this heresy is that Pelagianism stresses the efficacy of the will. As one sympathetic observer puts it, 'Pelagius' doctrine is intimately at home in a philosophy of freedom and of the natural good, which presupposes an essentially optimistic conception of our capacities and makes way for a thoroughgoing apology of moral humanism' (De Plinval 1943: 250). Which, at first glance, looks much like what we have got out of *Meditations* IV and, so, would seem to be reason for associating Descartes with a form of

Pelagianism. I proceed, however, to offer grounds for thinking that such an association would, in fact, have been inappropriate, with regard to the humanism, the optimism and the natural good. And I suggest that that inappropriateness accounts for the accusation's not having been made.

A distinction of levels

Let us begin with the humanism to which De Plinval refers.

There are only two texts in which Descartes mentions Pelagianism by name, and it may be that he had 'very little understanding of what the anti-Pelagian excitement was about' (Menn 1998: 66 n. 42). Both are in his letters to Mersenne (27th April 1637, CSMK: 56 and March 1642, CSMK: 211) and might, therefore, have circulated among Parisians interested in Descartes' doings. But they are basically private communications. Consequently, they would not serve to head off the accusation that we are interested in among his other correspondents nor, *a fortiori*, among the polemists of Utrecht and Leiden.

In these letters, Descartes notes that some (unspecified) people have thought him a Pelagian. But he does not consider directly the possible similarity between Pelagianism and his views on the efficacy of the individual's will in forming true beliefs. Rather, he takes a programmatic stand against there being any relation between what he has to say and the subject-matter of the heresy (letter to Mersenne, 27th April 1637, CSMK: 56; AT I: 366: '[. . .] *je parle* [. . .] *seulement de Philosophie morale et naturelle, où cette Grâce n'est point considerée*'). He draws a distinction between, on the one hand, natural and moral philosophy, which is concerned with natural efforts, and, on the other, theology, which discusses grace and the supernatural (letter to Mersenne, March 1642, CSMK: 211; AT III: 544: '[. . .] *cette Gloire étant surnaturelle, il faut de forces plus que naturelles pour la mériter*'). Even if there are superficial similarities between what he has to say about the natural realm and what a Pelagian would say about the supernatural, they do not leave Descartes open to the charge of Pelagianism, because he has said nothing about the knowledge of God that is not equally said by all theologians (AT III: 544: '[*e*]*t je n'ai rien dit touchant la connaissance de Dieu, que tous les théologiens ne disent aussi*').

Moreover, the protestations he makes in private about this particular heresy are congruent with his public statement, in the letter to the Doctors of the Sorbonne, that the *Meditations* is concerned with philosophy and not with theology (CSM II: 3).[35] Of course, there is *natural* theology in the *Meditations*, in that natural theology investigates the existence and essence of God. Rather, the theological questions that Descartes is not wishing to get involved in are those of revealed religion: the issues of the particular action of God in relation to sacred history. Likewise, in the *Conversation*, he denies knowing whether or not man was immortal before the Fall, leaving the question to the theologians (*Con.*, CSMK: 353; AT V: 178).

If the reading that I have offered of *Meditations* IV is correct, then the whole business of belief-getting calls for the concurrence of God: the ideas that are clear and distinct are so because God made them so. The creation of the eternal truths means that we could not have the knowledge we get by the natural means of enquiry without the action of God. Though it depends on no special revelation, of the sort we contemplated in connection with enlightenment, the results of enquiry might be thought of as involving an 'ordinary revelation'. Where an analogue of special revelation might be with the repeated miracle of the Eucharist, the analogue of ordinary revelation would be the continuous miracle of the conservation of the world in existence.

In one of the letters just referred to, Descartes denies that the knowledge of the existence of God that can be gained by the use of reason makes us deserve supernatural glory (to Mersenne, March 1642, CSMK: 211; AT III: 544: '[. . .] *on peut connaître par la raison naturelle que Dieu existe, mais je ne dis pas pour cela que cette connaissance mérite de soi, sans la Grace, la Gloire surnaturelle*'). All that natural reason can do is prepare unbelievers for faith, but not make them gain heaven (AT III: 544: '[. . .] *ce qui se connaît par raison naturelle* [. . .] *peut bien servir à préparer les infidèles à recevoir la Foi, mais non pas suffir pour leur faire gagner le Ciel*'). In the light of this, though enquiry may be meritorious, it is restricted to the here-and-now. If the ultimate human goods are to do with salvation, then the 'humanism' attributed to Descartes' conception of natural enquiry is a restricted thing – perhaps adding a third grade of conditionalness to the two ways we have already seen in which doxastic rectitude has a hold over us.

We may put this the other way about.

One of the reasons why Pelagius' views caused trouble when they were first proposed was that they tended to deny not only an intercessionary role for the Church (Woerther 1847: 520B-1A), but also the centrality of Christ as the Saviour (De Plinval 1943: 155). Without the special redemptive function of the Passion, admission to eternal life would be open even to those who are not part of the Church. In his anti-Pelagian polemic *De Natura et Gratia*, St Augustine cites the cases of virtuous heathen (*Nat.*, 2 and 10), as well as the Old Testament patriarchs (*Nat.*, 42–4) and unbaptised babes (*Nat.*, 23) as among those for whom Pelagius wished entry into Heaven to be possible. But, as established at the Synod of Diospolis (415) and at the Council of Carthage (418), baptism is a necessary condition of salvation (Grossi 1969); and even the Virgin Mary seems to be in a precarious position relative to this doctrine (Vossius 1618: 632a-5b). This it may be one of the reasons why, as a matter of common observation, Pelagianism is a very common view among persons who believe that they are orthodox Catholics.[36]

If someone is puzzled, for instance, why Dante puts the great philosophers of antiquity in Hell (*Inferno* IV, esp. 129–51), the answer is that they are not redeemed within the sacred history of Christianity: without salvation, they are not capable of righteous action. To reject this exclusiveness is to assert that there is at least 'grace of congruity', whereby observation of the moral law is within the power of the individual. This assertion is tantamount to Pelagianism.

But there is no reason to think that Descartes subscribes to it. If we think of him as an obedient but unzealous Catholic, we can understand why he nowhere asserts such a humanistic position and why he nowhere denies its contrary. Moreover, if there had been any suspicion of his adopting a position that could be seen as downgrading the role of the Church, Descartes would surely have been charged by his Catholic readers, of whatever sect, with one or other form of Protestantism; which, again, we do not find.

Man's fallen state

Now for what De Plinval calls the optimism in Pelagius' heresy.

Despite their close interconnections and their complex connections with other positions, we can pick out two main strands of thought that would justify an accusation of Pelagianism. One is to do with the relation of the Biblical Fall to our current state; the other is to do with the ease of our willing rightly.

As to the former of these, the Pelagian position is that Adam's sin does not mean that the whole of humanity is conceived in sin; as he says in the 'Letter to Demetras', Adam's sin harmed his descendants by example, not by contagion' ('*Adæ peccatum exemplo posteris nocuisse, non transita*'). At most, Adam created only the form of wrong-doing (Commentary on *Romans*, V, 16: '*Adam solam formam fecit delicti*'). The motivation for this is to allow room for denying the absolute depravity of human nature as a result of the Fall from Eden. To attribute my sins to Adam would be to deny my responsibility and thus to grant myself a certain moral latitude. In these terms, there does seem to be an element consonant with Pelagianism in *Meditations* IV: God is not responsible for our errors because we are; we are responsible because we do not limit our wills to what is clear in our intellects. But even in anti-Pelagian overdrive, St Augustine is prepared to assert that much: God certainly is not responsible for our sins (e.g. *Lib. Arb.*, III, 6, 18: '*Deo non deputanda peccata*'), because the only proximate cause is the will and no other cause is called for (e.g. *Lib. Arb.*, III, 17, 48: '[*v*]*oluntas est causa peccati*'; III, 22, 63: '[. . .] *nec ulla ulterior peccatorum causa quærenda*').

One crucial point at which St Augustine and Pelagius differ here is over the relation of our souls to Adam's. Though he concedes in *De Libero Arbitrio*

(III, 20, 59) that there is no authoritative Catholic doctrine on the origin of souls, St Augustine ends by supporting a form of the doctrine, which has come to be called 'traducianism' (Abbagnano 1946: II, 78–9), that all humans have inherited the original taint from Adam (*Civ.*, XIII, 14). By contrast, Pelagius upholds the view, which he takes to be expressed in *Romans*, V, 15, that each of our souls is directly created by God and so have only a relation of resemblance to Adam's (quoted by St Augustine in *Imp.*, 61: '*imitatione transisse, non generatione peccatum*'). Though he says surprisingly little about the matter, we would expect Descartes' position to be closer to Pelagius' than to what became the orthodox view: in regarding each mind as an individual substance, we would expect him not to embrace Augustinian traducianism. Nevertheless, by considering how Descartes could reconstrue the Biblical story as recapitulated in the life of each individual, we can see that creationism is compatible with a pretty radical sort of incorrigibility.

In caricature terms, Adam goes to work in the Garden, his intellect and his will in harmony with his Creator's will. However it comes about, the Fall involves his willing to do what he has imperfect understanding of. He need not will wrongly; all that is necessary is that what he wills is wrong.[37] Thereafter, the two faculties are out of kilter. They cannot be reformed into the unity that is in God. Whereas before the Fall, the concord of intellect and will was fully internalised and unreflective, afterwards, it is only by dint of scrupulous inspection of his every action that Adam can avoid further error.

For all that it is a caricature, this account follows fairly closely the sort of story that it is quite common to find recounted in the seventeenth century. It is, for instance, not dissimilar from the account of the progress of knowledge that Descartes encountered at school: his Jesuit teachers offer a version of human history on which the Fall is an essential factor in determining the powers of the mind (Collegium Conimbricense 1606: 1 col. 2–2 col. 1). Likewise, in Martinus Schoockius' anti-Cartesian *Admiranda methodus*, the stress is on the loss of Adam's previous perfect knowledge of all things (Schoockius 1643: 212). Combining both Cartesianism and declared Augustinianism, Malebranche sought in his *Traité de la Nature et de la Grâce* to work out a similar exercise in Biblical Cartesianism (e.g. Malebranche 1680: 47–51) 'in all seriousness' (Menn 1998: 318 n. 14). At the other end of the scale of claims to Catholic orthodoxy, it is the explanation that appears as the most general cause of man's misery in the second paragraph of Burton's *Anatomy of Melancholy* (Burton 1621: 81), and that Joseph Glanvill gives of the limits of our intellectual powers in the chapter of *Scepsis Scientifica* devoted to 'Our Decay and Ruine by the Fall' (Glanvill 1665: 4–8). The list could go on.

We all find that we are in Adam's postlapsarian case in the fact that we find in ourselves two distinct faculties involved in judgment: intellect and will.

If they were one, we would be as Adam was and as God is. What is strongly anti-Pelagian in this vision of human depravity is that it is in our constitution not to be without sin and error, even though, as we have seen, our faculty for judging is perfect of its sort. If the schism on which the theodicy of *Meditations* IV depends is the marker of our fallen condition, then we can to that extent understand why the charge of Pelagianism would not stick to Descartes: he sees that every human being, as a matter of fact, is party to the doxastic vice of credulity by having acquired in childhood beliefs that derive from the senses.

Nature and virtue

Lastly, the naturalness of willing the good.

The other main strand of thought that would justify the charge of Pelagianism is the thesis that it is wholly within our power to choose the good. Like the denial of the transmission of Original Sin, this is motivated by a perception of human responsibility and the theodicidic desire to avoid imputing human misdeeds to God as their ultimate cause. It is heretical on the grounds that it gives rise to the thought that a mortal can deserve Heaven without grace and, hence, that God is a mere spectator to salvation. As already noted, this is a position that Descartes explicitly denies occupying. Still, there remains the question of whether, in any given case of choice about belief, we can do the right thing.

Descartes and Pelagius share a source in their thinking about the moral strength of our free choice, namely the Stoicism that we saw in considering the *Passions* (see Pohle 1913). The view that both take about our capacity to be in control of the situation is that, indeed, we can choose rightly. And each offers an argument of roughly the same sort in defence of this. Pelagius argues that, if the commands that God issues are possible for us, then we can live without sin if we want. In a passage corresponding to Pelagius, *De possibilitate non peccandi*, 3, St Jerome offers the following dilemmatic argument:

> Either the things that God requires are possible or they are impossible. If they are possible, then it is in our power to do them if we wish; if they are impossible, then we are not guilty if we do not do what we cannot do. Hence, whether what God requires is possible or impossible, man can be without sin, if he wishes (St Jerome, *Dialogus adversus Pelagianos*, I, 27: '[a]ut possibilia Deus mandata dedit, aut impossibilia. Si possibilia, in nostra potestate est, ea facere, si velimus; si impossibilia nec in hoc rei sumus, si non facimus, quod implere non possumus. Ac per hoc, sive possibilia dedit Deus mandata, sive impossibilia, potest homo sine peccato esse, si velit').

Add to that the principle that no one is obliged to do what is impossible (*'ad impossibile neminem obligari'*), which Vossius describes as a 'vulgar dictum' (1618: 718a). 'Ought implies can'; from which it follows that we can obey God's commands if we want. In much the same way, concerning his beliefs, even about the doubtful matters of the senses, Descartes argues from divine benevolence and truthfulness to the thesis that he could not have false opinions that he is unable to correct with some other God-given faculty; thus, he can have a certain hope of finding the truth about them (*Med.* VI, CSM II: 55–6). If we used our wills aright, we could always climb out of particular errors.

Whereas for a position like Pelagius', there is a symmetry between doing the right and avoiding the wrong, on Descartes' position, we have to distinguish extricating ourselves from a given error and not falling into it in the first place. If I attend to an error that I have committed, I can correct it; with respect to beliefs, particular sins can be undone. But it does not follow that I can prevent myself from committing the same or similar errors by such acts of attention. To ensure such prevention, I would have to extirpate the whole habit that gave rise to the initial error. It is not to be expected that I should be able to do that, and Descartes gives no reason for supposing that I can. At best, I can seek circumstances in which my vicious habits do me little harm, and I can set myself objectives in which I do not pay attention to the tainted sources.

Some context for this difference can be found in the underlying anthropologies that are in play here. Pelagianism takes it that there is no insurmountable obstacle between man and God, in at least the respect that, on reaching the age of reason, a person can choose to obey the moral law (De Plinval 1943: 228–30). On the other hand, we have seen that, for Descartes, we all develop defective habits of belief-formation in childhood and continue to be subject to the same influences thereafter. In the terms offered in the latter part of *Principles* I, by the time we can take stock of our vicious propensities, we have already accumulated many errors. The extent of our error means that it is hard to imagine our being able to do more than cultivate a small patch of properly-acquired ones: no more than a patch, never a whole Garden. In the postlapsarian terms just referred to, it confirms the fracture that is our lot. In this way, though error is not natural, human beings are de-natured by the fact of having to grow up in the first instance without the use of reason. That is, reaching the age of reason is no guarantee that we will be able to impose reason on all our actions and habits.

Our first taste of credulous belief ruins us for ever. Even though doxastic sin is a thing of the will and not of nature, by the time we come to understand what is required, we are well lost to the acquisition of virtue. At its gloomiest, this line of thought leads to the conclusion that any creature that needs to impose doxastic rectitude on itself will fail. If it needs to try, then it is already fallen; if fallen, then it will have made errors; if it has made errors, then it cannot realign will and intellect by bringing about a habit, trait, characteristic or ἕξις that ensures virtue.

Part III

Defect

6 The modes of scepticism

Locating scepticism

Let us turn now to consider some of the various facets of scepticism.

In the scheme I am developing, the word 'scepticism' is a tag for the doxastic vice of not acquiring true beliefs though they are available to be acquired. Such a usage has all the air of a definition, and I offer it as such. But, where 'credulity' and 'rectitude' are words with little currency as terms of art, that definition of 'scepticism' runs up against the fact that considerable scholarly and philosophical attention has been paid to the phenomena that call for the use of the name. It might, therefore, have been better to choose a less interesting word for the vice opposed to credulity and rectitude. For instance, 'diffidence', 'mistrust' or 'over-caution' would have done. Choices like these would have added to the unfamiliarity of the picture I am giving of Descartes' epistemology. Granting that on those (relatively few) occasions when it is not a strawman or a mere tag, 'scepticism' is shorthand for a manifold of interrelated but fissiparous tendencies, I stick with the word in the interests of connecting both with historical debate and with going concerns in early seventeenth-century philosophy.

The difficulty here is at least twofold: on the one hand to do with what scepticism was before Descartes and on the other to do with what it has come to be perceived to be since. The former of these aspects has at least something to do with ways of adopting or inventing terms for some of the more important phases through which the refusal of knowledge passed, particularly in late antiquity. Thus, it is not surprising to find some taxonomy into Early (or 'Practical') Pyrrhonist, and passing through Probabilist (or 'Critical') Methodic and Academic versions (see, e.g. Sextus Empiricus 1933: xxx; Sedley 1980: 8–10; Striker 1980: n. 1). Even taking over the name 'scepticism' is tendentious: 'sceptic' was the preferred self-description of neo-Pyrrhonians, though we also encounter words such as 'aporetic', 'zetetic' and 'ephetic' (Diogenes Laertius 1925: IX, 70; Sextus, *PH*, I, 7) and phrases such as 'those who suspend judgment' (Plutarch, *Adv.Col.*, 1122). The latter aspect, to do with how scepticism has been viewed since, afflicts us more closely, alas.

Many studies of Descartes rightly emphasise the fact that he was working in an intellectual environment in which a revival of ancient scepticism was taking place. Accordingly, his contribution has been seen as being wholly or primarily directed to stemming this tide (e.g. Curley 1978). So, to explain why Descartes deploys arguments of a sceptical character at the beginning of his operations in epistemology, it has been argued that his aim is to show that, ultimately, scepticism runs into trouble (Williams 1983), because we encounter truths that we can find no sustainable reasons for doubting (Curley 1978: 115–23), because we can find a non-circular validation of reason (Frankfurt 1970: 170–80), or because the criterion of clear and distinct ideas can be grounded in divine benevolence (Kenny 1968: 186–99; Wilson 1978: 313–15; Flage 1999: 210–13). Despite the variety of understandings of Descartes' tactics, there is a widespread and, I think, correct perception that his strategy is to invent and respond to an extreme form of scepticism to show that, after all, knowledge is possible: scepticism is used as a tool to show where we can find knowledge that is immune to further doubt.

This perception has given rise to the idea that what Descartes did in inventing what has come to be known as 'demon scepticism' is specify a rather sad thing called 'the *philosophical* problem of our knowledge of the external world' (Stroud 1984: 1, emphasis original). And, if there is, as Kant tells us (1781: 34), a scandal over the lack of an adequate response to this problem, there is room for those who think that what Descartes did was invent a 'method of doubt' (Gibson 1932: 35–9) and also for those who would take the opening moves of the *Meditations* as a model of philosophical procedure (e.g. Unger 1975: 8–9). Again, the perception of Descartes' strategic use of scepticism has given rise to the further idea that the 'refutation' of demon scepticism is the determinant of his success in his enterprise of making the world safe for knowledge-gathering by expelling sceptical threats once and for all.

But there is something partial in each of these developments of the basic perception, though taken together they can be used to build up a balanced picture. A failure to refute an extreme form of scepticism is a poor argument in favour of other, unspecified, forms; and a successful refutation of an extreme form is a very poor argument against less extreme forms. My aim, therefore, is to show how Descartes responds appropriately to the various threats and opportunities that sceptical argumentation offers.

To do this, in line with the definition of scepticism given above, the following two chapters offer a picture of the roles, both positive and negative, that it can play both (i) in correcting credulity, by invoking the modes of ancient Pyrrhonism; and (ii) in demarcating rectitude, by observing the formal characteristics of madman, dreaming and demon scepticism, as set out in *Meditations* I.

The first move is to show how scepticism can be used to correct the credulity that has been at the centre of our discussion so far. In the last two chapters, we saw why Descartes thinks that, with sufficient attention, any given credulous belief can be weeded out: if the will is so powerful as to be able to resist even ideas that seem to be irresistible, it can certainly resist the deliverances of the senses, which can easily be shown to be feeble. But the argument about the powers of the will does not show that I could develop the *habit* of discounting the deliverances of the senses.

As already noted in Chapter 1 and several times since, there are important structural differences between credulity and scepticism that influence the ways each is to be treated. One is a matter of timing: I was, as a child, subject to credulity before I could begin reasoning about how good my beliefs were. Once I discovered the nature, extent and source of my credulity, I saw I could and ought to do something about it. Granting that we are always under some pressure from the senses, what attitude should we take to that pressure, especially outside the circumstances Descartes thinks are propitious for enquiry? After examining the motivations and methods of one classical form of scepticism, we shall see that Descartes endorses an argument-schema against a wide range of credulous beliefs, and that the sorts of postures of non-committalness that were recommended by the ancient sceptics fit neatly onto what Descartes has to say about everyday life. He also adopts sceptical strategies with others, both in face-to-face confrontation with a living interlocutor (De Chandoux) and when dealing with the dead who have handed books down to us.

Verbally, then, Descartes is a sceptic: scepticism is a corrective to credulity, and credulity is a more troublesome vice both to uncover and to cure than scepticism ever could be. But Descartes opposes scepticism where scepticism is a refusal of *acceptable* beliefs, where it really is vicious. Scepticism is really vicious when we are in the conditions propitious for enquiry and it prevents us from gaining beliefs to which we are entitled. At the end of this chapter, therefore, we consider briefly what makes for propitiousness in the conditions of enquiry.

In the next chapter, I presuppose the conditions that permit us to allow scepticism free rein as a test for the acceptability of the ideas we find in our intellects. To begin with, I describe a scheme of the relations between the hypotheses that Descartes considers in *Meditations* I and the sets of beliefs they cast doubt on. The demon hypothesis sets a very high standard of the acceptability of beliefs; but Descartes does not offer any argument to show that we could know that the hypothesis is false. For all we know, there might be a demon. Rather, his strategy is to show that there are some beliefs that meet and exceed the standard the demon hypothesis sets, and that are therefore knowable even if there is a demon.

By considering what the demon could interfere with in the acquisition of belief, I home in on the privileged source of beliefs that are immune to such interference. This source is within us. When we come, in the last four chapters of the book, to look at what rectitude amounts to, we shall see the effects on Descartes' notion of science that arise from scepticism about the senses and from the privilege given to what is *a priori*, intuited and innate.

Modes and modishness

Dogmatism and disappointment

Relative to credulity, which has its roots in the biological constitution of human beings, scepticism is a superficial habit. When it is not a merely tedious party trick, it is the result of some reflection and some effort of will. In every case, it is a chosen posture. When it is a vicious habit, it can be combated by the adduction of arguments and reasons because it is, generally speaking, under the control of the person who espouses it.

One significant motivation for espousing scepticism is the avoidance of dogmatism, here understood as the species of credulity that prematurely systematises insecure beliefs. A person who has been put on her guard against insecure beliefs has grounds for wishing to avoid further error, especially of the sort where the object of belief is one where demonstrably secure beliefs are hard to come by. To avoid further error, a person who is aware of her own tendency to credulity may make an effort to direct her attention away from its usual objects and to attend either to something else or to nothing in particular. If she attends to something else, it may be because she believes (rightly or wrongly) that that alternative source of beliefs is less likely to lead her into error or, indeed, is such as to discourage dogmatic credulity. Of course, this move may simply replace one dogmatic stance with another. If, on the other hand, she seeks to direct her attention away from every source of potentially dogmatic belief, her aim may be a generalised suspension of judgment.

We know that, in the ancient tradition, there was an image in circulation to picture the relations between a state of generalised suspension of judgment and the overarching life-aim proposed an variously elaborated by all the schools of the Hellenistic period (Sedley 1983). The desideratum went by the name of ἀταραξία, variously translatable as freedom from passion, tranquillity, quietude, calmness or unmolestedness. For Sextus Empiricus, this unmolestedness follows from suspending judgment as if by chance, as a shadow follows a body (*PH*, I, 29).[1] Presumably, what is meant is that the shadow follows the body as incidental to the body, though it is always present;[2] analogously, unmolestedeness is incidental to the state of suspension, though it is its constant companion (see Annas 1994: 352–4). It is regarded as incidental in that Sextus does not pretend to have an explanation of how a shadow is caused nor of how unmolestedness is caused. Just so, there is an element of the unexplainable in the famous case of Apelles' throwing a sponge at his painting and obtaining the desired effect (Sextus, *PH*, I, 28; on which Annas 1985: 168–71); it simply happens that the one appears to follow the other.

Nevertheless, Sextus does supply at least the sketch of an explanation when he observes that a person who forms beliefs of a dogmatic sort will be forever running into disappointments and perburbations on account of his excessive attachment to his opinions (Sextus, *PH*, I, 27; also texts in Long (ed. 1987: 468–73)). One thing that is wrong with dogmatic beliefs is that, being formed by insecure means, they are apt to turn out to be false or, at least, in conflict with other beliefs that we form. Moreover, when we discover these discrepancies, the discovery itself is upsetting (Striker 1990). If what we said about the control of the passions in Chapter 2 is anything to go by, this fear of double trouble also finds a home in Descartes' thought about the avoidance of desires over whose fulfilment we have no power: disappointment is worse than merely not getting what you would have wanted if you had really wanted it.

Acquiring sceptical ability

If a person must learn how to resist the sources of potentially credulous belief that crowd in on him, it is a matter of some importance what exercises he does in order to learn. Given that credulity is deep-rooted, and perhaps ultimately ineradicable, the resistance to be acquired ought to be set up as a habit in the learner. This means that what is needed is training and practice, rather than the one-off admission of some proposition or other. In terms of the Aristotelian distinction between what we acquire by instruction (intellectual virtue) and what we acquire by habituation (moral virtue), what we are looking for is closer to the latter: something that can become 'second nature'. In this respect, an acquired sceptical ability should work independently of the operation of the intellectual virtues, because it should be like a skill or art.

It is easy to see that the mere exercise of the will from time to time is an inadequate response to what is called for. What we need is not merely to be able to control our response to this or that sensory stimulus, but to have the right sort of response to the senses as a source of stimuli. This requires us to develop an attitude that makes the discounting of the senses our norm. An appropriate sort of habituation is offered by the sceptical 'modes' or 'tropes', of which we have evidence about a variety of lists in ancient writers (see Annas 1985: 29).

Let us follow the way our most abundant source, Sextus Empiricus, proceeds. He introduces an enumeration of the ten modes that he attributes to the older sceptics; in the *Outlines of Pyrrhonism* (I, 36) he does not even venture who these might have been; in *Against the Mathematicians* (VIII, 345), he supposes Ænesidemus as a source. He does not commit himself to the exhaustiveness of the list or the soundness of the schemata (*PH*, I, 35: οὔτε περὶ τοῦ πλήθους οὔτε περὶ δυνάμεως αὐτῶν διαβεβαιούμενος). He does, however, think that what he is introducing are arguments: λόγοι (e.g. *PH*, I, 36, 40).

To illustrate their argumentative force (*PH*, I, 39: δύναμις again), Sextus goes through them in copious and exhausting detail in an exposition of a vast range of supposed contrarieties that take up fully half of the sections of *Outlines*, I, from 40 to 163, out of a total of 241. Though he makes some general observations about the relativisations that the various modes involve (I, 38–9), it is worth noting that he nowhere gives the sort of schematisation that scholars of the text naturally want to give (Striker 1983: 128). This might seem a curious omission if we were supposing that each of the samples of contrariety were meant to provide a cogent reason for someone learning how to become a sceptic by suspending judgment about this or that. Yet, if the modes had to be regarded as being of the form:

(1)   x appears F in respect S;
(2)   x appears F* in respect S*;
therefore
(3)   we cannot be secure about whether x is F or F* (Annas 1985: 25)

then they would be manifestly inadequate as probative arguments for suspension of judgment, if only for some of the reasons canvassed in considering Descartes' discovery of his own credulity at the beginning of *Meditations* I: (1) and (2) will only seem to be in conflict to someone who has faith in something other than appearances. In any case, Sextus himself gives over *Outlines*, II, 144–92 to considerations that are meant to undermine the notion of proof (ἀπόδειξις).

So as not to have to attribute to Sextus the idea that an argument like (1)–(3) is anything but manifestly inadequate, we need some other explanation of his tedious compilation and repetition. If we bear in mind that the aim of the procedure is the production of a habit rather than the sort of notional assent to a proposition that Newman calls 'profession' (187

52–60), the fact that Sextus supplies such a mass of illustration can be accounted for in terms of a distinction made by Jonathan Barnes between the 'material' and the 'formal' modes (Barnes 1990): Agrippa's modes of hypothesis, regress and circularity are given the latter tag and those of relativity the former. A formal mode is aimed at the recognition of some epistemological principle, such as that every warrant for a belief stands in need of warrant for itself, thus instituting a regress of warrants (*PH*, I, 166). We shall return in the next chapter to consider what use Descartes makes of analogues of these types of argument. By contrast, the material modes are meant to wear down our tendency to think that we can easily get secure beliefs.

The result of the process of attrition by the material modes ought to be the inculcation of a readiness or ability to find for every F an F* that makes F seem less than secure. The ability or capacity Sextus refers to ($\delta \acute{v} v \alpha \mu \iota \varsigma$: e.g. *PH*, I, 8, 9, 11) had better not depend on the proposition that all appearances are as credible as each other. For obvious reasons, that proposition is one relative to which appearances *pro* and *con* could be lined up and, thus, it would come to seem no more secure than its contrary, namely, that some appearances are more credible than others.[3] Rather, what underlies Sextus' harping on the contrarieties is the desire to accustom us to treating appearing F and appearing F* as if they were as credible as each other, as if they were 'equipollent' (*PH*, I, 10: $\iota \sigma o \sigma \theta \acute{\epsilon} v \epsilon \iota \alpha$), which he defines as equality with regard to belief and disbelief. Equipollence expresses the state of resourcelessness in belief-formation to which the neophyte is reduced *after* going through a stack of the cases Sextus proposes.

If this is what is going on, it is quite proper that, in seeking to illustrate the workings of the modes, scholars offer a manifestly inadequate schema like (1)-(3) above, and then add some proposition about equipollence, not by way of premise (but see Hookway 1990: 8), but as an inference-principle. What the inference-principle corresponds to is one's readiness or ability to treat appearances in a certain way.

A further trouble with the claim that all appearances are equipollent is that, *prima facie*, it is not true. Indeed, Sextus himself is clear that some of the reasonings a sceptic brings forward are more credible than others (e.g. *PH*, III, 281); but it may be that these differences in strength are assimilable to a medical model of the purposes of argumentation (Nussbaum 1994: 296–8; Hankinson 1995: 272–301). Nevertheless, the habit involved in bringing us to regard all appearances as equipollent requires us to learn to see them as all having just one grade of credibility.

Setting aside in this context the idea that all appearances should be accounted wholly credible, there seem to be two lines that could be taken to cultivate a vision on which conflicting appearances seem equipollent. One is to aim at regarding them each as having some grade of credibility, but never sufficient to justify belief-formation. The other is that of regarding them all as having no credibility at all.

In favour of taking the former line there is the fact that the modes' deployment of alleged data presupposes that those data themselves have some credibility, however exiguous and contested. Let us take the supposed effects of jaundice on vision (*PH*, I, 44). Though a person with jaundice does not see snow as yellow, as Descartes seems to think (*Resp.* II, CSM II: 104), the effect that the adduction of this alleged fact is supposed to have is that of putting me in doubt about the matter. If I cannot rebut it straight off, perhaps because I have never had jaundice, then it serves as a marker of my lack of right to be certain about the whiteness of snow. This lack of right is meant to be brought home to me not just by an apparent conflict between the appearance (to me, now, in good health) of the snow's whiteness and the appearance (for all I know straight off, to someone with jaundice) of its yellowness, but by the fact that that conflict is itself embedded within sets of beliefs and appearances that seem to be pulling in different directions.

On this line of thought, if a mode involves the contraposition of two appearances (or ensembles of appearances), simple division will give each as half-credible; if there are three contrasting appearances (or ensembles), then a third. The arithmetic here might seem an arbitrary way of starting: there is no obvious reason why we should begin by supposing a principle of indifference. But given that, like other troubles, appearances never come singly, the shove here is towards thinking that if we cannot tell how many we ought to be taking into account, then each is reduced to some indistinct, and so, for simplicity's sake, equally distributed denominator.

Even if, instead of the simply arithmetical principle of division of credibility, we hang on to the idea that some appearances initially seem more credible than others, once the appearances begin to proliferate, we still come to be robbed of all reason for preferring one over the others. There is 'nothing more' (οὐ μᾶλλον) to be said for one rather than for the others (De Lacey 1958: Woodruff 1988: 146–53).[4] By following this approach, the person who is acquiring sceptical ability is enjoined to envisage some consideration or considerations that would countervail the appearances in favour of any incipient belief, and then to see them as having no less weight than the initial appearances (e.g. *PH*, I, 10, 200–2; II, 103, 130; see Striker 1980: 105–15). In this way, all the appearances that Sextus details are reminders of considerations that ought to have more weight than we are habitually inclined to give to them: as much more as is required to bring them into equipollence with the appearances that we normally trust.

On the other line of thought, the 'nothing more' runs in the opposite direction. The over-abundance of appearances reduces the credibility of each of the appearances to which we normally trust effectively to zero.[5] Here, Sextus' battering us with the variety of (real and merely apparent) appearances is aimed at alerting us to the way in which 'nothing more' can mutate into 'nothing at all'. The appearances all become quite incredible.

Though it is of intrinsic interest to try to determine which sceptical thinkers and writers tend in each of these directions relative to various types of subject-matter and for various purposes (see Burnyeat 1980b, 1984; Frede 1979, 1984; Barnes 1982), our present aim is to apply the models they suggest to Descartes.

A scepticism to live by

At the outset of *Meditations* I, Descartes avows his credulity and sets himself to overturn his opinions (*Med*. I, CSM II: 12). But we also saw in considering his discovery of his credulity that Descartes does not, and could not properly, rely on anything like the material modes of contrariety to make that discovery. Nor, I suggest, is his operation in rejecting the deliverances of the senses to be directly compared with the account just offered of Sextus' exhaustiveness. For, Descartes explicitly refuses the idea of running through his beliefs one by one, because this would be an infinite task (*Med*. I, CSM II: 12; AT VII: 18: '[*n*]*ec ideo etiam singulæ erunt percurrendæ, quod operis esset infiniti*'). Instead he takes aim at the principles that have hitherto supported the edifice of his beliefs. In this respect, he offers something more like the ancient sceptics' formal modes, whose contours will occupy us in the next chapter. All the same, we can see his subscription to a 'once-bitten-twice-shy' maxim as a 'nothing at all' reading of 'nothing more' arguments: if I have no more reason to accept this or that sensory deliverance while I recognise that some sensory deliverances are insecure, then I have no reason to accept any sensory deliverance.

In taking aim at the principles on which his former opinions were built, Descartes does not directly confront those opinions or the difficulty of suspending assent to them. This procedure illustrates an important difference between his project and that of the ancient sceptics. Whereas they sought, in varying ways and degrees, to cultivate suspension of judgment about a large range of widespread beliefs and belief-forming habits for the purposes of living differently, Descartes does not seek to put himself in any permanent condition of suspension with respect to the matters that come under attack in *Meditations* I.

In line with a distinction that we shall elaborate below, Descartes isolates the hyperbolic doubts of *Meditations* I from the everyday affairs in which he continues to rely on the senses for information about the dispositions of objects such as tables and bits of wax for letter-sealing (Burnyeat 1984: 225ff.). The separation here is permissible because the Cartesian enquirer has put himself in a secluded situation outside everyday affairs. He does not have to apply his doubts about the senses to ordinary life, because, while he is enquiring, he is holding ordinary concerns in temporary abeyance: 'Descartes has to insist that his doubt is strictly theoretical and methodological, not practical, precisely because he believes that the judgments of ordinary life *are* put in doubt by the sceptical arguments' (Burnyeat 1984: 248, emphasis added).

Until he has found some satisfactory way of quelling or circumventing his doubts Descartes has to make do with an interim code of conduct for an approach to ordinary life of the sort set out in *Discourse* III.[6] In the prefatory text to the *Discourse*, the interim morality is said to be derived from the methodical precepts that are set out in *Discourse* II (CSM I: 111; AT VI: 1: '[. . .] *la morale que j'ai tirée de cette méthode*'). But there are three principal reasons for thinking that there is no such derivation.

One is the simple fact that there is no discernible logical relation between the precepts of *Discourse* II and the maxims of *Discourse* III.

A second is that, in the 'Letter Preface' to the French version of the *Principles,* the code is properly described as 'imperfect', as such that one might follow it until one finds a better (LP, CSM I: 186–7; AT IXB: 15: '[. . .] *morale imparfaite, qu'on peut suivre par provision pendant qu'on n'en sait point encore de meilleure*'), whereas the precepts, though they may need some *ex post* metaphysical underpinning, are not reconsidered or subject to replacement. If the code is revised, then the method that is alleged to follow from it must be revised too; the method that the code is alleged to follow from is not subject to further revision; therefore, either the code is not subject to revision (is not 'interim') or it does not follow from the method. Furthermore, Descartes is pretty certain that even the roughest discoveries in morality will come well down the proper sequence of enquiry, after the settling of many questions of metaphysics and physics (CSM I: 186). Nothing that depends on settling them is settled. Hence the interim code could not be derived from the method, because the required derivation would have to have settled all the intervening questions of metaphysics and physics. And a third reason for treating the alleged derivation with caution is that, as Gilson has documented in detail (Descartes 1925: 246ff.), at least the third maxim is clearly derived from an independent source, namely Stoicism. It is worth dwelling also on the sceptical origins of the first maxim.

Following the code is a makeshift for living while one enquires in the hope of finding something that is not subject to sceptical attack (Beyssade 199 146). The maxims are recommendations for dealing with practical affairs the absence of secure sources of belief. Until one locates such sources, one has, nevertheless, to get on with life. Hence, one has to act, though one does not have to treat the springs of one's actions *as* one's own.

In some matters, the laws and customs of the place one happens to find oneself will provide guidance. Hence, it is well to follow them (*Dis.* III, CSM I: 122; AT VI: 23: '[*l*]a première [sc. *maxime*] était d'obéir aux lois et aux coutumes de mon pays'). Though Descartes speaks of the laws of 'his' country, as a Frenchman on the move in the narrated time, he would not obey French laws wherever he was but those of the various countries through which he passed, appropriating as he goes. As an Englishman should be uncommitted to the superiority of driving on the left and would do well to stick to the right in France, so one ought to be prepared to follow others' laws and customs (*Dis.* III, CSM I: 122; AT VI: 23: '[. . .] *il me semblait que le plus utile était de me régler selon ceux avec lesquels j'avais à vivre*'). Even the most bizarre arrangements for dealing with, e.g. roundabouts should be acted on because, in some such matters, what is important is not that the rule should be, in any abstract way, correct, but that everyone should have the same expectations. Though one may harbour suspicions about the rules of precedence that are likely to command general acceptance and would thus reduce fatalities if adopted, all that is called for is outward behaviour of the sort that is said to be recommended when in Rome: doing as the Romans do.

Likewise, on matters not governed by law or custom, Descartes seeks the most moderate and least extreme opinions (*Dis.* III, CSM I: 122; AT VI: 23: '[. . .] *en toute autre chose, suivant les opinions les plus modérées, et plus éloignées de l'excès*'). The policy is one of following the most level-headed men, by observing what they do rather than what they say.[7] While he allows that this has practical advantages,[8] he also speculates that such opinions are likely to be the best available, since all sorts of excess tend to be bad (*Dis.* III, CSM I: 123; AT VI: 23: '[. . .] *vraisemblablement les meilleurs, tous excès ayant coutûme d'être mauvais*'). But he distances himself from assenting in any full-blooded way to the beliefs he is prepared to mimic. For, he envisages cases – even before he makes any of the systematic discoveries he hopes to derive from his concerted enquiry – in which he should have to give up the guides on which he acts.[9]

In the second of his maxims, Descartes puts a prudential brake on the readiness to change one's mind even about matters where one might expect all belief to be in some measure doubtful.[10] The point is that, in practical affairs, it may be better to pursue one consistent, moderate, line, though it be mistaken, than to act incoherently; his imagery is that of a person lost in a forest, who ought to walk in a straight line, thus ensuring that he doesn't double back on himself (*Dis.* III, CSM I: 123); and, he declares, a little further on, that, in adopting this policy, he is not imitating the sceptics, who doubt for doubting's sake and pretend to be forever in a quandary (*Dis.* III, CSM I: 125; AT VI: 29: '[*n*]*on que j'imitasse pour cela les sceptiques, qui ne doutent que pour douter, et affectent d'être toujours irrésolus*').

In regarding the moderate opinions he has picked up as a stop-gap, Descartes is committing himself not only to a sort of dissociation from his own actions, but also to the sort of conservatism that has frequently characterised the lifestyle that sceptics have aimed at (Sextus, *PH*, I, 23–4). The sceptic can never be a radical because she cannot throw herself into one line of thought or action, in the face of an opposition that she recognises as such (Popkin 1960: Chapter 3; Penelhum 1983). Suffice it to think again of Hume in this connection (also Unger 1975: 242–6).

In regarding his interim code of conduct as interim and as centrally concerned with the conduct of affairs that have no essential bearing on the enquiry he envisages, Descartes concedes that the Pyrrhonist approach to decision-making under uncertainty may represent the most painless option.

So long as one has to act and does not have secure beliefs about the objects of that activity, one may get by with what is to hand. And Descartes holds on to the religion in which, by God's grace, he has been brought up (*Dis.* III, CSM I: 122; AT VI: 23: '[. . .] *retenant constamment la religion en laquelle Dieu m'a fait la grâce d'être instruit dès mon enfance*'); this is not just a matter of its customary force (Descartes 1925: 235), because Descartes remained a Catholic even when he was not among Catholics, in the Netherlands (Descartes 1963–73: I, 592–3 Alquié n.): he takes it that being born to Catholic parents is a good fortune that it would be futile to put aside. In this respect, too, Descartes' sceptical tendency in his first maxim is an echo of the purposes to which his pretty immediate predecessors had put what they had learnt from Sextus and others: some polemicists, such as the younger Pico della Mirandola (Copenhaver 1992: 245–50), hoped to render philosophers' dogmas uncertain and thus to clear the way for divine grace, while others, such as Francisco Sanchez, Pierre Charron (Rodis-Lewis 1995: 71–6) and, perhaps, Montaigne (Popkin 1960: 37–41) supposed that the most obvious theological rival – Protestantism – would give way before sceptical attack much more easily than Catholicism would.

Since, as he recognised, Descartes never did get very far with producing many practical principles (bar the preliminaries set out in the *Passions*) from any source of beliefs that he was prepared to regard as secure, it is fair to picture him as having cultivated a sort of Pyrrhonist suspension of judgment with respect to the types of affairs that could not be directly determined by his methodical enquiry. This refusal to commit himself has emblematic expression in his comparison of himself with an actor, who proceeds behind a mask ('Preliminaries', CSM I: 2; AT X: 213: '*larvatus prodeo*'), and in his adoption of Ovid's dictum that he has lived well who has kept himself well hidden (letter to Mersenne, April 1634, CSMK: 43; AT I: 286: '*bene vixit qui bene latuit*'). But we can see it at work not only in Descartes' standing disregard for what can be got out of books, but also in his reaction to his encounter with De Chandoux in the late 1620s. Since the latter is something of a microcosm of the former, we may consider it first.

The encounter with De Chandoux

As is well known, towards the end of his last prolonged stay in France (1625–8), Descartes gravitated towards the Augustinian movement represented at Paris in the Oratory founded by Cardinal de Bérulle. At some point,[11] he was invited to be part of the audience of a talk given by the alchemist/chemist N[icholas] De Chandoux. De Chandoux is a rather shadowy figure: one established fact that commentators seem to enjoy reporting about him is that he ended badly: he was hanged for counterfeiting, his conviction proving incompetence at transmutation, one supposes.[12]

Nor do we have much information about the content of De Chandoux' talk, beyond the vague description that it was an exposition of his 'new philosophy' (letter to Villebressieu, CSMK: 32; AT I: 213: '[. . .] *le discours de M. de Chandoux touchant sa nouvelle philosophie*'). But it is not wild to suppose that it may have been of neo-Epicurean inspiration in opposition to Aristotelian physical theory; that, at least, would have been a live option (see Joy 1978: 66; Jones 1989: Chapter 7). Though it is just a supposition, if De Chandoux was setting out some form of Atomism, then we can explain Descartes' dissatisfaction with what was said, and the response he sought in his audience. As a rival to Scholasticism, De Chandoux' views would suffer from the same defect as what they were meant to replace: dependence on (credulous) empirical techniques. Relative to the method he took himself to have discovered as having the same certitude as arithmetic (Baillet 1691: I, 163; cf. *Reg.* II, CSM I: 13), all such projects would be doomed to be merely true-seeming or plausible ('*vraisemblable*', '*plausible*'). If so, Descartes' response was to follow in the Arcesilaus' and Carneades' footsteps and to argue *in utramque partem*. First, he took one of De Chandoux' best-received theses and piled up a dozen equally probable arguments against it; and then he took one, presumably Scholastic, thesis that was not accepted by those present and defended it with just as many equally probable arguments.[13]

Many commentators have properly seen that this first (and last) public display on Descartes' part, in which he gave some specimens of his method, had a decisive influence on his subsequent career, encouraging him to follow his own bent (Baillet 1691: I, 166: '*son naturel*') and set his thoughts down in writing. Descartes' performance can be seen as virtuosity in the school exercise that he had experienced at La Flèche of devising arguments for and against any position (De Rochemonteix 1889: IV, 21–6). If he was only re-enacting standard debating techniques, we might be puzzled by the astonishment that we are told attended his speech. His audience ought to have been fully familiar with what he was doing – after all, it is the standard format of the scholastic *summa*.

Against that, we may set the fact that Descartes' challenge was framed in terms of what seemed most certain and what seemed most evidently false. What is revealed by the even-handed approach to Aristotelianism and its (presumably) Epicurean rivals is Descartes' readiness to use sceptical tools to combat the credulity he finds in both. His use of those tools is based on the pretension to having discovered an approach to enquiry that is proof against them. Correspondingly, the response that he sought – and, by all accounts, obtained – from his audience was that they should, first, suspend judgment as between De Chandoux and the Schools (Baillet 1691: I, 165); and, then, accept the superiority of Cartesian principles, which they should recognise as better founded, truer and more natural than those that the learned have hith-erto accepted (letter to Villebressieu, summer 1631, CSMK: 32; AT I: 213: '[. . .] *mes principes sont mieux établis, plus veritables, et plus naturels que des autres qui sont déjà reçus parmi les gens d'étude*').

Though Descartes nowhere gives an argument to show that anything not derived from an application of his principles will fall foul of scepticism, that claim is a clear presupposition of his polemic against the things that the learned accept – in particular against the idea that the techniques and objects of erudition provide us with anything that is not a product of the most helpless credulity.

Descartes' polemic against learning

One common enough image of Descartes is of his having had 'a denial of history as his first and last word' (e.g. Bannan 1960: 416). And this is certainly what emerges from his polemic against learning. I call it a 'polemic' rather than a thesis, doctrine or argument because it is a slightly scattered thing, traceable in all his writings except the *Meditations*, at least in part because the types of doubtfulness that infect what can be derived from book-learning are but a pale foreshadowing of the worries that occupy *Meditations* I.

Its absence from the *Meditations* can also be explained by the fact that, from fairly early in the planning of that work, it was intended to be published with the *Objections* of educators and authorities (letter to Mersenne, 23rd December 1639, CSMK: 142; cf. Marion 1994a, 1995). Descartes would antagonise potential supporters if he denigrated the practices of which they were professional exponents. So, in preparation for responding to them, h sought to get (back) up to speed with scholastic terminology by readin

Eustace of St Paul's *Summa Philosophiæ* (letter to Mersenne, 11th November 1640, CSMK: 156 (abridged); AT III: 232). This is material that he puts to use in the *Replies*, where he does make use of scholastic and Biblical quotation to establish the orthodoxy of his position.[14]

In his review, in *Discourse* I, of the things he had learnt at school, Descartes says that philosophy gives us the means to speak plausibly ('*vraisemblablement*') about all things and to make less well-educated people admire us (*Dis.* I, CSM I: 113). The first of these assertions is presumably a crypto-quotation from the beginning of Aristotle's *Topics* (I, i, 100 a 18–20);[15] it serves two purposes in establishing Descartes' connection with the tradition, while also distancing him from it with the slightly scornful reference to plausibility, which is reinforced by the second assertion's insinuation of scholars' vanity. The insinuation is spelt out when, in *Discourse* VI, he explicitly connects the vanity of appearing to be omniscient (*Dis.* VI, CSM I: 147; AT VI: 71: '*la vanité de paraître n'ignorer rien*') with a preference for what is merely plausible ('*vraisemblance*') and for having a reputation for learning (also *Reg.* II, CSM I: 11; AT X: 362–3).

Although there are some concessive passages in which Descartes sees a positive, propedeutic, role for book-learning (e.g. *Reg.* III, CSM I: 13),[16] it is noticeable that his concessions tend to be set at least implicitly against the background of his distinction between the 'speculative' philosophy taught in the schools and his own 'practical' undertaking (*Dis.* VI, CSM I: 142; AT VI: 61: '[. . .] *au lieu de cette philosophie speculative qu'on enseigne dans les écoles, on en peut trouver une autre pratique*'; cf. *Reg.* IV, CSM I: 18–19). The first term of this distinction is denigrated as supplying a mere rag-bag of probable argumentative techniques that are appropriate to the competitive drive of immature minds (*Reg.* II, CSM I: 11; cf. Plato, *Gorg.*, 484C–5E). By contrast, the 'practical' philosophy is to do, not with defeating other people in dialectic, but with gaining power over nature (*Dis.* VI, CSM I: 142); this does not require that a person have any acquaintance with books. Indeed, he goes so far as to suggest to Mersenne that the *Discourse* and its accompanying works should have in their blurb an invitation to those who have not studied at all (March 1636, CSMK: 51). What Descartes would prefer as his ideal reader is a person who has some inclination for algebra and geometry, but who has not been given the standard training in those subjects (*Reg.* XIV, CSM I: 58).[17]

His hostility to the normal course of studies, to which he himself had been subject, is in some measure reflected in the fact that the *Discourse* was first written in French, where that vernacular is identified with the use of unsullied natural reason, over against musty old books (penultimate paragraph of *Dis.* VI, CSM I: 151);[18] and, in general, he sees no advantage to be gained from the unnatural task of learning the classical languages, over against living tongues, even if the latter be Ladin or Low Breton (*Re.*, CSM II: 403;

AT X: 503: '[. . .] *un honnête homme n'est plus obligé de savoir le grec ou le latin, que le suisse ou le bas breton*'; cf. *Dis.* I, CSM I: 114; AT VI: 7). What is supposed to be wrong with learning from books? At the least it would seem to be a great perversity for one who is able to read to give up what seems like a resource in knowledge-gathering. Why should it be that those who give themselves to it have their judgment sapped about easy things (*Reg.* IV, CSM I: 16; *Lum.* VI, CSM I: 92) and are even unable to explain what they are reputed to be experts in (*Reg.* XII, CSM I: 48;[19] *Dis.* VI, CSM I: 147)?

A short answer is that, according to Descartes, all one learns from books is history (*Reg.* III, CSM I: 13).[20] And he could reasonably rely on a perception of history as a discipline in which certainty is hard to come by (see Grafton 1990: Chapter III), and, what is more, as a discipline by which human knowledge is never increased. In one image he offers, such learning can never lead us beyond the contents of the books that we study, as ivy can never rise above the trees that give it support (*Dis.* VI, CSM I: 147). While this image is certainly suggestive, we might be looking for an argument to flesh it out. I think that we can pick out the materials of a sceptical trope from a range of Descartes' remarks and can set them up as a pair of dilemmatic arguments aimed at showing that the conflicting testimonies to be found in books cannot be judged by a person whose intellectual equipment is formed by reading.

The first dilemma is this. Either the books one reads are by one hand or they are by many.

If a would-be philosopher were to read only the works of, say, Aristotle in the search for a view of the world, then she might obtain the provisional contentment of following him whom she deems to be wiser than she is (*Dis.*, II, CSM I: 118). As it happens, there are very few people who get such a restricted diet. And only the remotest chance would bring such a person to find an author all of whose opinions he could believe at the various stages of his life (*Dis.* II, CSM I: 118). So, even with just one author/authority, the fact of a person's mental development would seem to give rise to different attitudes. Even if an author were wholly believed by a person over the whole arc of her life, there would still be no guarantee that his opinions were any more trustworthy than what she could discover for herself (CSM I: 180).[21] In any case, there is the important thesis, to which we shall return in Chapter 9, that it is only by seeing things for oneself that one really comes to understand them (*Dis.* VI, CSM I: 146; AT VI: 69: '[. . .] *on ne saurait si bien concevoir une chose, et la rendre sienne, lorsqu'on l'apprend de quelqu'un autre, que lorqu'on l'invente soi-même*').

On the other hand, if the books one selects, or has selected for one are by many hands, then it is inevitable that contrariety of opinion will emerge.

Descartes reports that he had learnt at school that there is no belief so odd or untoward, but it has been held by some philosopher (*Dis.* II, CSM I: 118; AT VI: 16: '[. . .] *on ne saurait rien imaginer de si étrange et si peu croyable, qu'il n'ait été dit par quelqu'un des philosophes*'). He does not make clear how he learnt this. It may have been from observing the standing difference of opinions among the learned (ibid.: '[. . .] *les différences qui ont été de tout temps entre les opinions des doctes*'). Or it could have been from Cicero, whom he certainly read (*Div.*, ii, 58, '[*n*]*ihil tam absurde dici potest, quod non dicatur ab aliquo philosophorum*'). But the thought was something of a commonplace at the time; it is quoted, for instance, by Montaigne (1580: 528), by Hobbes (1651: 34) and Pascal (1670: § 507).

Thus, Descartes describes how, having completed the studies that, in the ordinary way, would qualify him as learned, what he felt was disillusion, because there was no knowledge of the sort he had hoped for (*Dis.* I, CSM I: 113),[22] a knowledge that would, in the end, dissipate his doubts and correct his errors (*Dis.* I, CSM I: 113; AT VI: 5: '[. . .] *je me trouvais embarrassé de tant de doutes et d'erreurs*').

In the face of the difference of opinion, and the fact that some opinions seem to be wild, we ought to adopt Sextus' stance of treating those that might hitherto have seemed reasonable as 'no more' credible than the wild ones and of treating those that seem wild as if they were 'no less' credible than the others in the lists. We should arrive at a state in which we view them all as 'equipollent' and thus be encouraged to suspend judgment about them. For books 'teach not their own use' (Bacon 1625a: 797): they provide no criterion – a word to which we shall return – for deciding which of the conflicting appearances is to be accepted in the face of the others.

It is no way out of the confusion that constitutes the second horn of this dilemma to try to total up the testimonies on each side of a disputed matter, meaning to follow the opinion of the majority (*Reg.* III, CSM I: 13; cf. Arnauld 1683: 345–7). For, the matter may be one on which only a philosopher of a speculative bent feels in need of having an opinion (*Dis.* VI, CSM I: 147). Moreover, since the various authorities to whom one might turn are not independent of each other, but are themselves subject to fashion (letter to Dinet, CSM II: 392),[23] a whole tradition can be enfeebled. As he says at the outset of the *Passions,*

> because what the ancients taught is so paltry and for the most part so unbelievable, [. . .] I can have no hope whatever of coming close to the truth except by keeping well away from the paths they followed (*Pass.* I, 1, CSM I: 328; AT XI: 327–8: '[. . . leg. *puisque*] *ce que les anciens ont enseigné est si peu de chose, et pour la plupart si peu croyable,* [. . .] *je ne puis avoir aucune espérance d'approcher de la vérité qu'en m'éloignant des chemins qu'ils ont suivis*').

The image that emerges is one of the sciences as like an artefact – a painting (*Re.*, CSM II: 406), a house (*Dis.* III ad init., CSM I: 122) or a city (*Dis.* II, CSM I: 116) – to which many labourers have contributed to produce a less than satisfactory overall effect. And the moral to be drawn is that we have to start from scratch and on our own. If, therefore, we make progress neither by trusting to one author nor by getting involved in the point-by-point business of discussing the various conflicting views (*Dis.* V, CSM I: 131), there is no profit to be had from reading.[24]

The second dilemma is this. Either what we find in past philosophers' writings forms part of the practical philosophy or it does not.

If it does, then it will be arrived at in due course (*Reg.* VIII, CSM I: 29–30). In that case, the books are superfluous. And, again, discovering for ourselves is not just a source of intellectual satisfaction and a proper exercise of the soul (*Reg.* X, CSM I: 35; LP, CSM I: 180), but, ultimately, the only way we really come to understand. The picking up of stray pieces of information or opinion cannot replace enquiry in accordance with method.

If, on the other hand, there is material in books that would not be discovered by pursuit of the practical philosophy, then either it is not true or it is not genuinely intelligible to us. Setting aside the cases in which books may contain revealed truths of theology, which may be beyond our ken anyway (*Pr.* I, 25, CSM I: 300),[25] virtually the only occasions outside the *Replies* on which Descartes cites any author as an authority are when he refers to the novelties of writers reporting experimental results.[26] The explanation, presumably, is that, while some sorts of experimentation may be done second-hand,[27] the findings in question ought to be regarded as ancillary to the orderly business of building up a body of science, as set out, for instance, in the *Principles*: whenever thinking is called for, we had better do it ourselves.

If learning were necessary for the sort of enquiry that Descartes proposes, the enquiry could not succeed without it. But, he takes himself to have had considerable success without it. So, by *modus tollendo tollens*, learning is not necessary. Further, it is not desirable because it distracts attention from what is clear and necessary, to issues that create more problems than they solve,[28] and that are merely casual, haphazard and time-consuming (preamble to *Re.*, CSM II: 401;[29] *Dis.* VI, CSM I: 142–3). Thus, Descartes supposes that reference to the writings of our philosophical predecessors is a snare likely to lead us to consider matters about which all philosophers are as ignorant as the rest of humanity and about which it is therefore reasonable to suspend judgment indefinitely.

By way of comment on this sceptical posture towards the Scholastic discipline of reading and debating as a preliminary to the formation of an opinion, I would venture that Descartes offers one of the founding myths of what we have come to think of as modern philosophy: of the philosopher as engaged in an enquiry that can be pursued independent of any particular intellectual or cultural baggage.[30] It would take us too far afield to consider even a small portion of the ramifications and effects of this myth in post-Cartesian philosophy. Suffice it for present purposes to stress, first, that Descartes seems satisfied with the argumentative force of the sceptical tropes when applied to enquiries not conducted in accordance with doxastic rectitude; and second, that he nowhere makes any attempt to rehabilitate any canonic of intelligent reading. His scepticism about learning came on him at an early age and never left him; it is a case of circumscribed but intransigent Pyrrhonism.

Retreat to method

We have already had several occasions to call on a distinction between the principles that may govern our ordinary life and what must dominate in enquiry properly so-called.

In one respect, the affairs of ordinary life – crossing the road, doing the shopping, getting a book published, laying siege to a town and the like – can be described as 'practical'. Relative to these, Descartes recommends as unassuming a way of carrying on as possible, probably to the exclusion of the more daring of them. Affairs that are practical in this respect fall within the sphere in which, roughly, Pyrrhonist attitudes and reactions are appropriate. In another respect, Descartes distinguishes his own philosophy from that of the Schools, saying that his is practical and not speculative (*Reg.* IV, CSM I: 18–19; *Dis.* VI, CSM I: 142), because it should, when complete, protect us against all the ills that flesh is heir to. In this latter respect, the edifice of knowledge that Descartes is aiming to build up cannot admit of approximation, doubt or error.

The building of this edifice requires the enquirer not to be worried about the relative reliability of notions that are approximate, doubtful or erroneous. She should therefore put herself in a position in which she can suspend the sorts of activities about which she has ideas with those features. This suspension of activity lies behind a characteristic feature of Descartes' operation. For, he is very insistent in describing what he thinks are the best circumstances in which a person can go about the business of enquiring in earnest. Unlike so much of the Western tradition in philosophy, he does not think that enquiry is best done as Socrates does it, in *viva voce* dialogue with others, as Aristotle does it, by the sifting of the views of the many and the wise, nor, as many have thought in the more recent past, by taking over what they think is the best practice of the social or physical sciences.

Rather, Descartes opts for isolation and seclusion.

Several commentators have seen that Descartes' guidelines for ensuring the most propitious circumstances for enquiry resemble in various ways the conditions laid down for the conduct of a Jesuit retreat, with which he will have been familiar from his school-days.[31] Many of these resemblances are, indeed, very striking and, in some cases, could hardly be accounted for at all without seeing Descartes as directly influenced by his teachers. What is more, they help us to appreciate that his operation presupposes a model of human activity that is not purely philosophical in the technical sense that is common today.

But there is room for caution about an overneat assimilation (Rubidge 1990). For instance, it would be hasty to move from the fact that the *Meditations* is self-consciously divided into 'days', like the timetable of a Jesuit retreat (Beck 1965: 28ff.; Garin 1967: 160; Rée 1987: 19–24), to an overall rereading of the *Meditations* as a 'structured transformation of the meditational mode' (Rorty 1986: 17). I therefore restrict some of the more prominent similarities to endnotes, and aim primarily to offer a motivation for what Descartes prescribes in terms of the rectitude he is aiming at, and the principal means he adopts for cultivating it.

Let us consider two aspects of the relation between ordinary life and setting oneself to the business of enquiry. On the one hand, a moment of reflection may be called for in order to get the rest of life into some sort of order;[32] on the other, one might choose a life that is itself secluded and dedicated to enquiry.

The former of these kinds of retreat need not itself be dedicated to enquiry, but to the consideration of what to do about the fact that humans are rather poorly equipped to know how to act fully rationally. This sort of preliminary seclusion may be regarded as similar to the retreat that Descartes was presumably sent on in his final year at La Flèche in order to discern what would be his life's work (Thomson 1972: 64). It also comes out in what he reports at the beginning of *Discourse* II, about finding himself in Germany, in the winter of 1619, with no one worth talking to and no cares or passions to disturb him (CSM I: 116; Baillet 1691: I, 80–6). So he spent whole days communing with himself.[33] In the particular case, as we know from Baillet (1691: I, 81f.; cf. CSM I: 4), this self-absorbed activity issued in a dream one of whose key elements was a line from Ausonius asking what path he should follow in life ('*quod vitæ sectabor iter?*'). But, what with his comings and goings in the subsequent years, we find him as late as the summer of 1622, presumably in or near Poitiers (Baillet 1691: I, 106), still trying to fix the style of life that would most suit him.[34] Given his earlier reflection that, at the age of 23, he was not fully mature,[35] he returns towards the end of *Discourse* III (CSM I: 125) to note the preferability of preparing himself for his programme of research by travelling around rather than by shutting himself away. Nevertheless, the resolves of 1619 remained with him. Even if Descartes did not arrive at a settled determination until his interview with Bérulle, what he was looking for was a once-for-all commitment.

What he arrived at was a decision to try to reduce as far as possible the spheres in which he had to act on approximate, doubtful, or erroneous notions. By the age of 32, he took himself to be in full possession of his reason (*Pr.* I, 1, CSM I: 193; AT VIIIA: 5: '[. . .] *integrum nostræ rationis usum haberemus*'). He thereupon decided to abstract himself from the region where he would have to take account of pressing or doubtful matters (*Med.* I, CSM I: 12; AT VII: 17–18: '[. . .] *mentem curis omnibus exsolvi, securum mihi otium procuravi*'). The solution he hit on was to move to Holland. Anywhere abroad might have fitted the bill (letter to Picot, 2nd February 1643, AT III: 616), so long as it ensured that the neighbours would not make nuisances of themselves.[36] Holland presented several advantages. It was a place where he knew few people (*Dis.* III, CSM I: 125).[37] Descartes was active about keeping away from acquaintances (see letter of Saumaise, 3rd April 1637, AT X: 554–5), and frequently changed his address, perhaps to ensure that his whereabouts should not become too well known. The country was wealthy and outwardly peaceful (*Dis.* III, CSM I: 125; letter to De Balzac, 5th May 1631, CSMK: 31–2) and the Dutch were not inclined to interfere with or disturb him (Pagès 1996; Spallanzani 1999).

How did Descartes hope that the cultivation of doxastic rectitude would benefit from this situation?

First, and most obviously, having nothing else of any urgency to attend to, he can devote all the time that he can make use of to his studies (and sleep for the rest). This is the advantage of a gentleman who has taken measures to ensure that his private income will not either intrude on him or dry up (Baillet 1691: I, 116–17). In this, Descartes differs little from what we find Aristotle saying in the last book of the *Ethics* about the preconditions of the intellectual exercise that is the highest good for man: whether we call it σχολή (*EN*, X viii, 1177 b 4–5), '*otium*' (*Med.* I, CSM I: 12; AT VII: 17–18) or '*loisir*' (*Dis.* II, CSM I: 116; AT VI: 11), it is a freedom from disturbance that holds worldy worry in abeyance and permits full concentration on the matter in hand.[38]

More specifically, the meditator can concentrate on the defects that he has found in himself. The defects we are interested in are credulity and scepticism. Though we saw that the initial discovery of credulity calls for some contortions,[39] the state of seclusion permits the meditator not to have to act on what he has acquired from such tainted sources. That being so, there is little motivation for him to take them as seriously as he would if he would have to were out 'in the world': they tempt him that much less because they do not present themselves as the presuppositions of his actions.[40] He can thus take a step further than Pyrrhonist detachment. In addition to distancing himself from his habitual beliefs, he can examine their shortcomings all the more dispassionately.

Similarly, the scepticism induced by the procedures of the *Meditations'* first day means that, until such doubts as can be resolved have been resolved, he should have no other projects on hand. Those procedures should induce real doubt, especially about the senses as we see in the incantation with which *Meditations* III opens (CSM II: 24). So, only someone who has set all other activity aside for the duration could hope to get on with the enquiry undistracted by their promptings. How serious and longlasting these doubts are will occupy us in the next chapter. For the present, the important point is that no action whatever of the meditator could be described as rational until at least some of those doubts have been resolved, as at least some of them are as the *Meditations* proceeds.

Third, the removal from distractions means that the meditator is put in control of which sources of ideas he will pay attention to. His environment is a matter of no account, both because he has relieved himself of commitment to it and because he has given himself reasons, to do with the hypothesis of a malicious demon,[41] for thinking he is not in any reliable contact with it. So, he can attend to the things that he can get hold of irrespective of what merely appears to crowd in on him. The seclusion of the enquiry-retreat allows the subject to overcome himself rather than fortune.[42] What this means is that the retreatant is made responsible for guiding himself out of the ignorance and perplexity that is the normal human lot. The seclusion is supposed to have the effect of stiffening our resolve to assent in a full-blooded way only to those ideas that are fully in our intellects; in this way, '[t]he guidance of the will is the ultimate objective of meditation' (Hatfield 1986: 48) Furthermore, unlike Hume at the end of the first book of the *Treatise*,[43] we are supposed to carry away from the enquiry the results that can be applied to ordinary life and to apply them there when we can.

The preference for what is unchanging is itself one of the fixed biases of Western philosophy from Parmenides onwards; but Descartes' version of it, as embodied in his description of the best conditions for enquiry, adds perhaps a new twist. For him, it is by looking at what is invariant in the stock of our ideas that we can overcome the contingencies of what we happen to have acquired as a result of individual experiences. The invariance in question is both from time to time in a person's life and from person to person: not only do I always have at my disposal the common notions from which an orderly enquiry begins, but everyone, in order to be able to think at all, has the same natural light with with to see (letter to Mersenne, 16th October 1639, CSMK: 139; AT II: 598: '[. . .] *tous les hommes ayant une même lumière naturelle*'). The effect of this comes out most strongly in *Meditations* III when the meditator sorts his ideas into those that are innate, those that are adventitious and those that are invented (*Med.* III, CSM II: 26).[44] If, as we shall see, only the innate are to be regarded as proper objects of our attention, then it may seem no accident that an enquiry conducted in seclusion privileges them; vice versa, only if one has a prior commitment to what is innate will one think that the best sort of enquiry is conducted as if one were living in a desert (*Dis.* III, CSM I: 125; AT VI: 31: '[. . .] *j'ai pu vivre aussi solitaire et retiré que dans les déserts les plus écartés*'; also *Re.*, CSM II: 405).

In short, if doxastic rectitude involves attention to what is normally shouted down by the senses, then we need silence to hear what it says.

7   The form of scepticism

Standards

Belief-defeaters

Supposing an enquirer who is in a situation of seclusion and has no aims other than those of obtaining beliefs in accordance with doxastic rectitude, this chapter offers an account of the argument of *Meditations* I and some suggestions about where this leaves Descartes. The claim is that the structure of the argument is such that Descartes does not need to exclude the possibility that there is a malicious demon bent on, and frequently successful in, deceiving him. Knowledge is possible even if there is such a demon; but this means that most of what we generally think of as knowledge is no such thing.

The reconstruction of the underlying dynamic of the *Meditations* adapts some terminology that has some currency in recent writing on epistemology; but, so far as I know, it has not been applied in any detail to Descartes. I begin by describing an adaptation of the machinery of 'belief-defeaters' (Pollock 1974: 40–3; 1987; Moser 1989).[1]

In the sceptical trope already called on, the appearance of a round tower is supposed to be a belief-defeater relative to the appearance of a square tower, and vice versa. In the adaptation of this terminology to be suggested for present purposes, the 'vice versa' is important. The round look (from afar) is supposed to cast doubt on the square look (close up); and the square look (close up) does, as we tend to think, cast doubt on the round look (from afar). Though we do, as a matter of fact, tend to discount the view from afar in favour of the view from close up, the sceptical application of the machinery of belief-defeaters is meant to lead us to be even-handed about these relativisations. If we have reached just that grade of reflectiveness at which roundness and squareness are in some sort of conflict, then we might be led to suppose that we cannot get beliefs about the tower's shape on the sole basis of the looks it presents.

Perhaps the even-handedness comes out more clearly at a higher level of sophistication. For instance, someone might say that the Third Man Argument is a belief-defeater relative to the Theory of Forms, and vice versa. While Aristotle presents the Third Man Argument as his refutation of the Theory of Forms (*Metaph.*, A 9, 990 b 15–17), the continuing attractiveness to Platonists of the Theory of Forms – including to Plato, who had his own version of its supposed refutation (*Parm.*, 130 E–1 E) – might be a reason for thinking that the Third Man Argument does not refute it, and that it is not the refutation that Aristotle thought it was. The conclusion would be that the issue cannot be resolved by arguments of the sorts used by Plato and Aristotle.

In what we cited Barnes (1990) as calling the 'material' modes of ancient scepticism, there is mutual defeat of appearances and no belief is formed: we are encouraged to suspend judgment when we find that there is conflict between two or more of the testimonies of sorts to which we had previously been apt to trust.

Standard-defeaters and defeater-eaters

Generalising the notion of a belief-defeater, we can see it as one member of a family of structures that includes also what I shall be calling 'standard-defeaters'. The standards in question are standards of doxastic acceptability. For instance, a person may take it as a standard of doxastic acceptability that some idea should have come to her through the senses. This is someone for whom, *inter alia*, seeing is believing. The standard she adopts corresponds to a whole set of beliefs, all deriving from one type of source. What I am proposing to call a 'standard-defeater' is a hypothesis that renders doubtful all the beliefs in that set or from that type of source, without necessarily itself being put in doubt by the beliefs in the set or from the type of source. Not necessarily 'vice versa'.

Where the belief-defeaters of the sceptic's material tropes involve the counter-balancing of more or less actual testimonies, a standard-defeater, as I am seeking to define it, employs a more permissive modality. Let us consider a simple – and not yet Cartesian – case.

Either I am wearing blue-tinted glasses or I am not. If I am and have grounds for believing that I am, then I have grounds for believing that the things I see as looking green would look yellower (redshifted) if I took the glasses off. If I am not and have grounds for believing that I am not, then I have grounds for believing that the things I see as looking yellow would look greener (blueshifted) if I put the glasses on. My wearing or not wearing the glasses affects the ways things look; the beliefs I form on the basis of the ways they look are affected by the beliefs I have about whether I am wearing the glasses or not.

In the normal run of things, we can tell whether we are wearing sunglasses or not by pretty direct means: from the feel on the nose, in peripheral vision, or by remembering putting them on or taking them off. These direct grounds are also grounds for the sort of discounting we do when forming beliefs about the colours of things. For someone who is wearing blue-tinted glasses and who, despite the belief that she is wearing the glasses and on the basis of the greenish look of some sunflowers, forms the belief that the sunflowers are green, the glasses will stand as an actual defeater with respect to that belief. They are more than the belief-defeaters of the material tropes because they affect a whole set of beliefs about colours: everything gets shifted down the spectrum. But they are not yet what I am homing in on as the most interesting sort of standard-defeater.

Consider now the case of a person who is not wearing blue-tinted glasses but who, having an anæsthetised nose, a weakness for wrap-around glasses and a poor memory, has no direct grounds for belief about whether she is or not. Faced with some greenish-looking sunflowers, she supposes that she must be wearing sunglasses and, so, that the sunflowers would look yellower if she took the glasses off. But she is mistaken. The sunflowers have opened immature and really do look green. Yet some knowledge about (normal) sunflowers and the indirect supposition about the sunglasses were her grounds for discounting the green look of the sunflowers.

Suppose that she learns of her error on this and other occasions. She then weans herself of her tendency to form beliefs on the basis of the looks of things and to make inferences about the conditions under which she is perceiving. Having no grounds, direct or indirect, for belief about whether she is wearing the glasses, she is again presented with some sunflowers. They look greenish to her. In the absence of a ground for disbelieving that she is wearing blue-tinted glasses, this look is inadequate to lead her to believe either that they are as they look to her or that they really look yellow.

In this last case, the trick is played by the epistemic possibility (i.e. so far as the person knows) of a hypothesis that would, if true, defeat all the beliefs in a certain set. This is a standard-defeater that throws doubt on all the beliefs from a given source so long as the hypothesis that there is interference with the deliverances normally used for belief-formation might, for all we have grounds to believe, be true.

Generalising again, we can give the following definition of the relation of a standard-defeater to a set or type of source of beliefs:

(A) If G is a ground for potential beliefs $p_1 \ldots p_n$, then D is a defeater of $p_1 \ldots p_n$ iff the conjunction (G and the absence of a ground for disbelieving that D obtains) is not a ground for $p_1 \ldots p_n$.

The term 'ground' is being used on all three occurrences to mean the same as 'appropriately non-credulous source', and the set of potential beliefs $p_1 \ldots p_n$ is taken both distributively and agglomeratively. If the appearances to the senses of a sunflower are grounds for beliefs about its colour, then the sunglasses defeat those beliefs if and only if those appearances together with a lack of reason for disbelieving that I am wearing sunglasses, leaves me in doubt about the colour of the sunflowers. If (A) is an adequately inclusive statement of what a standard-defeater is, it will encompass also belief-defeaters of the more 'material' sort; for, where we have grounds for believing that a defeater obtains, we lack grounds for dismissing it.

A further bit of machinery. We may define a 'defeater-eater':

(B) If G is a ground for potential beliefs $p_1 \ldots p_n$ and D is a defeater of $p_1 \ldots p_n$, then E is an eater of D iff the conjunction (G, D and a ground for believing that E obtains) is a ground for $p_1 \ldots p_n$.

There are two crucially distinct ways in which an eater can satisfy (B).

In the one case, E is a reason for dismissing D. We can call this a 'devourer' of the standard-defeater. In the case of the sunglasses, if I can check, for instance by feeling my nose, that I do not have sunglasses on, then I can dismiss the hypothesis that my vision is blueshifted (by sunglasses) and so can believe that the sunflowers are the colour they look.

In the other, the eater is consistent with the presence of the defeater, but gets round it and allows some beliefs in the apparently-defeated class to be formed without vicious credulity. This is the relation of a 'nibbler' to a belief-defeater. Though I realise that I have the sunglasses on, and hence that my vision is being interfered with, I can discount in an approximate way for the blueshift and suppose that the sunflowers would look yellower to me if I took the sunglasses off, and that yellow is the colour they really look. What is more, there are many beliefs about the flowers that I can continue to repose faith in, though they are derived from sight; I can, for example, count the petals, which does not depend on colour vision.

The distinction between a devourer and a nibbler is crucial because it represents the difference between (i) the falsity of a standard-defeater, and hence the possibility of gathering grounded beliefs in accordance with the standard; and (ii) the consistency between the truth of the standard-defeater and the possibility of gathering grounded beliefs in accordance with another (generally, more stringent) standard. We shall see that this distinction makes all the difference to how we understand Descartes' handling of the different standard-defeaters that he brings into play in *Meditations* I.

Though the *Meditations* requires no more than the iteration of (A) and (B) to arrive at a defeater-eater-defeater, there is no obvious reason why, for some dialectical purposes, the sequences of doubt and resolution should not be of any arbitrary length.

Meditations I presents us with three and a half standard-defeaters. The integral hypotheses are:

(i)   that I am mad;
(ii) that I am dreaming; and
(iii) that I am the dupe of a very powerful and cunning malicious demon bent on, and frequently successful in, deceiving me.

Each of (i)–(iii) stands in the relation (A) to sets of beliefs. Descartes' movement through them is from the one that seems most likely and is least wideranging to the one that is most far-fetched but of virtually unlimited scope: standard-defeaters are empirically credible in inverse proportion to their generality. But, in accordance with (A), we do not need to find any of them in the least believable, so long as we lack an eater to show either that they do not obtain (devourer) or that, even if they do obtain, some of the beliefs they might seem to jeopardise are, nevertheless, acceptable (nibbler). As the *Meditations* progresses, Descartes indicates what he thinks are appropriate eaters of (i) and (ii): (i) is nibbled and (ii) is devoured. Though we shall see that his treatment of (ii) is less than satisfactory, there is an important exegetical point to be made from the fact that he nowhere offers any devourer of (iii); at best, the God of *Meditations* III nibbles (iii).

Standard-defeaters in the *Meditations*

Madness

The hypothesis that I am mad gets the shortest and least careful treatment of the three integral standard-defeaters encountered in *Meditations* I. It is introduced to defeat a defeater-eater of the half-defeater.

The half-defeater is the incomplete reference to the occasional deceptiveness of the senses concerning tiny and distant objects (*Med.* I, CSM II: 12). This reference is incomplete because it is subordinated, even grammatically, to the assertion that there are many other things, although from the same type of source, that one just cannot doubt (*Med.* I, CSM II: 13; AT VII 18: '[. . .] *de quibus dubitari plane non potest*'). Since I cannot doubt that I am sitting here with a piece of paper under my hand, the incipient (material) trope that Philo of Alexandria dubbed 'from places and positions' (*De Ebrietate*, 183) is nibbled.

Put in terms of the definitions of defeaters and eaters above, this fragment of argument comes out as follows. First the defeater. If the senses are my grounds for beliefs about physical objects, then the fact that I am deceived about tiny and distant objects defeats my beliefs about physical objects, because the conjunction of the sensory appearances and the absence of a ground for dismissing the possibility that I am now deceived leaves me without a ground for believing the senses. But the defeater-eater kicks in immediately. It depends on a distinction between not relying on the senses in unfavourable circumstances (when perceiving tiny and distant objects) and relying on them in favourable ones (when perceiving medium-sized things in one's vicinity). Though my beliefs about tiny and distant objects are defeated by the occasional deceptiveness of the senses about them, the standard-defeater is nibbled by the fact that that deceptiveness does not infect my beliefs about medium-sized things in my vicinity. The defeater-eater is a nibbler because it does not show that we can trust the senses about tiny and distant objects. It just sets a slightly more stringent standard for the credibility of the senses: we should limit ourselves to medium-sized things in our vicinity.

Thus, there is a moment at which the narrator of the *Meditations* reinstates beliefs derived from the senses so long as they are gathered under favourable conditions (see Frankfurt 1970: 30). But it is just a moment: the impetus is towards doubt about the distinction between the favourable and the unfavourable.

The standard-defeater of madness raises the spectre that I might believe that I am sitting here with a piece of paper under my hand, even though I am in fact doing something quite different. For, there are people who have similar delusions (*Med.* I, CSM II: 13). The set of these beliefs includes those to do with my position among medium-sized pieces of dry goods, my social rank, my clothing and the gross constitution of my body. In introducing the beliefs derived from the senses that he cannot doubt, the narrator adds 'and the like' (CSM II: 13; AT VII: 18: '*et similia*').

Though he does not specify the type of likeness, it is not hard to see that the set of beliefs that is jeopardised is very large and can be summarised as the beliefs of commonsense, in something like G.E. Moore's sense (1925), and described as the things that 'every or nearly every sane adult, who has the use of all his senses (e.g. was not born blind or deaf) knows or believes' (Moore 1962: 280), where the reference to sanity is not casual. All the members of this set are defeated by the standard-defeater that derives from the possibility that I might be mad. So long as I have inadequate grounds for disbelieving that I am at present suffering from some sort of mental aberration that could lead me into error about any (or even all) of my commonsensical beliefs, the beliefs that might have arisen as a result of such a disturbance are rendered insecure.

The hypothesis of madness defeats trust in the commonsense beliefs formed even in the favourable conditions that were implicit in the eating of the half-defeater from 'places and positions'. Descartes is cursory in dismissing this standard-defeater, almost as if he were treating it as standing in need of some evidential support. For, all he says is that he would seem just as mad as those who suffer from delusions if he took them as an example for himself (*Med.* I, CSM II: 13; AT VII: 19: '[. . .] *sed amentes sunt istis, nec minus ipse demens viderer, si quod ab iis exemplum ad me transferrem*'). This might seem too easily-won a bill of health: the narrator seems to be simply taking his belief in his own sanity as an appropriate eater of the insanity hypothesis.

Nevertheless, we can see from the form of the thing that the narrator takes himself to be justifiably confident in his own sanity, which is then taken to be a devourer of the hypothesis that he is mad. If common sense is the ground for the mass of his ordinary beliefs (acquired in favourable conditions) and the hypothesis of madness is a defeater of them, then his sanity is an eater of that defeater. If he is justified (on, perhaps, the grounds of the favourableness of the conditions of their acquisition) in believing commonsense things that seem to be inconsistent with his being is insane, then he can continue to trust to common sense. Rather than try to offer grounds for belief in his freedom from delusion, the narrator of the *Meditations* draws on a similarity between madness and dreaming to introduce his second standard-defeater.

The similarity is meant to be that in both madness and dreaming we are befuddled. Michael Williams (1986: 127–8) appositely notes some precedents in Sextus (*PH,* I, 104) and Cicero (*Acad.,* II, 27) for this assimilation, and adds a third term that is interestingly absent from the *Meditations*: drunkenness. One might easily think that drunkenness, or some other states of intoxication, would have better individuated confusion *of the senses* than do delusional madness or dreaming. For, these latter seem to involve some higher grade of elaboration of sensory inputs than drunkenness (sometimes) does: they hide their true source better. When drunk, I can, for instance, be aware of my inability to focus or reliably to locate even largish objects, such as bottles, relative to my outstretched hand. Moreover, there is some oddness in the thought that dreaming (directly) involves the senses at all; at most we have a sort of delayed and skewed perception of the sort Hobbes regards as 'caused by the distemper of some inward part of the body' (1651: 17).

How does the hypothesis concerning dreaming function as a standard-defeater? What sets of beliefs does it defeat?

Dreaming, an uneaten defeater

In the four paragraphs of the Latin version of *Meditations* I in which the dreaming hypothesis is most closely considered (CSM II: 13–14),[2] there is a pretty clear scansion into the following steps:

(a) an acknowledgement that one can be persuaded in a dream that one is in a waking condition;
(b) the posing of dreaming as a standard-defeater relative to a potential defeater-eater;
(c) a specification of the class of defeated beliefs; and
(d) the separation of the defeated class from beliefs not defeated by the hypothesis of dreaming.

In the paragraph corresponding to (a), the narrator notes how frequently a dream persuades (AT VII: 19: '*persuadet*') him when asleep that he is sitting dressed by the fire, though he is in fact lying undressed between the sheets. Two crucial ingredients for this as a standard-defeater are, first, that what he is reporting seems to be some sort of experience;[3] and, second, that, if he formed a belief in accordance with it, that belief would be false.

The first of these ingredients is meant to be equivalent to the claim that there are dreams of the sort frequently called 'lucid' (e.g. Cottingham 1986: 31–2). If there are lucid dreams, then there are sleeping states that can involve states of being, *inter alia*, persuaded. Descartes himself was an occasional lucid dreamer (see Baillet 1691: I, 80–6); but that is not essential to his case for dreams of the given sort to pose problems for other experiences of many sorts. His own history of lucid dreaming would give him evidential support of a sort that is strictly superfluous to the idea that one can have an experience that one cannot, while awake, be sure is not a dream state. It is icing on the cake of a standard-defeater that it should be, or have been, actual in the enquirer's own life.

Nor is it any objection to the hypothesis that our passage raises that many dream states are, as J.L. Austin waywardly put it, 'dream-like' (1962: 48–9); for it is irrelevant to the case in hand that '[i]f dreams were not "qualitatively" different from waking experiences, then *every* waking experience would be like a dream' (ibid.: 49, scare-quotes and emphasis original). It is enough that there could be one un-'dream-like' state that is, or, for all one knows, could be, a dream state. And there is, at least, no *prima facie* reason to rule such a possibility out; the lack of such *prima facie* grounds is enough to make the dreaming hypothesis fit the notion of standard-defeat set out schematically in (A) above.

Let us spell this out. I may suppose that a certain experience, *e*, is such that I would, in the usual run of things, not think that *e* is derived from a dream state or, even, think that *e* is not derived from a dream state; I therefore treat *e* as an experience that I can trust for the purposes of forming beliefs about the way the world is; now I raise the possibility that *e* is, after all and despite being un-'dream-like', derived from a dream state; if I find no ground (other than my usual trust to such experiences) to show that *e* is not derived from a dream state, then I have no ground for believing that *e* is trustworthy for the purpose of forming beliefs about the way the world is.

The particular contents of the dream state need not correspond to any experience of sitting dressed by a fire. Except for dreams that place the dreamer asleep in just the right state of night attire and in just the right bed (i.e. that happen to correspond to the way the world is), any lucid dream will do. With that exception, there need be nothing dully domestic about the dreams, so long as belief in accordance with them would be false.

To these two ingredients, we have to add the notion that there may be cases in which one might not be able to tell whether or not one's current experience differs qualitatively from an experience of which one subsequently learnt that it was a dream state. In terms of belief-formation, this is the possibility that I might now be acquiring beliefs in accordance with promptings from the same sort of source that, in the past, I discovered to have been a dream. If this is a possibility, then there could be states that I could get into and that, for all I know at the time I am in them, could be dream states. And this is more than an abstract possibility: it is part of fairly common experience. It is so most conspicuously in cases of my being unsure about whether some present experience that has all the qualitative feel of a memory (cf. Shoemaker 1970) is to be referred to a more or less lucid dream or to a waking experience of the sort I normally trust to (cf. Dennett 1976). I can, for instance, be haunted by a dream as if it had been something that happened to me.

To repeat, the permissive modalities here turn what might easily seem to be a silly argument into one that does license something just as threatening as Descartes' conclusion. What he says is that we can see no certain signs that enable us to distinguish sleep from waking (*Med.* I, CSM II: 13; AT VII: 19: '[. . .] *video nunquam certis indiciis vigiliam a somno posse distingui*'). What I suggest is that the machinery of the standard-defeater of dreaming licenses the conclusion that we can see no certain signs that enable us to distinguish an experience that ought to be referred to the content of a dream from one of the sort to which we usually trust, because it involves a waking experience (under favourable conditions). This conclusion does not, of course, mean that we can never distinguish; indeed, Kenny (1968: 29) says that in the oral presentation of the passage of *Sense and Sensibilia* cited above, Austin claimed that there were 'about fifty' criteria for distinguishing. Rather, however numerous they may be, the signs by which we do so are not, individually or collectively, *certain*: they do not give us grounds for dismissing outright the possibility that we may be being deceived by an element derived from dreaming. Nor can we even dismiss outright the possibility that the elements by which we may be being deceived ought to be referred to a dream that we are currently having.

One of the ways that lucid dreaming can be distinguished from the more ordinary sort of incoherent, disconnected and unnarratable dreaming is that it is the sort in which the dreamer may seem to be posing herself the question of whether she is currently dreaming or not, and even give herself a negative reply. So, there is no excessive contortion in her now considering whether she might not be in the position she remembers seeming to have been in when she was, in fact, dreaming. Contortion perhaps. But not excessive.[4] For instance, I can seriously doubt now whether the belief I have now that I have switched off the gas is prompted by a dream (or, more likely, in this case, an imagination of a habitual action, which I do not currently recall) or by the experience of actually switching off the gas. Indeed, I can be so serious about this doubt as to go and check: the doubt can prompt a fairly rational worry about gas leaks.

So, fearing the worst, the narrator of the *Meditations* draws us into his fears (*Med.* I, CSM II: 13; AT VII: 19: '[*a*]*ge ergo somniemus*' – from imperative to collusive first-person plural). Once we have allowed that, for all we can reasonably dismiss straight off, we may be dreaming, the narrator outlines the particulars ('*particularia*') that may well not be true: that our eyes are open, that our heads move, that we can stretch out – or even that we have – our hands or even any body at all (CSM II: 13). As with the madness hypothesis, what we are given at first are samples of beliefs that we might come to on the basis of a dream, but that might well not be true.

The samples Descartes cites fall into two classes corresponding to earlier references he has made. On the one hand, there are the cases of having one's eyes open and being in a certain bodily condition; these were defeated by the madness hypothesis and then reinstated when that was devoured by the (supposed and conceded) fact of the narrator's sanity. On the other hand, there are actions. The moving of the head is, earlier, taken to be a sign that one is not asleep (AT VII: 19: '[. . .] *non sopitum est hoc caput quod commoveo*'). Likewise, the stretching out of the hand is earlier said to be done 'deliberately and knowingly' ('*prudens et sciens*').

The expectation would be that, if one is to be in control of (what appears to be) one's body, then what one is in control of cannot be a dreamt object. The presupposition is that even the most lucid of lucid dreams will not allow us to (even appear to) intervene on the scene. If this were so, then the appearance of effectual action would be at least a nibbler relative to the standard-defeater of dreaming. But the expectation is dashed and the presupposition is discounted. Descartes seems to be treating states and actions on a par: the potential eater is left undeveloped and the defeater is left in place.

Instead, a futher individuation is given of what is defeated by the hypothesis of dreaming. The first part of this is, again, given by way of samples of what, in *Meditations* III, come to be classified as the ideas I make for myself.[5]

The unifying feature of the samples is stated in the fourth paragraph ((d) above) of our passage as being a matter of their compositeness (*Med.* I, CSM II: 14). But in (c), the kind is said to be that of the nature of body taken generally and its extension (*Med.* I, CSM II: 14; AT VII: 20: '*natura corporea in communi ejusque extensio*). By *Meditations* VI, and perhaps by the time of the wax example at the end of *Meditations* II, it comes to be allowed that the ideas that have to do with extended substance *qua* extended are neither adventitious nor invented; but, while the threat of the dreaming hypothesis is still in force, any beliefs we form about instances of that substance have to be counted as being defeated.

In the move from (c) to (d), Descartes gestures at a distinction between, on the one hand, the shape, quantity, size, number, place and time of extended bodies,[6] and, on the other, the simplest and most general features of them, which are the subject-matter of sciences like arithmetic and geometry (*Med.* I, CSM II: 14). The former class is made up of the objects of sciences like physics, astronomy and medicine, which are in some way doubtful (AT VII: 20: '*dubias quidem esse*'). I could dream a bit of physics, or some other non-simple matter, in such a way as to induce a belief that is mistaken. As samples of the latter class, Descartes cites the facts that, whether I am asleep or awake, two and three make five and that a square has no more than four sides; these are simple matters without which an experience would lack the coherence necessary for my being likely to mistake it for a waking state of the sort I usually trust to. Though one might have dreams in which such simplicities seem to have broken down, these would be less-than-lucid, and so not the dreams that are causing the worry.

In short, within *Meditations* I, dreaming is taken to be a standard-defeater of all non-simple beliefs, because the grounds that I might have for those beliefs are such that, if I were or had been dreaming, I could be mistaken about them. Beliefs about simple matters are the only beliefs that are excluded from the generalised doubt that dreaming induces. They are nibblers of the dreaming hypothesis, because they satisfy a more stringent standard of acceptability than the standards of, say, physics, and this standard can be met even in dreams.

The distinction between the simple and the non-simple is not fully worked out; for instance, Descartes seems to need to count among the simple things the causal principles of *Meditations* III, which do not get a mention until they are put to work. But, it is enough to be going on with to see the basic thrust of *Meditations* I, and, therefore, why Descartes invokes a standard-defeater stronger – and less believable – than the hypothesis that he might currently be dreaming.

But, before moving to consider the demon, we should see how effectively Descartes deals with the dreaming hypothesis later in the *Meditations*.

After introducing the dreaming hypothesis in *Meditations* I, Descartes pays the matter no further attention until the very end of the book. It is worth stressing the contrast with the earlier standard-defeaters. The fact of deceptiveness of the senses with regard to tiny and distant objects is immediately put in its place by the nibbler that appeals to my trustworthy perception of medium-sized objects in my vicinity. Likewise, the madness hypothesis is ridiculed without further ado and is regarded as devoured. But dreaming is set out relatively at length and left in place: the threat it poses to knowledge of non-simple matters is in force throughout the *Meditations*. This means that the operations of establishing the essence and existence of himself, of God and of extended substance are all carried forward consistent with or in the face of the hypothesis that the meditator is dreaming.

It is only in the final day's meditation that Descartes returns to consider whether he can discount the hypothesis. To see what happens, we need a little context.

Meditations VI gives an extended account of the meditator's capacity for rectifying his understanding of sensations that arise within his body, such as pains that could be in phantom limbs and thirsts that could be dropsical (*Med.* VI, CSM II: 58–61). Descartes does not aim to show that that capacity is error-free, even when properly used. Nothing in his treatment corresponds to what we saw in connection with proper use ('*ut recte utor*') in *Meditations* IV. That would be more than the weakness of human nature allows (*Med.* VI, CSM II: 62; AT VII: 90: '*naturæ nostræ infirmitas*'). But the correlations between sensations and their causes mislead us much less than they help us in matters to do with bodily well-being (*Med.* VI, CSM II: 61). For, bodily pain is a case where we need to act.[7] Thus, the way we are set up is, all things considered, the most convenient for human health and, so, not unworthy of God (CSM II: 60–1; AT VII: 87–8).

On these grounds and for these purposes, the hostility to sense-derived ideas that was centre-stage in *Meditations* I and II is relaxed: when it comes to pain, we cannot afford the minuteness with which we inspect the matters we consider when building up the edifice of secure knowledge.

In the midst of these considerations, we find a passage that it is hard to connect with the rest of the long last paragraph of *Meditations* VI. Out of the blue, the narrator announces that he has the means to explode as laughable the hyperbolical doubts of the preceding days (CSM II: 61; AT VII: 89: '[. . .] *hyperbolicæ superiorum dierum dubitationes, ut risu dignæ, sunt explodendæ*'). That is, in the terms we are using, he reminds us of the standard-defeaters of *Meditations* I and promises us an eater that will devour them. What makes it hard to connect this promise with its context is that it is very hard to see what the eater amounts to.

The defeater-eater the narrator takes himself to have can be set out as six conditions joint satisfaction of which would be sufficient and is necessary for virtuous assent to some sense-derived idea. If a sense-derived idea, P, is to inform me of how things stand, I can accept P as giving me knowledge and exploding my earlier doubts, only if:

(i) I perceive distinctly when and where P comes to me (AT VII: 90 '[. . .] *res occurrunt, quas distincte, unde, ubi et quando ihi aveniant, adverto*');[8]

(ii) I can connect P with the whole of the rest of my life (AT VII: 90: '[. . .] *cum tota reliqua vita connecto*');

(iii) I am certain that I am awake and not asleep (AT VII: 90: '[. . .] *plane certus sum, non in somnis, sed vigilanti*');

(iv) I have checked all my senses and found no other sense-derived idea, Q, such that Q conflicts with P (AT VII: 90: '[*n*]*ec de ipsarum veritate debeo vel minimum dubitare, si postquam omnes sensus* [. . .] *ad illas examinandas convocavi, nihil mihi, quod cum cæteris pugnet, ab ullo ex his nuntietur*'):

(v) I have checked with my memory and found no memory, Q, such that Q conflicts with P (as (iv) with '*memoriam*' in place of '*omnes sensus*'): and

(vi) I have checked with my intellect and found no idea, Q, such that Q conflicts with P (as (v) with '*intellectum*' in place of '*memoriam*').

Without going into the details of these conditions, it is easy to see that, even taken separately, they are extremely stringent, and that, taken jointly, they could be met only by the ideas of a person to whom error and credulity were entirely foreign. From the very beginning of the *Meditations,* the narrator admits that the beliefs he has arrived at and the ideas he has entertained form a disconnected, incoherent and confusing hodge-podge in which approximateness, doubtfulness and error are indiscriminately mixed in with the rest. Without this admission, his efforts would be silly. With it, (i)–(vi) become unfulfillable. Indeed, the whole fabric of the *Meditations* is built on the fear that, for every idea whatever (including, first of all, those derived from the senses), a defeater can be envisaged that casts doubts on its source. Unless we can find an eater either that devours the defeater by showing it to be an unreal fear, or that nibbles it by showing that some of the apparently defeated ideas are, after all, acceptable, then the defeater continues to threaten the whole class of beliefs.

Given that general observation, it might seem, the finale of the *Meditations* is rather more perplexing than it is frequently taken to be. Indeed, there seems to be a tendency to say that these considerations can be summarised as 'a resolution of the dream problem' (Dicker 1993: 177), even though no account is given of how the resolution is effected. And others have thought that here we have the reintroduction of an 'empiricist principle' that 'brings empirical data before the tribunal of reason' (Flage 1999: 251), even though no account is given of how any such data could be found anything but guilty. Let us, nevertheless, look more closely at what Descartes says about the thought that we might be dreaming; i.e. (iii).

We might be surprised to find the narrator saying that his inability to distinguish waking from sleeping was his foremost reason for doubting (*Med.* VI, CSM II: 61).[9] Even if he thinks that he has found a certain way of distinguishing dream states from waking states, he is still not out of the woods. His intellect has not, as he says it has, examined all the causes of his falling into error (CSM II: 61; AT VII: 89: '[. . .] *jam omnes errandi causas perspexit*'); for, astonishingly, he has left aside the malicious demon, which could, if it existed, cause the narrator to fall into error if he assented to any idea that seemed as if it could be sense-derived.

All the same, what Descartes offers as a defeater-eater of the dreaming hypothesis is a tyro's response. He says that the experiences of dreams are not joined up by memory as waking states are (*Med.* VI, CSM II: 61; AT VII: 89: '[. . .] *cum reliquis omnibus actionibus vitæ a memoria conjugantur, ut ea quæ vigilanti occurrunt*'). But this misses the point of the original hypothesis. For, the scare the narrator gave himself in *Meditations* I was that, for all he knew to the contrary, there might be states that seem enough like waking states to be taken for such, but that are in fact dream states, and that he might be in one now. The dream states about which he might make such mistakes are precisely those that do seem to be joined up appropriately.

Hobbes, who himself offered a similar line of thought to Descartes' barely ten years later (1651: 17),[10] raises the question in the *Third Objections* of whether a person might not dream that his dream hangs together ('*cohærere*') with his ideas of a long series of past events (*Obj.* III, obj. ult., CSM II: 137). To which Descartes replies that the connection would not be real (*Resp.* III, resp. ult., CSM II: 137). That is, indeed, what the person wants to be sure of; but he is not going to get appropriate assurance from what may be a merely apparent coherence. However we set it up, coherence can be faked in a dream or by the malicious demon either by reproduction of the regularities we are used to, hanging falsehoods together (with or without a sprinkling of truths), or by having phony regularities appear to us normal. Neither way of faking coherence can be got around by Descartes' lame appeal to what real coherence would be.

Though some commentators have suggested that Descartes would have sufficiently defended human reason if he could establish some criterion of coherence (Frankfurt 1970: 170ff.), it is hard to understand how he can answer this need by citing ideas that are connected even in some positive way by memory as waking experiences are. This would be nothing other than the coherence of our habitual dependence on the senses, which was exactly the object of the crisis in *Meditations* I. Even by the end of *Meditations* VI, the narrator still has virtually no guidelines for distinguishing conflict from consistency among ideas, especially among ideas derived from or through the senses. Without some account of how physical objects *should* look, there is no obvious procedure for checking one idea against any other; hence, a criterion of coherence is unenforceable or it presupposes that all the problems have already been solved.

In short, Descartes' claim to have found an eater of the dreaming defeater is not acceptable. It may be that the hypothesis that I may, at any given moment, be dreaming is meant to be eaten by the general considerations about divine benevolence relative to bodily well-being. If so, all the serious epistemological problems will have simply been ducked and coherence will have to do for the purposes of reducing pain. This does not respond adequately to the question of the standards to be applied in an enquiry in accordance with doxastic rectitude, where we are supposing pain not to be an issue.

Still, dreaming is not the reason that dictates the investigation of whether we can get rid of the 'very slender and, so to speak, metaphysical grounds for doubt' (*Med.* III, CSM II: 25; AT VII: 36: '[. . .] *valde tenuis et, ut ita loquar, Metaphysica dubitandi ratio est*') about the simple things of arithmetic and geometry, and that sets the terms of success in that investigation. The most powerful reason for doubt raised in *Meditations* I and subsequently is not dreaming, but the malicious demon. This hypothesis is not even faced in *Meditations* VI and is not exploded as laughable by anything said there.

The demon's reach and the criterion

Descartes' move to the introduction of the malicious demon passes through a set of reflections about the relation of the simple truths of arithmetic and geometry to the possibility that one might be deceived about them by some agent. The reflections lead him to set aside the possibility that such an agent could be a good, and therefore veracious, God. They are intended to head off the objection, which seems to have bothered only Burman, that there might be some conflict between the power of the demon and his being malicious (*Con.*, CSMK: 333).[11] Let us suppose, then, that the demon does not have to be supremely powerful, but only very powerful. Though they fill nearly two AT pages (VII: 21–2) and thus account for nearly a quarter of the text of *Meditations* I, these reflections are in some measure a mere preamble to the brief drama of the demon.

In the Latin version, the demon hypothesis occupies only the first half of the paragraph that runs from AT VII: 22 to 23; in the French, it has a paragraph to itself (AT IXA: 17–18), where it is slightly elaborated and separated from the closing animadversions about how hard it is to keep calm and focused on the idea that one might actually be mistaken about all the matters about which mistake is in any way possible. The supposition that there might be a malicious demon bent on, and frequently successful in, deceiving me,[12] functions as a standard-defeater in the following way.

So long as I have no direct grounds for dismissing the possibility that there is such an agent, the mere hypothesis of his power, cunning and efforts to deceive me succeeds in rendering at least all the beliefs defeated by the dreaming hypothesis doubtful. Descartes uses the vocabulary of dreaming to describe what would be before his mind if he were in the grip of such an agent: he says that he is treating all external things as if they were nothing but the trickery of dreams (AT VII: 22: '*ludificationes somniorum*'); vice versa, we encounter descriptions of dreaming as if it were a form of insanity (Oswald 1987: 201) The list of such external things picks up what was already covered by the earlier standard-defeaters: the sky, the earth, colour and shape were already mentioned in connection with dreaming (compare CSM II: 15; AT VII: 22 with CSM II: 14; AT VII: 20–1); and the parts of the body mentioned point back to the madness hypothesis (compare CSM II: 15; AT VII: 23 with CSM II: 13; AT VII: 18–19). And, in turn, these samples recur at the beginning of *Meditations* II (CSM II: 16; AT VII: 24: '[. . .] *nullas plane habeo sensus; corpus, figura, extensio, motus, locusque sunt chimeræ* [. . . AT VII: 25] *mihi persuasi nihil plane esse in mundo, nullum cælum, nullam terram, nullas mentes, nulla corpora*').

But it is not until *Meditations* III that the malicious demon's extra reach is made evident. There, the narrator reintroduces the easy and simple things of arithmetic and geometry that he had been thinking about, such as that two plus three make five and the like (*Med.* III, CSM II: 25). Though he can see no direct reason for doubt about these matters when he is thinking about them, he recognises that he cannot yet be sure that there is not some agent who could be deceiving him about them. So long as he cannot be sure about that possibility, there remains an indirect reason for doubt, a reason that we have already heard Descartes calling 'very slender and, so to speak, metaphysical' (CSM II: 25).

We may express the situation in the format of the definition (A) above. Whatever grounds we might have for any belief that we could be deceived about, the possibility that there is a malicious demon and the absence of an adequate reason for dismissing that possibility, taken together mean that our grounds are inadequate for the formation of any non-credulous belief. I add, in a preliminary way, that dismissing the hypothesis that there is a malicious demon is a very ticklish matter. One conspicuous reason why it is ticklish is that, if we have to have grounds to show that there is no demon, then they are precisely the sorts of things with which a demon could interfere. Hence, any state of assurance that there is no demon could itself be a deception worked by the demon: how better could such an agent secure his ends than by convincing us that he does not exist?

The dialectical position at this point seems to be this. Dreaming functions as a standard-defeater of all the narrator's beliefs about bodies and their sensible properties. The *cogito* manœuvre at the beginning of *Meditations* II opens the way to clearness and distinctness as a provisional nibbler of dreaming, and it comes to be used as an acceptance rule that provides moral certainty (*Med.* III, CSM II: 25).[13] Though the simple matters of arithmetic and geometry are clear and distinct, so long as we have no reason for believing that they are such that, however much some agent tried to deceive us about them, we have some guarantee that trumps such deception, they ought to be regarded as defeated by the possibility that there is a malicious demon.

The first commentators – with the usual exceptions of Gassendi and, later, Bourdin – make hardly any fuss about Descartes' invocation of the demon. Indeed, Hobbes, acknowledging the correctness of *Meditations* I, complains only that the material about dreaming is old hat (*Obj.* III, i, CSM II: 121, citing Plato, presumably with in mind *Theaet.* 157E–8E and *Rep.* X, 602 C–3 B); and he seems hardly to have noticed the novelty involved in the extra hypothesis. Presumably this acquiescence is in large measure accountable for by the demon's seeming to be an extension of the well-known sceptical challenges of madness and dreaming.

Yet 'extension' is a bit approximate. So it is worth comparing what we have been saying about standard-defeaters with one of Sextus' approaches to the supposition that, relative to some types of questions, there may be a guarantee against credulity. The point of the comparison is to get clearer one importantly novel feature of Descartes' use of scepticism.

The supposition that there is a guarantee against credulity is the supposition that there is a 'criterion' (*PH*, II, 14–21; cf., I, 21–4). Sextus distinguishes a variety of uses of this word and homes in on the sense, which he calls 'very special' (*PH*, II, 15: ἰδιαίτατα), in which it means every technical standard for apprehending non-evident matters (*PH*, II, 15: πᾶν μέτρον καταλήψεως τεχνικὸν ἀδήλου πράγματος). What makes matters non-evident for Sextus is that they require us to take up sophisticated and argued positions of the sort that are the special province of those whom he calls 'dogmatists' or 'professors'. At least, this is the implicit contrast with the evident matters that concern action (*PH*, I, 21) and in which we are governed or guided by our natures (sensation, thought and passion), by tradition or by the arts that have been handed down (*PH*, I, 23–4).

Sextus' non-evident matters are those that come up in the process of speculative theorising. They are the matters in which a criterion in the very special sense would have application to resolve disputes already under way among the supposed experts. But disputes do not arise among experts about, e.g. whether I have hands or a body at all, nor about whether there is an earth or the sky, nor yet about whether things have shape or colour. The existences of such things are evident matters, though their true natures and the means by which we can become acquainted with those natures are non-evident. This distinction seems to correspond in some measure to that between the simple and the non-simple matters that are separated by the dreaming hypothesis.

But there is another distinction in play here. With his application of the standard-defeater of the malicious demon to matters that Sextus might have called those of common sense, Descartes moves the frontier between what counts as 'external' to him, to include his own body, and what counts as 'internal', to restrict it to his own subjective states (Burnyeat 1982: 37, 40–1, and 44). Even if Descartes' talk of 'external' matters does not map directly onto what the ancient sceptics had to say about non-evident matters, it is still worth considering Sextus' argument against the 'very special' sense of the criterion.

At *Outlines*, II, 18–20, Sextus attributes the belief that there is such a criterion to the Stoics and others, and the belief that there is not to Xeniades of Corinth and to Xenophanes of Colophon. We therefore have a dispute about a non-evident matter, at least in the respect that, if it is to be resolved at all, it will have to be resolved by the application of a technical standard of apprehension. But the existence of such a standard is itself a non-evident matter and stands in need of just the disputed criterion if it is to be judged without credulous precipitancy. Thus a regress is launched.[14] As it is a regress of justification, the defender of the criterion cannot appeal to any standard that would be appropriate to resolving the dispute in his favour about this non-evident matter. Hence, he cannot win the argument against a suitably obstinate opponent. Note, however, that Sextus has not shown that there is no criterion, only that establishing that there is one cannot be done by means that pass through any non-evident matters.

As we have seen, the standard-defeaters that Descartes brings forward function so long as we cannot give an appropriate ground for rejecting the various hypotheses. The 'vice versa' of the material tropes does not hold unrestrictedly. Despite the sleight of hand one might suspect in his rejection of the madness hypothesis, Descartes does not, in *Meditations* I, allow it as an appropriate ground for certainty that I am not dreaming that I can, e.g. (seem to) control my head and hands, or for certainty that I am not the dupe of a malicious demon that I clearly and distinctly perceive that, e.g. two plus three makes five. The demand is that defeater-eaters – whether devourers or nibblers – outstrip the uncertainty introduced by their respective standard-defeaters. With the move to ('transcendental') scepticism about everything that is not a subjective state, which is the product of the demon hypothesis,

Descartes renders resourceless any challenge to that standard-defeater that is not an elaboration of subjective states.

The strategy, therefore, of *Meditations* III is to show that the acceptance rule of clear and distinct ideas does yield a genuine criterion of truth in the light of a demonstration that the narrator could not be in the subjective state of having the idea of God that he says he has unless there were an agent that, being good and therefore veracious, underwrote just those ideas that are clear and distinct. We might find the working out of the demonstration less than compelling; but the objective is clear: it is to put a stop to the sort of regress that Sextus plays on, by finding a guarantee independent of beliefs that the demon could interfere with. Like many moderns, the ancient sceptics would not accept that Descartes' finaglings with 'objective reality', 'material truth', 'eminent containment' and the rest of the concepts deployed in *Meditations* III are anything but non-evident. But that need not bother Descartes. He has already gone further than them by casting doubt on matters that they would count as evident: they stand accused of dogmatism about whether they have bodies. All that Sextus gives is a general argument against assenting in theoretical matters; what Descartes gives is a theoretical argument against assenting to anything that is not a subjective state or an elaboration out of the presuppositions of having subjective states.

The *Meditations* has thus raised the stakes, and the meditator has no options apart from solipsism and the exploration of the states he finds in himself (or: himself in).

Demonic powers

How the demon deceives

The power of a demon to deceive me depends on there being in me ideas with whose arising in me he is able to meddle. If he is to meddle, then there must be some stage in the process of their arising at which he can operate. Wherever he can operate, belief in accordance with ideas that could have been so meddled with is credulous and, so, improper: not knowledge. The processes with which a demon could meddle include all those that are not guaranteed by God's veracity. Hence, wherever the arising in me of an idea is the product of a process that would allow a demon to operate, I ought, for the purposes of the science that Descartes has in mind, to withhold assent. That is, I ought to be sceptical.

At its most generic, a process is a non-unit set of stages. Even at this very generic level, we can pretty quickly see both how sense-derived ideas stand, and what is required of simple truths to secure them against a possible demon.

All the sense-derived ideas I have arise within my mind at the end of a causal process; in the case of perceptual ideas of external objects, the process begins outside my body; in the case of sensations, it may begin within. In either case, there are many stages in these processes of transmission. There may be a demon that has the power to interpose extraneous elements to, subtract from or simply alter what is being transmitted without my being able to tell from the nature of the end-product. So long as I cannot dismiss the possibility that there is such a demon, all the ideas I seem to have derived from the senses must, for the purposes of science properly so-called, be regarded with fierce suspicion.

As to the simple matters of geometry and arithmetic, we must make a distinction. On the one hand, if we are considering a mathematical notion that we have picked up, e.g. at school (*Dis.* II, CSM I: 119; *Reg.* IV, CSM I: 19), then the proximate genesis of the idea indicates that a demon – or, indeed, some lesser power, such as the ordinary sort of maths teacher – could have imposed a falsehood in place of a truth. For, strictly speaking, the truths of mathematics cannot be learnt from another person: either we see them for ourselves or we do not see them at all. So, on the other hand, there are mathematical truths whose truth we can see for ourselves. Although truths such as that two plus three makes five are in one respect complex, because composed of more than one idea, Descartes indicates that this sort of complexity can be ironed out. What he offers is the thought that, by passing and repassing before the mind in a continuous motion of thought ('*cogitationis motus*') the parts of a (relatively) complex proposition, we can come to intuit the whole as if it were simple (*Reg.* VII, CSM I: 25).[15]

If, by these means, it is possible for us to embrace in a single thought a complex matter, then what is removed is any sense of there being a chain of reasoning leading up to it (*Reg.* VII, CSM I: 25; AT X: 388: '*conclusionum intermediarum concatenatio*'; cf. *Dis.* II, CSM I: 120; AT VI: 19: '*chaîne des raisons*'); for, in a chain, there are links and a demon could interfere with the transmission from one to the next. In this way, the only results of inference that are permissible are those that can be intuited as if they were immediate (cf. Gaukroger 1987: 116–26); only then will the intellect be able to stretch out to new truths (*Reg.* VII, CSM I: 25; AT X: 388: '[. . .] *hoc enim pacto* [. . .] *ingenii* [. . .] *capacitas quadam ratione extenditur*'), which are sure to be free from demonic interference.

Even so, on the model of belief-formation examined in Chapters 4 and 5, the final member of the set of relevant stages would be that at which assent is given to an idea. So, whenever there is a gap between the presentation of an idea in the intellect and the affirmation by the will, there is a stage at which a demon could meddle. For this reason, any idea that does not command spontaneous and unhesitating assent is one that, for all we know, is not guaranteed against his intrusions. This requirement need not be that, at first presentation, a great light flow from a given idea, but only that, on some presentation, it command spontaneous assent and, thus, be regarded as invulnerable.

So long as, for all he knows to the contrary, he may be being deceived by a malicious demon about all the matters that he derives from any non-unit process, whether causal or inferential, Descartes' narrator offers motivated doubt that extends to every idea that he must, in any way, *acquire*. If a properly-conducted science is to cohabit with that enduring possibility, then Cartesianism requires us to be sceptical of every idea that is not guaranteed by the divinely-underwritten criterion of clear and distinct ideas.

What we have to work out, then, is how long we are going to be in ignorance about whether or not there is a malicious demon: will science always have to cohabit with the possibility that there is one?

A veracious God, not a voracious one

In admitting that, in dreams, the things that appear still have some shape and so on, Descartes admits that there are some ideas that nibble dreaming as a standard-defeater; when clearly and distinctly perceived, the simplest matters of arithmetic and geometry are not defeated by the hypothesis.

A defeater-eater that nibbles by vindicating some of the apparently defeated beliefs is very different from an eater that devours the standard-defeater by showing that the threat it poses can be dismissed. Dreaming is a standard-defeater that would be devoured by any reason (i) that is exempt from that defeater; and (ii) that shows that we are not dreaming. We saw that it was hard to understand Descartes' apparent effort to find such a devourer which did not end up being either inadequate, because applicable only to the avoidance of pain, or simply unfulfillable by any being that needs such a guarantee.

Likewise, the demon would be devoured by any reason (i) that could not be imposed on us by him; and (ii) that disproves his existence. This looks like a promising approach. For instance, some recent discussions have focused on the respects in which we might be unable to believe that there is a demon. Given that we know many things inconsistent with the truth of the hypothesis, it is one that we cannot seriously entertain (Nozick 1981: 207ff.). In our adopted terminology, the hypothesis is treated as an ordinary belief-defeater, which is itself defeated by our everyday certainties about, e.g. the gross constitution of the world around us. Others have argued that it is not possible for us even to entertain anything that is, strictly speaking, the thought that there is a malicious demon (Putnam 1977; and 1981: Chapter 1).[16] But Descartes does not even seek such a devourer. Instead, the only argument he gives is aimed at defending the thesis that some ideas are exempt from interference by a malicious demon: there is a nibbler.

The demonstration he offers in *Meditations* III that responds to the demon threat is aimed at establishing that there is an agent (God) that vindicates only clear and distinct ideas. All other ideas, including the obscure and confused ideas of sense, are subject to the continuing epistemic possibility of demonic interference; assent to them is credulity.

It may appear scandalous to say that the final position of the *Meditations* excludes sense-derived ideas as possible sources or objects of knowledge. But we can arrive at that conclusion by another route, which is meant to be more charitable to Descartes than an attempt to wrench a defeater-eater of dreaming out of the unconvincing considerations about coherence at the close of *Meditations* VI. Unfortunately, the alternative I wish to propose is at odds with a reading that has been accepted by some of the most acute recent Cartesian commentators. Their reading seems uncharitable because it attributes to Descartes a key move that is unwarranted.

In setting out Descartes' 'validation of reason', H.G. Frankfurt expresses himself as follows: 'the proof that God exists precludes the existence of a Demon' (Frankfurt 1970; cf. Beck 1965: 142). The justification given is derived from the impossibility that there could be two omnipotent beings, though we have already seen signs of Descartes' caution in not supposing that the demon is omnipotent, but just very powerful. Likewise, A. Kenny, introducing considerations on the coherence of the demon hypothesis, refers to 'the reason Descartes later offers for its refutation, namely, that it is incompatible with the existence of a veracious, benevolent and omnipotent God' (Kenny 1968: 36), though the 'later' is not flagged or the incompatibility spelt out. For B. Williams, it follows from God's not being a deceiver, 'that the malicious demon who was suggested as a universal cause of error does not exist' (Williams 1978: 163); similarly, N. Kemp Smith: 'this hypothesis of an evil Genius has been shown to be inconsistent with what immediate experience discloses to us viz. the existence and nature of God' (Smith 1952: 289). M. Gueroult puts an analogous claim in terms of alethic validation, when he writes of 'the proof of divine veracity, destroying the hypothesis of the malicious demon at its roots' (1953: I, 287).

This looks like a consensus of the wise on the thought that Descartes does something to preclude, refute, exclude or destroy the hypothesis of the malicious demon. There is less than universal consent about how the alleged incompatibility is to be formulated (Curley 1978: 42 n.); and there is reason for doubting that any of the alleged incompatibilities can be found spelt out in Descartes. As it happens, none of the judgments cited in the last paragraph is accompanied by a reference to any particular passage of his writings. At the very least, there is this fact: after the beginning of *Meditations* II, Descartes does not return to consider the possibility that there is not a demon or to reconsider the possibility that there is. Nor, in the *Replies* to the objectors who raise questions about the demon (as already noted, Gassendi and Bourdin), does he try to argue that there comes a moment at which the possibility of there being one can be suspended.

There may, as a matter of fact, be incompatibilities between the existence of the sort of God argued for in *Meditations* III and V, and the existence of the malicious demon of the sort hypothesised. But Descartes does not himself argue for any such incompatibility in the *Meditations* nor, to the best of my knowledge, in any other text published or unpublished. If people have grounds for defending an interpretation of his philosophy that does involve his offering, or being committed to, arguments that show that there is not or could not be a demon, it seems to me that the burden of proof is on them to illustrate those grounds.

So far as I am aware, no one has yet removed that burden. The thesis that Descartes views the existence of the malicious demon as compossible with the existence of a veracious God may be widely held: by the many rather than by the wise just cited. But I am not aware of its having been as explicitly and emphatically supported as I aim to do here.

There are general grounds for thinking that Descartes would not find a hypothesis of the sort incoherent. Indeed, the existence of the Devil was (and is) a widespread positive belief to explain not only the sin and evil in the world but also the forty-odd references to him, under various names, in the New Testament, not to mention his very early appearance in *Genesis* to get the interesting part of human history going. Even so, the supposition of such a being's actual existence is more than is needed for the standard-defeater. Without going to the extreme of attributing to him a Manichean belief in a principle of darkness on a par with divine benevolence, there is no reason to suppose that Descartes would have seen any overall inconsistency between the existence of a veracious God and that of an agent bent on and powerful enough to deceive so weak and credulous a creature as the *Meditations*' narrator.

When he poses himself the question of whether there is a God and, if there is, whether He can be a deceiver, Descartes' narrator does not set himself to show that there is any incompatibility between the actual or possible (for all he can prove) existence of a deceiving demon and the existence of a God.

At the point in *Meditations* III where he poses this question, he is addressing a single issue, albeit presenting two aspects. What he says might be translated as follows:

So long as that (reason for doubting) is still to be removed, I should take the first occasion to examine whether there is a God and, if there is one, whether He can be a deceiver (*Med.* III, CSM II: 25; AT VII: 36 '[*u*]*t autem etiam illa* [sc. *ratio dubitandi*] *tollatur, quamprimum occurret occasio, examinar an sit Deus, et, si sit, an possit esse deceptor*').[17]

To someone who is anxious to find an incompatibility of the sort needed, there might seem to be a slight grammatical possibility that the Latin raises questions with two separable subjects: whether there is a God and, (even) if there is, whether there can (also) be a deceiver. Thus it might occur to someone to suppose that the subject of the second '*sit*' is '*Deus*', but that of the '*possit*' is '*esse deceptor*', taken to mean something like 'an existing deceiver'. A defence of this reading would have to appeal to some principle of Latin grammar alien to me. But, grammar apart, there are at least three grounds that certainly exclude so unwarranted a reading.

One, trivially, is that Descartes uses the singular in saying that, so long as he is in the dark about this matter, he will not be able to be sure about anything else (AT VII: 36: '*hac enim re ignorata non videor de ulla alia certus esse unquam posse*'). The matter he wants to know about is whether such a God as he might discover could be a deceiver.

Second, the French version of the passage is very clear about taking the question to concern whether or not God can be a deceiver (AT IXA: 28–9: '[. . .] *je dois examiner s'il y a un Dieu* [. . .]; *et si je trouve qu'il y en ait un, je dois examiner s'il peut être trompeur*'). The French passed under Descartes' hands, and is often thought to represent a reliable reflection of his considered views. Here, a significant change in wording would have been called for to give the sense that what is at issue is the compatibility of God's existence with the existence of a deceiver. The anti-compatibilists would need something like '*s'il peut y avoir un trompeur*', which we have no reason for putting in place of what the text says.

Third, more philosophically, the argumentation of *Meditations* III is directed only at establishing two theses, namely:

(a)   there is a God; and
(b)   He is not a deceiver.

I should expect it to be common ground that he is trying to establish both (a) and (b). There is notoriously room for discussion about how far he succeeds in establishing (a). But that is not at issue. And Descartes takes himself to have established (b) when he says, in clear reference to God at the end of *Meditations* III, that it is adequately clear that He cannot be a deceiver (CSM II: 35; AT VII: 52: '*satis patet illum fallacem esse non posse*'). Those who wish to defend the incompatibility of the existence of God with that of the deceiving demon, have to illustrate that there is some argument, in *Meditations* III or elsewhere, for a third thesis, namely:

(c)   there is no deceiver.

It will not do to say that the arguments in favour of (a) and (b) establish (c) because, crudely, they do not. (c) does not follow from (a) and (b) nor does it follow from any of the considerations that Descartes adduces in favour of (a) or (b); to argue for (c) from (a) and (b) is to argue badly.

It is uncharitable to attribute (c) to Descartes on the grounds that he argues for (a) and (b), because it is uncharitable to attribute obviously bad arguments to people unless one is forced to. Here we are not forced to. To argue from what Descartes does take himself to have established in *Meditations* III to (c) is to attribute to him an obviously bad argument. Descartes does not give any argument, good or bad, in *Meditations* III or, so far as I know, elsewhere, to suppose that (c), nor does he give grounds for attributing to him any (good) argument to show that (c).

Descartes pays no further attention to any question to do with whether there might be any agent other than God that is a deceiver. And, to repeat, he does not set himself the question of whether or not there is any sort of incompatibility between the existence of a non-deceiving God and a malicious demon. He leaves the possibility open, in just the way that my not being a Frenchman leaves the possibility open that there are Frenchmen. Likewise, it would be uncharitable to attribute to my friend a belief that there are no Frenchmen on the grounds that she believes that I am not one.

There being a God who is not a deceiver does not, for all Descartes tells us, imply that there is no deceiver: at the end of the *Meditations,* we know no more about whether or not we might be deceived about all or any of the ideas that are not guaranteed by God's veracity than we did at the beginning of the second day. God's not being a deceiver does not mean that I cannot be deceived, but only that I cannot be deceived *about any matter that I have on His authority*. It is therefore worth recalling which are the ideas that I can have on His authority. They are only the ideas that are, and that I perceive to be, clear and distinct, from which a great light flows, and to which I freely and spontaneously assent once I have clearly and distinctly perceived them. These are a sub-set of the ideas that I find in my intellect. All other ideas are such that I might be deceived about them especially if there is a malicious demon, and about which I do not know whether or not I am deceived, because I do not know whether or not there is a malicious demon.

In terms of the distinction between types of standard-defeater-caters, the position that I am thinking of as uncharitable to Descartes attributes to him the thesis that God is a devourer of the demon hypothesis. This requires it to be shown not only that there is an incompatibility between the existence of God and the existence of the malicious demon, but also that Descartes somewhere offers an account of such an incompatibility. It is more faithful and more charitable to regard Descartes' God as a nibbler of the demon hypothesis: the existence of a veracious God does not exclude, preclude, refute or destroy the hypothesis of the malicious demon. Even if there is a malicious demon who renders all my *other* sources of potential belief doubtful, I can be certain about clear and distinct ideas because they continue to be guaranteed by God.

How scepticism is a vice

We began the last chapter by recalling how it has seemed that scepticism was a – even *the* – public nuisance in Descartes' day. What we have ended up with is an account on which sceptical manœuvres are properly applied to almost all the sources of our beliefs. We are meant to suspend involvement so far as possible in everyday affairs and to cultivate (Pyrrhonist) indifference to them. And we are meant to conduct the enquiry to which the *Meditations* is a prelude in such a way as to allow that demon scepticism's threat to knowledge is in force.

One moral that might be drawn from this situation is that scepticism is not a vice. And we have already seen that scepticism is not a vice in the way that credulity is. It is not the sort of thing that is likely to become a habit or a matter of second nature, it is not forced on us by biological necessity, and it is not the sort of attitude that can be unconsidered. It is nevertheless a vice in that it declines a serious interest in the beliefs that we are, even on Descartes' exigent scheme of things, permitted and required to assent to. If so, we have to be clear about the way in which, in the definition from which we started at the beginning of the last chapter, scepticism is 'the doxastic vice of not acquiring true beliefs though they are available to be acquired'.

The Pyrrhonist sceptic's generalised refusal of non-evident ideas is vicious because, as Descartes aims to show, attention to the notions that are available to us can lead to the elaboration of doctrines that are immune to the onslaughts of the 'material' tropes. In any case, global scepticism, which says that nothing can be known, not only refutes itself, but is refuted by the fact that I can know, among other things, that I exist. Hence it is a position to which we should not be attracted. Furthermore, by arguing for the truth of clear and distinct ideas underwritten by a benevolent God, even in the face of a malicious demon of great power and cunning in deceiving him, Descartes does everything that could be asked to outstrip the sceptical arguments directed at showing that there could be no criterion. He does so by offering a criterion that he thinks could only be doubted by a person who did not *want* to get out of the state of ignorance and perplexity that the sceptic wishes to emphasise.

Here, then, is the vice of scepticism: it is the vanity of wanting no one to get out of the hole that it is easy to think we are all in, and the sloth of refusing to look for ways of getting out of a hole it is easy to get into.

Nevertheless, it has not been popular to visit on Descartes so wide-ranging a capitulation to scepticism. For he would seem to have failed to defeat the enemy of what is generally thought of as knowledge. So there seem to be only two plausible ways of understanding the position. On one, Descartes simply forgot about the threat that the demon poses. In that case, Cartesian epistemology would be a mere muddle. This was why some early interpreters thought that Descartes was a miserable failure in the fight to vindicate 'any foundation so solid that it could not be shaken by some of the standard gambits from the arsenal of Sextus Empiricus' (Popkin 1960: 210). Either through self-deception or in an attempt to deceive others, he turns out to be a '*sceptique malgré lui*' (ibid.: title to Chapter X). On an alternative understanding, the fact that the possibility of the demon is nowhere excluded means that we need to reconstrue what is to count as knowledge, because most of us do not attain anything that deserves the name (cf. Scott 1995).

The trouble that some observers have seen lurking in the second line of thought is that it seems to land Descartes with a doctrine that has been called 'lunatic apriorism' (Frankfurt 1978: 29; also Clarke 1982: 83–7), according to which all knowledge that counts as such must be 'spun' out of the basic principles of metaphysics (also Kenny 1968: 206, 213; Williams 1978: 256, 265–8). From the adjective 'lunatic' we see that it has seemed improper to attribute to Descartes any such doctrine; it would be better if we could find some non-lunatic doctrine to fit his case, and, so, a doctrine that is not apriorist.

In the last three chapters below, I set out an account of how to apply the method that is the direct subject of the next chapter. In giving this account, I attribute to Descartes a theory that may properly be called 'apriorism'. I also seek to show that, though it does have elements of spinning physics out of metaphysics, it is nevertheless not – at least in context – lunatic. Rather, I shall take a leaf out of the books of commentators who have located Descartes' position as fitting into a tradition stretching back to Plato and as part of an Augustinian trend in seventeenth-century France (Abercrombie 1938: Chapter 5; Gouhier 1978; Clark 1992; Menn 1998; Janowski 2000: esp. 141–9). These sorts of contextualisations need not establish any specific causal link between, on the one hand, Plato or Platonism and St Augustine or Augustinianism, and, on the other, Descartes. After all, St Augustine's Illumination theory was itself based on an indirect link with Plato, through sources that were '*libri Platonicorum*' (*Conf.*, VII ix, 13) meaning, principally, Plotinus, plus Cicero's translations and digests (Augustine, *Acad.*, III, 18, 41; Courcelles 1968: 168ff.). But it embarrasses no one to think of St Augustine as a Platonist. Likewise, though there is reason for doubting that Descartes was particularly well acquainted with St Augustine's writings (Gouhier 1924: 290; Rodis-Lewis 1950: 33–5),[18] it has been justly observed that, 'Augustine was part of the background against which Descartes and his contemporaries defined themselves' (Menn 1998: x), which explains why he was pleased to be told on occasion that the ideas he expresses are in accord with St Augustine.[19] What appeal to this background can help us to see is how, in the face of similar intellectual pressures, Descartes works out his position in ways that are anything but 'lunatic'.

Already in eighteenth-century France, among Descartes' supporters, there was a tendency to overlook or downplay his innatism. As G. Rodis-Lewis has illustrated (1951), the 'Discours préliminaire' to the *Encyclopédie* (1751) takes firmly against this part of his theorising. Likewise, in the articles on 'idea', 'innate' and 'first principle', there is considerable disquiet about how to get around this pretty evident part of Descartes' doctrine without having to brand him as in some way backward (see Spallanzani 1990: 133–47). And it is interesting to note that a full-scale study of the reception of Descartes in the Enlightenment (Schouls 1989) omits the question altogether.

The embarrassment felt about attributing to Descartes a doctrine that can be called 'apriorism' – and that consequently gets put down as 'lunatic' – may be traced to the influentialness – both in eighteenth-century France and since – of the anti-innatist polemic in Book I of Locke's *Essay* and of the cultural matrix of modern science into which its empiricist message has been incorporated (see, e.g. Yolton 1956: Chapter 1). The presumption has got itself accepted that, unless we can give the causes of an idea, it is somehow suspect. We saw in Chapter 5 how this presumption leads to a sort of passivity or determinism about belief-formation. Here, I observe that it also has the effect of leaving the field wide open for the demon, if there is one. The causation of adventitious ideas is just the sort of thing that a sceptic can capitalise on to show the shakiness of what an empiricist wants to palm off on us as knowledge. And it is no surprise that scepticism was on the rise in Descartes' day precisely because the empirical sciences were making unprecedented progress. For, empiricism as an epistemological doctrine is the sorry tale of finding scepticism a 'problem' (again, Stroud 1984: 1).

Because, that is, the popular aim is to show that Descartes' treatment of scepticism should allow him to 'champion a modified empiricist principle at the end of the *Meditations*' (Flage 1999: 7), the tendency is to say that 'the *fact* that an idea is innate appears to bear little or no epistemic importance' (ibid.: 49) because clearness and distinctness is the only criterion of truth and, so, innateness would be redundant (ibid.: 52). While many commentators see why there must be at least some types of enquiry in which, for Descartes, innate ideas are essential (e.g. Smith 1952: XII; Grosholz 1991: Chapter 7; Garber 1992a: Chapter 2), it is disappointing that others are unsure why any enquiry whatever should centre entirely on ideas that we are supposed to be able to find in ourselves (e.g. Williams 1978: 132–5; Wilson 1978: 168–72), hardly discuss the matter at all (e.g. Frankfurt 1970; Curley 1978), or attribute to Descartes doctrines that are diametrically opposed to what, on the reading I shall be proposing, he clearly and repeatedly declares he is doing (e.g. Clarke 1982: 2, 8, 10, 35–6, 83–4, 92, 103). But this is to leap ahead.

Either we do not take the cataclysm of *Meditations* I seriously or we see why, in taking it seriously, Descartes has to find sources of science other than in the confused and obscure deliverances of the senses. To suppose that he has, in some simple way, the means to shore up the cataclysm is not only to ignore some distinction between 'devourers' and 'nibblers', but also to underestimate his willingness to envisage a total renewal of his doxastic habits. The ominous reasons he supplies for doubt cannot be simply brushed aside; if anything that should be counted as secure science is to get going, those reasons call for an overhaul of what knowledge is. So, Descartes has to choose between the sceptical capitulation of solipsism, and thoroughgoing innatism. In trusting uniquely to the clear and distinct ideas he finds illuminated in himself by God, Descartes establishes a standard of assent-worthiness that both exhausts the resources of the classical Pyrrhonist and yet appears to admit of progress in the investigation of the essential characteristics of the created world. Even if this seems to surrender to the sceptic everything he might have wanted, the Cartesian project can be seen as wholly redirecting attention away from the matters on which the doubts of *Meditations* I have any purchase, and towards those that not even a demon could meddle with.

This re-direction begins with the denial that it is possible to be in doubt about one's own existence. Where it goes from there is all to play for.

Part IV

The mean

8 *Tota methodus*

Direction and method

We come now to the matter of what Descartes has to say about how to enquire virtuously. Our principal text is a well-known passage of about a hundred and seventy words from *Discourse* II (CSM I: 120; AT VI: 18–19; AT VI: 550) in which Descartes puts forward four precepts that he says he thinks are adequate for the proper conduct of his enquiry (AT VI: 18: '*je crus que j'en aurais assez des quatre*'). This will seem in some ways disappointing. Not just for the usual reason that it is hard not to be dull in talking about virtue. But also because what Descartes has to say seems perfunctory, being both brief and schematic; indeed, one commentator has observed that the instructions Descartes gives are proposed more as a riddle than as guidance for the reader (Liard 1882: 12). A major and enduring complaint, made by Leibniz and taken up others,[1] has been that nothing this short could constitute an illuminating guide. Against this criticism, I offer a partial defence of Descartes. The defence is only partial because the following chapters explore how the message of our passage can be applied without its being a guide, but allowing it to be illuminating. If I am to succeed in my partial defence of Descartes, what I have to make plausible is the idea that a method may be a procedure that can be rigidly applied without necessarily being fully expressible as a body of doctrine.

To throw more light on the passage of the *Discourse*, we shall be referring also to parallel texts in, most prominently, the *Rules*. By way of preliminary, it is worth noting how Descartes uses a significant word near-neologistically, in the titles of these two works.

Descartes' French word for method ('*méthode*') first appeared in the language in the sense of collection of rules or normative principles for the discharge of a skill in a passage of Rabelais of 1546 (*Larousse*); its absence from Huguet (1925) might indicate that, as a Rabelaisianism, it was not regarded as decent French. The currency of the word derived from its use in medicine, where, with one of those nice turns, it denoted a very strong form of traditionalism (Lloyd 1983: 183ff.; Frede 1983). In the sixteenth century, the word '*methodus*' was taken up by logicians and others in a sense, added to the Greek sense of 'a way of getting through', to mean something like a systematic arrangement of knowledge for use. These are developments that have been much studied (see Gilbert 1960; Stephens 1975: Chapter 2; Jardine 1988; Garber 1992a: 30–62; Dear 1998). Even so, its absence from Niziolius (1588) might indicate that it was not regarded as proper Latin.

In employing '*méthode*' in a sense in which a method could be described as 'analytic' or 'synthetic', namely – to be going on with – that in which it means a manner of proceeding in the sciences, Descartes is pretty certainly an innovator in French. Yet it is worth remembering that he does not refer to synthesis once in either the *Rules* or the *Discourse*. Although he does talk of '*methodus*' in the *Rules*,[2] he occasionally uses the simpler, but etymologically analogous, word for a way or route ('*via*').[3]

Likewise, one version of the title of the *Rules* specifies that what should happen to the mind is that it take on 'direction'.[4] While the cognate verb was not rare in classical Latin, the noun ('*directio*') was so (Lewis and Short). In later Latin, its primary use was legal, meaning a right or a claim, making its appearance in this sense in 1054 at the Council of Narbonne (Niemeyer 1976). Although St Thomas uses the adjective '*directivus*' in something like Descartes' sense (Blaise 1975), it is charming to find that '*directio*' had some currency as a term for the west–east movement of heavenly bodies in epicycle theory (Latham 1965), which is perhaps as far as one could get from Descartes' attempt to convey singleness of purpose, aim, concentration, focus, resolve and the like.

What makes up the 'direction' are rules and what makes up the 'method' are precepts (*Dis.* II, CSM I: 119: 'techniques'; AT VI: 17: '*préceptes*'; AT VI: 549: '*præcepta*') or instructions (*Dis.* II, AT VI: 17: '*instructions*'). These are jussive or imperative notions, rather than descriptions, presupposing that the person to whom they are addressed is already party to the sort of enquiry Descartes has in mind.

The *Rules* gives indications about the application of the intended set of thirty-six rules and it has been conjectured that the work was abandoned when Descartes became discouraged at the seemingly endless proliferation of these practical hints (Descartes 1925: 196). The *Discourse*, by contrast, presents its four precepts flatly, leaving the application of them to be seen from the development of the text and from the *Essays*.[5] Nevertheless, for reasons we shall examine at the beginning of the next chapter, there is nothing in the first part of the *Rules* that is not, in one way or another, implicit in the precepts and unfolding of the *Discourse*.

Descartes' route to this summary version is only spelt out negatively, in terms of the shortcomings of the subjects studied at school, some of which we reviewed in Chapter 6, and which he would have had in mind also when composing the *Rules*. If justification were to be given for the greater compression in the *Discourse*, it would presumably be in terms of his analogy between the sciences and the laws of the land: a country is better governed by few, even imperfect, laws strictly applied than by many that have arisen as *ad hoc* responses to disorder (*Dis*. II, CSM I: 120). This demands that anyone who is to operate the method should share not only Descartes' aims, but also the requisite alertness to the pitfalls that humans have to negotiate.

We have already noted, and shall explore further in the following chapters, that Descartes is committed to the thesis that all humans have a sufficiency of the materials out of which to construct the science he is aiming at. The notions on which attention is to be focused are in an important respect constitutive of the act of thinking. The question is: what can and should we do with the materials we have? This is a matter of the power of judging well or capacity for distinguishing the true from the false, the 'good sense' or 'reason' with which *Discourse* I opens and which is subsequently said to be naturally equal in all men (*Dis*. I, CSM I: 111).[6] Such inequalities as there are among humans are to be located either in their natural ability (*Reg*. IX, CSM I: 34; *Dis*. I, CSM I: 111–12) or in their taste for this sort of exacting enquiry (cf. *Reg*. X, CSM I: 35). Those who are just cleverer will get on more quickly, though they are more likely to go astray: in a tortoise-and-the-hare sort of way, excess of skill can subvert virtue. Those who are ready to stick with the task may get further with it (*Dis*. I, CSM I: 111).

Thus, Descartes insinuates an equality between himself and his reader, indicating that no factor either external or internal is an abiding or insuperable obstacle to the prosecution of the project in hand. The only reason why someone might fail in it is by a failure of application. This is a message we have already heard. On introducing his precepts, Descartes repeats it, speaking of a 'firm and constant resolution' (*Dis*. II, CSM I: 120; AT VI: 18: '*ferme et constante résolution*') not to fail even once to observe his precepts.

What, then, are they?

The first precept – evidence

The first precept falls into two parts. One is to do with truth and the sources of error. The other is to do with the relation of clearness and distinctness to doubtfulness.

The first part can be rendered:

> The first [sc. precept] was never to take anything as true that I did not evidently know to be such: that is to say, carefully to avoid rushing and

conservatism (*Dis.* II, CSM I: 120; AT VI: 18: '[*l*]*e premier était de ne recevoir jamais aucune chose pour vraie, que je ne la connusse évidemment être telle: c'est à dire, d'éviter soigneusement la précipitation et la prévention*').

The two sources of error that Descartes identifies here are those that arise from the time constraints that apply in ordinary life, but not in the circumstances of the secluded enquiry. Each of what I have rendered as 'rushing' and as 'conservatism' has a variety of causes, and these causes overlap with each other.

In addition to various forms of inattentiveness or overeagerness (cf. *Reg.* XIII, CSM I: 54), rushing (*la précipitation*) may be the result of a sort of vanity that induces us to form opinions where we would do better to be honest about our ignorance.[7] In such cases, what is in play is a readiness to affirm what we do not really understand which, as we saw in Chapter 4, is at the basis of all error. In ordinary life, this readiness is understandable as a response to time-urgent demands on our attention; but in seclusion, we can dictate our own pace, and we can watch ourselves forming beliefs, as it were, in slow motion.

Conservatism (*la prévention*) is the vice of holding on to opinions one already has in such a way as to prevent the formation of new ones. This is sometimes characterised as a matter of prejudices, meant not in the sense of blanket judgments, but just in that of already having beliefs that are not subjected to scrutiny (*Pr.* I, 71, CSM I: 218; AT VIII: 35: '*præjudicia*'). If I have already formed a certain belief, I will be apt not to reconsider it or to change it unless I am challenged. Cartesian seclusion permits, and this precept requires, me to challenge even matters that I did not think it worth reconsidering or changing my mind about.

While rushing gets us beliefs for which we might have less than adequate warrant, conservatism keeps the beliefs we happen to have, whether we initially had warrant for them or not. Use of the beliefs we already have is also a species of rushing: rather than go out and re-examine a given matter, we make do with what we already have because it is quicker to do so. Conversely, the ways in which we form our beliefs about matters where it is better to have some belief than none may be upshots of the beliefs that we antecedently hold fixed. For instance, if I already have a lot of beliefs about the colouredness of things, such as pieces of wax, I may allow myself to be rushed into judging that there is redness in this ball simply because it would be such a chore to undo all the others.

The reciprocal relation between rushing and conservatism is not that which holds between two opposed vices relative to a virtue: both are excesses in belief-acquisition and, being forms of inadvertence (*Reg.* II, CSM I: 12; AT X: 365: '*inadvertentia*'), causes of credulity. Their corrective is caution or care

(*Dis.* II, AT VI: 18: '*soigneusemente*'),[8] which is expressed by the effort to lay aside our most ingrained doxastic habits by the invocation of reasons for generalised doubt, as gestured at in *Discourse* IV and more fully rehearsed in *Meditations* I.

Descartes offers no argument for the claim, implicit in his 'that is to say' connecting the clauses of the first part of his first precept, that, so long as we are careful, we can take as true the things we evidently know to be such. But it is not obvious that he owes us such an argument. On the one hand, the claim seems fair enough: if something is, indeed, known to be true, then it is true and there need be nothing amiss about my taking it as such. On the other, as the *Discourse* unfolds, explanation is given of how being evidently known by me is a sign that a thing is guaranteed to be so by a veracious God.[9] Even if this explanation is not available at the stage of the work here under consideration, it nevertheless provides what we earlier called an 'indirect validation' for associating what is evidently known with what is true. If, therefore, we avoid the principal sources of error, we will be able to locate some things that we find we can evidently know to be true.

To the extent that the method is a means for the discovering of the truth of things, the fact of something's being true, as offered in the first part of the precept, can figure only proleptically in the specification of that means. Consequently, evidently knowing something to be true cannot be a means, but is rather a mark of success. So, we are looking for the marks of the things that we can include in our judgments that will lead to that sort of success.

What is involved in evidently knowing something to be true is spelt out in the second part of the precept:

> [. . .] and not to include in my judgments anything more than what would present itself to my spirit so clearly and so distinctly that I should have no occasion to cast it into doubt (*Dis.* II, CSM I: 120; AT VI: 18: '[. . .] *et de ne comprendre rien de plus en mes jugements, que ce qui se présenterait si clairement et si distinctement à mon esprit, que je n'eusse aucune occasion de le mettre en doute*').

A couple of linguistic observations.

One is that this passage is separated by a mere semi-colon from the patch I have been thinking of as the first part of the precept. This punctuation might be regarded as dictated by the colon that precedes the 'that is to say'. On the other hand, Descartes' use of the 'was' ('*était*') at the beginning of his list as governing the infinitives in all four precepts, means that he could, with grammatical or stylistic consistency, have started a new sentence and raised the number of precepts to five. Roth makes a similar suggestion in his (1937: 69ff.) but, with a view to exploiting an analogy with Bacon, divides the clauses around the 'that is to say' and jettisons what I am thinking of as the second part. The fact that Descartes keeps the parts together, and separates them by a paragraph break from the other precepts, presumably means that he regards them as correlated.

Again, there is something a little unsettling about the shift from the infinitive structure of the first part to the conditional of the second.[10] Where, in the first part, there is strong suggestion that there are many things that Descartes does evidently know, in the second, there is at least a hint that he is still waiting for something to present itself clearly and distinctly, and consequently to be immune to doubt.

Given the importance that clearness and distinctness have in Descartes' account of what knowledge is, it is worth remembering that there is some variation in his terminology as between the *Discourse* and the other texts in which the pair have a central part to play.

The differences in formulation may amount to very little. After all, it would be extravagant to expect a set of texts written over a period of more than fifteen years in two languages and by a variety of hands to be utterly uniform on a matter where Descartes was introducing and manipulating nascent terms of art, rather than following some antecedent usage. There is also room for doubt about whether it is proper to help ourselves to the stipulations in *Principles* I, 45–6 about how 'clearness' and 'distinctness' should be used in order to expound the assertions he makes using them or their analogues in the *Rules*, the *Discourse* and the *Meditations*. Except in the *Principles*, Descartes is not generally concerned to define his terms.

Rules II defines knowledge as certain and undoubted awareness (AT X: 362: '*certa et indubitata cognitio*').[11] This is echoed by what we find in *Meditations* II, where the result of the *cogito* manœuvre is held to be the most certain and most evident piece of awareness the narrator has (AT VII: 25: '*certissima evidentissimaque*'; cf. AT IXA: 20: '*plus certaine et plus évidente*'), which is reiterated as what is certain and unshakeable (*Med.* II, CSM II: 17; AT VII: 25: '*certum et inconcussum*'; AT IXA: 20: '*entièrement indubitable*'). Later, in *Meditations* III, when the acceptance rule of clearness and distinctness is adopted, the terminology recurs in what the secondary literature would lead us to think are its canonical forms, using both the adjectives 'clear' and 'distinct' qualifying the noun 'perception' (CSM II: 24; AT VII: 35: '*clara quædam et distincta perceptio*'; AT IXA: 27: '[. . .] *nous concevons fort clairement et fort distinctement*'), and the adverbs 'clearly' and 'distinctly' modifying the verb 'to perceive' (AT VII: 35: '[. . .] *valde clare et distincte percipio*'). This, presumably, is the usage that the *Principles* belatedly regulates, and that we have in our passage of the *Discourse*.

Still, the reference to knowing evidently in the French version of the first part of the first precept is rendered in De Courcelles' Latin as certain and evident awareness (AT VI: 550: '*certa et evidens cognitio*'), which may be more or less indirectly based on *Rules* III's recommendation that we attend only to what we can clearly and evidently intuit (CSM I: 13; AT X: 366: '*quid clare et evidenter possimus intueri*').

Though minor, such variations indicate that, even if, in the first precept, there is some gap between knowing something evidently to be true and there being no occasion for casting it into doubt, Descartes sometimes treats the two things as close to identical or effectively interchangeable. More importantly, he seems sometimes to think of clearness as going with certainty or unshakeability. Consequently, it may not be too hazardous to see knowing something evidently as including the certainty underpinned by the absence of there being any occasion for casting it into doubt. The difference between the two parts of the precept would thus be justification for distinguishing them; but they are parts of a single precept.

The distinction that appears to be operative here can be set out in terms of the difference already noted between knowing something evidently as the success aimed at, and the avoidance of rushing and conservatism as the marker of procedures that lead to that success. In the second part of the precept, the success-term is the having of clear and distinct ideas, and the marker here is that there is no occasion for casting them into doubt.

If knowing something evidently is, as we have also seen, closely associated with having a clear and distinct idea of it, then the apparent doubling in the precept can be explained by the notion that the absence of occasion for casting into doubt stands to knowing as the avoidance of rushing and conservatism does; namely, as markers of procedures that lead to success. Consequently, having an occasion for casting into doubt stands to what I may take to be true as rushing and conservatism do; namely, as a vice in belief-formation. In this case, it is the defect vice of not taking as true what I may properly take as true: the vice, that is, of giving succour to the sceptic, the person who will find occasions for doubt if anyone will.

The second precept – analysis

The presence of the implicit reference to scepticism in the first precept can be put another way, in terms of the 'more in my judgment' to which Descartes refers. Presumably, what he is thinking of as 'more' are judgments such as those that include in the idea of extension also that of colour, or in the idea of mind also that of body. These would be ideas in which, if we follow for a moment the terminology of the *Principles* (I, 46), distinctness is lacking: in them, the clear content is not sharply separated from everything else (AT VIIIA: 22: '*ab omnibus aliis ita sejuncta*'). Where distinctness is lacking, there is occasion for doubt. When we bite off more than we can chew, our inability to chew should stop us swallowing.

This is spelt out in the second precept, as follows:

> [. . .] to break down each of the difficulties I would examine into as many bits as could be and as would be called for in order the better to resolve them (*Dis.* II, CSM I: 120; AT VI: 18: '[. . .] *de diviser chacune des difficultés que j'examinerais en autant de parcelles qu'il se pourrait et qu'il serait requis pour les mieux résoudre*').

Again, we have a formulation that leaves open the possiblity that the enquirer has not yet encountered any difficulties, because the enquiry is not yet under way. We are thus reminded that the precepts are preparatory to the investigation and are meant to be neutral relative to what might turn up.

In the *Rules*, we are offered a direct link between what Descartes says in his second precept and the narration given in the following pages of the *Discourse*, which describes how he practised applying his precepts. In *Rules* IX, we are told that

> we must direct the attention of our mind totally to the smallest and simplest [CSM: 'most insignificant'] things, and ponder them at length until we have habituated ourselves to intuiting the truth clearly and perspicuously (*Reg.* IX, CSM I: 33; AT X: 400: '[*o*]*pportet ingenii aciem ad res minimas et maxime faciles totam convertere, atque in illis diutius immorari, donec assuescamus veritatem distincte et perspicue intueri*').

The sorts of things that have the requisite simplicity include the basic truths of algebra and geometry; and those who practise paying attention to them to the exclusion of all other become perspicacious (*Reg.* IX, CSM I: 33; AT X: 401: '*perspicaces*') or, more simply, wise (*Reg.* X, CSM I: 34; AT X: 403: '[*u*]*t ingenium fiat sagax, exerceri debet*').

Though Descartes certainly does think of the truths of mathematics as providing the model of what he demands knowledge to be like (e.g. *Dis.* I, CSM I: 114), it does not follow that he holds all genuine knowledge to be fundamentally mathematical in nature. What is of interest to him is the degree of certainty that mathematics offers, and the search is on to find *other* fields where that degree can be reached. To begin with, he says, at school, he thought that mathematics merely subserved the mechanical arts, such as those of fortification and siege-laying (Descartes 1925: 129). Subsequently, however, their utility is that of giving the mind practice in

dwelling on truths (*Dis.* II, CSM I: 120; AT VI: 19: '[. . .] *qu'elles accou-*
tumeraient mon esprit à se repaître de vérités') and not putting up with false
reasonings. In both cases, mathematics is regarded as subsidiary, as a means,
as contributory to something else in ways that are familiar enough from
Plato, who distinguishes between maths-for-war and maths-for-philosophy,
for instance, at *Rep.* VII, 522 B–523 A. Though there is some sense in which
knowledge of the Good is knowledge of something with an essentially mathematical structure (540 B; on which Burnyeat (2000)), Plato also regards
mathematics as a *preparation* for dialectic (531 C–2 D). In this last respect,
Descartes values it for setting up appropriate intellectual habits, those
involved in analysing problems until they become resolvable (for habituation,
see *Con.*, CSMK 351–2). Thus, it is not so much to learn mathematics that
Descartes studies mathematics, as to acquire and instil in himself the mathematician's virtue.

The second precept's reference to the breaking down of difficulties raises
a question of how small the bits have to be to enable resolution. In the *Rules*,
the answer seems to be 'superlatively'; but, in the *Discourse*, we have an answer
that is more concessively comparative: the bits need only be as small as is
necessary to ease the resolution, which is explicit in the Latin (AT VI: 550:
'*commodius*' for '*mieux*'). In large measure, this difference, if it needs explaining at all, can be accounted for by the greater prominence in the *Rules* of the
doctrine of simple natures, which we might summarise as the thought that all
intuitable ideas are of the same degree of complexity as each other (e.g. *Reg.*
VI, CSM I: 21). At least one element of this doctrine comes through in the
Discourse, in the claim that, when a truth is genuinely grasped, it is equally
well grasped by everyone – including a child – who grasps it at all (*Dis.* II,
CSM I: 121; cf. Craig 1987: 18–20, 29–30). While nothing in the doctrine of
simple natures is strictly inconsistent with what we find in the *Discourse*, it is
also worth noting two other differences.

One is, again, that in the *Discourse*, we are tooling up for an investigation.
That being so, we do not know in advance what amount of breaking down
may be necessary or desirable. It turns out that there are some matters that
we can resolve and directly intuit. So we come to see that it is unimportant
whether the bits into which we divide them are the smallest possible or just
small enough for us to make use of. The other is that, if we are accustoming
ourselves to perceiving the things that we perceive in better focus and more
distinctly (*Dis.* II, CSM I: 121), then we would expect that the truths that, to
begin with, we found too complex to grasp all at once, we come, after some
practice, to see in a single sweep: in the terminology of the *Rules*, a '*cogitatio-*
nis motus' (e.g. *Reg.* VII, AT X: 387, 388).

To get a better picture of what is meant by simplicity, we proceed to the
third precept.

The third precept – order

Like the first, the third precept can be divided into two parts, the first of which runs:

> [. . .] to guide my thoughts in an orderly way, beginning with the objects that are simplest and easiest to know so as to rise step by little step to knowledge of the most complex objects (*Dis.* II, CSM I: 120; AT VI: 18: '[. . .] *de conduire par ordre mes pensées, en commençant par les objets les plus simples et les plus aisés à connaître, pour monter peu à peu, comme par degrés, jusques à la connaissance des plus composés*')

and corresponds to the bold claim of *Rules* V:

> [t]he whole method consists in the order and arrangement of the things to which the mind's attention [CSM: 'eye'] must be turned for us to discover some truth (*Reg.* V, CSM I: 20; AT X: 379: '[*t*]*ota methodus consistit in ordine et dispositione eorum ad quæ mentis acies est convertenda, ut aliquam veritatem inveniamus*').

This is not the only place in the *Rules*, at which Descartes says something to the effect that he is giving the whole of the method (e.g. *Reg.* VI, CSM I: 21; XII, CSM I: 39). And this is not surprising given the close interrelations among the rules, as among the precepts. Though a tradition, beginning with Baillet (1691: II, 404–5) and continued by Marion (1974 and Descartes 1977), of giving order a certain primacy in Descartes' thought, there is little reason to take literally the idea that it is the whole of the method. Like the second precept, *Rules* V says that the first move towards resolving a problem is gradually to reduce convoluted and obscure propositions to simpler ones (*Reg.* V, CSM I: 20; AT X: 379: '[. . .] *hanc exacte servibimus, si propositiones involutas et obscuras ad simpliciores gradatim reducamus*').

One troubling thing about this demand is that it either elides or deliberately takes a stand against an important and very prominent Aristotelian distinction about order in science, namely that between the things most knowable to us and the things most knowable in nature (*Phys.*, I i, 184 a 17–19). What makes it troubling is not merely that Descartes could not have been ignorant of this distinction, coming as it does at the very outset of the *Physics*, and of its crucial importance, but that he makes no attempt to mollify a reader who will have it in mind. Where Aristotle allows that the objects of sense-perception are, in one sense, better known, being more immediately present to us, and affirms that the purpose of enquiry is to get to things that are intrinsically more luminous (*Phys*, I i, 184 a 21: σαφεστέρα τῇ φύσει), more explanatory, and necessary, Descartes proceeds as if the two orders of knowability and, hence, of simplicity, straightforwardly coincide. In making no concessions to the distinction, Descartes is once again denying that sense-perception gives us knowledge of any sort.

The things that are simplest and easiest to know are those that are *like* the truths of algebra and geometry. The feature these are supposed to have that makes them readily analysable is that they can be presented in such a way as to contain no extraneous or superfluous concepts. Thus at *Rules* XIII, Descartes exemplifies what he has in mind by abstracting a problem about sound into the terms of a problem purely (AT X: 431: '*præcise*') about the lengths of cords, and in the next chapter, we shall see how he applies the procedure to the more difficult case of the rainbow. The removal of all that is superfluous is the first step to overcoming what *Discourse* II calls a 'difficulty' ('*difficulté*') and what the *Rules* calls a 'question' (e.g. AT X: 430: '*quæstio*'). If we leave a difficulty undivided, then we will keep the habit of thinking (wrongly) that we know things, though we do not intuit them as distinctly as we do those things we are most distinctly aware of (*Reg.* IX, CSM I: 34; AT X: 401–2: '[*a*]*ssuescant* [crucial word] *igitur omnes opportet, tam pauca simul et tam simplicia cogitatione complecti, ut nihil unquam se scire putent, quod non æque distincte intueantur, ac illud quod omnium distinctissime cognoscunt*'). Practice at analysis helps us kick that habit and replace it with the habit of taking as true only those things that we intuit as distinctly as we do the simple truths of algebra and geometry.

If we are to solve difficulties or answer questions, Descartes recommends, in the second and third precepts, first, to break them down and, then, to put the bits in order. The products of the process of breaking down are ideas that we can include in a single intuition or sweep of thought ('*cogitationis motus*'). The test for whether an idea can be so included seems to be, in the *Rules*, whether it contains only a simple nature and, in the *Discourse*, whether it is so clearly and distinctly presented as to be as simple and easy to know as the truths of algebra and geometry. The putting back together of these ideas has to be done in sequence if, at each stage, we are to be able to include the whole in a single sweep of thought (cf. Gaukroger 1987: 48–60). At each stage, our capacity for containing ideas in a single sweep of thought is enlarged (*Reg.* VII, CSM I: 25; cf. *Dis.* II, CSM I: 121).

In the image implicit in the third precept of a flight of stairs ('to rise step by little step'), the rearrangement of what was previously a difficulty and has now become intuitable is possible only if we start at the bottom step and take the others in order. The image is set out more explicitly in *Rules* V (CSM I: 20), where it is contrasted with an attempt to leap to the top of a building. This is one of a rather mixed bunch of kinds of lack of orderliness. The others cited in *Rules* V include not learning from Theseus in the maze, following the astrologers in conjecturing about the effects of the heavens before understanding their motions, trying to study mechanical arts without physics, and being like those philosophers who, ignoring the need for investigations, expect the truth to spring from their heads like Minerva from Jove's. Descartes' need to express these kinds of disorder in such varied terms is an indication that there is more than one way to muddle the relations between the simple and the complex.

In the analogy of the stairs, presumably what is being pointed to is not only that there is a proper sequence but also that each of the steps ought to be as easy or as difficult as any of the others, and that each is easier than trying to take too many at a time. Easier and more secure.

The point about the astrologers and the mechanics who know no physics must be that they jump the gun. In the one case, Descartes might hope unargued that a reader might scorn astrologers' pretensions to knowledge. In the other, he is offering a similarity with the sort of rough-and-ready empirical knacks which will never give assurance in advance that, say, a bridge will hold up or a siege engine will work.

A slightly different point is being made about the philosophers; it is not so much that they have reversed the proper sequence, but that they are not doing anything with what they have in their heads. If what we said towards the end of the last chapter is right, then Descartes might himself be regarded as one who aims to get the whole of knowledge out of what is available within his own head; nevertheless, he takes it that work, application, habituation and attention is needed to turn what is available there into genuine knowledge. Not just any old thing that pops into one's head will do. The philosophers under attack are offering the first thing that comes to mind, just as the slaveboy in Plato's *Meno* gives a variety of mistaken answers to the questions he is asked before he gets on to the track of right opinions, which are themselves only the threshold to knowledge. After the geometrical interrogation, Socrates attributes to the boy true opinions (85 C: ἀλεθεῖς δόξαι), which are likened to the images of a dream and contrasted with knowledge (e.g. 85 D: ἐπιστήμη) that would be the result of repeated interrogation on many sides of the question. The genuine article has to be elaborated out of the simplest verities and it takes work to get to those.

As to Theseus, the vice of wandering unaided in a maze corresponds more closely to the second part of the third precept, which can be translated as: '[. . .] and even imposing an order among the things among which there is no natural precedence (*Dis.* II, CSM I: 120; AT VI: 18–19: '[. . .] *et supposant même de l'ordre entre ceux qui ne se précèdent point naturellement*'), where the 'imposing' is subordinate to 'to guide my thoughts' at the beginning of the precept.

There thus seem to be difficulties in which there is no distinction between the simple and the complex. Yet, from what we have already seen, a difficulty is, virtually by definition, a complex matter, and complexity is, equally by definition, the jumbling together of simples. It follows that anything that poses a difficulty must be the jumbling of simples; hence there will be a natural precedence, once we have broken the thing down into its simple constituents. So, it would seem unnecessary to impose an order where there already is one.

While this holds good for the genuine sciences, in which Descartes supposes that all the things that can be objects of human knowledge follow one from another as the truths of geometry do (*Dis.* II, CSM I: 121; AT VI: 19: where the key verb is '*s'entre-suivent*'), it does not hold for rather less exalted mental operations. A case Descartes offers, to which we shall return in considering moral certainty in Chapter 10, is that of decrypting a secret writing (*Reg.* X, CSM I: 35–6). Though he does not say how one should proceed, e.g. by supposing 'e' to be the most common letter, he has it in mind that the imposition of an order discourages us from wasting time in guessing.

One thing wrong with guessing is that it is an inefficient way of getting to the right answer. It does generate many answers, but we may have no way of discriminating among them. In a similar way, Theseus' adoption of the thread allows him to traverse the maze without needing to know anything about its topology. Guessing is also a bad habit; and those who practise it may even daze the light their reason (Gilson in Descartes 1925; *Reg.* X, CSM I: 36; AT X: 405: , '[those who guess] *hebetarunt tamen ingenii lumen*'). Though playing at decryption may be just a game, practising doing it with method accustoms us to knowing the truth of things: it is good for our intellectual fitness.

The fourth precept – reconstruction

In the *Rules* (*Reg.* XIII, CSM I: 51–2), Descartes makes a distinction, which does not appear in the *Discourse* but to which we shall return in the next chapter between questions that are 'perfect', where we are already in possession of all the information necessary for a solution, and those that are 'imperfect', where there is some unknown, which we may not be able to identify straight off. One case in which there seems to be no distinction between the simple and the complex, but where something is unknown, is that of anagrams (*Reg.* VII, CSM I: 27; cf., on riddles, *Reg.* XIII, CSM I: 53). To count as methodical, the solution of these requires not so much that we impose an 'imaginary' order on them (Descartes 1925: 209), as that we follow the fourth precept:

[. . .] to make such exhaustive enumerations and such general reviews everywhere as to be assured of not leaving anything out (*Dis.* II, CSM I: 120; AT VI: 19: '[. . .] *de faire partout des dénombrements si entiers, et des revues si générales, que je fusse assuré de ne rien omettre*').

As with clearness and distinctness, Descartes' terminology and use of it in other places throws a slightly flickering light on what the fourth precept is about. The closest parallelism is in *Rules* VII, which says,

[f]or the consummation of our knowledge, each individual thing that has to do with the undertaking must be surveyed in a sweep of thought that is continuous and at no point interrupted, and be included in an adequate and orderly enumeration (*Reg.* VII, CSM I: 25; AT X: 387: '[a]d scientiæ complementum oportet singula quæ ad institutum nostrum pertinet, continuo et nullibi interrupto cogitationis motu perlustrare, atque illa sufficienti et ordinata enumeratione complecti').

'Enumeration' ('*enumeratio*') is used in a somewhat narrower, but more fully articulated, sense in the *Rules* than its French counterpart ('*dénombrement*') seems to be in the *Discourse*. In the *Rules*, 'enumeration' seems to collect a variety of argument-forms connected with techniques of exhaustion and induction: in *Rules* VII, it is hitched with a mere '*vel*' to '*inductio*' (AT X: 388). The adequacy that Descartes demands of an enumeration involves its covering all the relevant material, and this sense of almost any sort of principled listing seems to be at the back of his mind in the *Principles* (*Pr.* I, 48, CSM I: 208–9). Thus, in the example he gives in *Rules* VII, if we wish to show that the rational soul is not bodily, then the enumeration suffices if we can show that the rational soul cannot be assigned to any of an exhaustive array of classes of bodily things. Likewise, an enumeration can be adequate if, on the basis of an argument from an arbitrary case, something can be proved of a whole set.[12]

As Garber has ingeniously illustrated (1987: 123–40), the beginning of *Discourse* VI seems to require an understanding of enumeration that includes also eliminative arguments and many-termed disjunctive syllogisms. And the Latin version of the fourth precept unpacks two types of enumeration: those that seek middle terms; and those that go over the parts of the difficulties specifying that they should be not only complete but take the parts one by one (*Dis.* II, AT VI: 550: '*singula enumerarem*'). Presumably, the extra specifications given in the Latin version respond to this enlarged understanding. The first, referring to the finding of middle terms, may be an acknowledgement that what Descartes is thinking of are demonstrations from arbitrary cases, where the middle term in question defines the appropriate set. The second, referring to going over the parts of the difficulty, would then apply, in conjunction with the third addition (i.e. demanding that the parts be taken one by one), to cases like that of an anagram: when we have all the possibilities before us, we have all there is to resolve the difficulty.

For these reasons, an enumeration is described as the most certain form of proof other than intuition (*Reg.* VII, CSM I: 26), though we might want to say that intuition is not really a form of proof, but of intellectual perception.

What Descartes calls a 'review' ('*revue*') in the *Discourse* pretty clearly corresponds to the *Rules*' notion of surveying in a single sweep of thought ('*cogitationis motus*') all the things relevant to the enquiry. Where a review is meant to be comprehensive ('*général*'), more dynamic attributes are required of the sweep of thought: that it be continuous and at no point interrupted. These two attributes are associated in the passage that immediately follows the *Discourse*'s enunciation of the precepts where Descartes speaks of long chains of reasoning (AT VI: 19: '*chaînes de raisons*') in just the terminology he deploys in the *Rules* ('*catena*', e.g. *Reg.* III, AT X: 369; *Reg.* VII, AT X: 390).

When we are solving a problem, the bits that we break it down into (second precept) need then to be put back together in good order (third precept). What we have before our minds is an ensemble of intuitions, each of which is clear and distinct and to which we may properly assent (first precept). But the ensemble itself cannot be all taken in at once. So, to enable us to do so, we must find a way of encompassing the whole in a single thought, to make up for the infirmity of memory (*Reg.* VII, CSM I: 25; AT X: 387: '[. . .] *ideoque memoriæ infirmitati continuo quodam cogitationis motu succurrendum esse dicimus*').

One objection to relying on memory, and, hence, reason for wishing to eliminate any role for it in methodical enquiry, is that memory is fallible: in the terms of the *Meditations*, it is just the sort of thing that the demon can interfere with. The emphasis that Descartes puts on the continuous and uninterrupted nature of the review arises from the demand that the whole be as error-free as each of the parts, because a chain is only as strong as its weakest link (*Reg.* VII, CSM I: 26). Any inference that takes time to perform raises the spectre of our having misremembered the premise(s): it is a process that the demon could meddle with. Hence, the practice of making reviews is aimed at emulating clear and distinct perception, which is essentially present-tense. Just as, for Descartes, all deduction aspires to the status of intuition, so the parts of deductive arguments need to be gathered so as to be perceived all together, as a clear and distinct whole.[13]

In the third precept, Descartes says simply that it is by guiding ('*conduire*') his thoughts in an orderly way that he will rise ('*monter*') to knowledge of the complex; he does not use the terminology of deduction and intuition that we find in the *Rules*. The absence of this vocabulary from the *Discourse* can be explained by noting (i) that the enumerations he refers to *are* the very argumentative structures that make the chains of reasoning chains, connecting the links; and (ii) that the reviews are rehearsals of these leading up to the performance of an intuition of the whole.

The importance of the fourth precept can be put in terms, again, of what it guards us against.

If the moment of drawing up, perhaps by writing down,[14] enumerations of the simple bits resolved out of complex difficulties is the real business of constructive argumentation, then the habit that the fourth precept is primarily aimed at correcting is that of not presenting the structure of one's thought perspicuously, or of drawing (even sound) inferences at random. In one respect, this vice can be regarded as an excess in belief-formation. As with the case of Theseus in the labyrinth, the important thing is that the beliefs that are formed – the turnings taken – should add up to something that can come, in the end, to be seen as globally directional. From another point of view, Descartes has a defect in his sights here: without the enumeration that underlies the whole procedure, the enquirer will fail to have appropriate assurance about matters to which she would be entitled to assent. Likewise, the running through of reviews is a corrective to the tendency to thinking that a conclusion has been definitively established, though the steps by which it was arrived at are no longer available.

There is both excess and defect in the vices that the fourth precept is directed against. The excess is that of believing what one does not have present warrant for. The defect is that of failing to have that warrant present.

The precepts viewed as correctives

In summary, *Discourse* II offers in a very brief span the outline of what doxastic rectitude guards against. The outline is distilled into four precepts that presuppose that the enquirer is already warned as to the dangers of credulity and scepticism, and that he is in a suitable situation, both as regards his outer affairs and as regards his willingness to meditate seriously, to concentrate.

The particular vices against which the precepts alert the enquirer are, in the order that they appear in the text:

(i) not having clear notions;
(ii) biting off more than one can chew;
(iii) muddling what is obvious with what is not; and
(iv) thinking one has completed an intellectual operation though one cannot rehearse it at will.

These do not carry us very far. They underdetermine any particular enquiry. To avoid a sense of anticlimax about where the method might lead, we must look at how Descartes takes it to be applied to the gathering of knowledge about the world. This is the much-contested issue of Cartesian 'philosophy of science' or 'scientific method'. It would be impossible to cover all the questions raised and suggestions made about the status and nature of Descartes' contributions to mathematical and physical knowledge. So, in the next chapters I propose to look at a few of what I take to be the most crucial phases of what is going on.

The overall order of the three chapters further exploits the idea that following the method is acting on or out of a virtue. A virtue requires some sorts of behaviour, is consistent with others and prohibits others again. Doxastic rectitude demands that we give assent only to what we can know to be true. It permits us to pay some attention to what is useful to arriving at the truth. And what it forbids is the false. So far, again, so uninformative: all the interest lies in what, for Descartes, fits these categories.

What demands does rectitude make?

Given the continuing epistemic possibility that there is a malicious demon of great power and cunning bent on deceiving him, Descartes has no choice but to concentrate on the ideas that he finds in himself and that he perceives clearly and distinctly. In a properly-conducted enquiry, there is no point at which this standard is relaxed. Consequently, we can understand why he offers a range of images according to which all the parts of a completed science depend on the metaphysical foundations set out in the *Meditations* and in the first book of the *Principles*. The next chapter will try to make literal some of Descartes' preferred images for expressing this relation of dependence. We shall see that the nature of the dependence does, indeed, make it seem that the whole of what is genuinely knowledge forms a system that we may call 'deductive'. This very unpopular position is, however, only part of the picture.

Rectitude also permits us to take into account models and hypotheses that are not, strictly speaking, objects of knowledge. In Platonic terms, they are matters of opinion (δόξα). Yet they enable us to elaborate theories that can subsequently be incorporated into the body of science proper. By examining some cases of Descartes' operations with this notion in Chapter 10, we shall see that there must be some third way between the two inadequate options of, on the one hand, an apriorism that gets called 'lunatic' because it 'spins physics out of metaphysics' and, on the other, a form of the 'hypothetico-deductive method' that just happens to be popular among those who wish to attribute it to Descartes.

In the last chapter, I wish to pay some further attention to a matter that has already cropped up from time to time: what should be done when a conflict threatens between the outcomes of properly conducted science and the positions of revealed religion. This seems to be covered by what doxastic rectitude excludes: if a view is forbidden, then there is a duty not to assent to it. We have already seen, in considering the role of the will in forming beliefs, that we have the ability to do this; and we shall see how the readiness to do it affected the course of at least one of Descartes' enquiries.

9 Rectitude and science

Virtue and method

As they stand, the four precepts of *Discourse* II give very little guidance about how to proceed in the sciences. In Leibniz' observation, cited at the beginning of the last chapter, they seem to amount to no more than a recipe in which one is told to take what one needs and do with it what is called for to get what one wanted.

There is nothing wrong with the observation. But is it a criticism? In this chapter, I argue that it is not. It is the complaint of someone who wants a method to be the sort of thing that could be implemented mechanically. But that want is misplaced. It is misplaced absolutely because the adoption of so global a thing as a method for refounding the whole of human knowledge could not itself be a mechanical matter: the want is unfulfillable. For Leibniz, the idea would be that an adequate picture of enquiry ought to specify the calculations necessary for arriving at the truth about any matter whatever. But, for Descartes, such a desire misses the way that any properly conducted intellectual operation cannot be mechanical (see again Hacking 1973).

Nevertheless, Leibniz' observation draws attention to a feature that we would expect in a synoptic account of a virtue. We may bear in mind how, at the beginning of his account of the intellectual virtues, Aristotle forestalls the criticism that his remarks about the virtues are too general.

He says that the formula, 'a virtue lies in a mean between two vices', for all that it is true, is quite unenlightening (*EN*, VI i, 1138 b 25–6). By analogy with the tightening or relaxing of a bow-string or with tuning a lyre, we have to have some standard (1138 b 23: ὅρος); by analogy with medicine, it is useless to be told to take what a medical expert would prescribe when we do not know what he would prescribe (1138 b 29–32). In reply to the complaint that the structure of the virtue theory does not on its own tell us much about what a given virtue consists in, we say that, if something is really a virtue, then only its genuine possessors, acting on particular occasions, fill in the details.[1]

If it's a virtue, then rectitude or following the method is not a formula or an algorithm. One way of saying this is that Aristotle denies that virtue is a τέχνη (Nussbaum 1986: 291–8; cf. MacIntyre 1981: 89ff.); another comes out in the comment that Sarah Waterlow Broadie makes on *EN*, II i, 1103 b 34–4 a 11: '[t]here is no recipe for 'functioning well'. It is functioning in accordance with right reason or *orthos logos*, but no one can say in advance what the *orthos logos* for a particular situation might be' (Waterlow Broadie 1991: 60).

In one respect, the latter part of this comment is surely right when we remember Aristotle's insistence that exactness is not possible in ethics. But there is a downgrading of what is involved in following a recipe to something less engaged than any self-respecting cook would allow. For, even the making of so simple a thing as an omelette may be said to involve a recipe, though there are many more or less satisfactory ways of following it. Nevertheless, the ruling idea here is that there is a built-in or conceptual indeterminacy in the definition of a virtue relative to its opposed vices (see McDowell 1979: 147–53; Watson 1990: 59–61). In this way, the cause for Leibniz' complaint about what is involved in an effort to follow the precepts of *Discourse* II supports the idea that Descartes' is concerned with a virtue.

The underspecification of what would satisfy the demands of 'method' is one sort of reason for thinking that what is in play is more like a virtue than something that Leibniz would recognise as a decision-procedure by calculation. But we may also put this the other way round and follow up, what we earlier touched on, why Descartes abandoned the project of the *Rules* and, instead, gives so brief an account of the method in the *Discourse*.

In April 1630, Descartes tells Mersenne that he has abandoned the writing of some treatises, among which one is pretty surely the *Rules*. Some commentators have sugggested that the reference is to the *Dioptrics* (Schuster cited in Gaukroger 1995: 181 n. 90; though Schuster dropped the suggestion in his 1980: 80 n. 161), and others have seen in the reference to plural treatises versions of *The World*, the *Dioptrics* and the *Meteors* (CSMK: 21n.). Though one or more of these surely underwent redesign in 1629–30 (letter to Mersenne 18th December 1629, CSMK: 14), we can see from the sort of reason he gives for the abandonment that he must be talking about a fairly abstract work. Hence, we may accept the consensual identification of the *Rules* as the writing that was abandoned (see Gouhier's 'Notice' to Descartes 1939: xxv)

The reason Descartes gives for the abandonment is that he has discovered that he has learnt rather more than he could fit into his original scheme;[2] the analogy he uses is that of a man who, after beginning to build a house, comes into unhoped-for wealth and so, because of his changed status, decides to start from scratch with a plan that is more fitting to his fortunes (letter to Mersenne 15th April 1630, CSMK: 21; the image of the house returns at the beginning of *Dis.* II). And he says that what he has been working on is important because it concerns his learning what is necessary for the conduct of his life (CSMK: 21; AT I: 138: '*nécessaire pour la conduite de ma vie*'). That is, at least one of the treatises is left incomplete because it is insufficiently capacious and because it concerns matters that are not of merely technical interest, but are really fundamental to his overall project.

Towards the end of *Rules* XII, we are given a sketch of the plan of the book as projected, which was to be divided into three groups of twelve rules. The first twelve rules, which we have entire, have to do with the simple propositions, consideration of which readies our powers of thought for the more distinct intuition and the wiser grasp of other objects (*Reg.* XII; CSM I: 50); the second group, of which we have about three-quarters, has to do with questions that are perfectly understood (CSM I: 50; AT X: 429: '*intelliguntur perfecte*'); and the last dozen, about which we have only hints, would have been about questions that are not perfectly understood. The distinction on which turns the difference between the second and third parts of the original project of the *Rules* is spelt out in terms of three jointly necessary positive characteristics that perfectly understood questions have. These are that we should distinctly perceive:

> (i) in advance what will count as a solution; (ii) what exactly our deductions are based on; and (iii) how to prove that the solution and the premises depend on each other in such a way that neither can vary in any respect while leaving the other invariant (*Reg.* XII, CSM I: 51; AT X: 429: '[. . .] *distincte percipimus: nempe, quibus signis id quod quæritur possit agnosci, cum occurret; quid sit præcise, ex quo illud deducere debeat; et quomodo probandum sit, illa ab invicem ita pendere, ut unum nulla ratione possit mutari, alio immutato*').

From the hints that we are given in the second group of rules, it seems that what Descartes has abandoned by April 1630 is to do with matters that go beyond what can be expressed in terms of extension and shape (*Reg.* XIV, CSM I: 58); to do with the rather broader application of the principles already set out (*Reg.* XVI, CSM I: 69–70); and to do with illustrating the techniques for treating unknowns as if they were known (*Reg.* XVII, CSM I: 71).

Everything in the precepts of *Discourse* II is contained in the rules of the *Rules'* first part, and very little of it reappears in the second and third parts: in setting out the precepts, I needed to cite only from rules I–XII (plus just a couple of clarifications from XIII).[3] It would seem, then, that the *Discourse* is a narrower cell than the fully worked-through *Rules* would have been. If the

Discourse represents the more capacious house that was fitting to Descartes after his windfall of knowledge, why is there nothing in the *Discourse* corresponding to the rules that would have made up the last third or two-thirds of the *Rules?*

The answer must lie in the fact that the *Discourse* is by way of an adjunct to the other treatises that Descartes published in 1637: the *Dioptrics,* the *Meteors* and the *Geometry,* which, as just noted, were under way in one form or another in the early 1630s. The *Discourse* is an adjunct to these writings not just because it ended up with a separate pagination from them in the first edition but because Descartes himself calls it a 'preface' (letter to Huygens, November 1635, CSMK: 50; to Mersenne, February/April 1637, CSMK: 53) a 'notice' (letter to Mersenne, February/April 1637, CSMK: 53) or a 'project' or 'plan' (letter to Mersenne, March 1636, CSMK: 51). In the last cited passage he also says that the *Discourse* discloses a part of his method (AT I: 339: '[e]n ce Projet *je découvre une partie de la* Méthode'); from which we might infer that there is at least part that is not disclosed.

The absence from the *Discourse*'s methodological statement of rules that are appropriate to, say, geometry must be explained by that treatise's adjunct status. For, in *Rules* XII, immediately after sketching the plan of the work, Descartes says that perfectly understood questions are generally abstract and almost always of an arithmetical or geometrical nature (CSM I: 51), meaning that they are not the simple propositions with which the first dozen rules deal (see Israel 1990: 447–59). Even if the *Discourse* does not talk about geometry, the *Geometry* does. So we should not expect the *Discourse* to contain precepts that (in the plan of the *Rules*) come after those applicable to studies that themselves come after the precepts (set out in *Discourse* II) applicable to simple propositions.

Two morals are to be drawn from this. One is that, though the precepts of *Discourse* II can be regarded as having universal application (as do the rules of the *Rules*' first part), their universality does not make them sufficient as a guide in any field whatever, not even in the mathematisable subjects discussed in the essays of 1637. The other is that, even if the precepts do not determine any particular implementation, that should not discourage us from seeking the sorts of fit there might be between their summary formulation in *Discourse* II and the enquiries that Descartes conducts in ways that he regards as being in accordance with them, so as to see the outlines of a general doxastic virtue, namely, rectitude.

This latter moral has knock-on effects for a historiographically influential image of Descartes' procedure. This is the image of Descartes as unfurling a small set of premises by use of a single, tightly-defined foundational method to arrive at all the sciences he investigates. It is the image that emerges from the way that Spinoza's account of Descartes' principles

(Spinoza 1663) employs the *mos geometricus*, as if that were somehow the natural form of what is being expounded; and, with the reservation already noted, it is what is imputed to him by Leibniz: the criticism implicit in what Leibniz observes is that a calculating method of the sort that Descartes *ought* to have wanted *ought* to be available.

In the hundred years up to the middle of the twentieth century, it was the dominant image of Descartes in France and, quite apart from what Kant says, has been a major reason why Descartes has been classified as a 'rationalist'. Thus, C. Renouvier's *Manuel* explicitly endorses as Spinozistic Descartes' (Renouvier 1842: 51); similarly L. Liard takes the clarity of mathematics to be the whole of the method (Liard 1882: 65–6), and O. Hamelin's *Le Système* – not a chance title – takes the practical sciences to be *'applications'* of the principles of metaphysics (Hamelin 1910: 21). And this tradition extends down at least to M. Gueroult, who says that 'there is no good philosophical demonstration that is not mathematical' (Gueroult 1953: I, 12), implying that mathematics supplies the sole ideal for the methodical prosecution of philosophy, a point on which we have already had occasion to express caution.

But, since the publication of Jean Laporte's magisterial *Le Rationalisme de Descartes* in 1945, there has been a noticeable trend towards downplaying the extent and nature of the rationalism in question. At first, the extent of the rationalism attributable to Descartes was limited by a growing willingness to make exceptions to the matters to which the method is meant to apply. Where, in an earlier period, there was a tendency, again most marked in France, to see Descartes either as a hero of anti-clericalism (e.g. Cousin's dedication to Descartes 1824–6; Cousin 1845: vii–viii; Bouillier 1842: 15, 73, 79 &c.; Bordas-Desmoulins 1853) or as a dissimulator of his less-than-orthodox theological commitments (e.g. Gilson), questions of religious faith came to be seen to be among the areas on which Descartes would not trespass, at least in public. We have already seen some of these (e.g. with respect to the doctrine of the creation of the eternal verities, or to Pelagianism), and shall see some others in Chapter 11.

But there has been a much greater change in perceptions of the nature of Descartes' procedures in the physical sciences. The tendency, strongest among some recent Anglophone commentators, has been towards finding in Descartes elements of the empirical and experimental practices that are frequently used to explain the success of some seventeenth-century developments in astronomy, optics, mechanics and physiology. Several very able commentators have found strongly empiricist presumptions lurking in what he has to say. As we proceed, we shall consider how these should be taken. It may be that saving Descartes from the accusation of rationalism has been a way of making sense of his canonical position as the founder or father of modern philosophy, including those philosophical positions that have no time for anything that deserves the name of rationalism. But this is too big an issue to address here.

The main question to be faced is: how is Descartes' scientific enterprise meant to function? Though I do not pretend to know the truth about some of the matters on which Descartes takes himself to have come to definite conclusions, I want to examine how what he offers fits with his programmatic statements. I proceed by considering, first, what doxastic rectitude requires, second, what it permits and, third, what it prohibits. Responding to the first and last of these are, predictably enough, the *true* and the *false* respectively. Responding to the second is a category that does not seem to have been given much attention in the literature, that could be called the helpful, the handy, the useful or the opportune, and that, translating pretty directly from Descartes' French, I shall call the *expedient*. The remainder of this chapter will be occupied with the true; the next with the expedient; and the last with the false.

What rectitude requires

Where to begin

The first part of the first precept of *Discourse* II tells us not to take anything as true that we do not evidently know to be such, and the second part associates this evidence with having no occasion to cast anything we include in our judgments into doubt. We have occasion to cast into doubt anything that could be interfered with by a malicious demon. The demon could interfere with any idea that we acquire by any process, causal or inferential. It very quickly follows that we should not take as true any idea that, in the tripartition of ideas in *Meditations* III, comes to us from without or that we make for ourselves (*Med.* III, CSM II: 26). This leaves only innate ideas.

That should be that: we should take only innate ideas to be true. Hence, doxastic rectitude requires us to attend only to the ideas that we find in ourselves independent of any experience or imagination. But there are two outstanding problems. One is that we need some reason for thinking that we can get knowledge at all. And the other is that, looking for it exclusively among innate ideas immediately lands us with having to attribute to Descartes the view that we have seen called 'lunatic apriorism'. To begin showing that it is not lunatic, though it may be apriorism, we should recap the rationale for Descartes' position, and thus explain why he thinks that at least some innate ideas are, indeed, trustworthy enough to satisfy the first precept of *Discourse* II.

First, negative. Scepticism about the senses, whether modelled on the 'material' tropes or supercharged by the demon, provides grounds for thinking that some other source is needed if we are going to get anywhere in building anything secure in the sciences. As we have see, even Hobbes allows that the uncertainty of the senses has been a commonplace since Plato (*Obj.* III, CSM II: 121). So we must either resign ourselves to uncertainty or reject the senses as a place to look for certainty.

More positively, when he is able to hold the senses to some degree in abeyance, Descartes finds that there remain some notions that do not seem to be derived from the senses and that do, indeed, seem to be pretty certain. We saw that the simple truths of arithmetic and geometry look as if they fit the bill. But even these are infected with a degree of doubtfulness: they could be interfered with by a malicious demon because, though simple relative to arithmetic and geometry, they involve some complexity. They are composites of genuine simples and have to be arrived at by a process of ratiocination. They might, therefore, be regarded as ideas that we make for ourselves, though what we make them out of may well be innate.

Yet, there are some ideas that involve no complexity. In the *Rules*, Descartes calls these the 'common notions' (*Reg.* XII, CSM I: 45), where their commonness is a matter of their being applicable both to bodies and to spirits. There, they are associated with the 'simple natures'.[4] In the *Principles*, the term 'common notions' recurs (*Pr.* I, 50, CSM I: 209), and they are described as being the most general things (*Pr.* I, 48, CSM I: 208; AT VIIIA: 22: '*maxime generalia*'). In each of these places, Descartes gives a list of samples of the notions that fall into this class though it is neither possible nor necessary to give a full enumeration of the truths that can be made out of them (*Pr.* I, 49, CSM I: 209). The list given in the *Rules* includes existence, unity and duration, and that in the *Principles*, substance, duration, order and number. The differences between the lists is not as important as the generality of the categories Descartes is referring to, which he says is the level of the highest genera of things (*Pr.* I, 49, CSM I: 208; AT VIIIA: 23: '*summa genera rerum*'). In this, he is no doubt picking up Scholastic discussion of transcendental terms that, ultimately, leads back to the various abstract divisions we find in Plato: at *Sophist*, 254B–5E, the Eleatic Stranger lists being, rest, motion, same and other as the 'Five Highest Kinds'; and at *Philebus*, 23C–7C we find a categorisation into limited, unlimited, mixed and cause of mixture. These are meant to represent the most basic elements of conceptual combination, which is just the sort of role that Descartes attributes to the common notions.

The common notions could not be derived from any other ideas. On the one hand, he says that they are the elements and rudiments of thought (*Con.*, CSMK: 347; AT V: 165: '*elementa et rudimenta*'). On the other, they could not be arrived at by processes like abstraction or induction, however those are to be thought of, because those processes themselves presuppose existence, unity, number and the like. For this reason, Descartes indicates that such simple concepts are antecedent to any intellectual activity whatever (*Re.*, CSM II: 417–18). They appear to be pretty pure potentials of the sort that he refers to in the *Notes* as a faculty for thinking (ad 12, CSM I: 303; AT VIIIB: 357: '*facultas cogitandi*'). But we still have to do something with them.

Descartes calls the mode of generation by which we get thoughts out of these notions 'composition' (*Pr.* I, 47, CSM I: 208; AT IXB: 23: '[. . .] *ex quibus cogitationes nostrae componuntur*'). Though he does not expand on this procedure elsewhere, the idea must be that the common notions are not themselves predications but, as Frege would say, 'unsaturated' (Frege 1923: 55–6: '*ungesättigt*'; cf. Dummett 1973: 245–63). They may then be composed to come up with truths whose simplicity is such that we can perceive their truth simply because, as we saw in considering the role of the intellect in belief-formation, we fully understand what is presented to us.

The first truths to emerge from the composition of the common notions are what Descartes variously calls the foundations of metaphysics ('*les fondements de la métaphysique*', e.g. in LP, CSM I: 187; AT IXB: 16; letter to Mersenne, November 1633, CSMK: 41; AT I: 271), the principles ('*principes*'/'*principia*', conspicuous in *Pr.*), the primary truths ('*premières vérités*', e.g. *Dis.* V, CSM I: 131; AT VI: 40) or the entry points ('*initia*', letter to the reader of *Med.*, CSM II: 8 ('foundations'); AT VII: 9; also αἴτιον and ἀρχὴν, *Resp.* IV, CSM II: 166; AT VII 237). They stand to what is deduced from them as axioms stand to theorems in mathematics; in the terminology of the *Meditations*, they are said to be manifest by the natural light (e.g. *Med.* III, CSM I: 28; AT VII: 40: '*lumine naturali manifestum*'). An example of such axioms would be the principle that nothing comes from nothing, which Descartes cites in a variety of contexts to much the same purpose.[5] This example can be used to make two points.

One is that Descartes' attachment to the axiom does at least mean that he would not offer us a picture of enquiring on which we get something out of nothing. If, as a result of enquiring in accordance with doxastic rectitude, knowledge comes to be out of what was previously not knowledge, then the knowledge must have come to be out of what was the material of or potential for knowledge. And if, as we have seen, the Cartesian enquirer cannot draw the material of knowledge from outside herself, then there must be within herself the that-out-of-which knowledge can come to be. Hence, if enquiry is to bring knowledge to be, there must be within the enquirer the that-out-of-which of knowledge. This is what Descartes is identifying when he tries to isolate the simple notions from which the axioms – including the axiom that nothing comes from nothing – are composed.

The other point starts from the fact that the axiom cited has long since become a commonplace: Aristotle recognises it as a shared formula in the

Physics (I iv, 187 a 34 and viii, 191 a 31). Suppose that someone first encounters it, say, reading Parmenides. In one respect, the person can learn that nothing comes from nothing: she sees Parmenides' words and comes to believe what they say. But there is also an important respect in which she does not learn that nothing comes from nothing *from her reading*. It may be that that axiom has been brought to her attention by her reading, but there is also the respect in which that truth should be biddable without those contingent means. If she is really to understand what Parmenides says, she must understand it as he did: for herself. In considering what doxastic rectitude permits in the next chapter, I shall pin down more accurately how the 'respects' I have been referring to come out in practice.

In short, innatism is a way of avoiding having to be forever squabbling with potential sceptics and is also a way into an order of ideas that are unavailable for virtuous assent other than by ratiocination.

Over the rainbow

The common notions are the that-out-of-which the primary truths are composed. Some of these primary truths are general, such as the Parmenidean axiom. Others are particular, such as the *cogito*. These primary truths satisfy the first precept of *Discourse* II. Once more, they do not seem to take us very far.

To get things moving, we need at least the second and third precepts, to do with analysis and order. These procedures ensure that the guaranteedness of the primary truths is preserved to the further ideas we draw out of them. As we saw, the reference to simplicity in the notion of analysis in the second precept could best be brought out by considering what orders of simplicity there are. Postponing for a moment some of the considerations that have occupied the literature to do with what is involved in turning the chains of reasoning (referred to in the fourth precept) into intuitions, with the standing of syllogistic inference, and with the relations of analysis to synthesis, I mean to go a step further and consider a case in which Descartes sets analysis and simplification to work.

Offering as examples of imperfectly understood questions the problem of the nature of the magnet and the problem of the nature of sound, Descartes refers in *Rules* XIII to a procedure that he calls 'reduction' or 'abstraction'. He claims that from these cases it is easy to see how all imperfect questions can be reduced or abstracted to perfect ones (*Reg.* XIII, CSM I: 52; AT X: 431: '[e]x *quibus facile percipitur, quomodo omnes quæstiones imperfectæ ad perfectas* reduci *possint*', emphasis added). Similarly, in rule XVII, he says that magnitudes are not further reducible, implying that other things are reducible to magnitudes (CSM I: 70), and the remaining fragment of rule XXI requires that many equations should be reduced to one (CSM I: 76); the terminology of abstraction appears in *Rules* XII (CSM I: 41; AT X: 413: '*abstrahamus*').

This is clearly a close relative of what is in play in the notion of resolution, referred to in the second precept of *Discourse* II. What the reduction or abstraction is performed on stands to the result of the procedure as an unknown stands to a variable that is substituted for it (Joachim 1957: 85–8). As we are promised in *Rules* XVII, the operation permits us to treat as known what is, at present, unknown (CSM I: 71). However, the text (as we have it) of the *Rules* treats the examples it offers in a very summary way: contrary to what he says, it is far from easy to see what reduction or abstraction is. Yet, I offer the treatment of rainbows in *Meteors* VIII as a pretty well worked-through case of this procedure; and Descartes himself takes his exposition to be a sample ('*échantillon*') to show how his method works (letter to Vatier, 22nd February 1638, CSMK: 85). But, where some commentators have taken the sample to be a sample of 'the fundamental methodology of present-day science' (Beck 1952: 214) or an effort to find an 'explanation on the basis of his laws' (Flage 1999: 107), I suggest that the background conception of enquiry is very much at variance with empirical approaches to science and makes no essential reference to laws.

The question about rainbows is imperfect because it lacks all three of the positive distinguishing characteristics of perfect questions referred to in *Rules* XII. First, the rainbow is described as a marvel of nature: just the sort of thing that has left many unsure about what would put an end to enquiry about it (*Met.* VIII, AT VI: 325; also I ad init., AT VI: 230–1). Second, unless we are properly prepared, it is unclear (not 'distinctly perceived') what we should base our deductions on: for instance, Descartes has to appeal to what he has already argued about the roundness of drops of water when suspended in a vapour (*Met.* VIII, AT VI: 325; appealing to II, AT VI: 240 and the whole of V). And, third, we do not know which variables will make a difference to the others: towards the end of his discussion, Descartes takes on the artificial production of irises by means of fountains, and admits that the handling of this calls for skill (*Met.* VIII, AT VI: 344: '*il faudrait de l'adresse et de la dépense*').

Though he does not deal directly or systematically with the last of these imperfections (to do with the reciprocity of premises and solution),[6] Descartes' approach to the question of rainbows turns on at least two phases that it is surely proper to call 'reduction' or 'abstraction' (Gaukroger 1994: 52–3).

The first of these begins by discounting the dimensions of the individual drops of water in the cloud that forms the rainbow, because the result is much the same (*Met.* VIII, AT VI: 325). In one respect, this looks like an empirical observation. If it were that, it would be wrong because, as it turns out, if the drops are very small (less than 0.1mm diameter), the colours become superimposed and the resulting white effect is known as a fogbow or Ulloa's ring. So if this were an instance of 'the fundamental methodology of present-day science', we would have a minor disaster on our hands. Rather, we should represent it as an abstraction from questions of size, which are *counted* as being irrelevant for the purposes in hand. In doing so, Descartes follows accepted practice,[7] and substitutes for the cloud a large glass carboy filled with water (*Met*. VIII, AT VI: 325). Like everyone using the technique, Descartes has to ignore the refractions due to the glass, an inconvenience that could be overcome by examining a sphere of water in conditions of weight-lessness and trusting to surface tension. Again, he cannot be trusting to observation to get him what he wants. That is, he abstracts from the large number and the small size of the drops that make up the vaporous region where the rainbow is to be seen, and he discounts the empirical interference of the instruments employed. Rather, in the diagram that illustrates his dis-cussion, he superimposes the circle that interests him, in its turn a representative of the carboy, on the portion of the air-and-water in front of the observer. Even if we call this a 'super-droplet' (Flage 1999: 101), it is not by experimenting that Descartes can achieve his understanding of it.

Among the problems that these initial moves leave to be resolved are, first, the constancy of the angles at which the bands of the spectrum appear (with water, $\pm42°$ and $\pm52°$) and, second, the finding of some account that does not make the traditional sort of reference to the light's being 'weakened' or 'darkened' as it passes through the globe of water. Because he does not have access to an articulated account of the differential refrangibility of white light, Descartes' responses to these problems are, for all their experi-mental detail (tables, *Met*. VIII, AT VI: 337–40), incomplete. He does not, that is, have the means either to explain why the angles are as they are nor to account for the sequence of the colours.

Yet his approach is to appeal to the prismatic effects of refractions and reflections which can be applied by simple iteration to understand not only the primary rainbow, but also the inverted secondary one and, by extension, also the higher orders (Boyer 1959: 200–19). This marks a further stage of abstraction or reduction to simplicity: he began by abstracting a single large sphere from a fog of droplets; and here he abstracts from both the shape and the substance with its particular refractive index (though he does not call it that).

In place of his sphere of water, he recalls that the colours of the spectrum can also be separated by a triangular glass prism (*Met*. VIII, AT VI: 329). He proceeds to show that the rainbow-effect can be obtained independently of the curvature of the surface of the drops (AT VI: 330), and independently of their being drops of water. For the only relevant factor is that there should be a difference in refractive index between two media.[8] The effect he seeks in this case depends on no reflections and on only one refraction (AT VI: 330); in this way Descartes has reduced at least the problem of the production of colour to one that he thinks he can deal with in the mechanical terms of the speed of rotation of the particles of the subtle matter that he says he has described in the *Dioptrics* (*Met.* VIII, AT VI: 331). Yet there is, in fact, very little in the *Dioptrics* that directly concerns the generation of colours, except a reference in discourse V (CSM I: 168; AT VI: 132) forward to the *Meteors'* discussion of rainbows. What he does give is a physical solution in terms of the speed of rotation, so that the parts of the subtle matter (to which we shall return) that tend to spin much more quickly cause the colour red, those that tend to do so a little less quickly cause yellow and so on for green, blue and violet or purple (*Met.* VIII, AT VI: 333–4). He thus proposes a five-member spectrum that omits orange and indigo (unless that is what he means by *incarnat*), as in the modern Munsell calibration of hues (see also *Des.*, CSM I: 323).

It is not to his purpose in the *Meteors* to go on to explain why the different particles rotate at different speeds or how and why these differences map onto perceived colours. These questions need to be addressed at an altogether higher metaphysical level, perhaps by reference to the account of God's overall benevolence in *Meditations* VI (CSM II: 56ff.). Nevertheless, it is no mean achievement to have got from a 'marvel of nature' to the knocking about of the tennis balls that the *Dioptrics* offers (CSM I: 155–63), and thus to have rendered the imperfect question with which Descartes began about the nature of the rainbow as the (potentially) perfect question of what motions are taking place.

How does a case like this help us to understand the applicability of the precepts of *Discourse* II? Since they do not supply a method for the framing or the applying of the simplifications that Descartes makes in the *Meteors*, we might say either that the precepts constitute an incomplete expression of the method, or that the operation of rendering questions perfect is not itself 'methodical' in some strict (Leibnizian) sense. Perhaps it does not matter overmuch which we say. Either way, we have the idea that the path of methodical enquiry cannot be set out in advance by precepts or rules: again, just the turn of phrase that often comes up in describing action in accordance with virtue (see Waterlow Broadie 1991: 60, as cited above; Von Wright 1963: 145). In other words, the procedure of *Meteors* VIII may be described as a 'somewhat confused mass of experiment and reasoning' (Garber 1992b: 298) and this might tempt us to doubt that it 'fit[s] into the rather rigid mold of Descartes's method' (ibid.); but the method does not generate the processes by which we turn an imperfect question into a perfect one. Rather, it supplies guidelines to seeing whether those processes have succeeded or not.

Faced with the rainbow, Descartes is in a position not dissimilar from that of Meno's slaveboy faced with the relations between a given square and various constructions on it (*Men.*, 82Cff.). He is not sure what moves will get him nearer to an overall understanding. By making some suppositions that simplify the problem, for instance of how to double the area of a square, he can arrive at an account of the puzzle that satisfies and that might be extended to other problems. In each case, the approximateness of the object of direct empirical examination is no obstacle to progress. Looking at scratches in the sand has no more essential role in finding out about the geometrical relations that hold between a square and the square con-structed on its diagonal than does the examination of the water-filled carboy in understanding the rainbow. We cannot tell from just looking at the rainbow or even at the carboy which are the suppositions that do, in the end, lead to a solution. Rather, it is by seeing the rainbow in the simplified way suggested by the carboy, that Descartes can see how a solution is to be had.

The *Discourse* does not offer any precepts other than those that can be applied to the propositions of the sort that that book itself handles, namely those that, because of their abstractness, can be called simple. When we do have simple propositions of an appropriate sort, we have knowledge and, in accordance with the first precept, we can know that we do. By the time the precepts are applicable, much of the work of enquiry has already been done: if we are in possession of simple propositions, then we have already succeeded in the arduous part of the enterprise. But how we are to get to those simple propositions is not a matter that can be predetermined. The more concrete or specific a problem is, the more complex propositions it will involve. But the complex is made up of simples. What must be at work in get-ting from the former to the latter is a certain sort of *perception* of which factors can be ignored (the size and number of droplets) or of the lowest common denominator (the difference of refractive index between two media).

That perception, as such, is uncodifiable. Which is not to say that it is arbitrary: in the case of the rainbow, the sameness of effect is a heuristic justification for the moves Descartes makes. Yet, if the set of puzzles that could be posed for resolution is itself indeterminable or contingent, then there is not going to be a precept or set of precepts that covers every even-tuality. To hope that there could be any finite set of rules for dealing with a potentially infinite variety of complexity is to make the unfulfillable demand that we have heard Leibniz and others making. Though it may be that the project of the *Rules* had ambitions to satisfy at least part of that demand, I suggest that the skimpiness of the precepts of *Discourse* II can be seen as adequate precisely because the demand cannot be fulfilled in any global way.

The shape of completed science

The tree in the 'Letter-Preface' to the Principles

The operation of *Meteors* VIII renders simple and knowable what is, at first, complex and unknowable. But the knowable simples are plural. For them to be understandable, for them to form a science, they must be arranged into some sort of structure and their interrelations must be made perspicuous. This is what is involved in the application of the fourth precept. The structure Descartes has in mind is set out in the well-known simile of the tree of knowledge in the 'Letter-Preface' to the French edition of the *Principles*.

With its obvious Biblical resonance (*Genesis*, 2: 17), its use in setting out the Aristotelian categories (Porphyry, *Isagoge*, 4, 17–31) and in graphic representations of, for instance, supposition theory (see Spade 1982: 196), the tree has had a long history as an image for the interrelations of the sciences which extends from Bacon to the *Encyclopédie* and into the Hegelian jungle. So it may not be that much of an accident that Elzevier put a tree on the title-page of the second edition of the *Meditations* (Amsterdam, 1642). But rather than draw it, Descartes describes it.

The text in which the simile is embedded is a contrivance, appearing to be a letter to the reader used as a preface posing as a letter explaining what is in the book that the ostensible addressee, Claude Picot, has already slaved over translating out of Latin. It is also strangely composed as a report for Picot's use on what Descartes would have written: from the beginning of the second paragraph, the ruling verbs are in the anterior conditional (*'j'aurais voulu'*, etc.). Nevertheless, it should be taken seriously as expressing Descartes' aspiration: the 'Letter-Preface' does make an effort to explain in layman's terms the subject, aim and benefits of the book to which it is appended (LP, CSM I: 179).

Descartes proceeds from reflection on the word 'philosophy', through a description of what should answer to the name, to a thumb-nail sketch of the ways that the search for first principles has been corrupted. He then states two conditions that the true principles of philosophy should meet. One, corresponding to the first precept of *Discourse* II, is that they should be very clear (CSM I: 183; AT IXB: 9: '[. . .] *ils sont très clairs'*). The other, which Descartes is very insistent on in this text, is that one can deduce everything else from them. On these principles depends the knowledge of everything else (CSM I: 179; AT IXB: 2: '[. . .] *que ce soit d'eux que dépende la connaissance des autres choses'*); from them one can deduce all the other things (CSM I: 183; AT IXB: 9: '[. . .] *on en peut déduire toutes les autres choses'*); and the knowledge of everything else that exists in the world can be deduced from them (CSM I: 184; AT IXB: 10–1'[. . .] *on en peut déduire la connaissance de toutes les autres choses qui sont au monde*). This is not casual talk, and it deserves a word.

There is much to discuss about Descartes' uses of the notion of 'demonstration'; these range from the etymological 'pointing out', as in the case of the exhibitions of one's own and, I suspect, of God's existence in the *Meditations*, to rather more formalisable senses of 'proof' that turn up in the scientific writings (Clarke 1982: 207–10). But there is a much narrower variety to be found in his use of the notion of deduction. Descartes is not being random in specifying the relation between that from which deduction proceeds (the principles) and that which is deduced (the other things). The relation is, precisely, that the former can be known without the latter, but not vice versa (LP, CSM I: 179–80; AT IXB: 2: '[. . .] *en sorte ils puissent être connus sans elles, mais non pas réciproquement*').

The denial of reciprocity is a clear sign that Descartes' idea of deduction is rather different from what a modern logician would recognise; trivially, he has to deny that the relation of any proposition to itself can be one of deducibility. And the denial has two important consequences: not only does it imply that the principles cannot be deduced from the things later in the order that is being set up, but it is to be taken in the sense that what can be deduced from the true principles of philosophy cannot be known unless it is deduced from them: the principles are the only source of knowledge properly so-called. This is 'apriorism': it is the claim that, in the order of virtuous enquiry, knowledge of the principles is prior to knowledge of all other things: and nothing can be known unless it is deduced from the first principles. It is Descartes' doctrine about what he thinks he is doing, whether it is 'lunatic' or not.

To proceed with the 'Letter-Preface'. After giving some advice about how to assess and how to read the *Principles*, he explains, what we saw in considering the third precept, that a reader who practises on mathematics will limber up for metaphysical questions (CSM I: 186; cf. *Reg.* XII). This leads to swift summary of the parts of philosophy, whose relations are brought out in the simile we are interested in:

> [t]hus, philosophy taken as a whole is like a tree, whose roots are metaphysics, the trunk physics and the branches that come out of this trunk are all the other sciences, which boil down to three main ones, namely, medicine, mechanics and morals (LP, CSM I: 186; AT IXB: 14: '[a]*insi toute la philosophie est comme un arbre, dont les racines sont la métaphysique, le tronc est la physique, et les branches qui sortent de ce tronc sont toutes les autres sciences qui se réduisent à trois principales, à savoir la médecine, la méchanique et la morale*').

Here we have at least the following notions. Philosophy is a whole. There are determinate relations among the parts. To get from some parts (e.g. metaphysics) to others (e.g. medicine), one must pass through a third (physics). Some parts (the 'other sciences') are parallel to or divergent from each other, though they have an origin in common (physics).

This simile models *completed* science. A person in possession of it can move freely from the lower parts to the upper and vice versa. The difference between the two directions is the difference between analysis and synthesis. That is, for a person in possession of the whole of science, the parts of the tree are as perspicuously related as the nodes of, say, a genealogical chart: every element is in its place, which is determinable in relation to every other. Though analysis and synthesis have different roles to play in the process of discovery, they are symmetrical once knowledge has been acquired. As Arnauld and Nicole say in the midst of an exposition of bits of the *Rules* and the *Discourse*, analysis and synthesis differ from each other as the proof that a given person is descended from St Louis starting by showing that so-and-so is his father, and so on backwards, differs from the proof starting with a son of St Louis and so on forwards (Arnauld 1775–83: XLI, 376): the way up is the way down.

So far, so static. At the beginning of the following paragraph of the 'Letter-Preface', Descartes introduces learning as an ordering principle:

> Now, as we do not pluck fruits from the roots or the trunks of trees but only from the ends of their branches, just so, the main usefulness of philosophy derives from the parts of it that we must learn only at the end (LP, CSM I: 186; AT IXB: 15: '[o]r, *comme ce n'est pas des racines ni du tronc des arbres qu'on cueille les fruits, mais seulement des extrémités de leurs branches, ainsi la principale utilité dépende de celles de ses parties qu'on ne peut apprendre que les dernières*').

The fruits in question are the benefits of medicine (health), mechanics (power over inanimate objects: *Dis.* VI, CSM I: 142–3), and morals (generosity, as we saw in Chapter 2).

It is useful here to reiterate Descartes' anti-Aristotelian identification of the order of simplicity in nature with what is simple to us, and what he says about the need for a properly conducted enquiry not to miss out any stages – not to try to leap in a single bound to the top of a building. Once we have cleared our minds of the preconceptions and prejudices that have encumbered it since childhood, we are left with material out of which the principles of metaphysics are the first things that can be elaborated. From those principles, we can proceed step by step (cell by cell?) through physics and whatever adjunct sciences are necessary to reach the goods that are promised by the truly practical philosophy Descartes is advertising. The point, therefore, about the principles' being knowable without the later things but not vice versa, must concern the process of discovery, where direction is all.

The place we start is with the roots, with metaphysics. At this point we see that the tree-simile is hard to take literally: a tree does not grow from its roots, but from a seed; and a tree whose roots are exposed dies. But on we press.

How to climb the tree

Analysis, then, is just whatever it is that gets us from the principles of metaphysics to the goods of medicine and the rest. The direction of analysis is the direction of deduction. And this gives us a second, and very strong, reason for thinking that Descartes' notion of deduction is very different from what we recognise today. For it might be doubted that any procedure that should be called 'deduction' can get us these goods without cheating, without our helping ourselves to knowledge to which, in accordance with the precepts, we have no just claim. If there is no such procedure, Descartes' undertaking is 'trivially hopeless from the start' (Williams 1978: 204). Though it may, indeed, be ultimately hopeless when all is said and done, I wish to head off an objection, which has acquired some currency in recent literature, to the use of analysis as a – *the* – tool for discovery.

The objection is this. If the procedure of analysis is deductive and truth-preserving, then it cannot involve the addition of information. The goods of medicine involve information that is not in the principles of metaphysics. Therefore, the goods of medicine cannot be deduced from the principles of metaphysics.

If Descartes is maintaining that the goods of medicine can be obtained by deduction from the principles of metaphysics, then, unless he has not taken account of the objection, either deduction is compatible with the addition of information, or the goods of medicine do not involve information that is not in the principles of metaphysics. It would be uncharitable to Descartes to think that he was blind to so obvious an objection; so, his innatist apriorism must involve some negotiation either with the 'epistemic value of deduction' (Gaukroger 1987: 116–26), or with the true content of the principles of metaphysics.[9] Or both, as it turns out.

As to the question of charity, it is well enough known that Descartes objects to syllogistic reasoning on the grounds that it can only tell us what we already know (e.g. *Reg.* X, CSM I: 36–7; *Dis.* II, CSM I: 119). This is an analogue of the objection to analysis as both deductive and productive of the goods of medicine from the principles of metaphysics. It is, therefore, highly unlikely that Descartes would not have seen the point of the objection to analysis; so it is highly likely that his conception of how we get from the principles of metaphysics to the goods of medicine is meant to be immune to the objection as stated. Syllogistic reasoning may be one model for synthesis, for the recapitulation of knowledge already acquired (Barnes 1969); but presumably it is not the only one.

The biggest difficulty with the principles of metaphysics is that they look uninformative: they do not seem tell us much about the actual constitution of the actual world. The goods of medicine, by contrast, involve a great deal of information about very specific parts of a very specific world: human bodies as they happen to be configured here and now. If the principles of metaphysics do in some way contain the goods of medicine, then what we need is some way of isolating the latter within the all-inclusiveness of the former. The techniques for this sort of isolation will concern us when we come to consider the role of experience as an expedient in the sciences. For the time being, let us concentrate on the sort of epistemic advance that Descartes thinks we make in applying analysis to the principles of metaphysics.

'Epistemic advance' is what leads to new knowledge (Gaukroger 1987: 5, 118 &c.). The newness in question must, for Descartes, be something like an idea's newness in being presented as a suitable candidate for non-credulous assent, though the idea might have been previously present to us buried in our minds. In turn, the being 'buried' is a matter of being implicit, latent or potential in the things that we have clearly and distinctly before our minds, illuminated by a great light and so on. An alternative vocabulary that has been proposed for this kind of latency is that of some of the ideas that we find in the clutter of our mind forming 'open systems' (Scribano 1997: 99). Here the contrast is between a notion like that, say, of a triangle on which we can get going with analysis, discovering what is implicit in the idea, and one like that, say, of a winged horse, which, being invented by us, contains only what we put into it and is thus 'closed' to further analysis.

Thus, the fact that the hypotenuse subtends the largest angle is closer to the 'surface' in the general idea of a triangle than the fact that the internal angles of any plane triangle add up to the sum of two right angles, and we have to dig down further still to reach the fact that the square on the hypotenuse of a right-angled triangle is equal to the sum of the squares on the other two sides (*Med.* V, CSM II: 47). It is by analysis of the general idea of a triangle, that is, by digging down into it and seeing what must hold of certain sub-types of it (planeness, plane right-angledness and so on) that we build up knowledge in geometry (*Resp.* IV, CSM II: 158–60). This holds even if there is nothing that fits the shapes we investigate (*Med.* V, CSM II: 44–5) and even if we cannot imagine a certain shape, such as a chiliagon, with sufficient distinctness to distinguish it from others, such as myriagons (*Med.* VI, CSM II: 50).

To illustrate this, I appeal again to Plato and consider a step he exhibits, trying to leave out of account the form of pre-existence that he is seeking to shore up by the argument.[10] In cross-examining the slaveboy in the *Meno*, Socrates does not give him information about the properties of squares, but at most about what the parts can be called, as when he says what the adepts' word for the diagonal is (*Men.*, 85A). Rather, he takes it that he is enquiring into what the soul has already understood (*Men.*, 81D). We might say Plato is trying to illustrate how the slaveboy can learn without being taught, though Plato makes the distinction between the verb to recall (ἀναμίμνισκω) and the verb to enquire or ascertain (μανθάνω; *Men.*, 82B; 82E; 84A; 85B). In guiding the slaveboy, Socrates is using the knowledge that he has to mind about squares, but this is employed only to reduce the number of false turnings that the boy makes, and Socrates' questioning helps him to understand for himself that these turnings are false (*Men.*, 82D, 83E, 84A). Had the slaveboy hit on those questions for himself, as we may suppose Pythagoras did, then his answers could have been the same. In this respect, the only material essential to the demonstration is the slaveboy's capacity to answer Socrates' questions. The slaveboy's possession of that capacity is taken to imply that he was always in a state of knowing (*Men.*, 85D: ἀεὶ καὶ ἦν ἐπιστήμων); then Socrates generalises the model from geometry to all other subjects (*Men.*, 85E: καὶ τῶν ἄλλων μαθημάτων ἁπάντων).

It is sometimes regarded as a problem for this sort of general application of the model that it suffers from 'sheer implausibility' (Gaukroger 1987: 121). That is, it requires us to say that a person who can come to know some geometry already knows all the geometry there is to know and, generalising, that any being that can come to know anything already knows everything there is to be known.

Put like that, plausibility does seem to be a problem.

To avoid the problem, we should not put it like that, and should recall the reasons why Descartes wants analysis to be the tool for enquiry in general: it uses only clear and distinct ideas, and it does not depend essentially on any ideas that are either adventitious or made by us. To start with, the only clear and distinct ideas we have are the principles of metaphysics; so it is by analysis of them that we are going to get other ideas that satisfy Descartes' demands. Though the results of the analysis are, in one sense, 'in' those ideas, they are, in the image I have offered, buried. That means that we may not yet have them available to us for assent in accordance with doxastic rectitude: they are clear and distinct only insofar as they are true and known by God. As we proceed with analysis, we come to perceive them clearly and distinctly. In this sense, no information is added when they yield the results of analysis. But, at the beginning of our enquiry, they are not clear and distinct to us and are not known by us.

We are not adding information but following the contours of the ideas themselves;[11] and those contours are not matters of our choice. With the ideas we make for ourselves, such as that of Pegasus, it is up to us to choose to add the wings to the horse; but with innate ideas, such as that of a triangle, we can choose to attend to this or that sub-type, such as plane right ones, but we cannot choose what features such triangles have in virtue of their membership of the sub-type. Those features are established by God in His creation of the eternal verities and impressed on our minds by Him in accordance with His veraciousness. Perhaps *that* is implausible, but it is certainly what Descartes argues for, most centrally in *Meditations* III and, as we have seen in some detail, IV.

Granted this respect in which Descartes thinks the principles of metaphysics do contain all other knowledge and in which analysis is the tool by which we can obtain it, the difficulty of the apparent uninformativeness of the principles of metaphysics can be inverted: the difficulty is that they contain too many lines of information, among which it is hard to know which apply to the actual world and, in the case of the goods of medicine, to human beings as they happen to be constituted.

We shall return in the next chapter to consider the expedients we can use to find which of the truths that God has made available to us are applicable to our situation. First, however, there are two matters to be considered. One concerns the overall structure of Descartes' tree: for there are some curiosities to be noted in the relation between the way he sets out the interrelations of the sciences and some parts of his practice. The other concerns a clarification of what is meant by the direction of analysis being the direction of discovery from the principles of metaphysics to the other things that, if they are going to be known at all, have to be known by being deduced from those principles.

The discreet charm of stuff-types

The description that Descartes gives of the interrelations of the sciences is very summary. What he wants to get across is the basic and exhaustive division of the tree at, as it were, ground level between the things that are non-material substances and those that are material. In this way, the objects of metaphysics are themselves described as 'metaphysical' (LP, CSM I: 184; AT IXB: 10: '*immatérielles ou métaphysiques*') and are used to deduce the general form of material bodies (ibid.: '*je déduis la vérité des autres choses*'). Given this level of generality it is perhaps unfair to puzzle too tenaciously about the oddities. But some missed beats are telling, especially when the fourth precept of *Discourse* II plainly enjoins us not to leave anything out.

A query has been raised about there being no announced place for (pure) mathematics in this structure (Garber 1992a: 53 and n. 41). One suggestion is that it ought to be fitted in between metaphysics and physics: that is, at ground level (Gaukroger 1980: 124–5). But this would overlook the way that, being non-material, the objects of mathematics must themselves be as 'metaphysical' as mind and God are: in Platonic terminology, they are forms (Schmaltz 1991). It might also be suggested that mathematics is present throughout the tree: it's the sap, so to say.

Similarly, there is room for doubt about the relative placings of the sciences further up the tree; medicine, mechanics and morals seem to be disconnected and can be pursued separately (Rodis-Lewis 1992c: 251). Thus, there comes a point (at the end of physics), when there is no longer any particular order to be followed. Though mechanics might have some input for medicine, and medicine might have some input for morals, Descartes does not seem to envisage any straightforward sort of reducibility here. Being concerned in large measure with mind and divine command, and therefore with the non-material, morals had better be related as directly as possible with metaphysics, perhaps even skipping physics.

Again, we might raise an eyebrow about the apparent absence of anything corresponding to chemistry in Descartes' account. Two general reasons for not expecting him to allot it a special place are, first, that the scheme itself is very general, and, second, that the theory of matter on which the development of chemistry actually depended when it did acquire some autonomy in the late eighteenth century was (being Democritean) at variance with Descartes' official or philosophical theory of extended substance. We can allow ourselves to say a little more about this, though the full story would be very complex.

There is something like open-order chemistry in the discussions in *Principles* IV 57–143 of the various types of stuff we come across from time to time, such as the exhalations that make up what we now think of as the fortunate parts of the theory of hydrocarbons, where Descartes counts sulphur and clay in with tar and petroleum (*Pr.* IV, 76). This material is anecdotal and unsystematic – a common enough complaint against even the aspiration of post-Mendeleev chemists to be theoretical and systematic: their stories are too short. But, as Descartes hints in *Discourse* V, these are the things that emerge from a review of inanimate bodies and plants (*Dis.* V, CSM I: 133–4).

A modern expectation is that, ultimately, chemistry should be reducible to, or explicable in terms of, physical structures and interactions: what makes different types of stuff different and what makes them combine in characteristic ways has to do with their inner constitution. But it does not seem that Descartes sees it that way. If a theory of the sorts of stuff there are is supposed to come between physics and the more specific matters of biology, then chemistry ought to be fairly far up the tree of the sciences and ought to encompass different chemical types doing different types of jobs. Instead, Descartes introduces his snippets of chemistry in rather a muddle, and in such a way that translations and editions that present themselves as 'philosophical' tend to edit this material fairly severely.[12]

In the parts of the *Treatise on Light* where he introduces a sort of chemistry, he begins with what seems to be a sham confrontation with Aristotle's account of the hot, the cold, the wet and the dry. He makes a rather generic reference to what 'the philosophers' think (*Lum.* V, CSM I: 88; AT XI: 23: '*les philosophes*'), though the version that he sets up to knock down bears only the vaguest resemblance to what we find in Aristotle. Yet we can be sure that Descartes was familiar with Aristotelian physical theory, both from the fact that he studied the *Physics, On Generation and Corruption* and *De Cælo* at school (De Rochemonteix 1889: IV, 30; Gilson 1913b: 156–8), and from his letter to Villebressieu of summer 1630 (CSMK 33 (abridged); AT I: 217ff.).

What he offers in place of the caricature scholastic account is a three-element theory. The first two, Fire and Air, are both regarded as fluids, the former as finer and more penetrating than anything else in existence (*Lum.* V, AT XI: 24: '*Feu, comme une liqueur, la plus subtile et la plus pénétrante qui soit au Monde*'), and later as being made of parts each with some size and shape (*Lum.* V, AT XI: 24–5). Descartes does not envisage water as an element, but he uses its most conspicuous property (fluidity) as a feature of two others. There is also the implication that the parts of Fire have neither size nor shape, or that they are not parts properly so-called, being more like points or ranges of a continuum. The third element, Earth, is defined as being much more lumpy and sluggish than Air as Air is than Fire (*Lum.* V, AT XI: 25: '[. . .] la Terre, du quel je juge que les parties sont d'autant plus grosses et se remuent d'autant moins vite à comparaison de celles du second [leg. élément, sc. Air] que font celles-ci à comparaison du premier*').

As even commentators anxious to recruit Descartes for modern science have had to concede, this scheme is 'not very convincing' (Clarke 1992: 262). And it has been ingeniously suggested that the three elements are introduced in the Descartes' theorising about light because they correspond to the three moments of the production (Fire), transmission (Air) and reflection and refraction (Earth) of light (Gaukroger in Descartes 1998: xvi). But this still leaves unanswered questions about the status of Descartes' move and about its relation to other parts of the tree of knowledge. For, a theory of this sort has no obvious advantages over its contemporary rivals and is just as arbitrary as they are. For instance, he preserves the Aristotelian idea that each element has its natural place (*Lum.*, V, AT XI: 28: '[. . .] lieux dans le monde qui leur sont particulièrement destinés*'; cf. *Phys.*, V vi or *Cæl.*, I viii). Moreover,

Descartes must be differentiating the elements not so much in respect of their motion as in their motility: their disposition or ability to move at specified speeds. That is, a bit of Air moves more quickly than a bit of Earth, not because it is, say, less heavy, less bulky or less dense, but because it is Air. If so, there is a fundamental feature of motion that is not caught by Descartes' official version of the fundamental laws of kinetics, namely, what makes the difference between the motion of Air and that of the other elements.

The theory of elements gets alternately taken up and dropped in Descartes' effort to account for the physical interactions of the visible world. And Descartes indicates that the employment of the theory would make the account he aims to give too boring (*Lum.* V, CSM I: 90; cf. *Lum.* VII, CSM I: 98). It appears not to be called for in the 'fable' of the world that is set a-spinning in *Treatise on Light* VI, and to whose status we shall return below. For, in the fable, matter is defined in a philosophical, abstract or stripped-down way (*Lum.* VI, CSM I: 91; AT XI: 33: '*dépouillé*').[13] But the elements recur in Chapter VIII to explain the differential behaviour of different parts of the cosmos he is imagining. Though he continues to say that he is not concerned with matter as wood, stone or metal (*Lum.* VI, CSM I: 91), it is not clear that his appeal to stuff-types should not fall foul of the objections he makes to the more traditional theory. Similarly, when he makes a further stab, at *Principles* III, 52, towards reintroducing the theory of the basic types of stuff, his exposition is still-born, having no progeny in what follows; likewise at *Principles* IV, 3 and following.

We have, then, an uncertainty about the relation between, on the one hand, considering physics as ultimately identical with geometry, which is a doctrine that we find from the *Rules* (e.g. *Reg.* II, CSM I: 13) through to the latest writings, such as the *Principles* (*Pr.* II, 64, CSM I: 247; also *Con.*, CSMK: 343), and, on the other, the possibility of discriminating some fundamental elements, albeit in terms of a single, perhaps ultimately qualititative, *differentia*, namely, their generic motility. Worse (from the modern point of view), in the accounts on offer in the *Treatise on Man* and in the *Description of the Human Body*, there is no essential reference to what the parts of the body are made of in explaining how they interact: for instance, the behaviour of the nervous system is regarded purely as a matter of string-pulling (see the figure reproduced at CSM I: 102). What seems to be lacking is the hierarchy we have become accustomed to of the atom (as that word has been hijacked), the molecule and the cell.

There seem to be two options for Descartes here. Had the *Principles* been expanded to include an account of animate matter (cf. *Dis.* V, CSM I: 134), he might either (i) have given some description of how his three elements combine or are concocted to make such things as flesh, bone, muscle and the rest; or (ii) have introduced an extra element, or even extra elements, to deal with the types of stuff that seem to defy ready reduction to Fire, Air and Earth. Neither of which is pretty. Perhaps Descartes would have thought of something better; but he did not.

In short, while the tree is meant to picture order among the sciences, Cartesian element-theory appears to be an instance of mismatch: the theory is introduced either too soon or too late to help physics, and is not put to work in biology.

Causes and effects

Passages like those we have discussed from the *Meteors* on the rainbow and from the *Treatise on Light* on element theory have give the impression to some commentators that Descartes was engaged in science in 'our current sense of the term "science"' (Clarke 1982: 5) or that he was a 'practising scientist who, somewhat unfortunately, wrote a few short and relatively unimportant philosophical essays' (ibid. : 2). Indeed, this was a view that not a few self-styled Cartesians in the seventeenth century took of the matter (Clarke 1989). What they understood by it was that hypotheses have a crucial role in enquiry into the constitution of the world and that those hypotheses have to be inferred from and tested by observation and experiment in order to discover the laws that govern the world.

From the gist of what we have seen so far, and from the account we shall give in the next chapter of the heuristic role that Descartes allots to hypotheses, there is reason for thinking that the impression of a Cartesian 'hypothetico-deductive method' must be an inadequate interpretation. On one crucial point of that interpretation, I wish to gather here some of the evidence that Descartes held, rightly or wrongly, that the proper order of discovery runs from causes to effects and not vice versa. I arrange this sprinkling of evidence in chronological order over Descartes' career, in the hope of showing that the idea of deducing all other things from the principles of metaphysics is a constant in his vision of the nature of discovery.

Presaging the third precept of *Discourse* II, on the distinction between the simple and the complex, *Rules* VI cites being a cause as one of the features of a pure and simple nature (*Reg.* VI, CSM I: 21). Granting that there is a correlativity between causes and effects, corresponding (in terms not used in the *Rules*) to the difference in direction between analysis and synthesis, Descartes asserts that if we want to know the nature of the effect, we must first know the cause and not vice versa (*Reg.* VI, CSM I: 22; AT X: 383: '[. . .] *si quæremus qualis sit effectus, oportet prius causam cognoscere, et non contra*'). Given that analysis is the direction of increasing knowledge, effects must be deduced from causes; and the sciences of obscure matters must proceed from the things that are simple and obvious to us (*Reg.* IX, CSM I: 34; AT X: 402:

'[. . .] *ex facilibus tantum et magis obviis, scientias quantumlibet occultas esse deducendas*'). So, causes first, because causes are simple.

Writing to Mersenne a little after the abandonment of the *Rules*, Descartes describes the *a priori* as the natural order of knowledge, of which he says, mixing his metaphors rather enthusiastically, that analysis is 'the key and the foundation of the highest and most perfect science that humans can have of material things (letter of 10th May 1632, CSMK: 35; AT I: 250: '[. . .] *la clef et le fondement de la plus haute et la plus parfaite science que les hommes puissent avoir touchant les choses matérielles*').

There are several passages in the *Discourse* in which Descartes indicates that the procedure adopted in the sciences involves their borrowing their principles from first philosophy.

One is in *Discourse* I, where he diagnoses the instability of earlier investigations into nature to be a consequence of their resting on insecure foundations (*Dis.* I, CSM I: 115). When he refers to the sciences he was taught at school, the structure of 'borrowing' recurs in *Discourse* II. Here, he takes the dependence relation to be a feature of all well-conducted enquiry: his own reformed and refounded science should stand on stabler and more certain principles (*Dis.* II, CSM I: 121–2). These considerations lead him, at the beginning of *Discourse* V, to speak of there being a whole chain of truths that he had deduced from the basic metaphysical principles (*Dis.* V, CSM I: 131: AT VI: 40: '[. . .] *toute la chaîne des autres vérités qu'j'ai déduites de ces premières*'). The principles in question are those operative in *Discourse* IV, though he is very reticent about stating what they are (*Dis.* IV, CSM I: 126–7). The metaphysical principles are first in order of knowledge; and they are simple. They also permit Descartes to discover laws that lead him to more useful and important truths than everything he had hitherto learnt (*Dis.* V, CSM I: 131). This is as clear an indication as any that Descartes regards the theories he was developing, both in *The World* (i.e. *Lum.* and *Des.*) and in the essays published with the *Discourse*, as deductive; deduced, that is, by analysis from the primary metaphysical truths. He therefore takes the movement to be from causes to effects.

Descartes allows that the exposition of the *Discourse* does not itself show the deductions from the primary truths of metaphysics; and he says that he expressly decided against such a mode of exposition (*Dis.* VI, CSM I: 150; AT VI: 76: '[. . .] *j'ai voulu expressement ne la pas faire*'; cf. letter to Mersenne, 11th March 1640, CSMK: 145). His reasons, we gather, are (i) that he did not wish to get embroiled in arguments with the learned on disputed matters (*Dis.* VI, CSM I: 141–2, on which more in Chapter 11 below); and (ii) that he did not wish to give succour to those who would get carried away with half-understood ideas (*Dis.* VI, CSM I: 150).[14] But he is not denying that this *is* his procedure when he says that his principles are proved by their effects:

experience making most of these effects very certain, the causes from which I deduce them serve not so much to prove them as to explain them; but on the contrary, it's the former [sc. the causes] that are proved by the latter [sc. the effects] (*Dis.* VI, CSM I: 150; AT VI: 76: '[. . .] *l'ex-périence rendant la plupart de ces effets très certains, les causes dont je les déduis ne servent pas tant à les prouver qu'à les expliquer; mais, tout au contraire, ce sont elles qui sont prouvées par eux*').

Some commentators take this passage to be an indicator that Descartes' procedure is experimental (e.g. Alquié in note ad loc. in Descartes 1963–73: I, 614; Clarke 1992: 236–4). But this cannot be right, because he is saying that he *has* deduced effects from causes.

As I return to explain, the physics that he was enabled to do by the simplification in the *Treatise on Light* gets him more effects than do his efforts to work on the actual world. Even so, he is trying to demonstrate effects from their causes and to show the seeds from which, and the manner in which, nature must produce those effects (*Dis.* V, CSM I: 134; AT VI: 45: '[. . .] *démontrant les effets par les causes, et faisant voir de quelles semences, et en quelle façon, la nature les doit produire*'). As he explains to Morin, each of the effects could also be proved (in the sense of demonstrated to be as it is) by its cause (letter of 13th July 1638, CSMK: 107; AT III: 198: '[. . .] *qu'on sache que chacun de ces effets peut aussi être prouvé par cette cause*').[15] Taking this into account, the way that the effects might 'prove' the causes is like what is sometimes misunderstood in the dictum that an exception proves a rule: it is test of it, not evidence for it.

Furthermore, one might doubt that the phrase 'most of these effects' in the passage just quoted from *Discourse* VI has been taken seriously enough. At the least, it leaves open the possibility that some effects may have been deduced that experience does not make certain. These would be effects that can be known certainly, through their causes and independent of experience. In similar vein, a little earlier in *Discourse* VI, he says that he can predict many effects from his principles and know straight off that the former are deducible in various ways from the latter, though sometimes he is unsure which derivation is the one actually in operation (*Dis.* VI, CSM I: 144). There remains the problem, which we shall address in the next chapter, of finding the right deduction; but the selection is clearly a selection among deductions.

In this connection, it may be useful to bear in mind a thought expressed by Spinoza in his discussion of definitions in the *Correction of the Understanding* (Spinoza 1926: XIII). The thought is that, when one is dealing for instance with a triangle, there is such a thing as its perfect definition. For Spinoza, as for Descartes, this is to be identified with the essence of the *definiendum*, in such a way that the definition can be used for analysis of it. Thus, it might be that, of two proposed definitions of a triangle, one is perfect and one imperfect; both can be used to make some deductions that seem to fit the triangles that we see; but it is only the perfect definition that allows the 'connection of the understanding to reflect the connection of nature' (ibid.). In appealing to this potent thought, I am not suggesting that Descartes is as Spinozistic as Spinoza seems to have thought he was. Rather, the idea is that the correct identification of the principles from which to deduce the effects of nature is crucial to Descartes' enterprise: the first metaphysical principles stand to what is deduced from them as the definition of a geometrical figure stands to the various properties that can be dug out of it.

There is a great deal in the *Meditations*, especially and notoriously III, about causes. And one might have to concede that there is some respect in which, in arguing from the existence of a contingent being (himself) to the existence of a necessary being (God), Descartes' operation might be described as '*a posteriori*', moving from effect to cause. I have two reservations – grumbles really – about this concession.

One is that the sort of argument he is giving is not meant to discover God's existence from something prior in the order of knowledge; on the contrary, he says God's existence is much more evident than the existence of anything perceptible (*Resp.* I, CSM II: 77; AT VII: 106: '[. . .] *Deum existere multo evidentius esse putavi, quam ullas res sensibiles*'). The cause is really a given, even if there are persons who need to have it *pointed out* to them, which may be the sense of 'demonstration' in the title of the *Meditations*. If any type of argument deserves the name *a priori*, it will be the type that gets called 'ontological' and discovered in places like *Meditations* III (and with more justification V; Barnes 1972: 15–16).

The other grumble is that, within the operation of *Meditations* III, we have not yet got to the level at which the sciences start to fan out and the order of causes and effects can be made perspicuous, with, e.g. the simple and general bits of physics clearly preceding the more specific bits of mechanics. The doctrines that make up metaphysics seem to hang together pretty much as a piece: order really begins when, in the image of the tree, we get above ground level. In this respect, God's essence is a first principle that is, at most, *primum inter pares* with the other common notions. And if His essence has that standing then so too does His existence.

Nevertheless, the shape of the sequel to metaphysics is spelt out at the end of *Meditations* V:

> I see for sure the certainty and truth of all knowledge depending on a perception of the true God in such a way that, before being acquainted with Him, I could not perfectly know anything about any other thing

whatever (*Med.* V, CSM II: 49; AT VII: 71: '[. . .] *plane video omnis scientiæ certitudinem et veritatem ab una veri Dei cognitione pendere, adeo ut priusquam
illum nossem, nihil de ulla alia re perfecte scire potuerim*').

As cause of all things, God must be known before His effects; and those
effects can only be properly known through knowledge of Him. For an atheist, the dispiriting consequence is that he can only make a hypothetical
profession of Descartes' physics, stripped of all certainty (Gueroult 1954:
112; Janowski 2000: 74–8). The atheist does not know the cause of the suppositions he makes in physics and, so, does not know them perfectly.

We have already seen enough from the 'Letter-Preface' to the *Principles* for
us not to be in doubt about what he thinks is the right direction of proof in
science proper; and, in the next chapter we shall examine some relevant
material from the end of part IV. But, for now, we may add this from the end
of part II:

> [. . .] I shall admit as true nothing [concerning matter] that has not been
> so evidently deduced from those common notions, whose truth we
> cannot doubt, as to be regarded as a mathematical demonstration. And
> given that all the phenomena of nature can be explained in this way, as
> will be made plain in what follows, no other principles of physics seem
> to be acceptable, nor even choiceworthy (*Pr.* II, 64, CSM I: 247; AT
> VIIIA: 79: '[. . .] *nihilque de ipsis ut verum admittere, quod non ex communibus
> illis notiones, de quarum veritate non possumus dubitare, tam evidenter deducatur, ut
> pro mathematica demonstratione sit habendum. Et quia sic omnia naturæ phænomena
> possunt explicari, ut in sequentibus apparebit, nulla alia physicæ principia puto esse
> admittenda, nec alia etiam optanda*; cf. the addition, at AT IXB: 102, that we
> have no reason to want any principles other than those Descartes is
> about to spell out).

It may be that Descartes does not carry this programme out. It may be that
he does not do so because no one could. And it may be that no one could
because humans do not, as a matter of fact, have the powers required to
carry the programme out. But that does not undermine its status as a programmatic statement, defining what rectitude in the sciences *would* be and
what it *would* get us.

From what we have seen in the foregoing chapters, it is a programme that
Descartes argues is within human powers. First, we saw him trying to show
that we can learn that almost all the beliefs and belief-forming principles,
especially concerning matter, that people have accepted come from the
tainted source of the senses. Then we saw his account of the intellect and
will, which he thinks are of such kinds and are so related that we are able to

admit as true only notions whose truth we cannot doubt. After that, there was the question of how we can secure ourselves against the bad doxastic habits that make us accept principles that are not really secure (and that, therefore, do not explain the phenomena of nature). We found that Descartes sets the standards so high that we must restrict ourselves to deduction or analysis, which is understood as an arrangement of small steps of seeing the rightness of the principles and of the things that follow from them. These principles are the explanations of the things of which they are the principles. By analysis, we expand our understanding from the uniquely intelligible principles of physics, which we find are within our grasp, to the other things of which it is proper for us to take cognisance.

This is the view that Descartes consistently expresses in works from the *Rules* to the *Principles*: it is an apriorism that is a fixed feature of his thought about the proper conduct of the sciences.

10 What rectitude permits

Moral certainty

Rectitude is austere in what it demands for some procedure to be counted as virtuous: the metaphysical first principles are the *only* starting-points we can trust and analysis is the *only* way we can get knowledge properly so-called out of them.

But we have already seen several ways that rectitude is not unconditionally obligatory. Humans have purposes other than those that are dominant in enquiry as described in Descartes' philosophical writings. One purpose of this sort was proving the freedom of the will by suspending assent to a clear and distinct idea (Chapter 5 above) Others, such as the avoidance of pain by following the teachings of nature (*Med.* VI, CSM II: 56), do not presuppose the state of seclusion that enquiry demands.[1] These latter cases can be grouped together as having as their upper limit a grade of certainty that Descartes calls 'moral'. After considering how high this upper limit is, I shall move to consider whether any use can be made of matter with that grade of certainty within the austere business of knowledge-getting.

We saw in Chapter 7 that there is something alarming about the way that, at the end of *Meditations* VI Descartes appears to relax his demands on what is to count as knowledge. Although no belief that any human has formed would fulfil the criteria that he sets out, he seems to be trying to circumvent the threats to knowledge posed by the possibilities that, for all we know to the contrary, we may be dreaming or the dupes of a malicious demon. The suggestion was made that paying attention to the promptings of the body is an acceptable shift because, as with the forms of childish credulity reviewed in Chapter 3, those promptings are aids to our survival. The apparent relaxation of Descartes' standards of assent-worthiness should, therefore, be understood not as a vindication of what the senses tell us about the world, but as an acceptance, in the light of general divine benevolence, that we can learn how to conduct ourselves even in an environment about whose true nature the senses do not give us reliable information (Menn 1998: 366–80). Even if a hot poker is not really red, because redness does not truly belong to bodies, we can use the colour it looks as an empirical warning sign and thus escape a burning.

The *Meditations* finishes soon after Descartes offers these observations. But we can see how what is implicit in them from a work with broader aims: namely the *Principles*. The first part of the *Principles*, which in large measure recapitulates the whole of the *Meditations*, ends with a round-up of the causes of human error (*Pr.* I, 71–4, considered in Chapter 3 above). Descartes subjoins to his account of these causes a summary of the rules for philosophising, followed by an assertion that whatever God has revealed to us has priority over the results of the application of those rules (*Pr.* I, 75 and 76).

We then have to wait until the end of Part 4 of the *Principles* before we find anything resembling the considerations in the *Meditations* about the teachings of nature. When it does come, this analogue material is deeply embedded in Descartes' claim to have deduced, in the intervening nearly 300 AT pages, a great deal about magnets, fire and the make-up of the whole world from just a few principles (*Pr.* IV, 205, CSM I: 290). There is room for uncertainty about whether the main subject of Descartes' closing remarks to the *Principles* is the certainty we are allowed in using the senses for practical purposes or the certainty of the senses *as contrasted with* the certainty of Cartesian explanations of physical phenomena. Let us unpick what Descartes says, bearing in mind the variants as between the original Latin and the French translation of 1647. Because the French adds some substantial points, it makes sense to attribute them to Descartes and not to suppose that Picot is going beyond his remit as translator.

The title of *Principles* IV, 204 says that, when we are dealing with things that cannot be sensed ('*insensibilia*'), it is enough if we can explain how they could be, even if they are not really that way.[2] This move will put us in mind of the concession in *Principles* III, 43–7 that even if the hypotheses Descartes employs to account for heavenly movements are false, they can be used to explain the phenomena. This is a matter I return to in a moment.

For the time being, it is worth concentrating on the things that cannot be sensed, which are the indefinitely divisible quantities invoked to explain such phenomena as the growth of a tree from one day to the next (*Pr.* IV, 201, CSM I: 286). The characteristics of these can be assigned or learnt (*Pr.* IV, 203, CSM I: 288; AT VIIIA: 325: '*assigno*'; AT IXB: 321: '*j'ai appris*') by application of the basic principles of the constitution and behaviour of bodies. In agreement with what we saw on the tree of the sciences, mechanics is an outgrowth of physics (*Pr.* IV, 203, CSM I: 288; AT VIIIA 326: '[. . .] *nullæ sunt in Mechanica rationes, quæ non etiam ad Physicam cuius pars vel species est, pertineant*').

Therefore, the basic principles can be employed to work out what would be needed to get a certain effect.

To exemplify this move, Descartes makes two references to what we can know about the innards of a mechanism. In his first reference to it, at the end of *Principles* IV, 203, he has in mind the idea that, if someone knows about how, say, clocks can be made, then the sight of some of the parts will allow her to judge what the unseen bits will be like.[3] Here, the expert uses what she sees to fill in the gaps. Descartes uses the analogy to explain what he is doing when he explains the parts and effects that can be sensed ('*sensibilia*') by reference to their unsensed ('*insensiles*') causes and parts (*Pr.* IV, 203, CSM I: 288). We are meant to think that the range of judgments plausible to an expert about the unseen will be relatively narrow: there is a limited number of ways of completing the mechanism.

By contrast, in the following article, the reference to clocks makes a slightly different point. Here, the idea is that the effect (telling the time to a given degree of accuracy) can be achieved in a variety of ways, though the casings of the two clocks are identical (*Pr.* IV, 204, CSM I: 289). If we are looking only at the outside of the two clocks, we may not be able to tell that one runs by clockwork and, to take a more radically different case than Descartes envisages, the other is regulated by quartz. We are not trying to work out what else goes with a given sort of, say, escapement or remontoire, but trying to see what *could* keep time. As Descartes confesses, this analogy, when applied to all the possibilities that God could have come up with as the way of making the world work means that what we see does not determine a single outcome.[4] This he confesses happily enough, so long as the explanation he gives answers accurately to all the phenomena of nature (*Pr.* IV, 204, CSM I: 289; AT VIIIA: 327: '[. . .] *ut omnibus naturæ phænomenis accurate respondeant*'), and in the French version he declines to wonder which of the possible ways God could have operated is the one He has actually chosen (AT IXB: 322: '[without demanding that *all* the phenomena be accounted for] *sans m'enquérir si c'est par elles* [sc. *causes*] *ou par d'autres qu'ils* [sc. *effets*] *sont produits*'). Descartes is not concerned about the way the world actually works because he is interested in the grade of explanation that suffices for (AT VIIIA: 327: '*sufficiet*'), or is useful in (AT IXB: 322: '*utile*'), life, where that grade of explanation is contrasted with the true causes, which may turn out to be hidden from humans.

In the title of the French version and in the text of both the Latin and French of *Principles* IV, 204, which we have already cited in part, Descartes refers to Aristotle as seeking to do no more than explain how things could be. The passage he has in mind is from the *Meteorology* (I vii, paraphrasing 344 a 5–8); and the reference recurs in a letter to unknown recipient of 1644 or later (CSMK: 239). This is one of many places in which Aristotle offers the thought that we should be satisfied with an account on which all the phenomena harmonise (e.g. *Phys.*, IV iv, 211 a 11–12; *EN*, I viii 1098 b 10–12). But, broadly speaking, Aristotle takes the harmonisation of the phenomena to be a sign of the *truth* of the account: we should be satisfied because we have got to the bottom of things. In this respect, the *Meteorology* passage is 'exceptional in talking of a sufficient demonstration' (Lloyd 1996: 25); and in citing it, Descartes seems to be moving in the direction of an instrumentalist or anti-realist conception of the confirmation of his explanations in natural science: we should be satisfied because there's nothing more to say.

Though there is an obvious benefit for Descartes in referring to Aristotle to establish the respectability of his position on the at-least-moral certainty of his explanations, his implicit denial that humans have to be able to discern the way that God has set the world up is more closely reminiscent of an Epicurean view. For, in one report of Epicurus, we find the idea that, so long as there is no counter-evidence (οὐκ ἀντιμαρτύρησις), even a non-evident thing (such as the existence of void) that is consistent with what is perceived (such as that there is motion) can be believed.[5] Yet in the *Letter to Pythocles*, Epicurus himself says that someone who seeks to defend one explanation of the heavenly motions against others that account for the same phenomena is giving up natural philosophy and going in for myth.[6] What is instrumentalist in this position is the notion that, so long as we are attending only to the things that make a difference to our lives, we need no more than a story that fits the facts (Nussbaum 1994: 133–5). And, for Descartes, the anti-realism comes out in the thought that divine agency may, in many cases, such as those of natural teleology and special miracles, be beyond our ken (cf. *Pr.* I, 28): where we have a plurality of possible causes, we may as well remain open to all of them.[7] The plurality of candidate explanations, whether for the working of a clock or the motions of the heavens, means that some questions must simply remain open.[8]

At *Principles* IV, 205, Descartes says that his explanations are at least morally certain. In the French version, but not in the Latin, he defines moral certainty as the certainty that is sufficient for guiding our behaviour or that is as great as that about things we do not usually doubt in the conduct of our lives (*Pr.* IV, 205, CSM I: 289 n. 2; AT IXB: 323: '[*certitude*] *suffisante pour régler nos mœurs ou aussi grande que celle des choses dont nous n'avons point coutume de douter touchant la conduite de la vie*'; cf. *Dis.* V, CSM I: 139). That degree of certainty is *contrasted* with the certainty that we could not, absolutely speaking (*Pr.* IV, 205, CSM I: 289 n. 2; AT IXB: 323: '*absolument parlant*') or in relation to divine omnipotence (ibid. AT VIIIA: 327: '[. . .] *si ad absolutam Dei potentiam referantur*'), be deceived.

Descartes has two main problems here.

One is God's absolute power to create the world any way He chooses, and thus to produce the phenomena in any of many ways, among which we must seek a decision. Because his talking about 'what we do not generally doubt' so drastically lowers the standards of acceptability, I doubt Descartes is quite in earnest here or has amended his text without due attention to the implications of what is added in the French.[9] For, he is, and knows he is, offering a theory of the world that flies in the face of what most of us generally believe and have no inclination to doubt; so he cannot appeal to what we generally believe: he has to show that he has done better than that.

The other problem is that, where two explanations cover the same phenomena, there can be no 'argument to the best explanation' without taking into account previously formed canons of, for instance, simplicity. But Descartes does not have or offer any such canons for dealing with phenomena, other than the claim that his principles do explain them.

So, when, in the following article, he claims that his explanations are *more* than morally certain (*Pr.* IV, 206, CSM I: 290), he is backtracking into the view that it is their similarity to mathematical demonstrations, spun out of the most evident first principles, that makes them so. That is, they are the results of analysis. In the preceding articles (IV, 203–5), he makes a gesture at putting his findings on an empirical basis, but at *Principles* IV, 206 the emphasis is on the relation of the certainty of his explanations to their metaphysical foundations (*Pr.* IV, 206, CSM I: 290: AT VIIIA: 328: '[. . .] *innixi Metaphysico fundamento*'; AT IXB: 324: '[. . .] *elle est fondée sur un principe de métaphysique très assuré*'). In the Latin version, this comes out as effectively equivalent to their really constituting the only ultimately comprehensible accounts.[10] He hopes to have eliminated the threat of plurality and, hence, the attractions of anti-realism.

At an earlier stage in his thought, we find a nascent distinction between the explanation of some phenomenon, perhaps for practical purposes, and the truly philosophical explanation that is involved in giving the true grounds of things in general. In the latter case, plurality is not on:

> we can explain a given effect in various ways all of which are possible, but I think that the possibility of things in general can only be explained in only one way, which is the true one (letter to Mersenne, 28th October 1640, CSMK: 154; AT III: 212: '[. . .] *on peut expliquer un même effet en diverses façons qui soient possibles, mais je crois qu'on ne peut expliquer la possibilité des choses en général, que d'une seule façon, qui est la vraie*').

Here he is not claiming to be able to find confirmation of his principles from cases; rather, he is setting up the exclusivity of those very principles; as Alquié notes in this connection, 'he holds the principle of his physics for certain' (Descartes 1963–73: II, 270). If this distinction is still operative in the

Principles, however inexplicitly, it leaves moral certainty with no place in the system of completed science.

The examples of the moral certainty that suffices for the practical affairs of everyday life given in *Principles* IV, 205, can confirm the reading according to which any certainty, even if it is greater than moral certainty, that falls short of the certainty provided by analysis from first principles falls short of what is required in an enquiry in accordance with doxastic rectitude.

A case that appears in the French version (but again not in the Latin) is an instance of testimony: even if I have never been to Rome, I do not doubt that it is a city in Italy; yet it could be that everyone who passed this information on to me was mistaken (*Pr.* IV, 205, CSM I: 290). As it happens, this is a true belief. Suppose, analogously, that the belief that Budapest is a city in Bulgaria had got passed on to me. For all extra-Budapest and extra-Bulgaria (and, as it turns out, extra-Hungarian) purposes, I can regard this belief as certain: the error it contains gives me no cause for doubt, does not conflict with any other of my beliefs, impinge on my other activities, or cause me pain. So long as I keep well clear of Bulgaria and of Budapest, I can be morally certain of a belief that happens to be false. But there are experiences, such as those that crop up in trying to get to Budapest, that would reveal my error and would mean that my conduct was misguided. If I set off for Budapest by heading for Bulgaria, I shall soon find myself in a frustrating muddle. Thus, moral certainty has to be indexed to what I happen to have as my travel plans; which conflicts with the idea we have explored of Cartesian science as independent of such contingencies. Moreover, if testimony could provide moral certainty, then the senses could too. But what the senses provide cannot be directly incorporated into the body of completed science. *A fortiori*, testimony cannot either. Hence, moral certainty is inadequate to science proper.

The other case is perhaps closer to the question of the confirmability of explanations by fit with the facts. Here, Descartes supposes the decoding of a text by substitution of a given letter by the next in the alphabet (cf. *Reg.* X, CSM I: 35–6, cited in connection with the fourth precept). If the resulting text makes some sense, that vindicates the initial guess about the key (*Pr.* IV, 205, CSM I: 290; AT VIIIA: 327–8: '*conjiciens* [. . .] *conjectura*'; AT IXB: 323–4: '*deviner* [. . .] *conjecture*'). For it would be incredible (AT VIIIA: 328: '*incredibile*'; AT IXB: 323: '*n'est pas moralement croyable*') that some other message should have been encoded. Incredible, but possible (AT VIIIA: 328: '*fieri forsan possit*'; AT IXB: 323: '*il se pourrait faire*').[11] As with the Budapest/Rome case, suppose that the author of the text had employed another key than the one we use for decoding, encoding a different message than the one we have arrived at.[12] In that case, we shall not get his meaning; and, again, if the message happens to concern a matter of importance to us, our satisfaction with having got *a* sense out of the text may turn to dismay – regret or remorse – of just the sort that Descartes is trying to avoid.

In short, the sorts of hypotheses whose certainty is no more than what suffices for the purposes of life, and whose support is evidential rather than rational, suffer from all the defects that the refoundation of science is meant to overcome. When he says that his scientific explanations are more than morally certain, Descartes pictures them not as hypotheses to account for empirical data, but as consequences of demonstration, the outcomes of analysis from first principles.

The irrelevance of experience

There are two general reasons why we should not expect Descartes to hang anything of scientific value on attempts to justify or confirm an explanation by reference to the phenomena. One is that it is invalid; the other is that he thinks it is irrelevant.

The invalidity in question derives from an elementary logical observation. Suppose I have an astronomical theory that predicts an eclipse on a certain date: if the theory is true, then the eclipse will occur. Suppose that the eclipse occurs. What can I infer? Nothing, on pain of affirming the consequent. After all, my prediction could have just happened to coincide with what the heavens were going to produce anyway. Contrariwise, if the eclipse does not occur I can infer, *modus tollendo tollens*, the falsity of the theory.

I doubt that there is any good reason to think that Descartes would not have seen this asymmetry. And there are several reasons for thinking that he would have. One is that it is so elementary an observation. Nevertheless this elementary error has been regarded as attributable to Descartes: 'by deducing a description of a phenomenon from a law of nature [. . .] one proves the analysis that led to the discovery of that law' (Flage 1999: 44). Yet even Popper understood it. Another is that, in the scientific culture of Descartes' day, there was no special reason of the sort we seem to have been given by the subsequent successes of experimental science and by the mathematisation of probability and confirmation theory for thinking that empirical techniques could be used positively to support theories. Indeed, a major reason why Descartes wanted to find something more secure and apodeictic was the need to rise above the fray among those who were satisfied with 'saving the phenomena'. Recall his behaviour when faced with the opposition between De Chandoux and the Scholastics.

Granting that the hypothetico-deductive model is an invalid approach to theory confirmation, the *modus tollendo tollens* beloved of falsification theorists had better make sure that the negated consequences are better known than the antecedents they are set against. In the example cited above, I predict an eclipse and then rely on an imbecile or a liar to make observations for me. If my informant tells me there was no eclipse, I have not done a good job of testing the theory that led to the prediction. But I need not abandon it either.

We return, under the rubric of what rectitude forbids, to consider an important class of truths that Descartes thinks can falsify the products of analysis. For now, let us look at how science proper is immune to contradiction by empirical techniques. Descartes' position – that experience is irrelevant to science proper – is unequivocal, coherent and, in at least some of the cases he cites, correct.

One case in which he is pretty certainly right comes out in another of those squabbles with Gassendi.

Near the beginning of *Meditations* V, Descartes says that it is irrelevant to his understanding of the intrinsic properties of triangles that he should have sometimes come across, by means of the sense organs, bodies of triangular shape (*Med.* V, CSM II: 45; see Jolley 1990: 44–6). To which Gassendi objects that, if Descartes had been totally deprived of sensory functions, and been able neither to see nor to touch, then he would not have been able to have or form the idea of a triangle or of any other shape (*Obj.* V, CSM II: 223). In reply, Descartes offers Gassendi a choice. Either the whole of geometry is false (which is in conflict with the fact that many truths can be proved: *Resp.* V, CSM II: 262) or we do not get our ideas of shapes through the senses (see Guenancia 1998: 134–41). If the whole of geometry were false, what it would be false of is the gritty, granular world that we perceive, and that Atomists who were Gassendi's inspiration, theorise as the ultimate account of matter.[13] But, what Descartes takes geometry to be true of are figures understood not as substances but as limits (*Resp.* V, CSM II: 262).[14] So we do not arrive at those truths through the senses.

In any case, the straight lines and smooth curves of geometrical figures are simply not at the disposal of our senses. Yet, for instance, as both Aristotle (*De An.*, I i, 403 a 10–16) and St Augustine (*Sol.*, II, 19, 33–20, 35) argue, we can know of a plane that it touches a sphere only at a point. If some surface really were a plane, its planeness would not be perceptible as such. It would not be distinguishable from the unplane surfaces that we generally take to be plane, and the surfaces we take to be plane generally turn out, on microscopic inspection, to be lumpy (*Resp.* V, CSM II: 262).

This can be illustrated with the following anecdote taken from John Aubrey's brief life of Descartes:

> [a]ll the learned men made visits to him, and many of them would desire him to show them his [store] of instruments (in those days mathematical learning lay much store in the knowledge of instruments, and as Sir Henry Savile said, in doing tricks). He would draw out a little

drawer under his table and show them a pair of compasses with one of
the legs broken; and then for a ruler, he used a sheet of paper folded in
half.

(Aubrey 1975: 110)[15]

Some of this is surely bravado: we know, for instance, of the care he took
over getting an artisan who was expert at lens-grinding (Ferrier; see
Belgioioso 1999: 132–45). But the point is that fancy instrumentation will not
get you very far unless you grasp the principle it embodies: a fine pair of
compasses is no more an aid to the understanding of circles than one with a
broken leg. Because both are imperfect, just in different degrees.

The matter is raised also by Burman, who suggests that we create the idea
of the perfect triangle out of an imperfect one (*Con.*, CSMK: 344; AT V:
161: '[Burman . . .] *ex imperfecto illo triangulo effingis perfectum*'). To which
Descartes replies with the question of why we do not just form an idea of an
imperfect triangle (ibid.: AT V: 162: '[Descartes . . .] *cur illum imperfectum mihi
potius exhibet ideam perfecti trianguli, quam sui ipsius?*'). And, in response to
Burman's supposition that experience gives us the ideas both of the imperfect and of the perfect, Descartes says that it is because we conceive the
perfect that we can understand how imperfect the empirical shapes are
(ibid., '[Descartes . . .] *viso triangulo, concipio perfectum, ex cuius comparatione dein-
ceps illud quod video imperfectum esse animadverto*'). In his note on the point
(Cottingham in Descartes 1976: 96–7), John Cottingham aptly refers us to
Plato's *Phædo* (74 B) and suggests that Descartes is here operating a distinction
between positive and negative concepts of the sort we do find in the
Meditations. The point may be, however, that the idea of a perfect triangle is
just the idea of a triangle, whereas the idea of this or that imperfect approximation is an idea of what a triangularish thing might look like, kinks and
bumps, both above and below the sensory threshold, included, and is not the
idea of a *triangle* at all.

Going back again to the scratches Socrates makes in the sand in the *Meno*,
Descartes' point here comes out as follows. The squares and triangles under
the slaveboy's eyes are mere approximations to the geometrical figures that
are being investigated. Hence, the fact that, despite the scragginess of the
scratches, the slaveboy does get the drift of the demonstration means that the
demonstration calls on perfect figures. We can put this the other way about.
Suppose the slaveboy stops Socrates at a certain point and, whipping out a
ruler, sniggeringly shows that this is never a square and that diagonal does
not bisect it anyway. Would this show that the square on the diagonal of a
given square is not twice its area or whatever other particular feature
Socrates is trying to get across (see Lloyd 1992)?

If we go with Gassendi, we have to say that, yes, a geometrical proof is only as good as the instruments, including paper and pen, with which we construct it. And we will find ourselves in the company of those who say that the (geometrical) idea we have of a triangle is somehow an abstraction from the triangularish things we have seen. In that case, our friends will include Locke (1689: II, xii), Hume (1739–40: I, vii) and Mill (1843: IV, ii). Otherwise, to keep from the position that Descartes occupies, we might make a desperate lunge in the direction of conventionalism and say it's all a matter of definition, along with such as the early stages of Ayer (1936: Chapter 4) and Quine (1936). But, in either case, we are not going to be willing to say that geometry is true because of how plane right triangles are. If this is because we think we are being sophisticated about the limitations of Euclidean geometry, then we are pretty surely underestimating the range of Descartes' conceptual point. Namely, that whatever geometrical ideas we attend to under their geometric aspect, their interrelations hold irrespective of experience and can be dug into independent of it.

The slaveboy would not be doing geometry, understood as the investigation of the properties of limits, if he paid attention to the scratches in the sand. No observation of scratches, or of any more fine-grained diagram, can dislodge Pythagoras' insight into (Euclidean plane) triangles; likewise, there is no experience that could dislodge, say, the possibility of converging parallels in a Riemannian space. In neither case, is this a matter of definition, though the case has to be defined. For Descartes, it is a matter of the truths established by God and imprinted within us; and for any moderate realist it is a matter of what geometry is about and what (geometrical) analysis can get us.

As we saw Socrates applying the structure of learning in geometry to whatever we discover, so for Descartes what is going on in geometry is not an isolated case. Indeed, responding to objections to his optical theories, he treats a commentator who appeals to experience as laughable, contemptible and credulous, and quite beyond the pale. He explicitly draws the analogy between what goes for optics and what goes for geometry: the objector to the Cartesian theory of refractions who appeals to experiments is like someone who wishes to use a battered old setsquare to show that the angles of a triangle do not add up to 180° (letter to Mersenne, 9th February 1639, AT II: 497–8).[16]

It is as old a *topos* as any that experience can get you wholly the wrong answer even in an area, such as astronomy, where 'saving the phenomena' is regarded as necessary to the plausibility of a theory. Descartes is inventing nothing when he refers to the erroneous idea we get from the senses of the size of the Sun (*Dis.* IV, CSM I: 131; *Med.* III, CSM II: 27; *Resp.* VI, ad 10, CSM II: 296). He does not even have to explain his allusions to the phenomenon: everyone knows that we are badly placed on Earth to get an idea through the senses of the dimensions of the Sun, however much of a problem that may be for theories on which experience is given a primary role (Ben-Zeev 1984; Barnes 1989). If we are going to work out how big the Sun is, we have to go so long a way round that the reason why we prefer the astronomers' version over what we see is precisely the amount of calculation involved.

Things become a little trickier when we consider the laws of motion and their applications. Though Descartes does claim that they agree with all our experiences, there are a couple of places where he envisages our perceiving bodies moving in defiance of them. This is tricky because we have to consider at least two cases, which Descartes does not explicitly distinguish.

In one, we are dealing with bodies for which we have actually done the measurements of motion and seemed to find, for instance, that, after a certain collision, there was less motion in the world than before it. In such a case, the discrepancy between experimental data and what the laws of motion predict (namely, conservation of the total amount of motion) might be dealt with by supposing that the error lay in measuring instruments.[17] But suppose that such effects were invariant in a variety of experimental setups.

This, I take it, is the sort of case he has in mind in *Principles* II, 52. He is polishing off and commenting on his rules for the determination of a given body's motion. In the Latin, he says that the rules need no proof because they are manifest of themselves (*Pr.* II, 52, CSM I: 245; AT VIIIA: 70: '[*n*]*ec ista egent probatione, qua per se sunt manifesta*'). Being manifest of themselves means that the rules are more manifest than anything that is manifest through something else; including anything that is manifest through experience. As if to clear up all doubt about the matter, in the French version he replaces the short formula with the more fully unpacked thesis that:

> the demonstrations of all this are so certain that, even if experience were to seem to show the opposite, we would nevertheless be obliged to place more faith in reason than in our senses (*Pr.* II, 52, AT IXB 93: '[. . .] *les démonstrations de tout ceci sont si certaines qu'encore que l'experience nous semblerait faire voir le contraire, nous serions néamoins obligés d'ajouter plus de foi à notre raison qu'à nos sens*').

That is, if experimentation were consistently to show that a given type of collision produces a shortfall of motion, then the experiments, even if they were perfect of their kind, would be just wrong. When in conflict with what reason tells us, experiments are wrong because their kind is wrong: they do not produce anything that is manifest of itself.

In the same direction, in Chapter VII of the *Treatise on Light*, Descartes considers the attitude to take to the possibility of a discrepancy between the physics of the 'fable' and the motion of bodies in the actual world. He says that, even if everything our senses experienced in the real world seemed to be in manifest conflict with his first two rules of motion, the power of reason that taught me them seems so strong that I would not give up the belief that I am required to suppose them in the new world I am describing for you (*Lum.* VII, CSM I: 95; AT XI: 43: '[. . .] *encore que tout ce que nos sens ont experimenté dans le vrai monde, semblait manifestement être contraire à ce qui est contenu dans ces deux règles, la raison qui me les a enseignées, me semble si forte, que je ne laisserait pas de croire être obligé de les supposer dans le nouveau que je vous décris*').

This is a rather hedged position, asserting only that the physics of the 'fable' is the only one that reason could accept. It allows, that is, that the physics of the actual world could be so chock full of mysteries and wonders that humans can understand hardly any of it, which is certainly a possible outcome of divine omnipotence. As we shall see in the next chapter, this is just how Descartes thinks the actual world may be. But the point for present purposes is that, once again, experience is being put down: Descartes is not going to model what he hopes will be the best possible physical theory on it.

The other sort of case that we should distinguish is the normal case, in which we are dealing with stuff other than the parts of the world on which we can actually do the measurements and calculations. I take it that this is what he has in mind in the transition at *Principles* II, 52 and 53. In article 52, the priority of reason is asserted against even the best sensory evidence. In article 53, Descartes begins to deal with the fact that the actual world is not tidy: the bodies we are in (sensory) contact with are not as neatly isolated nor as perfectly inelastic as the theory calls for.[18] The things we see and feel are composites of the elementary, microscopic regions of matter that the laws do fit. In this sort of case, the appearance of conflict between his laws of motion and the data of experience can easily be explained away. This bit of explaining away requires us to say both that the things we see ('*sensibilia*') and that we can explain are to be explained by things we cannot see ('*insensiles*', '*insensibilia*': *Pr.* IV, 203–4) and that there are things we cannot explain among the things we see because there are too many things we cannot see. The promise of actually *giving* the explanation cannot be kept in many, perhaps all, actual cases.

There are thus clear indications that Descartes did not suppose that the results of analysis could be refuted by any counter-instance derived from experience. It might be doubted that he was right to assimilate all the sciences to the model of geometry. But it is reasonable to think that that is just what he did.

Admonitions

Empirical adequacy

What, then, should we say about Descartes' boasts that his theory fits the facts of experience?

In a general way, he is as entitled to them as any advertiser or politician is to her self-puffs. His theorisation of nature was not noticeably worse than many others on the market at the time; indeed, it was markedly superior to many in point of rigour and fecundity. If we think of him as in the race to take the office previously held by Aristotle, then, as already noted in considering the moral certainty of some explanations, he has to make appeals to recognised standards. The candidate who does not say she can solve crime *and* bring social justice will be beaten by the opponent who does: both reason and experience have to be satisfied. But we have seen that, if Descartes wins the election, experience will not be satisfied and should know its place.

So it is worth considering why, when he does mention the supposed fit, it is worth his while to do so. It is worth bearing in mind that it is sometimes hard to be sure whether, in the passages already cited where he speaks of 'phenomena' (e.g. *Pr.* II, 64, CSM I: 247; *Pr.* IV, 204, CSM I: 289;) or 'experiences' (e.g. *Dis.* VI, CSM I: 144, 150; letter to Mersenne, 9th February 1639, AT II: 497–8), he is referring to what actually happens or to what we perceive of what happens. For instance, in an early letter, he speaks of his determination to explain all the phenomena of nature, which he identifies with the entirety of physics (letter to Mersenne, 13th November 1629, CSMK: 7; AT I: 23: '[. . .] *je me suis résolu d'éxpliquer tous les phénomènes de la nature, c'est à dire toute la physique*'): here, he must mean what actually happens, though a little further up the same letter he refers to false suns (parhelia) as a 'phenomenon' presumably in the sense of what is perceived.[19]

In the *Treatise on Light*, Descartes says that his account squares with experience. He does so twice.

Near the beginning of the paragraph preceding his affirmation in Chapter VII that, if there were any conflict between the laws of the 'fable' and the actual world, he would choose the former, Descartes claims that his first two laws of motion are in full agreement with all experiences (*Lum.* VII, CSM I: 94–5; AT XI: 41: '[c]*ette règle, jointe avec la précédente, se rapporte fort bien à toutes les expériences*'). By this he means that we do not see bodies beginning or stopping moving without being pushed or arrested by something else. And this seems easy enough to refute: an apple falls off a tree, rolls a bit and then stops; it doesn't look as if it was pushed or obstructed. But that cannot be a refutation, because it is too easy. So Descartes must have in mind not *all* experiences, but only those that have to do with the bodies he is considering and in the way that he is considering them, namely as abstract projectiles. If we experienced *them*, then we would find no counter-instances to the laws. As it happens, of course, we do not have experience of the world of the 'fable'; so the point must be that, when we see the apple doing its thing, we should think about what is going on below the threshold of what we can see; then we will be satisfied. But this is not what we sense directly.

Again, in the incomplete Chapter XV, he is arguing that the face of the sky in the world of the 'fable' should look to its inhabitants just as ours does to us (*Lum.* XV, AT XI: 104). The account he is giving of the illumination of stars, comets and planets is not meant to be the true history of our world, because the world of the 'fable' is heliocentric, a point we shall return to in the next chapter. But that does not prevent Descartes from saying, experience shows us that something similar happens also in our world, and that, in any case, it would be hard to account for what does happen unless one adopts his theory of light (*Lum.* XV, AT XI: 109: '[. . .] *l'expérience nous montre que le semblable arrive aussi dans le vrai monde, et toutefois je ne crois pas qu'il soit possible d'en rendre raison, si on ne suppose que la lumière y soit autre chose dans les objets qu'une action ou disposition telle que je l'ai expliquée*'). The similarity here is between the way that light functions in the two worlds. Even if the places of the heavenly objects are different in the new world, our world probably being geocentric, the action or disposition of light is such that the same effects can be seen. So, the claim is that even if the places of the heavenly bodies *were* different, we *would* experience the same things that we do experience. This looks like an attempt to insinuate the theory of light by arguing from its effects: however the heavens are arranged, we get the same lights at night. But it is also a way of making the world of the 'fable' seem less alien, an appropriate sort of place as a testbed for the physics that analysis can excavate from our most basic notions.

We ought also to consider *Principles* III, 42 following, which we have seen is often regarded as a prime source for the idea that Cartesian science has an essential role for experience. Here, Descartes dedicates five consecutive articles to considering the status of the hypotheses about the motions of the heavens.

In III, 42 he asserts the doctrine that effects, namely all the things that we grasp here below on Earth, must be deduced from the most general causes (*Pr.* III, 42, CSM I: 255; AT XIIIA: 98: '[. . .] *ex iisdem* [leg. *causis generaliorum*] *etiam, illa omnia quæ in Terra cominus intuemur, deduci debent*'). He goes on to say,

> if we use only principles that we see to be very evident and deduce from them with mathematical rigour and the results closely agree with all the phenomena of nature, then it would be an insult to God to suspect that the causes thus uncovered were false (*Pr.* III, 43, CSM I: 255;

AT XIIIA: 99: '[. . .] *si nullis principiis utamur nisi evidentissime perspectis, si nihil nisi per mathematicas consequentias ex iis deducamus, et interim illa quæ sic ex ipsis deducemus, cum omnibus naturæ phænomenis accurate consentiant, injuriam Dei facere videremur, si causas rerum hoc pacto inventas, falsas esse suspicaremur').*

The insult would be that He should have created us so imperfect as to allow that if, to use a phrase we have already met, we were using our reason rightly ('*ut ratione nostra recte utendo*': AT XIIIA: 99), we could nevertheless make a mistake. In this, there is nothing *essential* about the agreement with the phenomena: all the emphasis is on the deductions and on the truths that reason uncovers.

In III, 44 Descartes redescribes the principles or causes as 'hypotheses', so as not to have to make an extra claim about their truth. Then he suggests that he will have done something of great value if all the things that he deduces from them agree with experience (*Pr.* III, 44, CSM I: 255). As he explains in the French, this agreement means that we can make use of the hypothetical causes to get the effects we want (*Pr.* III, 44, AT IXB: 123: '[. . .] *on s'en pourra servir en même façon pour disposer les causes naturelles à produire les effets que l'on désirera*'). But, as with the case of the agreement between the skies of the 'fable' and of the actual world, the manipulability of the natural world is not to be taken to mean that the hypothesised causes are the actual causes. Rather, it means that the agreement, being an agreement between distinct things, shows that the hypotheses are *not* true. Far from being 'confirmed' by agreement with experience the hypotheses are shown to be *false* by that agreement.

Descartes expands on this in the following article, where he makes the concession that the developmental account he is giving of the world is in conflict with a deliverance of reason, namely that God creates things perfect of their kinds (*Pr.* III, 45, CSM I: 256). This, too, is a matter that we shall attend to more closely in the next chapter.

Then comes the passage in which Descartes does say that only experience (and not the power of reason) should teach us which of the innumerable ways that God might have set the world up is the one He chose (*Pr.* III, 46, CSM I: 256; AT VIIIA: 101: '[. . .] *quia potuerunt ista innumeris modis diversis a Deo temperari, et quemnam præ cæteris elegerit, sola experientia docere debet*'; the French adds '*et non par la force du raisonnement*' (AT IXB: 124)). Since there are innumerable ways the world could be set up, no finite elimination of hypotheses will leave us with one that we can call true because it is the only one remaining that agrees with experience.

The way in which experience is meant to teach here is by providing a consequent in a falsificationist's conditional: if a hypothesis leads to a false consequent, then the hypothesis is false; but the converse does not hold and there is no reason in this text or elsewhere for thinking that Descartes supposed that it does. Specifically, there is no warrant for reading the claim that it is a necessary condition for the assuming of a hypothesis that its consequences agree with experience (*Pr.* III, 46, CSM I: 256–7; AT VIIIA: 101: '[. . .] *modo omnia, quæ ex ipso consequentur, cum experientia consentiant*') as if that claim also posited a sufficient condition for accepting the hypothesis and, in particular, for accepting it as a principle. He does not say that agreement with experience in any way confirms a hypothesis. After all, any unfalsifiable (but false) hypothesis will do that. Indeed, Descartes recognises in III, 47 that truths can be derived from falsities. Among such falsities will be the thesis about an initial chaos in the universe that he builds into the 'fable' of the *Treatise on Light*. Because we can validly derive truths from falsities, the faces of the heavens in the new world and in the actual can resemble each other, though one is false and the other true.

Descartes is regarding the hypotheses that he is allowing in as objects of *choice*, which we can pick up and drop freely for the purposes of doing a bit of physics. The hypotheses are less certain than experience; since experience is less certain than the principles derived by analysis from the common notions, hypotheses are less certain than principles, though they may happen to coincide in content with them. But they are no part of science proper.

Uses for scratches

So far, what we have seen about what rectitude permits has been pretty relentlessly negative. The bits of science we have been citing – kinetics, optics, astronomy – are those for which the prospects for mathematisation looked and look brightest. So it is not surprising that Descartes regards their full flowering as having both the certainty and the structure of mathematics. And this means leaving almost entirely to one side the deliverances of the senses. We might use experience or imagination to remind us of the things to be investigated, but they have no role in the deductions that make up science proper. Let us consider now the status of sciences that did not look, and still do not beyond a certain point, reducible to the simples of physics.

Part V of the *Discourse* contains an account of the movement of the heart and arteries; it is another part of Descartes' work that sometimes gets omitted in texts that aim to give us his philosophical writings.[20] It is a description of what we see with our eyes and can feel with our hands when we cut up a large animal (*Dis.* V, CSM I: 136). And we know that Descartes patronised the butchers of Amsterdam to get animal carcasses and that he attended a public anatomy demonstration in Leiden.[21] These goings-on are of interest for present purposes because he might seem to be appealing to the senses to get him knowledge. Yet I think that the knowledge that is to be got even here depends only indirectly on the senses.

To see what is going on, I appeal again to the passage of *Discourse* VI where Descartes admits there is a difficulty of working out which are the causes of the effects we see. It may be worth having this in full:

> these principles are so simple and so general that I notice hardly any specific effect that I cannot tell straight off can be deduced from them in a variety of ways, and that my biggest problem is normally that of finding out in which of these ways it depends on them (*Dis.* VI, CSM I: 144; AT VI: 64–5: '[. . .] *ces principes sont si simples et si généraux, que je ne remarque quasi aucun effet particulier, que d'abord je ne connaise qu'il peut en être déduit en plusieurs diverses façons, et que ma plus grande difficulté est d'ordinaire de trouver en laquelle de ces façons il en dépend*').

The difficulty is that the principles from which he deduces the effects are too general. We might almost say 'too generous'; the generosity is that of nature's power to produce many different things in accordance with the principles. If we are wanting the goods of medicine, we have to have some inkling of how the animals in the actual world are constituted. To find out how they are constituted, Descartes adopts what he calls an 'expedient' (*Dis.* VI, AT VI: 65: '*expédient*').[22] An expedient is a make-shift or a short-term measure; in the long run, the expedient has to be replaced with actual deduction from principles. In the case in hand, it turns out to be a version of the method of concomitant variation (ibid.: AT VI: 65: '[. . .] *chercher derechef quelques expériences, qui soient telles que leur événement ne soit pas le même si c'est en l'une de ces façons qu'on doit l'* [sc. *l'effet*] *expliquer, que si c'est en l'autre*').

We can distinguish perhaps four roles that the expedient of experimentation can nevertheless play.

One is that of giving us some temporary opinions on matters of urgent utility. With this in view, it makes sense for Descartes to say, as he does in the midst of describing how a large mammalian heart works, that there are many things to witness (AT VI: 52: '*qui témoignent*') that the true cause of the movement of the blood is the one he is describing. Witnessing is not proving, demonstrating or deducing from principles. In *Discourse* V, he issues a promissory note that the account of the heart he is setting out should in the end be overtaken by mathematical demonstrations. For those who do not know the force of mathematical demonstrations, he claims that the movement of the heart follows just as necessarily from the disposition of the organs as does the functioning of a clock (*Dis* V, CSM I: 136). Though it is not knowledge proper, the witness given by the effects may be enough to be going on with to get some general notions of anatomy until we have climbed far enough up the tree of the sciences to pluck the true fruits of medicine. And it may help save lives in the interim.

A second use for experiments that help us understand what sorts of animals there are, and how similar we are to them, takes seriously the fact that there are very many ways that nature could be. Of all the sorts of animals that there could be, we most want to know about those that there actually are and how they are made. We may suppose merely possible oxen whose hearts are different from those of actual oxen: they pump blood using the same mechanical principles – in Descartes' view, of rarefaction and condensation – but with a somewhat different disposition of valves and chambers. Such a supposition is an alternative way of causing the effects that take place in an ox before we get to see it opened up on the slab. If experiments help us to close in on actually instantiated cardiologies, we can pay less attention to the alternatives, all of which could be deduced from the primary truths, but most of which are of relatively little interest. For the purposes of practical, earth-bound medicine and veterinary practice, the physiology of merely suppositious animals ought to take second place to the deductions that refer to actual ones, and especially to actual animals whose innards are like human innards.

Descartes has this second sense in mind when he says that, the further one gets in the sciences, the greater the need for experiments (*Dis.* VI, CSM I: 143). The more variable the instantiation of a given cause, the more contingent the effects, and so the greater the desirability of excluding the non-actual.

A third role that empirical anatomy might play takes us once more back to Socrates and the scratches in the sand. The relations of squares and triangles are the sorts of relations where it is pretty obvious that there are interconnections. The obviousness is, in a sense, perceptual: you can just see, even by looking at imperfect squares and triangles, that the diagonal bisection of a given square will be related to a quarter of the square twice the area of the first. You can just *see* the relations are simple. The same does not hold of many irregular shapes that do not put you in mind of such things as squares and triangles; for instance, I would be hard put to construct geometrically a figure congruent with the wispy right eyebrow of Ginevra dei Benci, but exactly twice the area. That is why geometry starts with triangles and squares, and not with wiggly shapes *qua* wiggly. Seeing an ox heart as a pump and ignoring all the gore and other particularities is, I suggest, like seeing the scratches in the sand as squares and triangles and ignoring their imperfections. The heart looks like a bodily part whose workings we ought to be able to get an idea of: its constitution is gross and its connections with the tubing of veins and arteries are fairly open to view. At least, we can tell that we shall have much less difficulty with the heart than we shall with, say, the pancreas. Even so, there is no telling in advance that, in the finally completed science, cardiology comes before the treatment of the annexes of the alimentary canal. Just so, in the end an even-handed geometry may not give priority to Euclidean space over Riemannian ones, though that was the place for us to start.

Connected with the idea that experience and experimentation can help us see which bits of nature will yield most readily to rough and ready treatment, there is perhaps yet another role that Descartes' expedient can play. This is as scene-setting or stimulus to enquiry proper. As with the reduction of the rainbow to a single sphere, the experience that Descartes calls in aid is not itself meant to be the object of knowledge. Rather, it is a means to an analytical understanding; and while we are waiting for, or doing, the demonstrations, we do not yet have knowledge at all.

The sort of stimulus I have in mind here connects with a model St Augustine proposes concerning the relation between the use of words and the gaining of knowledge. In the *De Magistro*, he offers a dilemmatic argument about our being able to learn from signs. At 10, 33, the Augustine character cites the hapax '*sarabaras*' from the Bible (*Daniel*, 3: 94; cf. Bettetini in Augustine 1993: 189–90). On the one horn, we do not understand the sign, in which case we cannot learn from it (*Mag.*, 10, 35: '[. . .] *dicens "ecce sarabaras", discam rem quam nesciebam, non per verba quædicta sunt, sed per eius aspectum*'). On the other horn, we do understand, in which case we already know, and it is the thing and not the word that taught us (*Mag.*, 12, 39: '[. . .] *non verbis, sed rebus ipsis [. . .] discit*'). In either case, nothing new is taught to us when we learn the meaning of a word, because it is only if we know the thing a sign means that we can learn its meaning.[23] If this goes through,[24] we do not learn from signs at all. But it does not mean that language has no function in our gaining knowledge. If it meant that, then the whole business of St Augustine's book would be in vain: to establish *by dialogue* the claim that there is no teacher who teaches man knowledge except God,[25] St Augustine needs there to be something that is done by the words passing between his characters and between them and the reader. The something that words do need not be essential to the process of knowledge-gathering, though it may be helpful to us, given what we are like.

For St Augustine, the ultimate ground of knowledge is the divine inner voice (*Mag.*, 11, 38: '[*i*]*lle autem qui consulitur, docet, qui in interiore homine dictus* [sc. at *Ephesians*, 3, 14–17] *est Christus, id est incommutabilis Dei virtus atque sempiterna sapientia*'). Yet he allows that language is useful to draw our attention to the things that we shall see (*Mag.*, 10, 35). At *De Magistro*, 8, 21, the Augustine character describes what he is doing as playing, not for the sake of playing, but to train his powers and sharpen his mind (*Mag.*, 8, 21, '[. . .] *præludo tecum non ludendi gratia, sed exercendi vires et mentes aciem*'). By going through exercises of sophisms and digressions, the participants in the dialogue are directed to the matters of greater importance (Marrou 1938: 255–66). Later in the dialogue, St Augustine puts this notion of our being directed to such matters in the terminology of a warning or notice (*'admonitio'*). This terminology returns several times (e.g. *Mag.*, 8, 24; and 11, 36) and is resoundingly present in the dialogue's closing speech, where the interlocutor, Adeodatus, says that he has been taught by the admonition of Augustine's words only that with words man can only be admonished to learn (*Mag.*, 14, 46: '[. . .] *didici admonitione verborum tuorum, nihil aliud verbis quam admoneri hominem ut discat*'; also Madec 1975: 71; Doignon 1986).

We have already seen the idea that mathematics for Descartes has the propedeutic function of limbering up the mind and of accustoming us to high standards of doxastic acceptability. We may further apply the idea of the admonition to the way that the outcomes of experimentation offer experiences that are appropriately ordered and harnessed and that can prepare our minds to grasp the truths that we ultimately deduce from first principles. The appropriate ordering and harnessing of experience into the sort of research project that Descartes envisages, and seeks funding for, in *Discourse* VI may look at first glance like an enterprise in empirical science. But it does not itself yield knowledge any more than the slaveboy's wrong turnings do, as when he suggests that the side of the doubled square will be one and a half times as long as the original (*Men.*, 83E). What is more, even when put together in an orderly way, empirical results will only be the true opinions that are stirred up as in a dream and are the prelude to the work that will produce knowledge proper (*Men.*, 85C). This stage of enquiry is only necessary because we are habituated to looking to the senses. A properly attuned enquirer would not seek in the deliverances of the senses, however well arranged and harnessed, support for the truths that she acquires in accordance with doxastic rectitude, namely those that she sees clearly and distinctly as consequences of the primary truths.

11 What rectitude forbids

What might be false

For the purposes of enquiry to rebuild knowledge on firm foundations, we are so thrown down by the doubts raised about the senses that we shut our eyes, block our ears and withdraw our assent from them, and accustom ourselves to drawing our mind away from them so as to investigate primarily the attributes of God, which lead us to discover, by consideration of the clear ideas we have, the essence and existence of material stuff.[1]

At no point in this process do we open our eyes, unblock our ears or approach the deliverances of the senses as anything other than what might be false. So we should not believe them. And we should not appeal to them to disbelieve other things either.

This delivers an apriorism with the following dimensions. We begin and continue paying attention to ideas that are clear and distinct. These we find in ourselves and we find are true. They provide the materials out of which anything that we can know by natural means can be known. As we proceed, we come to know other things through the things we know first. These later things are effects whose causes are the primary truths of metaphysics. By citing, cross-referencing and explaining his texts, I have sought to illustrate that Descartes' apriorism has these dimensions. As a matter of history from Plato to Einstein, I have also indicated that an apriorism with these dimensions is not a rarity in the history of Western thought and certainly not an aberration specific to Descartes. And, as a matter of philosophy, I have sought to show that Descartes' position is a coherent and sensitive response to pressures that he feels are on any theory of knowledge worth pursuing. More than that to show that his apriorism is not 'lunatic' I cannot do.

What we have grounds for thinking is false

Abandoning the Treatise on Light

We come now to two cruces in the interpretation of Descartes that have to be dealt with sooner or later. In the present case, it is later. These concern matters that can be summed up in the following two questions. First, how much physics did Descartes think humans can do in accordance with doxastic rectitude and where do we find it done? And, second, what are we to do with the fact that there is conflict between at least one expression of an operation that might seem to be an operation in accordance with doxastic rectitude and some doctrines of religion?

The answers we give to these questions inevitably colour and are coloured by much else we think about Descartes' theory of enquiry and about Descartes more generally. So there is, generally speaking, very little to be done to make answers to such questions seem innocent: every reading of Descartes is tainted by the stand it takes (or conceals) on these matters. And, indeed, the answers I am about to come clean about have coloured what I have already said, for instance, about the standing of the 'fable' in the *Treatise on Light* and, more generally, about the tenor of Descartes' thought as a whole.

In summary, the answers I propose to our two crucial questions are these. To the first question, the answer is that humans encounter virtually insuperable obstacles in trying to do the physics of the actual world, and that, if there is an exposition of how to do it, it is not in the *Treatise on Light*, which Descartes regarded as false. To the second, the answer is that Descartes held that there is a source of knowledge that is not available by following the method, in accordance with doxastic rectitude or by natural means, that this source can provide knowledge that is more secure than anything that could be acquired by those means, and that this source is the special divine revelation to access which one must apply to the Roman Catholic Church.

To begin motivating these answers and to clarify the scansion of the next two sections, let us consider the abandonment in 1633 of the *Treatise on Light* and various other writings. Near the beginning of *Discourse* V, published four years later, he refers to these writings (CSM I: 131–2) and says that there were 'various considerations' (AT VI: 41: '*quelques considérations*') that stopped him publishing them. These considerations fall into two principal parts.

The first has to do with not wishing to discuss the many questions that are controversial among the learned (*Dis.* V, CSM I: 131; AT VI: 40: '*plusieurs questions qui sont en controverse entre les doctes*'). As we saw in considering Descartes' polemic against learning, one problem with entering such controversies is that it leads to indecisive disputes about 'speculative' matters.

And the indecisiveness arises from the fact of having to follow or refute opinions that are accepted among the learned (*Dis.* V, CSM I: 132; AT VI: 42: '*opinions qui sont reçues entre les doctes*').

The second, we read at the beginning of *Discourse* VI, is that he learnt that an opinion in physics, recently published by someone else, had been disapproved of by persons to whom he defers and whose authority over his actions is hardly less than that of his own reason over his thoughts (*Dis.* VI, CSM I: 141–2; AT VI: 60: '*j'appris que des personnes à qui je défère, et dont l'autorité ne peut guère moins sur mes actions que ma propre raison sur mes pensées, avaient désapprouvé une opinion de physique publiée un peu auparavant par quelque autre*'). The reference, of course, is to the condemnation of Galileo, about which some detail shortly.

One thing Descartes had learnt in learning that Galileo had been disapproved of was that the opinion in question was prejudicial ('*préjudiciable*') to religion or the state, which was something he had not previously imagined (ibid.). And this would be enough to make it mischievous to publish a work that appeared to contain that or a similar opinion.

A further point, which does not seem to have been made in the literature, is that Descartes does not say that he had been of the opinion that was disapproved of; nor does he exactly deny that he had been; rather, he says that he does not want to say that he had been of that opinion (*Dis.* VI, CSM I: 142; AT VI: 60: '[*opinion*] *de laquelle je ne veux pas dire que je fusse*'). One thing this must mean is that he was intending (in 1633) to publish an opinion that he does not wish (in 1637) to avow as his (in 1637). It may also mean that he was intending (before 1633) to publish an opinion that he subsequently (in 1633) learnt it was mischievous, because prejudicial to religion or the state, to avow as his own. But, more likely, it means that it was an opinion that he did not wish (before 1633) to hold even before he learnt (in 1633) that it was mischievous. And I suggest it was an opinion that he did not wish (in 1633) to hold as his own because he did not (even before 1633) hold it to be true and he subsequently (in 1633) learnt that it was not only false but mischievous.

To confront our two questions about the standing of Cartesian physics in the light of the abandonment in 1633 of the *Treatise on Light*, let us consider four theses that are expressed in that work and that, for differing reasons, Descartes had to regard as untrue descriptions of the world where we live. The four theses, to which I add tags for identification, are the following:

(i)   that the creation of the world in time, as described at *Genesis*, 1: 1ff., may not have been a unique event of its sort (the plurality of worlds);

(ii)   that God might create a world that is not fully formed and ordered (the hypothesis of chaos);

(iii) that suns are at the centre of planetary motions (the heliocentric hypothesis); and

(iv) that the Earth is a planet in motion of itself around the Sun (the first vortex theory).

And what I aim to show is that, for Descartes, natural means suffice to exclude (i) at least probably and (ii) certainly, and that supernatural means are both necessary and sufficient to exclude (iii) at least probably and (iv) certainly.

If I can succeed in making these claims plausible, then we seem to have some bad news either for operations that look like efforts to cultivate doxastic rectitude or for the whole of the foregoing exercise in describing Descartes' operation in terms of that virtue. In the one case, the bad news would be that doxastic rectitude does not suffice for getting us from firm foundations in the sciences to anything much else. In the other, it would be that the foregoing description must have got something seriously wrong about the nature of Descartes' operation. Nevertheless, I shall try to show how neither of these pieces of looming bad news is the moral to be drawn. Rather, we should think that the natural means that we have at our disposal for doing physics are very hard to apply to the actual world: the falsity of (i) and (ii) means only that a certain sort of shortcut in the sciences is not a genuine operation in accordance with doxastic rectitude. That is: the desire to find something secure in the sciences should not outrun itself. And the fact that Descartes held that (iii) and (iv) can, with varying degrees of certainty, be known to be false by supernatural means, does nothing to impugn operations in accordance with doxastic rectitude. Those operations are the best we can do on our own, though we may need external help to complete the picture.

A final clarification. Many of the things I have been describing in the foregoing chapters as Cartesian theory about enquiry by natural means can easily seem very queer indeed. They attribute to human beings a range of powers, such as the infinite power of the will or the capacity to deduce, in Descartes' sense, the whole of what can be known from what is imprinted in our minds by God. As already noted, especially in relation to innatism, the attribution of these powers can appear implausible because they might seem magical or unaccountable. But they are meant to be natural in the sense that they activate capacities that humans are alleged – by Descartes – to be endowed with by nature. As I have been envisaging it, the activation of these capacities is a matter of taming the disorderly propensities of childhood, the schoolroom and the wider world of experience (the vice of credulity), and of resisting the temptation to give up on beliefs altogether though secure beliefs are to be had (the vice of scepticism). If we could manage, however briefly and precariously, to tame these tendencies and resist that temptation when it is misplaced, then we would be building a habit of belief-formation to which we could trust, both to avoid error and to acquire important truths. As it turns out, humans in their fallen state cannot achieve rectitude as a habit; yet they can at least operate in accordance with its precepts in order to acquire the best belief-set that it is open to them to acquire on their own. The operations that are conducted in accordance with doxastic virtue are thus the natural means at our disposal. Other means by which we might be provided with truths that we are permitted or required to believe should be regarded as supernatural.

What we can know by natural means is false

In not wanting to say (in 1637) that he had been (even before 1633) of the opinion that had been disapproved of, Descartes is giving an indication of a feature of the *Treatise on Light* that would speak against its publication. This is that the description he gives in the 'fable' of the new world is not true of the actual world. It is not true of the actual world because it disregards some features of the actual world that are in conflict with what is built into the 'fable'.

Some of these features are absences that make a polemical point. Thus, in excluding the scholastic notions of form and quality (*Lum.* VI, CSM I: 91; AT XI: 33; *Dis.* V, CSM I: 132; AT VI: 43), he is claiming to be able to do physics better and more simply without them. Other absences, such as those of the human soul, natural teleology and miracles (*Lum.* VII, CSM I: 97) may be regarded as more or less accidental to the scheme. The exclusion of forms and qualities may be likened to the way in which, for instance, an experiment to show something about the acceleration of a ball-bearing under gravity is allowed to disregard such factors as magnetism and friction. We know that the fall of the ball-bearing is affected by these factors, but we count their operation as null for the purpose. The stipulated absences of manifestations of mind, human or divine, might correspond to the idea – not so often encountered in physics textbooks as in physics classrooms – that the ball-bearing experiment should not be wilfully interfered with: no catching the thing as it falls.

As he explains, for instance in his letter to Hyperaspistes (CSMK: 190), Descartes thought he had reasons for excluding from any ultimate description of the world the scholastic notions of form and quality, except as those notions apply to mind, as he tells Regius (letter of January 1642, AT III: 503–4). In constructing his world without them, he is, as Gaukroger puts it, showing 'that a world constructed in this manner [. . .] is indistinguishable from the actual one' (in Descartes 1998: xvii). That is, the exclusion of them is no more than a simplification or abstraction of the sort we saw in considering his treatment of the rainbow. By contrast, in excluding human and divine minds, he is setting aside things that are unpredictable by any physical law, and, in excluding natural teleology, he is setting aside things that are, being referred to God's purposes, inscrutable to humans (*Med.* IV, CSM II: 39; also *Pr.* I, 28).

These exclusions make only for the incompleteness of the 'fable'. In the simile that Descartes deploys in *Discourse* V, he is like a painter who cannot represent all the sides of a three-dimensional object on a flat surface; so he chooses to highlight just one side and show the others only insofar as they can be seen when looked at (*Dis.* V, CSM I: 132). Thus far, there is no trouble.

The trouble could have begun with Descartes' first move in the description of his new world in Chapter VI of the *Treatise on Light*. This is the positing of 'imaginary spaces' (*Lum.* VI, CSM I: 90; AT XI: 31: '*espaces imaginaires*'). Descartes is careful not to describe this space as actually infinitely extended, though the philosophers who invented the notion describe it that way (AT XI: 31: '*les Philosophes nous disent que ces espaces sont infinis*'). Rather, he says that, even if our imagination *seems* to stretch to infinity, we would do better to suppose that the matter with which God will have filled the 'imaginary spaces' extends beyond the region between the Earth and the main stars of the firmament (*Lum.* VI, CSM I: 90) in all directions up to an indefinite distance (AT XI: 32: '*s'étend bien au delà de tous côtés, jusques à une distance indéfinie*').

This description could have caused trouble because it might have been misunderstood as the positing of at least a potentially infinite space. Which in turn might have been seen as on a slippery slope to the view that a world could fill an actually infinite space. And Descartes is sure to have known from Aristotle's *De Cælo* (I, vi–vii) that there are impressive arguments against the coherence of such an idea. The existence and reputability of those arguments have two consequences. One is that a supposed world predicated on them would attract the controversy with the learned. The other is that a description of a world that depended on the notion of an actually infinite space – or anything that seemed to slide towards it – was in danger of incoherence.

This is why Descartes is careful in setting up the position. In fact, he was scrupulous enough about the question, fearing perhaps being tainted with Epicurean thoughts about an infinite universe (cf. Usener: 301; Lucretius, *DRN*, I, 958–97), to have checked with Mersenne on the point. What he had asked was whether Mersenne could tell him if there is anything determined in Religion, meaning the established doctrine of the Roman Catholic Church of the day, concerning the extension of created things, and specifically whether it is finite or infinite (letter to Mersenne, 18th December 1629, AT I: 86: '*s'il n'y a rien de déterminé en la Religion touchant l'étendue des choses créées, savoir si elle est finie ou infinie*'). He had wanted to know whether there was anything determined in Religion because, if there had been, the first move in the description of the world of the 'fable' would have been in trouble. The trouble it could have been in was the trouble of being in conflict with something determined in Religion. Quite what sort of trouble this trouble would have been we shall see in considering the cases in which Descartes' description *is* in conflict with something determined by Religion.

Mersenne, as good an authority on such matters as Descartes might have found, must have given him the green light. So, even if the spaces of the actual world are not indefinitely extended, the use of the 'imaginary spaces' does not run up against something determined in Religion. Nevertheless, he makes two moves that appear to run up against things that are determined in Religion or by reason or both. In one case, which I have tagged the question of the plurality of worlds, the appearance may turn out to be just that: the apparent conflict can, with some juggling, be resolved. In the other, tagged as the hypothesis of chaos, there is a matter that Descartes takes to be a truth of reason that really should cause him more trouble than he was fully prepared to face.

The question of the plurality of worlds comes out at the point at which Descartes says that, in the new world, he is going to lose sight of all the creatures that God made five or six thousand years ago (*Lum.* VI, AT XI: 32: '*perdre de vue toutes les créatures que Dieu fit il y a cinque ou six milles ans*'). In one respect, this might be taken to be equivalent to the exclusions already noted, of forms and minds. But there is another way to take the hypothesis that there is more than one possible Creation: in one possible Creation, God does not create, say, moistness, in another no badgers, and in another again no humans either. These are hypotheses that God could have created either more than one world or a world other than the one He did create.

The supposition of the world of the 'fable' may, therefore, presuppose the idea that the Creation is not unique. The claim that God is such that He makes only one world is intricately related to a resolution of the nature of His omnipotence and the ways in which His nature can be said to determine what He wills and, thus, does. Nevertheless, it can be said that Descartes surely knew, again from Aristotle (*Cæl.*, I viii–ix) and more generally from the tradition whose spokesman we can take to be St Thomas (*ST*, Ia, qu. 25 art. v), that the very idea of there being a world other than the world that God is described as creating at the beginning of *Genesis* is both subject to controversy among the learned (i.e. among those who have applied Aristotle to the Bible) and, possibly, incoherent.

Indeed, though there was controversy, it was *opinio communis* that there is no plurality of worlds. That is to say, authoritative statements like the Paris Condemnation of 1277 deny that one should deny God's power to create more than one world (Tempier 1277a: 34, condemning the proposition, '[*q*]*uod prima causa non posset plures mundos facere*'; see Grant 1974). And this left open the possibility that He is able to do so. But those who asserted that He has, as a matter of fact, done so ran into trouble. Less than forty years before Descartes was writing, one of the opinions Giordano Bruno was burnt for was the assertion that there is a plurality of worlds. Likewise, writing in the late 1640s, Descartes' first biographer, Pierre Borel, found it hard to publish on the Continent in favour of the thesis that the event recounted at the beginning of *Genesis* was not the only creation: only two copies of the Geneva edition (1657) of his *Discours* have survived censorship, though the English translation of 1658 has fared somewhat better. Thus, it is no way out of controversy with the learned about the plurality of worlds to talk about a world other than the one God did create. To do so is to take a position – and a widely condemned position at that – on a disputed question.

This leaves us with the question of what Descartes has in mind with his 'imaginary spaces'. If this is not an alternative Creation, it may be worth reconsidering why he makes the reference, already cited, to a space beyond the space between the Earth and the main stars of the firmament. For, the suggestion comes to mind that the 'fable' concerns a world that is new in the way that America has been said to be a new world: it was there all along, but over the horizon from us. That is to say, if the 'fable' is to avoid problems with the plurality of worlds, the 'imaginary spaces' will have to be *spatially* related to the space between the Earth and the main stars of the firmament: they may be located in what we might call deep or perhaps intergalactic space. Which would explain his saying in the *Discourse* that he is imagining God's creating enough matter for a world 'somewhere' (*Dis.* V, CSM I: 132; AT VI: 42: '*quelque part*'). Even if Descartes says that it is our thought that goes out from this World (*Lum.* VI, CSM I: 90; AT XI: 31: '[*permettez*] *à votre pensée de sortir hors de ce Monde*'), where thought goes, the body could follow.

If this is what Descartes means by his 'imaginary spaces', it implies that what he means by talking about the world where we are ('*ce Monde*') is perhaps misleadingly expressed by talk about the 'actual world', except for those to whom 'actual' really does function just like the spatial indexical 'here' (e.g. Lewis 1973: 86). That is, the actual world is just that bit of the manifold in which there may or may not be forms and qualities, and in which minds, both human and divine, are operative. But the point of his appealing to these other spaces would be that they are regions of space filled only with stuff that is appropriately stripped-down (*Lum.* VI, CSM I: 91; AT XI: 33 '*dépouillé*') to allow physics to be done on it. They are regions in which, if we were present in them, we would not have to abstract from what we have in front of us to the stripped-downness that is matter's essential *proprium*. Since we are not in them, Descartes conducts his thought-experiment by appeal to them as the regions in which his physics is meant to work unhindered.[2]

Let us, then, suppose that the spaces on which Descartes wishes to run his physics are imaginary in the sense of being accessible by the imagination, as Tucson is from here, and that they have the advantage from the point of view of physical theorising that they are uncluttered. The suggestion is that they are collocated in the same space as the Earth. Of course, this means that the universe as a whole is rather larger than was contemplated in the rather cramped theories handed down from antiquity, and it includes regions that are luxuriant (our world, with its minds and whatnot) and regions that present desert landscapes (the world where physics can work). But its being rather larger than was contemplated is not a very principled objection to imagining spaces that are as different from here as Tucson may be.

Pursuing what fills the 'imaginary spaces', Descartes describes the material substance that we recognise from his other writings and that is identifiable with extension (e.g. *Med.* V; *Pr.* I, 51–3). To this stuff, God then gives what we are told Pascal thought blasphemously close to a flick of the fingers (1670: 1001: '*chiquenaude*'), imparting motion that is then transmitted by 'the ordinary laws of nature' (*Lum.* VI, CSM I: 91; AT XI: 34: '*elles continuent par après leur mouvement suivant les lois ordinaires de la nature*'). Then he addresses the question of what the initial configuration is of the extended stuff. Or, rather, he tries to duck the question.

In one early printed version, the title of the chapter of the *Treatise on Light* that we have been considering contains the claim that the world of the 'fable' is,

> very easy to know, yet for all that similar to the one where we find ourselves, even down to the chaos that the poets have pretended preceded it (AT XI: ix: '*très facile à connaître, mais semblable pourtant à celui dans lequel nous sommes, ou mêmes au chaos que les poètes ont feint l'avoir precedé*'; cf. Descartes 1998: 21 n. 40).

Even if this text is not by Descartes himself, it faithfully represents what he says in the body of the chapter about the laws of nature being operative,

> even if God puts into matter no order or proportion, but makes it into a chaos more confused and muddled than the poets have been able to describe (*Lum.* VI, CSM I: 91; AT XI: 34: '*même qu'il ne mette en ceci aucun ordre ni proportion, mais qu'il en compose un chaos le plus confus et le plus embrouillé que les poètes puissent décrire*').

Likewise, describing this passage in *Discourse* V, he pretty much repeats the formula, saying that God shook the different parts of the matter of the hypothesised world differently and without order so that they made up a chaos as confused as any that the poets could invent (*Dis.* V, CSM I: 132; AT VI: 42: '*un chaos aussi confus que les poètes en puissent feindre*'). And in the French, but not the Latin, version of *Principles* III, 47 (AT IX B: 125), he again attributes the notion of chaos to the poets.

In these passages, the references may be to Hesiod (*Theogony*, 116), Plato or Lucretius and it might be interesting to follow up the ways in which the envisaged disorder is pictured as being brought into order, especially by comparison with the Platonic Demiurge of the *Timaeus* and with the quasi-evolutionary account that we find in, especially the second half (ll. 416ff.) of the fifth book of the *De Rerum Natura*. But there is a more urgent worry about supposing chaos.

This is that the mere supposition of it is in conflict with a fact, according to Descartes in the Latin version of *Principles* III, 45, that reason clearly persuades us of (CSM I: 256; AT VIIIA: 100: '*ratio naturale plane persuadet*') and, in the French version of the same passage, that natural reason absolutely persuades us of (AT IXB: 124: '[. . .] *la raison naturelle nous persuade absolument*'). This fact can be represented by the particular instance cited and by a general principle that Descartes states. The particular instance is that Adam and Eve were never children, but sprang into existence fully-formed. The general principle is that, in the light of God's enormous power, we cannot think that anything He does is other than in every respect perfect of its kind (AT VIIIA: 100: '[a]*ttendendo enim ad immensam Dei potentiam, non possumus existimare illum unquam quidquam fecisse, quod non omnibus suis numeris fuerit absolutum*').[3] This is a thought we have encountered before in considering the perfection of the faculty of judging; so it ought to occasion no surprise.

What this fact, especially taken under its guise as a general principle, implies is that reason rules out the supposition of anything's being created by God that is in itself disorderly or imperfect. If things are perfect of their kind at their creation, then they do not evolve out of chaos; we are persuaded by natural reason that they are perfect of their kinds at their creation; therefore, we are persuaded by natural reason that they do not evolve out of chaos.

The chaos that Descartes takes over from the poets might be regarded as a limiting case of a region in which order must come out of disorder in accordance with Descartes' ordinary laws of nature. In that case, it would have to be understood as a *reductio ad absurdum* against those who think that there is no way of getting order into the world without special providential or demiurgic activity. But that is not how Descartes seems to be using it. Rather, he is using it to show how his ordinary laws of nature work, by applying them to a region whose course of evolution is not interfered with by minds either divine (after the first shove) or human.

Yet the story of the working of the ordinary laws of nature is predicated on a supposition that, on Descartes' own estimate, is incoherent, in virtue of being in conflict with a fact that we are clearly persuaded of by reason. The 'fable' is not merely incomplete or a simplification that picks out the features of matter that are relevant to the basic laws of motion (though it may be intended to do that: Garber 1992a: 19). It is a 'fable' of the sort that we find in Æsop: frogs talk and suchlike nonsense.

But we can learn even from stories about talking frogs. In this case, the moral we might draw would be that, even if the laws of physics set out in the *Treatise on Light* were the best physical theory accessible to humans by natural means, it is hardly more than a skeleton. It is a shortcut to seeing which are the terms that should appear in a genuine explanation of physical phenomena. Thus, an explanation of any occurrence that makes reference to terms other than those embraced by the theory – conspicuously extension, motion and collision – has to justify itself either by appeal to derivability from the terms of the theory, or by reference to minds of one sort or another. If reference to other terms is ineliminable, the proposed explanation has to be rejected as not an explanation at all. In the cases where we have not actually done the calculations, we might feel that there is in play nothing other than applications and iterations of the basic laws of kinetics; *if* we did the calculations, then we *would* know the effects through the causes. Until we have done them, we do not know the complex by means of the simple; and so do not really know it at all.

The physics of the 'fable' might be found to apply to the more boring bits of the actual world. For instance, we might actually be able to do the calculations for some of the simpler goings-on on a well-made billiard table. Where we find that we cannot do the calculations, we are up against the limits of human knowledge of the actual world. Though someone might entertain the fantasy of Laplace (1795) to imagine a calculation of the whole history of all the pieces of stuff in the universe and their positions past, present and future, Descartes is quite clear that that is beyond human powers.

In his letter to Mersenne of 10th May 1632, Descartes sees it as a limitation of the Baconian, *a posteriori*, approach (AT I: 251: '*selon la méthode de Verulamius*') to the sciences that it goes beyond the grasp of the human spirit (AT I: 252: '*passe la portée de l'esprit humain*'). There are just too many bits of stuff to be taken into account. If so, appeal to experience is at best rarely going to get us enough material for us to do adequate calculations. As he sees at *Principles* III, 46, a given disposition, static or dynamic, of matter cannot be determined by reason alone (*Pr.* III, 46, CSM I: 256; AT VIIIA: 100–1: '[. . .] *quam magnæ sint istæ partes materiæ, quam celeriter moveantur, et quales circulos describant, non possumus sola ratione determinare*'). But this does not mean, as most commentators suppose, that there is an essential role for experience in science proper (e.g. Clarke 1982: 262). Rather, it means that, where we have to appeal to experience, we are very unlikely to get any knowledge.

Viewed positively, the 'fable' illustrates what rectitude demands as a standard of success in understanding physical interactions. Viewed negatively, it reminds us of the vanity of trusting to pseudo-explanations that do not limit themselves to ideas that we perceive clearly and distinctly.

What we can know by supernatural means is false

Natural means suffice to rule out the plurality of worlds and the hypothesis of chaos, the former being parlayed into an expansion of the dimensions of the universe and the latter being simply excluded by divine omnipotence. But it is to revelation that we must turn to see why Descartes was not prepared to avow as his own opinion either the heliocentric hypothesis or the first vortex theory.

But first another analogy between the scope of a moral virtue and that of the intellectual virtue we have been calling 'doxastic rectitude'.

There is a virtuous disposition of temperance, which has to do with bringing our appetites for various kinds of pleasure into line. Observance of the mean with respect to such pleasures will allow us to avoid the excesses of indulgence and yet get us the pleasures that we need to flourish. But this does not mean that we are free to take pleasures, even in the right measure and at the right time, wherever we want. A case might be that of adultery. If marriage is inviolably exclusive, then, for a married person to get her sexual gratification other than with her marriage partner would be wrong. In this, the Bible (*Exodus*, 20: 14) agrees with Aristotle (*EN*, II vi, 1107 a 14–17). Yet the inviolable exclusivity of marriage is not something that can be established by appeal to the nature of temperance; it is meant to flow from the sacramental or contractual nature of the ceremony that gives rise to it. The sacrament or the contract binds those who were party to it. This seems to mean that, if an unmarried person has voluntary sexual intercourse with a married one, it is only the latter who is an adulterer, because the former is not bound by the sacrament or contract. An unmarried person who does not believe that marriage is a sacrament, but a contract, may be giving the nonadulterous spouse grounds for breaking the contract, but appears, on this model, to be doing nothing that he is bound not to do (unless there is some general, and presumably independent, prohibition on fornication). Nevertheless, there are many people who would say that the unmarried partner is as guilty as the married one: the exclusivity of marriage extends to possible interlopers and the ban on adultery is absolute and binding on everyone: married persons are off-limits to everyone else.

Though the details – not to mention the ultimate correctness – of such examples may be controversial, extending in this case perhaps to social justifications of the institution of marriage and so on, the point I am trying to illustrate by reference to it is this: if there is an absolute prohibition on a certain type of action, then performance of it does not count as the proper exercise of a virtue. And this will apply similarly to *topoi* such as that of whether a burglar is exercising the virtue of courage in carrying out his daring plans (Davies 1998b).

In the epistemological analogue of such cases, if there is some belief that it is prohibited to hold, then, even if it seems like the exercise of doxastic virtue to acquire it, we can and should refuse it. We can because of the infinite power of the will to refuse even ideas that are as clear and distinct as they can be in the natural understanding; and we should because we should count it as false. And, as in the case of adultery, we shall find that Descartes regarded determinations that derived from the most straightforward readings of the Bible and Aristotle provided reasons for counting at least two astronomical theses as false.

It is worth distinguishing between the heliocentric hypothesis and the claim that the Earth is in motion of itself because of the difference in Descartes' handling of them. He persists, albeit conditionally, in the former, because it was not distinctly prohibited, but he abandons the first vortex theory (that of the *Treatise on Light*) on which the Earth's motion comes out true in favour of a new version of the theory (that of the *Principles*) on which it does not.

In the eighth chapter of the *Treatise on Light*, Descartes describes an indefinitely large set of physical systems, which he calls 'heavens' (*Lum.* VIII, AT XI: 53: '*cieux*'), that he boldly treats as analogous to the region between the Earth and the principal stars of the firmament. But they are separated from each other and from the region where we are precisely by the surface called the firmament (*Lum.* VIII, AT XI: 53–4: '*le firmament n'est autre chose que la superficie, sans épaisseur, qui sépare ces cieux les uns des autres*'). The limit marked by the firmament for each heaven is what holds the bodies within it: it is the outer member of the concentric nesting of vortices centred on the star of that heaven. In modern terms, it might be thought of as like a gravitational point-of-no-return, at which the attractions of two bodies are balanced, or, more trendily still, like an event horizon: it is not an obstacle to passage, but is the limit of a physical system. In this respect, though comets wander from heaven to heaven (*Lum.* IX, AT XI: 61–3), each heaven is a closed system for the bodies that make it up.

The description begun in *Treatise on Light* VIII is elaborated in the following chapters and ends, as we noted above when considering Descartes' claims to empirical adequacy, with the comparison in Chapter XV between the lights we see in the sky and what the inhabitants of the other heavens see in their skies. But that comparison is a comparison between *different* ways in which those lights can be secured. For Descartes is doing a sort of rational astronomy, attempting to reconstruct the notion of a heaven from that of the most basic motions and the action of light; this procedure requires him to set a star at the centre of each heaven. Though, as we shall see, he adjusted a part of the theory of the basic motions that underlies his rational astronomising, he did not feel it necessary in the *Principles* to offer an account of the distribution of the bodies in the sky of a world where rational astronomy describes how things are that is anything other than 'unmistakably Copernican' (Garber 1992a: 26).

What is unmistakably Copernican about the account of the heavens in the *Principles* is that the best that rational astronomy can do is produce an account of a *solar* system. For a rational astronomy, *where* things are is less important than *how* they act. So, the fact that there is a star at the centre of each of the heavens (other perhaps than ours) is, for Descartes, a mere consequence of his account of the action of light.

But having the star at the centre of such a system does not imply either that the rational astronomy is the true story of the heaven where we are, or that the Earth moves around the Sun of itself (i.e. in addition to its diurnal rotation). Of course, these latter two theses were also part of Copernicus' view of the heavens, which was expressed in his posthumous *On Revolutions* (1543) and which immediately caused controversy within the Roman Catholic Church. Even so, when Descartes was at school, the Jesuits illustrated to their students the heliocentric system as an ingenious hypothesis (De Rochemonteix 1889: IV, 39); and this may serve to explain why Descartes did not interrogate Mersenne about the teachability of the ensemble of doctrines in the way that we have seen he did about the potentially infinite extent of the 'imaginary spaces'.

The part of Copernicanism that caused most controversy was the part that says that the Earth moves. In 1616, it had been condemned by the consultants to the Index; though the decree does not name Galileo himself (Galilei 1890–1909, XIX: 322–3; Finocchiaro 1989: 148–9), he was undoubtedly its instance. And, in 1633, seven of the ten cardinals sitting at Rome as Inquisitors General issued a Sentence prohibiting Galileo's *Two World Systems* because it appeared to support the movement of the Earth (Galilei 1890–1909, XIX: 402–6; Finocchiaro 1989: 297–91).

There is no doubt that Descartes' knowledge (from November 1633) about, and his subsequent (by April 1634) reading of, this latter Sentence led him to suppress the *Treatise on Light*. But there is considerable difference of opinion about the motivation behind his reaction. There are, at bottom, four views one might take here. One is to say that Descartes was poised to burn these writings because he was afraid of being acted against by ecclesiastical authority. A second is to say that he held them in reserve because he was waiting for the Church to change its mind. A third is to say that he was waiting for a definitive outcome to the process involving Galileo. And a fourth is to say that, even though it had not reached a definitive outcome, the process involving Galileo gave him reason for thinking that Galileo's opinion was false.

To decide among these possible views, we need to assess the letters that Descartes sent to Mersenne in the relevant period (1633–4). The reason for this focus is that it is our best blow-by-blow source and that we can be pretty sure that Descartes was sincere with Mersenne, though we shall see reason for thinking that the converse does not hold. But we are hampered by two facts. First, the two men were having some difficulty communicating because of 'unreliable couriers' (letter to Mersenne, 22nd July 1633, AT I: 269: *'messagers infidèles'*),[4] and there was a hiatus in their correspondence (cf. letter to Mersenne, April 1634, CSMK: 42) at just the period that Descartes was making up his mind. So we do not have full documentation of the development of Descartes' thought. Second, as usual, we do not have Mersenne's letters. So we cannot be sure what information and advice Descartes received.

There is less to be said for the first of the four possible views than for any of the others. It has, nevertheless, been favoured in relatively recent Anglophone literature. Thus we find the vocabulary of Descartes' acting out of 'fear' (Sorell 1987: 36), being given a 'scare' (Keeling 1934: 22), being given cause for 'worry' (Hatfield 1993: 267), or being made 'cautious' (Grene 1985: 78). But, as has been rightly noted (e.g. J. Scott 1952: 24; Gaukroger 1995: 291), Descartes could have published freely in Holland, where versions of the thesis that the Earth moves were pretty commonplace, and even in France, where the writ of Rome was pretty regularly contested (McClaughlin 1979).

Descartes was silly in his letter to Mersenne of November 1633 to express surprise that Galileo, 'an Italian, and even well-beloved of the Pope' (letter to Mersenne, end November 1633, CSMK: 41; AT I: 271: *'qui est Italien, et même bien voulu du Pape'*), should have been the victim of a Vatican backlash against astronomical novelties. After all, it was only prominent Italians in Italy who could be brought to book, as Giordano Bruno's equal silliness, coupled with greater impetuousness, had already witnessed.[5] Yet it is not clear that Descartes' silliness on the point reflects any state of anxiety for himself or for the opportunites for spreading his doctrines. And one might be forgiven for suspecting that those who wish to attribute anxiety to Descartes do so either because they have an impression of him as basically cowardly or because they wish to emphasise, to the point of exaggeration, the power of the forces of reaction that he was struggling with. Or, perhaps inconsistently, both.

In favour of the second view mentioned – that Descartes was biding his time – there is the fact that, in April 1634, Descartes tells Mersenne that he has not entirely lost hope that the same thing will happen to the opinion about the movement of the Earth as happened to the (opinion about the) Antipodes, which had been condemned in a similar way long before, and then rehabilitated (CSMK: 44). On this view, Descartes continued to believe in the movement of the Earth, but would not pronounce publicly on the matter, even to the extent of showing Mersenne his manuscripts, until he was permitted to do so.[6] And this would explain why he did not act on his earlier half-intention to burn his papers (letter to Mersenne, November 1633, AT I: 270–1: '*je me suis quasi résolu de brûler tous mes papiers*'): no more than half an intention until the Church had had a chance to reconsider.

Not necessarily inconsistent with the second view, there is a third, proposed, for instance, by Gouhier (1924: 87–8). On this account, Descartes doubted that the Church had gone through the correct procedures for declaring heretical the teaching, even by way of hypothesis, of the movement of the Earth. This view would be based on two passages in a letter just cited (April 1634), in which he distinguishes between what the Inquisitors (letter to Mersenne, AT I: 285) or a sub-committee (ibid.: AT I: 288: '*Congregation particulière*') of cardinals can decide, and the way that a point determined by the Pope or a Council does become straightaway (ibid.: AT I: 285: '*incontinent*') an article of faith. Until a final ruling had been reached, it was not up to the faithful to express their views, though there was nothing to stop them holding them. But, once a final ruling has been reached, it is the duty of a good Catholic to reorganise his thoughts in accordance with the established teaching.

On this line of thought, there is room for saying that, strictly speaking, there was no Roman Catholic teaching on the question of the movement or stationariness of the Earth in 1633–4. Rather, what we have is, on the one hand, the least difficult reading of some passages in the Bible, such as *Psalms*, 104: 5; *Ecclesiastes*, 1: 5; and *Joshua*, 10: 12–13, from which it appears that the Sun is in motion around the Earth, and, on the other a fairly extended bit of argumentation in Aristotle (*De Cælo*, II xii–xiv) in favour of the conclusion (explicitly decided at 296 a 24–7 a 8) that the Earth is stationary. The overall agreement between these two authorities provides a presumption that what they agree on is the truth of the matter. Hence it is what a dutiful believer will believe, unless he thinks he has reason to the contrary. Though it might be attractive to think that Descartes may at some stage (during the composition of the *Treatise on Light*) have thought that he did have reason to the contrary, in which case he could have held onto the opinion he expresses in the 'fable' of the *Treatise on Light*. But he did not hold onto it. So this cannot be how he understood the position.

Between them, the second and the third options seem to me to attribute to

Descartes a defiance that I find it hard to read into the relevant letters. To the extent that he was, in Gaukroger's word, 'devastated' (1995: 292) by the condemnation of Galileo, he was so because he came to see that he had been on the verge of spreading a view that he had from the start (between 1629 and 1633) reason to think was false. That reason was that the agreement between the Bible and Aristotle is a reason for denying that the Earth moves. Not just because, as he learnt in 1633, prejudicial to religion or the state; but because false.

In addition to having reason to think the thesis that the Earth moves is false, there is the fact that Descartes held that, if this view was false, then so were the foundations of his philosophy because it was evidently demonstrated from them (letter to Mersenne, November 1633, AT I: 271: '*s'il* [sc. *le mouvement de la terre*] *est faux, tous les fondements de ma philosophie le sont aussi, car il se démontre par eux évidemment*'). That is, Descartes took his philosophy to include a deduction of the movement of the Earth. One thing that this plainly implies is that the disposition of the world is meant to be demonstrable from the foundations of philosophy. We have seen that his account of deduction cannot be identical to what we might want to say about relations of entailment or implication. But it does seem that if, *modus tollens*, the Earth does not move, then anything from which we can deduce (including in Descartes' sense of deduction) that the Earth does move is false. Nevertheless, we find commentators saying such things as: '[i]f physics were logically deduced from metaphysics, then by contraposition, the refutation of physics would imply a similar fate for the metaphysics. This option Descartes wishes to avoid' (Clarke 1982: 101).[7]

We might wish him to avoid it on his behalf; but, without his denying the appropriateness of the Roman Catholic Church as a conduit for special divine revelation, it is hard to see how Descartes can 'opt' out of it. That is, having been alerted to a problem about the movement of the Earth, he has to save the metaphysics by remodelling the physics. Which is just what we find him doing.

In the first letter to Mersenne in which the condemnation of Galileo is mentioned (November 1633, CSMK: 40–1), Descartes requests a year's grace before letting him see the manuscript. In that time, he means to rewrite (ibid., AT I: 272: '*revoir*'). He means to rewrite so as to remove the bad things (ibid., AT I: 271: '*mauvaises choses*'), and so that the opinions it expresses can be approved without controversy (ibid.: AT I: 271: '*approuvées sans controverse*'). In the next letter we have (February 1634, CSMK: 41–2), he says that he is ready to lose four years' work in order to render complete obedience to the Church, inasmuch as it has forbidden (AT I: 281: '*défendu*') the opinion about the movement of the Earth. In April of the same year (CSMK: 42–4), he says that he would not for anything in the world maintain even the demonstrations that he held to be most certain and evident against the authority of the Church (AT I: 285). This seems to me a clear assertion of the priority of that authority relative to what *solo* enquiry in accordance with doxastic rectitude can deliver.

In the same letter of April 1634, he seems to be responding to information furnished by Mersenne that a certain Ismaël Boulliau[8] had written a book proposing, if only hypothetically, the movement of the Earth. Descartes' response to this information is one of surprise or shock (AT I: 288: *'je m'étonne'*), because Boulliau is in holy orders and because Descartes has seen the Sentence against Galileo, which prohibits people from proposing, even by way of hypothesis (AT I: 288, quoting: *'quamvis hypothetice'*), the movement of the Earth. In the letter of 14th August 1634 (CSMK: 44–5), he reproduces more at length the text of the Sentence that he has seen and to which we have already referred; and it seems to be Descartes who emphasises the part of it that says that one may not regard the doctrine of the movement of the Earth as even probably defensible (AT I: 306: *'aut quasi eam doctrinam defendi posse uti probabilem existimaverit'*).[9]

Again, Descartes uses the same expression of surprise or shock (AT I: 324: *'je m'étonne'*) when, sometime in the summer or autumn of 1635 (CSMK: 49–50), Mersenne has told him that he, Mersenne, is intending to refute J.-B. Morin's book that Descartes calls *'Contra Motum Terræ'*.[10] I.e. Mersenne is going to argue against the stationariness of the Earth and, by implication, in favour of its movement. In their editorial note to this letter (I: 321), AT conjecture that Mersenne had not been entirely open with Descartes about his own penchant for heliocentrism, taken broadly. In any case, Descartes would not have feared Mersenne's censure were he to have persisted in thinking that the 'fable' of the *Treatise on Light* could be presented as somehow exempt from the Sentence he had seen. That is, Descartes seems to have thought that Mersenne, himself, like Boulliau, in holy orders, would abide by the terms of the Sentence and would interpret those terms to mean that defence, even hypothetically or for the purposes of probable debate, of the condemned doctrine and attack on the contrary of the condemned doctrine were both prohibited.

As late as the early 1640s, Descartes was trying to find out whether there there was any chance that the movement of the Earth could be taught. One approach was through Gabriel de Naudé to the Cardinal di Bagni (letter to Mersenne, December 1640, CSMK: 160–1), where Descartes says that he believes very firmly in the infallibility of the Church (ibid.: AT III: 259: *'croyant très fermement l'infallibilité de l'Eglise'*). At this stage, it is true, he is concerned that he is unable to detach the movement of the Earth from the rest of his philosophy, because the whole of his physics depends upon it (ibid.: AT III: 258: *'toute ma physique en dépend'*). If the movement of the Earth is prohibited, the physics has to be changed, because, as we have seen in the last two chapters, the whole system hangs together as a sequence of deductions of effects from causes. The other was through perhaps Mersenne or Ste Croix to Cardinal Francesco Barberini, who had been Papal Legate in France and had sat in the Congregation of Inquisitors that condemned Galileo, and was a nephew of Urban VIII.[11] And what he wants to know is whether the opinion about the movement of the Earth is permissible or not (letter perhaps to Dinet, March 1642, AT V: 544: '*liceat vel non liceat*'), where that will determine what he is to believe.

From these reactions and hopes, expressed in private correspondence with an interlocutor who was open to astronomical novelty (though Descartes may not have been aware just how open), it would seem that Descartes did believe that the Roman Catholic Church could identify false opinions in astronomy and other matters concerning the overall consitution of the universe better than he or Galileo could on their own.[12] Accordingly, we can understand why, between 1633 and the publication of the *Principles* in 1644, he reconsidered the matters discussed in the *Treatise on Light*, and developed the second vortex theory, on which the proposition 'the Earth does not move' comes out true.

If Descartes were to have followed Galileo, then he was not a good Catholic; but Descartes was a good Catholic; therefore, following Galileo was not a viable path. Unless he gives up on the authority of the Roman Catholic Church, the only serious alternatives he has are: (i) to reform the principles of his metaphysics in such a way as to avoid the false physical opinion; or (ii) to admit that the heavens are a mystery. The second vortex theory, which we find in the *Principles* is an attempt to do (i). The admission that the 'fable' of the *Treatise on Light* is not true of the actual world is a move in the direction of (ii),[13] and so is his resolution not to publish this material lest it mislead people into giving a hearing to the hypothesis that the Earth moves.

Commentators have noticed that, in his early writings, Descartes does not offer the sort of definition of motion that the format of the *Principles* requires him to give (e.g. Garber 1992a: 158). It is, nevertheless, clear that the conception of motion in the 'fable' of the *Treatise on Light* is fundamentally quantitative and geometrical, in contradistinction to the qualitative and broader Aristotelian notion of a change (κίνησις), of which local motion is just one sort (e.g. *Phys.*, III i, 200 b 34–1 a 9). It could not be other, given that the 'fable' excludes the forms and qualities – the 'natures' – on which the Aristotelian model essentially depends (see Waterlow Broadie 1982). Rather, Descartes takes motion to be simpler than the simples of geometry, the point and the line, because it can be used to define them (*Lum.* VII, AT XI: 40). Instead, he takes the notion of a place (ibid.: '*lieu*') as basic and says that we have movement when bodies pass from one to another and successively occupy all the spaces in between. Thus, in a given heaven, the planets are in movement relative to the central star and the firmament, because the relation between those two fixes which are the places within the heaven. Hence, if the Earth were a planet in a heaven of the sort that fixes places in this way, then it would be in movement relative to the central star (the Sun).

In the theory proposed in the *Principles*, motion and place are more carefully defined. At II, 24–5, Descartes distinguishes between the vulgar or catachrestic sense of motion as 'the action by which some body migrates from one place to another' (*Pr.* II, 24, AT VIIIA: 53: '*actio, qua corpus aliquod ex uno loco in alium migrat*') and what he takes to be its true or philosophical definition as

> the translation of one part of matter, or of one body, from the neighbourhood of those bodies that are immediate in contact with it and are thus held to be at rest, to the neighbourhood of other [*sc.* bodies] (*Pr.* II, 25, CSM I: 233; AT VIIIA: 53: '*translationem unius partis materiæ, sive unius corporis, ex vicinia eorum corporum, quæ illud immediate contingunt et tanquam quiescentia spectantur, in viciniam aliorum*').

The vulgar definition corresponds pretty closely to what, in the first vortex theory, is presupposed about motion. The true definition brings to light the respect in which, in the second vortex theory, motion is relativised to the contents of the neighbourhoods that are in contact with a given body. For the idea is that no *place* can be held to be fixed and immobile in any absolute sense. And a body like the Earth stays with the bodies in its neighbourhood.

In the account given in the 'fable' of the *Treatise on Light*, the planets are in motion both because they occupy successively different places in the heaven, relative to the star and the firmament, and because, in their circulation around the star, they displace the subtle matter that fills the heaven. This is illustrated in advance by Descartes' image in the fourth chapter of the *Treatise on Light* of the fish swimming below the surface of a pool: even if they move the water immediately around them and are in a plenum, the water they do move does not push all the water in the pool indifferently (*Lum.* IV, CSM I: 87; AT XI: 20: '[*l'eau*] *ne pousse pas indifférement toute l'eau du bassin*'). Thus, if the surface of the pool is unruffled, the fish are in motion relative to it.

By contrast, in the theory of the *Principles*, not only are the motions of bodies so thoroughly relativised to different understandings of place as to make the difference between motion and rest hang on our thought (*Pr.* II, 28; CSM I: 232; AT VIIIA: 55: '*loci acceptio varia est, ac pendet a nostra cognitione*'), but things that we might want to say are in motion may nevertheless be carrying with them the bodies that are in immediate contact with them (*Pr.* II, 33). Taken together, the relativisations that Descartes spells out in *Principles* II, 24 and 31 and III, 15, along with the claim, made at *Principles* III, 25, that movements within a given heaven necessarily carry along with them all the things contained in them (AT VIIIA: 89: '*necessario secum deferent alia omnia corpora in se contenta*'), there is a clear sense in which the Earth (like all the other planets) is at rest in the heaven just as a boat that is neither pushed by the wind or by oars and is not anchored is at rest in the midst of the sea (*Pr.* III, 26, AT VIIIA: 90: it is '*ut navis, nullis ventis nec remis impulsa, nullique anchoris alligata, in medio mari quiescit*'). Which is what Descartes spells out at *Principles* III, 28.

In the strict sense, already quoted from II, 25, the planets are not transferred from the neighbourhood of the parts of the heaven with which they are in immediate contact, inasmuch as those parts are to be considered as unmoved (*Pr.* III, 28, AT VIIIA: 90: '[*nullum*] *motum proprie dictum reperiri: quia* [*Terra nec planeti*] *non transferuntur ex vicinia partium cæli quæ illos immediate contingunt, quatenus istæ partes cæli ut immotæ considerantur*'). Descartes concedes a sense in which it is useful to be able to account the other planets as in motion. But not even in the vulgar sense should we say that the Earth moves unless we are going to get ourselves in a twist (*Pr.* III, 29, AT VIIIA: 91: '[*m*]*otum autem sumendo juxta usum vulgi, dicendum quidem est planetis alios omnes moveri* [. . .] *sed non, nisi admodum incongrue, idem de Terra dici potest*'), because, roughly speaking, if there is a privileged reference frame, it is that provided by the relative positions of the Earth and the fixed stars (ibid.).[14]

In short, though he has a job to accommodate the apparent movements in the sky (*Pr.* III, 15ff.), the intended physical realisation of the second vortex theory allows Descartes to assert that the Earth does not move relative to the neighbourhood of the bodies in immediate contact with it. As appears from the adjunct to the French version of *Principles* III, 29, the Earth moves no more than does a person who sleeps through a cross-Channel passage (AT IXB: 115: '[*si*] *nous semblons attribuer quelque mouvement à la Terre, il faudra penser que c'est* [. . .] *au même sens qu'on peut dire quelquefois de ceux qui dorment et sont couchés dans un vaisseau, qu'ils passent de Calais à Douvres*').

It thus seems that, when he came to apply his mind to defining motion in a way that he had not earlier done, Descartes saw a conceptual advantage in distinguishing the vulgar definition of motion from his slightly contorted philosophical account, and that the account he gives of the relativity of motion is to be understood as a consistent application of the arbitrariness of reference frames. The adoption of these two moves into his physics also has the advantage that, because they do not commit him to the movement of the Earth, he can hold onto his metaphysics and fall in line with what was required by the condemnation of 1633.

Though it does not come out false in quite the ways that the most straightforward readings of the Bible and Aristotle might lead us to expect, the

Galileian opinion about the movement of the Earth does nevertheless come out false. So Descartes is justified, in writing to an unknown correspondent sometime after the publication of the *Principles*, that he very roundly denies this movement (CSMK: 239; AT V: 550: '*je nie très expressément ce mouvement*'). Half-conceding that, at first glance, his denial may seem merely verbal (ibid.: '*c'est de parole seulement que je le nie*'), and attributing this to his continued subscription to the heliocentric hypothesis (ibid.: '*je retiens le système de Copernic*'), he makes one point about how the Church must view the astronomy of the ancients and one about how Biblical expressions are to be taken. As to the former, if the Tychonic system commits us to the movement of the Earth, and the Copernican does not, it is better to have a Copernican theory, explained as Descartes explains it (ibid.: '*expliqué en la façon que je l'explique*'), than to go back to Ptolemy. What is wrong with the Ptolemaic system is that is manifestly contrary to experience (ibid.: '*manifestement contraire à l'expérience*') and this gives Descartes reason for believing that the Church will not oblige anyone to believe it. As to the Bible, he says that the passages that seem to count against the movement of the Earth should not be taken as what we would call scientific statements about the nature of the world (ibid.: '*ne regardent point le système du monde*'). Rather, they are couched in or guides to what we say or the way we speak (ibid.: '*façon de parler*'). Descartes says that his account of the heavens does entire justice to these passages (ibid.: '*suivant le système que j'expose, je satisfais entièrement à ces passages*').

Descartes has less than apodeictic reason for thinking that the movement of the Earth is a false doctrine. It is less than apodeictic because the organs for the dissemination of Roman Catholic dogma could be the playthings of a malicious demon.[15] This is not equivalent to the claim that the Church itself could be an instrument of deception: if the stationariness of the Earth *is* the teaching of the Church, Descartes is bound to believe it. But, even so, that opinion was not established by the condemnation, as it stood in 1633, as the definitive teaching of the Church.

But we have reviewed indications in his correspondence tending to show that Descartes' attitude was that, even if the condemnation of 1633 was not definitive or the stationariness of the Earth was not an article of faith, it would be an error to believe in the movement of the Earth. Where 'error' means the same as 'false opinion' and not a view that is prejudicial to religion or the state, or merely ill-mannered, imprudent or unpopular. And I suggest that Descartes was interested in the avoidance of false opinions, and that he happened to believe that the Roman Catholic Church was a source of admonitions against some false opinions that it might be hard for the natural operation of the flimsy faculties of an individual human to discern unaided. That he believed this does, it is true, run counter to one image of him as a champion of the seventeenth-century 'Scientific Revolution'; but it is precisely images of that sort that can be put under pressure by consideration of what he said and how he acted.

In terms of the analogy with adultery suggested earlier, Descartes' position seems to be this. As a temperate man in pursuit of licit pleasures, he finds himself flirting with a certain woman. Subsequently, he learns that she is married. Though she seems willing enough, he recognises that it would involve him in adultery to have sexual intercourse with her. He consequently sets himself no longer to desire her. It is not his temperance that tells him that he should curb his desire, but a prohibition that is independent of the desires of either: the institution of marriage as inviolably exclusive. Natural enquiry in accordance with doxastic rectitude brings him to the verge of believing in the movement of the Earth. Subsequently, he learns that this is a prohibited view. Though it is a view that looks as clear and distinct as one could wish it to be, he recognises that avowing it as his own would involve him in error. He consequently sets himself to revise his opinion. It is not doxastic rectitude that tells him he should rewrite his physics to remove the bad things in it, but a prohibition that is independent of it: the authority of the Church to access special revelations about the gross constitution of the universe.

Thus Descartes aims to be obedient, to propose for others and to believe for himself only what is consonant with the doctrines of the Church.[16] Though he is generally confident that his philosophy will make better sense of its theology than any other system,[17] he is seeking to treat those doctrines as authoritative and, in particular, as more authoritative than what he can discover for himself. This might look like Jesuitry in the derogatory sense, already abroad in his day, of prevarication and mental reservation. But it can also be read as a sort of humility not often associated with Descartes. St Ignatius puts the point, notoriously or heroically, by saying that he should believe that what he sees as white is black if the Church should so decide (Loyola 1534a: 344–6).[18] I suggest that Descartes thinks the same: the Church had decided that the Earth does not move, so Descartes should and can set himself to believe that it does not.

Afterword

No book on Descartes could hope to give the whole picture. This is no exception, and I noted at the outset some specifically and canonically Cartesian questions that have been hardly touched on.

But there is also a picture bigger than even the most complete picture of Descartes, which has to do with why Descartes gets studied at all by modern philosophers. This, too, is a matter I have kept mostly quiet about. But I offer here a couple of theses that seem to be supported against the broader background by the snaps I have taken of bits of Descartes.

First, for all that I have tried to make his thought responsive to serious problems, Descartes ends up in many positions that it would be hard to imagine any modern philosopher willingly or professionally occupying. He is weird and unmodern. As history, this is what we ought to expect: Descartes did not have the doubtful benefit of having read the things that have gone on in philosophy over the last nearly 350 years, some of which were set off by readings of Descartes. If there are culprits for the mess that modern philosophy – particularly epistemology – is thought to be in, we should be looking to modern philosophers, not to Descartes, who was not one.

Second, it seems to me bad policy, both as history and as philosophy, to divide up the concerns of a thinker like Descartes in ways that would be alien to him. In the case in point, the separation of what he has to say about God from what he has to say about us, can lead to disaster. Specifically, the trend of recent, mostly Anglophone, philosophy is to regard the God-question as that of the validity or otherwise of various arguments, some of which can be found in Descartes, for His existence, and to treat the epistemology as a matter that can be taken up independently of whether there is a God or not. I was brought up an atheist and remain in the faith of my parents; and I expect that my experience is not so different from that of many philosophers brought up to detheologise philosophy; but it seems worth considering what Descartes, brought up a Catholic and remaining in the faith of his country, would have made of the separation. The disaster here is an unwillingness to see why he needs a God at all, and an amputation of the theory of knowledge just when it gets interesting. Descartes' questions about knowledge get answers of a sort that they require only by passing through a stage alien to us. The same goes, in spades, for the question of how much control we might have over the beliefs we form.

Third, Descartes' contributions to epistemology, as that subject has grown up, have very little to do with the most debated topics, to do with the possibility of there being something that is both empirical and knowledge. What he has to say about credulity could help us to redirect our thought about why such a possibility might seem paradoxical. And what he had to say about the bogey of scepticism seems to me to cut short a great deal of debate about a variety of allegedly wicked doctrines that get called 'foundationalist', but are generally nothing of the sort.

And fourth, it is not all that obvious, on the other hand, that modern philosophy is in quite the mess that it is often thought to be. In particular, it seems to me that there is no compelling reason to go in for the sort of 'end of philosophy' talk that is visited on us by persons who are dissatisfied with what they have got out of Descartes and others. If one does not want to do theory of knowledge, one is not obliged to; if one wants to do it in a new key, then one might be ready to rethink why caring about knowledge is better than not caring about it. Seeing what is weird and unmodern in Descartes can help to identify ways to rethink such questions, perhaps by going back to someone who is weirder and even more unmodern: perhaps Aristotle or, according to taste, Plato or Epicurus or Chrysippus, or even Sextus. But only after having exorcised what remains in us of modernised variants on Descartes.

In short, I think that Descartes is interesting because he is not the father of modern philosophy.

Notes

Introduction

1 Hume's observations on the virtues of footnotes as against endnotes are quoted and referenced by Grafton (1997: 102–3 and n. 7).

1 Intellectual virtues

1 Schneewind (1980: 182–5) discusses Grotius' objections to Aristotle's account of justice as a virtue on the grounds that it has no excess.

2 His 'Of Studies' appeared among the ten sketches published in the first edition of the *Essays* (1597); in the final, enlarged and altered version of 1625 (Bacon 1625a), it is printed as Essay L. For an elaborated textual history, see Bacon (1625b: on the rhetoric 143–8; text and variants 356–7; notes 598–600); on its medical imagery, Vickers (1968: 54–5). The best commentary I know of its pith is Samuel Johnson's essay, now bearing the misleading title 'The Rôle of the Scholar', first printed in *The Adventurer*, 85 (28th August 1753), reproduced in Johnson (1984: 269–73).

3 This is none too far from what Myles Burnyeat, thinking of Montaigne, describes as the 'country gentleman's interpretation' of Pyrrhonism in Burnyeat (1984: 231ff.).

4 D. Balme (in Aristotle 1972) translates the latter passage as one who is 'able to judge successfully what is properly expounded and what is not'; its opposite would be the ἀπαιδευμένος who demands proof of the Law of Contradiction in *Metaph.*, Γ iv, 1006 a 6–8. The sense of perspective is not, however, meant to lead to the Total Perspective Vortex conjured in the *Hitchhiker's Guide to the Galaxy*, which is (Leibnizian) prejudice in favour of the absolute.

5 In this vein, there is plenty to ponder in the following slightly pruned passage from M'Taggart (1930: 74–6):

> [. . .] to acquire true belief in religious dogma does require moral qualifications – in almost every case – in the seeker. But they are required, not to show us what the truth is – for that purpose they seem to me as useless to the metaphysician as to the accountant – but to prevent our turning away from the truth. In the first place, a man will scarcely arrive at truth on these questions without courage. For he must seek before he can find, and at the beginning of his search he cannot tell what he will find.
>
> And he also needs – unless he is almost incredibly fortunate – a certain form of faith. He will need the power to trust the conclusions which his reason has

deliberately adopted, even when circumstances make such a belief especially difficult or painful [. . .].

If we want to know the truth, then, we must have faith in the conclusions of our reason, even when they seem – as they often will seem – too good or too bad to be true. Such faith has a better claim to abide with hope and love than the faith which consists in believing without reason for belief.

6 Some of the material in this section appears in a different format in Davies (1998b).

7 Collegium Conimbricense (1593): disp. VII qu. III art. i: '[*u*]*numquodque secundum suæ* [sc. *humanæ*] *naturæ gradum perficitur, est illi secundum naturam conveniens; homo autem secundum gradum suæ naturæ virtutibus acquisitis perficitur et excolitur*'.

8 Also *EN*, III v, 1114 b 29; VI i, 1138 b 20. See Gottlieb (1994: 280–6) on the distinction between μετὰ λόγου ἀληθοῦς (e.g. at VI iv, 1140 a 20–1) and κατὰ τόν ὀϱθόν λογόν (cf. II iv, 1105 a 25–6). Also Audi (1995).

9 Also *EN*, II ii, 1104 a 27–b 3; II iv, 1105 a 22–6; III ii, 1111 b 6–7; III iii, 1113 a 9–14; III v, 1113 b 3–21; and X ix, 1179 b 31–1180 a 29. Cf. the formula of Collegium Conimbricense (1593: col 83): '*licet per unum actum gigni possit habitus virtutis; plerumque non gigni habitum virtutis perfectæ, nisi per multos actos*'.

10 *EN*, II vi: κατὰ δὲ τὸ ἄϱιστον καὶ τὸ εὖ ἀκϱότης (1107 a 7–8); cf. τὸ μέσον εἰαί πως ἄκϱον (1107 a 23); it is only πως because we normally contrast the centre with the extremes.

11 Taking a stand against the 'idols', Bacon says that they must be 'renounced and put away with a fixed and solemn determination' (1620: I, 68). Such formulæ presumably echo the renunciation of the devil and all his works in rituals of baptism.

12 In Hobbes (1651: I, 8), we likewise find the primary intellectual virtue of 'natural wit' requiring 'steady direction to some approved end'.

13 *Dis.* VI, AT VI: 62, speaking specifically of just one branch of knowledge (medicine): '*sans que j'aie aucun dessein de la mépriser, je m'assure qu'il n'y a personne, même de ceux qui en font profession, qui n'avoue que tout ce qu'on y sait n'est presque rien à comparaison de ce qui reste à y savoir*'.

14 For lack of swiftness, *Reg.* IV, AT X: 378–9: '*At ego, tenuitatis meæ conscius, talem ordinem in cognitione rerum quærenda pertinaciter observare statui, ut semper a simplicissimis & facillimis exorsus, nunquam ad aliam pergam, donec in istis nihil mihi ulterius optandum superesse videatur*'; for lack of fecundity, *Dis.* VI, AT VI: 71: '[. . .] *s'ils* [the '*meilleurs esprits*', loc.; cit.] *veulent savoir parler de toutes choses* [. . .] *ils y parviendront plus aisément en se contentant de la vraisemblance* [. . .] *qu'en cherchant la verité, qui ne se découvre que peu à peu en quelques-unes, et qui, lorsqu'il est question de parler des autres, oblige à confesser franchement qu'on les ignore*'.

15 *Pr.* I, 73, AT VIIIA: 37: '[. . .] *quia in primis annis, cum sensus et imaginationes occuparetur, majorem de ipsis quam de cæteris rebus cogitandi usum et facilitatem acquisivit*'.

16 *Pr.* I, 73, AT VIIIA: 37 gives '*difficultas*' and '*defatigatio*', which go easily enough into '*peine*' and '*fatigue*' (AT IXB: 60).

17 'Synopsis' to the *Med.*; CSM gives an absolute superlative 'the easiest route' (II: 12) to translate the indeterminate '*via facillima*' (AT VII: 12), though the French is plainly only positively superlative: '*chemin très facile*' (AT IXA: 9).

2 Reason and virtue in the *Passions*

1 Seneca, letter to Lucilius 76.11: '*quid est in homine proprium? ratio: hæc recta et consummata felicitatem hominis impelluit. Ergo si omnis res, cum bonum suum perfecti, laudabilis*

est et ad finem naturæ suæ pervenit, homini autem suum bonum ratio est [. . .] *hæc ratio perfecta virtus vocatur'*.

2 Letter to Princess Elizabeth of 1st September 1645, AT IV: 282: '[*c*]*ar il n'y a personne qui ne désire se rendre heureux; mais plusieurs n'en savent pas le moyen; et souvent l'indisposition qui est dans le corps, empêche que la volonté ne soit libre'*.

3 *Pass.* I, 17, AT XI: 342: '[. . .] *ce n'est pas notre âme qui les* [sc. '*toutes sortes de perceptions*', ibid.] *fait telles qu'elles sont, et* [. . .] *elle les reçoit des choses qui sont représentées par elles* [sc. '*passions*', ibid.]'*.

4 *Pass.* I, 46, AT XI: 363–4 '[. . .] *l'âme, en se rendant fort attentive à quelque autre chose, peut s'empêcher d'ouïr un petit bruit ou de sentir une petite douleur, mais ne peut s'empêcher en même façon d'ouïr le tonnerre ou de sentir le feu qui brûle la main'*.

5 *Pass.* I, 49, AT XI: 367–8: '[*i*]*l est vrai qu'il y a fort peu d'hommes si faibles et irrésolus qu'ils ne veulent rien que ce que leur passion leur dicte'*.

6 Note, again, the emphatic in '*elles n'ont point de raison*' (AT XI: 369); subsequently, animals are described as '*dépourvus de raison*' (AT XI: 370).

7 *Pass.* II, 144, CSM I: 379; AT XI: 436–7: '[. . .] *pour celles qui ne dépendent que de nous, c'est-à-dire de notre libre arbitre* [. . .] *nous en recevons toujours la satisfaction que nous en avons attendue'*.

8 See, for instance Chrysippus cited by Stobæus *Eclogues*, II, 7; Cicero, *Tusculan Disputations*, III, 14.

9 *Pass.* III, 161, AT XI: 454: '*la clef de toutes les autres vertus et un remède général contre toutes les dérèglements des passions*'.

10 *Pass.* III, 156, CSM I: 385; AT XI: 448: '[. . .] *il n'y a aucune chose dont l'acquisition ne dépende pas d'eux qu'ils pensent valoir assez pour mériter d'être beaucoup souhaitée'*. See Rodis-Lewis 1975.

11 Of the various types of contingency that we might be able to individuate, those that (falsely) seem as if they might have been brought about by an agent with some end in view are those that we are most likely to give the names of 'luck' or 'fortune'; cf. Aristotle, *Phys.*, II iv–vi, esp. [τυχή] ἔστι δ ἕνεκά του ὅσα τε ἀπὸ διανοίας ἂν πραχθείη καὶ ὅσα ἀπὸ φύσεως (196 b 22–3); cf. Wieland 1962: on 'as if' teleology: 144–6.

12 *Pass.* II, 146, CSM I: 380; AT XI: 439: '*Mais parce que la plupart de nos désirs s'étendent à des choses qui ne dépendent pas toutes de nous ni toutes d'autrui, nous devons exactement distinguer en elles ce qui ne dépende que de nous, afin de n'étendre notre désir qu'à cela seul* [*et*] *afin que notre désir ne s'y* [sc. of what is '*fatal et immuable*', ibid.] *occupe point*'.

13 *Pass.* II, 148, AT XI: 442: '[*vivre*] *en telle sorte que sa conscience ne lui peut reprocher qu'il n'ait jamais manqué à faire toutes les choses qu'il a jugées être les meilleures*'.

14 *Pass.* III, 153, AT XI: 446: '[*qu'on*] *sent en soi-même une ferme et constante résolution d'en* [sc. of the '*libre disposition de ses volontés*', [loc. cit.] *bien user, c'est-à-dire de ne manquer jamais de volonté pour entreprendre et exécuter toutes les choses qu'il jugera être les meilleures*'. We shall return to consider the use to which Descartes puts the epistemological '*ferme et constante résolution*' in the adoption of his '*préceptes*' in *Dis.* II (CSM I:120; AT VI: 18).

15 *Pass.* I, 49, AT XI: 368: '[*m*]*ais il y a pourtant grande différence entre les résolutions qui procèdent de quelque fausse opinion et celles qui ne sont appuyées que sur la connaissance de la vérité; d'autant que si on suit ces dernières, on est assuré de n'en avoir jamais de regret ni de repentir, au lieu qu'on en a toujours d'avoir suivi les premières lorsqu'on découvre l'erreur*'.

16 In reply to Bourdin's query Z in the *Seventh Objections and Replies*, Descartes appears to suppose that a bad belief can infect others as a bad apple can spread rot to the others in the same basket (cf. CSM II: 324); B. Williams suggests that

Descartes is guilty of using a bad analogy, one that can (only?) be shored up by offering some version of holism or by considerations about the deductive structure of belief-systems (1978: 59–60).

3 The vice of credulity

1 In the study of, most prominently, Plato and Aristotle, 'unitarianism', which can come in varying degrees of strength, is the thesis that these thinkers occupied just one view over the whole of their careers. It is opposed to the 'developmental' or 'genetic' hypotheses that have been used to explain perceived discrepancies between one text and another. I borrow the terminology for Descartes studies to label a difference between the pretty extreme unitarianism in, for instance, Martial Gueroult's writings and the strongly developmental stand of, for instance, Ferdinand Alquié. On the whole Anglophone commentators gravitate towards unitarianism, but rarely explicitly. I have no trouble with the idea that Descartes 'developed' in the period from his birth in 1596 and the time he began writing the things that have come down to us (1618); and I do suppose that there was a period in which he was getting his thoughts into order (say, 1619–37). There are some matters, such as the movement of the Earth, which we discuss in Chapter 11, in which his shifts of position as between the earlier period and the later are of interest in seeing how he rejigged his ideas; but I take it that they are much the same ideas that get rejigged and that the variations to be found in his core philosophical ideas as between the *Reg.* and the *Pass.* are primarily matters of emphasis, presentation and terminology. Where I think that matters of substance are at issue, I try to say so.

2 Although it is occasionally a little cumbersome, it is sometimes worth distinguishing between the narrators of the *Med.* and the *Dis.* and, therefore, between each of them and Descartes, who was the author of these texts. There being no such figure in play in the *Reg.*, the scientific essays, the *Resp.*, the *Pr.* and the *Pass.*, I feel unembarrassed about referring to Descartes as the voice in these texts. For uses other than those that I try here to exploit, to which a readiness to distinguish the narrators from their author can be put, see Marlies (1978: esp. 98–107 and 110–12); Rée (1987: 5–30); Kosman (1986: esp. 30–3); and Cavaillé (1994).

3 Here, I follow Haldane and Ross' translation (Descartes 1911: I, 144) of '*quam multa*'; likewise D.A. Cress in his version (Descartes 1980: 57); CSM may be rather overtranslating by rendering it 'the large number' (II: 12); likewise both Veitch (Descartes 1912: 79) and Sutcliffe (Descartes 1968: 95) construe it as an absolute 'many'; Anscombe and Geach (Descartes 1954: 61) give 'the multitude'; the Duc de Luynes is non-committal with '*quantité*' (AT IXA: 13). I am grateful to Robert Wardy for pointing out that the Latin will not bear the number's being very low, but even that will be an attributive notion.

4 Again, CSM and Veitch probably both go too far with 'highly doubtful' and Sutcliffe is (avowedly) following the French with 'what I had since based on such insecure principles could only be most doubtful and uncertain'; Anscombe and Geach refer to an absolute 'dubiousness'. Haldane and Ross, get both the first two assertions of the *Med.* almost dead right – bar a mild overtranslation of '*istis*' as 'on this basis'.

5 The French is rather more emphatic about the trust that the narrator put in the senses, saying not merely that he accepted as most true what he acquired from or through them, but adding the notion of assurance: '*le plus vrai et assuré*', AT IXA: 14.

6 The polemical use of the example can be traced at least to Diogenes of Oenoanda (Chilton, fr. 69), presumably responding to Plutarch *Adv. Colotes*, 1109a, or Sextus Empiricus, *PH*, I, 118 and *Adv. Math.*, VII, 208ff.; see also Lucretius *DRN*, IV, 353–63, who makes a suggestion to explain the phenomenon away.

7 There are puzzles about which of the standard (= Aristotelian (cf. *Metaphysics*, Γ iii, 1005 b 19–20)) relativisations apply at this point: 'at the same time' and 'in the same sense or respect' both seem to depend on theories of what sorts of things towers are and how they are related to times of being seen.

8 This line of thought has antecedents in Epicurean doctrine, cf. Epicurus, *Key Doctrine*, 23 (apud Diogenes, *Lives*, X, 146) and Lucretius, *DRN*, IV, 500–12.

9 *Pr.* I, 4, AT VIIIA: 6: '[. . .] *prudentiæ est, numquam nimis fidere iis, qui nos vel semel deceperunt*'; put in the negative in the French: '*il y aurait de l'imprudence de nous trop fier à ceux qui nous ont trompés*' (AT IXB: 27).

10 *Dis.* IV, AT VI: 32: '[. . .] *à cause que nos sens nous trompent quelquefois, je voulus supposer qu'il n'y avait aucune chose qui fût telles qu'ils nous la font imaginer*'.

11 *Search*, in a passage where Eudoxus makes explicit reference to credulity as the vice to be avoided; AT X: 510: '[. . .] *je trouve étrange que les hommes soient si* credules, *que d'appuyer leur science sur la certitude des sens, puisque personne n'ignore qu'ils trompent quelquefois, et que nous avons juste raison de nous defier toujours de ceux qui nous ont une fois trompés*' (emphasis added).

12 The French does not reiterate the reference to reason, replacing it with the notion of an occasion (*sujet*) of doubt: AT IXA: 14: '*mais, d'autant que la raison me persuade déjà que je ne dois pas moins soigneusement m'empêcher de donner créance aux choses qui ne sont entièrement certaines et indubitables, qu'à celles qui nous poaraissent manifestement être fausses, le moindre sujet de douter que j'y trouverai suffira pour me les faire toutes rejeter*'.

13 *Dis.* IV, AT VI: 31: [*mes*] *premières méditations* [. . .] *sont si* métaphysiques *et si peu communes qu'elles ne seront peut-être au gout de tout le monde. Et toutefois, afin qu'on puisse juger se les fondements que j'ai pris sont assez fermes, je me trouve en quelque façon contraint d'en parler*' (emphasis added: I follow Gilson's deflationary, non-technical, reading of '*métaphysique*' (Descartes 1925: 283)).

14 *Reg.* II, AT X: 363: '[. . .] *quotiescumque duorum de eadem re judicia in contrarias partes feruntur, certum est alterutrum saltem decipi*'; this assertion is then reinforced by '*ac ne unus quidem videtur habere scientiam*'.

15 In the mouth of Descartes' spokesman, Eudoxus, speaking of the Schools' method of exposition; AT X: 516: '*id, quod scio, debeo, eiusque adminiculo, ad agnoscendam rerum omnium, quas ibi edoctus sum, incertitudinem usus fui*'. Of course, the parallelism has much greater force if, with, e.g. Gouhier (1924: 155–8 and 139–20) and Kemp Smith (1952: 29–30) we follow Baillet (1691: II, 475; reproduced at AT X: 529) and date the work to the last years of Descartes' life; but in view of the powerful reasons for an early date put together by A. Bortolotti (1983: 139–53, 177–205, summarised at 219–23), I would not wish to hang anything on it.

16 *Pr.* I, 70, AT VIIIA: 34: '*nec ullam similitudinem intelligere possimus, inter colorem quem supponimus esse in objectis, et illum quem experimur esse in sensu*'. This doctrine is much developed in the *Lum.* (esp. I) and has come to be known as the 'error theory of colour'; for defence of this theory, and its attribution to a range of seventeenth-century figures, see Maund (1995).

17 From the very first words of *Pr.* I, 1, AT VIIIA: 5: '[*q*]*uoniam infantes nati sumus . . .*', through I, 47, AT VIIIA: 22: '*in prima ætate mens ita corporis fuit immersa*' to I, 66 as

just quoted, the theme is recurrent and echoes the '*ineunte ætate*' of the first assertion of *Med.* I.

18 *Pr.* I, 71, CSM I: 219 offers 'immersed' as a neutral rendering of '*immersus*' (AT
VIIIA: 36). Descartes' word choice recalls not only the passage from *Pr.* I, 47 cited
above but also his discussion with Burman (*Con.* (CB 9)) of a passage from the
Fourth Replies in which Cottingham (Descartes 1976) gives the chunkier rendering
'swamped' of the '*immersus*' of AT V: 150 (CSMK: 336), a translation that, in *Pr.*
I, 71 he reserves for '*imbutus*' (AT VIIIA: 36). Picot's French version gives '*offusqué*'
as an account of '*immersus*' and engages in periphrasis to avoid '*imbutus*' (AT
IXB: 59).

19 Letter to Hyperaspistes, August 1641, CSMK: 189; AT III: 422–3. This is one
relevant text not taken into consideration in the usefully uncluttered account
given by Marlies (1978: 91–5).

20 Cf. letter for Arnauld, 29th July 1648, CSMK: 356; AT V: 219: '[*v*]*erissime mihi
videtur, mentem, quandiu corpori unita est, a sensibus avocare se non posse, cum ab objectis exter-
nis vel internis vehementius percellitur. Addo etiam avocare se non posse, cum alligata est cerebro
nimis humido et molli, quale est in infantibus*'.

21 Of course, Descartes nowhere uses this terminology, which we owe to – or can
blame on – Locke (1689: II viii, 8–25). But it is not uncommon to find it invoked
in discussing his enterprise; e.g. by Laporte (1945: 63f.) Gueroult (1953: I, 131–3),
Kenny (1968: 204), Curley (1972), Williams (1978: 237–41), Grene (1985: 199),
Cottingham (1986: 142), Sorell (1987: 96), Wilson (1993). The respectability of
this practice is not in doubt; but it might be observed in a programmatic way that
the distinction that concerns Descartes is, rather, that between what we can have
clear and distinct ideas of and what we cannot. For elaborations of this, see
Wilson (1978: 76–92), Bolton (1986), Garber (1992a: 75–85), MacKenzie (1994)
and Flage (1999: 23–9).

22 The terminology of '*essential proprium*' is meant to render '*præcipuum attributum*'
(AT VIIIA: 25) or '*attribut principal*' (AT IXB: 48). It is an overtranslation. The
reason for it, in brief, is that, underlying *Med.* III, Descartes has a rather baroque
theory of how the intrinsic properties of some of our ideas – their being innate
and materially true, their having objective reality and clearness and distinctness – can combine to pick out (i) the *cogito* as representative of a substance that
must other than the idea of that substance; and (ii) the idea of God as representative of God in such a way that we can be assured that we are acquainted with
what is essential and peculiar to the substance in question. Elaboration and
defence of this interpretation counts as work in progress.

23 What Descartes seems to be treating as one are differentiated by Locke in the distinction he makes between a 'secondary' and a 'tertiary' quality. The former are
(wrongly) thought to be resemblances, whereas the latter 'neither are nor are
thought' to be such (marginal summary added in second and some subsequent
editions to *Essay* II viii, 24–5). Rather, a 'tertiary' quality is a bare power and not
an idea that has any 'conceivable connexion' (ibid.: 25) with the 'primary' qualities (e.g. the configuration of the surface of a body that reflects light in such a
way as to make me sense redness) that give rise to it.

24 Cf. *Med.* I, CSM II: 12; AT VII: 17; in *Dis.* III, he specifies the delay as fully eight
years (CSM I: 126; AT VI: 31: '*justement huit ans*'); if we take into account time for
actual research and the three years referred to at the beginning of *Dis.* VI (CSM
I: 141; AT VI: 60), we seem to come to either rather less than or considerably
more than the nine years Descartes approvingly (but rather shame-facedly)

quotes from Horace as the proper maturation time (letter to Mersenne, end November 1633, CSMK: 41; AT I: 272: '*nonumque prematur in annum*' (*Ars Poetica*, 388)).

25 On the progressive nature of the development of (some of) the relevant faculties, see *Reg.* VI, CSM I: 22–3; AT X: 383–4: '*Quia vero non faciles est cunctas recensere, et praeterea, quia non tam memoria retinendae sunt, quam acumine quodam ingenii dignoscendae, quaerendum est aliquid ad ingenia ita formanda, ut illas, quoties opus erit, statim animadvertant; ad quod profecto nihil aptius esse sum expertus, quam si assuescamus ad minima quaeque ex iis, quaedam ante percipimus, cum quadam sagacitate reflectere*'.

26 In the letter to Chanut, 15th June 1646, CSMK: 289 Descartes has given up hopes of eliminating death from the calculations, contenting himself, in classical fashion (cf. e.g. Plato, *Phaed.*, 64A–65A; Epicurus, *Letter to Menoeceus*, 124; Seneca, *Letter to Lucilius*, 54.6), to learn not to fear it.

27 Cf. the use of '*conversio*' by St Augustine, *Conf.*, III, 4, 7 and VII, 20, 26; for Plato's terminology, see Jaeger (1934); for a broad canvas of usages in antiquity, Nock (1933); for uses in the seventeenth century, Jolley (1990: 7–8).

4 The control of credulity

1 Lactantius, *De Ira Dei*, 13, 19 (picked up by Usener, *Epicurea*, 374); I am timid about conjecturing whom Epicurus (if Lactantius is to be believed) had in his sights; see also Sextus Empiricus, *PH*, III, 10–11.

2 As J.L. Mackie modestly concludes his survey chapter on the problem (Mackie 1977: 150–76), '[w]e cannot, indeed, take the problem of evil as a conclusive dis-proof of traditional theism, because, as we have seen, there is some flexibility in its doctrines [but] there is a strong presumption that theism cannot be made coherent without serious change in at least one of its central doctrines' (176).

3 Thus, the Anglican Bishop of Edinburgh blamed adultery on God with the words 'He has given us promiscuous genes', quoted in *Newsweek*, 29th May 1995: 11. Cf. Tierno (1997: 83–92).

4 *Med.* IV, AT VII: 52–3: '[. . .] *accurate animadverti* [the weasel verb of the last chap-ter again] *perpauca esse quae de rebus corporibus vere percipiantur*', and, in the French version: '[. . .] *j'ai si exactement remarqué qu'il y a fort peu que l'on connaisse avec certitude touchant les choses corporelles*' (AT IXA: 42). Such differences as there are between the '*connu*' and the '*perceptus*', and between the '*certain*' and the '*verus*' need not detain us.

5 The formula I adopt is that of Alexander Pope (1711: II, 325). There is an inter-esting variety of ways the dictum can be used to set up contrasts: to forgive (meaning others) is divine (Pope); to correct oneself is divine (Euripides, *Hippolytus*, 615); to persevere is diabolical (Augustine, *Sermons*, 164, 14) or, in more popular form, bestial (cf. Tosi 1991: 213); or, again, to persevere once is stupid, but twice damnable (Cicero, *De Inventione* 1, 39, 71); cf. Sophocles, *Antigone*, 1023–8, eloquently rendered by Lewis Campbell (1883): 'A man may err;/ But he is not insensate or foredoomed/ To ruin, who, when he hath lapsed to evil,/ Stands not inflexible, but heals the harm./ The obstinate man still earns the name of fool'.

6 E.g. Lucian, *Life of Demonax*, 7: ἀνθρώπου μὲν εἶναι ἁμαρτάνειν; Cicero, *Philippics*, 12.2.5: '*cuiusvis hominis est errare*', cf. Seneca, *Excerpta Controversiarum*, 4.3.

7 *Med.* IV, AT VII: 60–1: '[*p*]*rivatio autem, in qua sola ratio formalis falsitatis et culpae con-sistit, nullo Dei concursu indiget, quas non est res, neque ad illum relata ut causam privatio, sed*

tantummodo negatio dici debet, with the addition in the French of, '*selon la signification qu'on donne à ces termes dans l'École*' (AT IXA: 48).

8 This is the trend of CSM, Haldane and Ross (Descartes 1911: I, 8) and Anscombe and Geach (Descartes 1954: 157). It flourishes in Alquié's version, which supplies the notion that the things that have been revealed in a divine way come dressed (cloaked?) in a greater certitude: '[*ce*] *ne nous empêche pas* [. . .] *de croire revêtues d'une certitude supérieure* [. . .] *les choses qui nous ont été révélées*' (Descartes 1963–73: I, 90).

9 In this direction, Le Roy's French translation (in Descartes 1953: 45), and G. Galli's Italian (Descartes 1986: I, 24–5).

10 At AT VII: 56, it is called the '*facultas cognoscendi*' and '*intellectus*', corresponding to '*la puissance de connaître*' and '*l'entendement*' (AT IXA: 45); at *Pr.* I, 32, it is called '*perceptio*' and '*operatio intellectus*' (AT VIIIA: 17) corresponding to '*la perception de l'entendement*' (AT IXB: 39); at *Pass.* I, 17, (CSM I: 335; AT XI: 342) its contents are described as '[. . .] *toutes les sortes de perceptions ou connaissances qui se trouvent en nous*'. In speaking indifferently of the 'intellect', I am taking these correspondences to be identities.

11 At AT VII: 56, it is called the '*facultas eligendi*' (though the first edition carried the incoherent '*intelligendi*' (AT note ad loc.)), '*voluntas*' (57) or '*arbitrii libertas*' (ibid.), corresponding to '*puissance d'élire*', '*volonté*' and (in Clerselier's 1661 version, the pleonastic) '*liberté de franc arbitre*' (AT IXA: 45); in *Pr.* I, 32 we find '*volitio*' and '*operatio voluntatis*' (AT VIIIA: 17), corresponding to, again, '*volonté*' and '*l'action de la volonté*' (AT IXB: 39); at *Pass.* I, 17 (CSM I: 335; AT XI: 342) we have this faculty containing '[. . .] *toutes nos volontés*'. The same terminological indifference as in the last note applies.

12 *Med.* III, AT VII: 36–7: '[*n*]*unc autem ordo videtur exigere ut prius meas cogitationes in certa genera distribuam*'; AT IXA: 29 drops the reference to order. Although a little clumsy, the term 'cognitive state' is meant to cover everything that Descartes finds in his mind.

13 *Med.* III, CSM II: 26; AT VII: 37: '*ex his* [sc. the enquirer's *cogitationibus*] *aliæ voluntates, sive affectus, aliæ autem judicia appellantur*'; cf. AT IXA: 29. It might easily be wondered what the affections are doing on the 'will' side of this divide, in view of the passivity that is attributed to them in, e.g. the *Pass.* (cf. Cottingham 1986: 153). But, in his sixth response to the *Obj.* III (CSM II: 128), Descartes says rather tartly to Hobbes that '[*p*]*er se notum est aliud essere videre leonem et simul illum timere, quam tantum illum videre*' (AT VII: 182; cf. IX A: 142); and this might be used to explain the sense in which an affection is 'wider' (also in the modern epistemologist's sense) content than a perception; as *Med.* III says (CSM II: 26), it is '*amplius*' (AT VII: 37), which is made downright arithmetical in the French: '[. . .] *j'ajoute aussi quelque autre chose par cette action* [sc. *lorsque je veux, que je crains, que j'affirme ou que je nie* (ibid.)] *à l'idée que j'ai de cette chose là*'.

14 The term '*imago*' occurs in IV only once (at AT VII: 57) and that in a wholly different context: the enquirer's will is an image or likeness of God's (following the bit of *Genesis* alluded to above in connection with the naturalness of error (i.e. 1, 26)). In *Resp.* V, 5, Descartes only goes so far as to defend the thought that ideas are pictures by saying that they correspond to the forms of perception in the divine mind (CSM II: 127; AT VII: 181).

15 The frying pan from which it is meant as an escape is not only that the 'picture picture' is a very bad theory: mental contents had better not, especially for Descartes, have size, position, opacity or be anything other than what Anscombe

(1965) would call 'intentional'. It makes the having of an idea of God very difficult and a mess of the role of clear and distinct ideas. For context, see Ariew (1999: 58–76)

16 *Med.* IV, AT VII: 56: '[*n*]*am per solum intellectum percipio tantum ideas de quibus judicium ferre possum, nec ullus error proprie dictus in eo præcise sic spectato reperitur*', with the elaboration in the French (AT IXA: 45): '[. . .] *par l'entendement seul je n'assure ni nie aucune chose, mais je conçois seulement les idées des choses, que je puis assurer ou nier. Or en le considérant ainsi précisément, on peut dire qu'il ne trouve jamais en lui aucune erreur, pourvu qu'on prenne le mot d'erreur en sa propre signification*'.

17 *Med.* IV, AT VII: 54 '[. . .] *quamdiu de Deo tantum cogito, totusque in eum me converto, nullam erroris aut falsitatis causam deprehendo*', which the Duc de Luynes abbreviates to '[. . .] *lorsque je ne pense qu'à Dieu, je ne découvre en moi aucune cause d'erreur ou de fausseté*' (AT IXA: 43), thus specifying *where* no such cause is to be found. In Clerselier's 1661 revision, the suppressed clause is rendered '*et que je me tourne tout entier vers lui*', which might raise a puzzle about whether the narrator really is wholly occupied with God or is also incidentally concerned with himself; but the move is clear enough to be going on with.

18 *Med.* IV, AT VII: 56: '[. . .] *non tamen proprie illis* [sc. *ideis*] *privatus* [. . .] *sum dicendus, quia nempe rationem nullam possum afferre, qua probem Deum mihi majorem quam dederit cognoscendi facultatem dare debuisse*'; cf., making the same cut, AT IXA: 45: '[. . .] *on ne peut pas dire pour cela qu'il* [sc. *l'entendement*] *soit privé de ces idées* [. . .] *parce qu'en effet il n'y a aucune raison qui puisse prouver que Dieu ait dû me donner une plus grande et ample faculté de connaître, que celle qu'il m'a donnée*'.

19 *Med.* IV, AT VII: 56 (filling the gaps from the last note): '*sed negative tantum destitutus*'; AT IXA: 45: '*comme de quelque chose qui soit due à sa nature*'.

20 *Med.* IV, AT VIII: 57: '[. . .] *si facultatem recordandi vel imaginandi, vel quaslibet alias examinam, nullam plane invenio, quam non in me tenuem et circumscriptam*'; AT IXA: 45: '[. . .] *si j'examine la mémoire, ou l'imagination, ou quelqu'autre puissance, je ne trouve aucune qui ne soit en moi très petite et bornée*'.

21 *Med.* IV, AT VII: 57: '[. . .] *tantum in eo consistit, quod idem, vel facere vel non facere (hoc est affirmare vel negare, prosequi vel fugere) possimus*'; cf. AT IXA: 46.

22 *Med.* IV, AT VII: 57: '[. . .] *id quod nobis ab intellectu proponitur*' (passive voice); AT IXA: 46: '[. . .] *les choses que l'entendement propose*' (active voice).

23 *Med.* IV, AT VII: 58: '[*u*]*nde ergo nascuntur mei errores? Nempe ex hoc uno quod, cum latius pateat voluntas quam intellectus, illam non intra eosdem limites contineo, sed etiam ad illa quæ non intelligo extendo; ad quæ* [. . .] *facile a vero et bono deflectit, atque ita et fallor et pecco*'; cf., amplifying on '*latius*', AT IXA: 46: '[*d*]*'où est-ce donc que naissent mes erreurs? C'est à savoir de cela seul que, la volonté étant beaucoup plus ample et plus étendue que l'entendement, je ne la contiens pas dans les mêmes limites, mais que je l'étends aussi aux choses que je n'entends pas; auxquelles* [. . .] *elle s'égare fort aisément, et choisit le mal pour le bien, ou le faux pour le vrai. Ce qui fait que je me trompe et que je pèche*'. In the French, the will seems to be active in choosing, rather than the victim of the intellect's inadequacy.

24 *Med.* IV, AT VII: 57: '[*s*]*ola est voluntas, sive arbitrii libertas, quam in me experior, ut nullius majoris ideam apprehendam*'; cf. AT IXA: 45: '[*i*]*l n'y a que la seule volonté* [add.: '*ou la seule liberté de franc arbitre*' (Clerselier 1661) *que j'expérimente en moi être si grande, que je ne conçois point l'idée d'aucune autre plus ample et plus étendue*'.

25 *Med.* IV, AT VII: 57: '[. . .] *major absque comparatione in Deo quam in me* [*leg. voluntas est*], *tum ratione cognitionis et potentiæ quæ illi adjunctæ sunt, redduntque ipsam magis firmam et efficacem*'; cf. AT IXA: 45–6: '[*la volonté est*] *incomparablement plus grande dans Dieu,*

que dans moi [. . .] *à raision de la connaissance et de la puissance, qui s'y trouvant jointes la rendent plus ferme et plus efficace'*.

26 Although Descartes introduces the will in terms of being able to do or leave undone (CSM II: 40; AT VII: 57; AT IXA: 46), it is clear that it is a capacity for choice, and not a capacity for bringing a course of action to a successful conclusion: too often, we choose to do things we are not able to carry through.

27 Because Descartes wanted to exclude Gassendi's uncomfortable (or merely tedious) contribution from the first French edition of the *Med.* (1647), and it is excluded from AT IXA, the version I follow is Clerselier's (revised by Alquié in Descartes 1963–73: II 705–86): '*ces deux facultés* [*sont*] *d'égale étendue*' (753).

28 He employs the relatively rare verb '*allicere*', used, Lewis and Short (1879) tell us, by Cicero of the action of magnets (*Div.*, 1, 39, 86)

29 *Resp.* V, AT VII: 377: '[*m*]*ajoremque forte apud alios merebor fidem, quia id affirmo quod expertus sum, et quilibet apud se poterit experiri, quam tu, quæ idem negas ob id tantum, quod forte non experta sis*'; cf. '[. . .] *je trouverai plus de créance en l'esprit des autres en assurant ce que j'ai expérimenté et dont chacun peut aussi faire épreuve en soi-même, que non pas vous, qui niez une chose pour cela seul que vous ne l'avez peut-être jamais experimentée*' (Descartes 1963–73: II, 825).

30 *Resp.* V, AT VII: 377: '[*t*]*alia enim sunt ut ipsa quilibet apud se debeat experiri, potius quam rationibus persuaderi*'; cf. '*cela est tel que chacun le doit plutôt ressentir et expérimenter en soi-même que se le persuader par raison*' (Descartes 1963–73: II, 824).

31 See *ST*, Ia, qu.78 art. 1, where he distinguishes – in a way that brings to mind partridges in pear-trees – the three souls from the five powers of the soul and the four modes of living ('[. . .] *quinque sunt genera potentiarum animæ* [. . .]. *Tres vero dicuntur animæ. Quatuor vero dicuntur modi vivendi*'); for elaboration, see Cantin (1946). Nevertheless, at *ST*, Ia, qu. 76 art. 2, St Thomas clearly denies that the intellect is a separate substance, citing *De Anima*, III iv, 429 b 5, to the effect that it is separate only in respect of not depending on any particular organ.

32 *De An.*, II ii, especially, on the intellective soul, 413 b 27–8: ἀλλ' ἔοικε ψυχῆς γένός ἕτερον εἶναι, καί τοῦτο μόνον ἐνδεχεται χωρίζεσθαι, καθάπερ τὸ ἀΐδιον τοῦ φθαρτοῦ.

33 *ST*, Ia, qu. 83 art. 3 ad 3: '[. . .] *ista collatio quæ importatur in nomine electionis, pertinet ad consilium præcedens, quod est rationis*'; cf. Gilson (1924: 305–11).

34 The English translation (Tempier 1277c) follows Mandonnet's numbering (Tempier 1277b), in this case prop. 151. For the suggestion that Descartes may have been aware of at least some of the issues at stake in the 'Condemnation', see Osler (1994: 126).

35 Tempier (1277a: 194; 1277b: 151): '[*e*]*rror, si intelligatur mota ab alio scilicet ab appetibili vel objecto, ita quod appetibile vel objectum sit tota ratio motus ipsius voluntatis*'. Is this *ratio* an efficient cause or a final? Or is the objection that it must be the goodness of the desirable object that constitutes the reason?

36 Hyman and Walsh (Tempier 1277c) suggest that Tempier's target here is Aquinas, putting an 'A' number of the condemned proposition; that is, the '*aliorumque*' in the title of (Tempier 1277a) is coy in not naming so imposing a target. It has been noticed that the Condemnation is sometimes insensitive to the complexities of St Thomas' position: see Lottin (1942: I, 274–6). To explain the apparent insensitivity, it has been suggested that as plausible a target would be Roger Bacon; see Hackett (1997).

5 Reason, assent and eternal truth

1 *Med.* III, AT VII: 35: '[. . .] *jam videor pro regula generali posse statuere, illud omne esse verum, quod valde clare et distincte percipio*'; cf. the pluralising of subject and object at AT IXA: 27: '[. . .] *déjà je puis établir pour règle générale, que toutes les choses que nous concevons fort clairement et fort distinctement, sont toutes vraies*'.

2 I do not know of an argument to show that a rule adopted can only vindicate a criterion that employs the same terms as contained in the rule. At least, it seems plausible that a stringent rule might lead to a relatively lax criterion, for instance if a vindicator identified by the rule (in Descartes' case, God) were found to be gratuitously generous (e.g. with respect to the truths of faith) – or (*per impossibile* in the theological case) capricious. The converse would be excluded by the consideration that, if the vindicator of the rule (God) did not underwrite at least the ideas acceptable in accordance with the rule then the enquirer would leave a begged question about the acceptability of the rule.

3 *Med.* IV, AT VII: 58: '[. . .] *non potui quidem non judicare illud clare intelligebam verum esse*'; cf. AT IXA: 47: '[. . .] *je ne pouvais pas m'empêcher de juger qu'une chose que je concevais si clairement était vraie*'. This affirmation will come back to haunt us below.

4 *Med.* IV, AT VII: 62: '[. . .] *quoties voluntatem in judiciis ferendis ita contineo, ut ad ea tantum se extendat, fieri plane non potest ut errem, quia omnis clara et distincta perceptio proculdubio est aliquid, ac proinde a nihilo esse non potest, sed necessario Deum authorem habet [. . .] ideoque proculdubio est vera*'; cf. AT IXA: 49 -50, which supplements the idea's being a something (*aliquid*), with '*de réel et de positif*'.

5 E.g. *Med.* IV, AT VII: 58: '[. . .] *ratio in unam partem magis quam in alteram impellit*'; cf. the use of '*emporter*' as the verb whose subject is '*raison*' at AT IXA: 46.

6 I try to restrict use of the word '*cogito*' (i) to labelling the manœuvre that Descartes executes in various ways to establish the truth of the idea of his own existence in *Med.* II (CSM II: 17; AT VII: 25), in *Dis.* IV (CSM I: 127; AT VI: 32), at *Pr.* I, 17 (CSM I: 194; AT VIIIA: 7), in the *Search* (CSM II: 410, 412, 415, 416, 417; AT X: 515, 518, 521, 522, 523, 525) and to which he refers at *Reg.* XII (CSM I: 46; AT X: 421–2); and (ii) to labelling the exegetic *topos* aroused by the difficulty of saying just what it is that Descartes is doing in executing that manœuvre. For caustic criticism of (Gueroult's) loose usage, see Cottingham (1986: n. on 45 to text: 36).

7 I here presuppose only a minimal account of the *cogito* manœuvre, inspiration for which is owing to A.N. Prior, according to which 'there are thoughts which, if they occur at all, cannot but be true' (Prior 1965: 175), and the *cogito* is, thus, like the Law of Contradiction, backed by the self-refutation of its contrary. One exposition that seems to be in the same direction is (Stone 1993): "I am thinking therefore I am" means "My thinking this very thought is sufficient to constitute the fact that I exist". This proposition is not an argument for there is no inference; it entails that I exist without asserting that I do' (467).

It is one of the pleasures of teaching Descartes to undergraduates to hear them denying their own existences, but it does not reduce the workload of marking.

8 *Med.* IV, AT VII: 58–9: '[. . .] *ex magna luce in intellectu magna consequuta est propensio in voluntate*' (quasi-quoted also in letter to Mesland(?) of 2nd May 1644(?), CSMK: 233; AT IV: 116: '[. . .] *ex magna luce in intellectu sequitur magna propensio in voluntate*') cf. AT IXA: 47: '[. . .] *d'une grande clarté qui était en mon entendement, a suivi une grande inclination en ma volonté*'. The motor of the sequence is left quite unspecified; at *Pr.* I, 43 the Latin is purely paratactic, almost accidental: '[. . .] *quoties aliquid clare percipimus, ei sponte assentiamur*' (AT VII A: 21), though the French invokes our natures:

'[. . .] *nous sommes naturellement* [. . .] *enclins à donner notre consentement aux choses que nous apercevons manifestement*' (AT IXB: 43).

9 *Pr.* I, 45, AT VIIIA: 22: '[*c*]*laram voco illam* [sc. *ideam*] *quæ menti attendenti præsens et aperta est: sicut ea clare a nobis videri dicimus, quæ, oculo intuenti præsentia satis fortiter et aperte illum movent*'.

10 *Resp.* III, 13, AT VII: 192: '[*n*]*emo enim nescit per lucem in intellectu intelligi perspicuitatem cognitionis, quam forte non habent omnes qui putant se habere; sed hoc non impedit quominus valde diversa sit ab obstinata opinione absque evidenti perceptione concepta*'.

11 *Theaet.*, 190 A 4–6: [λ]όγον ὃν αὐτὴ πρὸς αὑτὴν ἡ ψυχὴ διεξέρχεται περὶ ὧν ἂν σκόπῃ [. . .] ὥστ' ἔγωγε τὸ δόξαζειν λέγειν καλῶ καὶ τὴν δόξαν λόγον εἰρημένον, οὐ μέντοι πρὸς ἄλλον οὐδὲ φωνῇ ἀλλὰ σιγῇ πρὸς αὑτόν. Cf. also *Phil.*, 38 E and *Soph.*, 263 E.

12 CSM II: 134–5 gives this translation without further ado or notice in all three places it occurs in the exchange between Hobbes and Descartes. Of course, the Latin does not contain any explicit functor; but the French does: '*soit que nous veuillons ou non*' (Hobbes, AT IXA: 149) and, perhaps belt-and-braces in this department: '*soit que nous voulions, ou que nous ne voulions pas*' (for both of Descartes' uses, AT IXA: 150).

13 This latter is Descartes' own explication, e.g. in *Med.* III in discussing the non-dependence of our sensations on the will; CSM II: 26; AT VII: 38: '*sive velim sive nolim, sentio calorem*'; cf. AT IXA: 30: '*soit que je le veuille, soit que je ne le veuille pas, je sens de la chaleur*'.

14 *Resp.* III, 13, AT VII: 192: '[. . .] *verbum enim*, nolentes, *in talibus non habet locum, quia implicat nos idem velle & nolle*' (emphasis original; for once, I have left the ampersand regularly produced by AT); cf. AT IXA: 150: '[. . .] *car cette façon de parler*, soit que nous ne voulions pas, *n'a point de lieu en telles occasions, parce qu'il y a de la contradiction à vouloir et ne vouloir pas une même chose*'.

15 In its canonical form – '*omnis peccans est ignorans*' – the dictum makes clear that the '*fere*' is to be taken in the strong sense (cf. the ambiguity of 'quite' in English). Kenny (1972: 23) adroitly notes that Descartes' source for it – probably at one remove – must be Aristotle (cf. *EN*, III i, 1110 b 29–30: διὰ τὴν τοιαύτην ἁμαρτίαν ἄδικόι καὶ ὅλως κακοὶ γίνονται), at a further remove it is surely Plato who, in turn, presents himself as reporting Socrates' views (cf. *EN*, VII i, 1145 b 25ff.) as expressed in various ways at *Charmides*, 165 C–75 A; *Laches*, 190–201; *Protagoras*, 354 E–7 E; *Gorgias* 468 E–70 C and 476 B–9 C.

16 The reference is to the end of *Med.* II; Descartes indicates that the wax was white before it was heated, associating its whiteness with its former sweetness and fragrance (CSM II: 20; AT VII: 30). My impression is that Descartes did not do his experiment: to get the white stuff for candles, the bees' product has to be cleaned and bleached. Some commentators have suggested yellow as the colour to which it changes (e.g. Wilson 1978: 81); again, it is my impression that it becomes near-transparent when melted; could this be what Descartes is ruefully admitting at *Pr.* II, 11 (CSM I: 227; AT VIIIA: 46)?

17 These distinctions and labels are derived from Kenny (1972: 28–30), who further distinguishes 'perversion' – as I did 'balance' – into 'simultaneous' and 'subsequent'; I take up a close relative of this distinction in a moment.

18 *Med.* IV, AT VII: 58: '[. . .] *si semper quid verum et bonum sit clare viderem, nunquam de eo quod esset judicandum vel eligendum deliberarem; atque ita, quamvis plane liber, nunquam tamen indifferens esse possem*'.

19 Letter to Mesland, 8th February 1645, CSMK: 246; AT IV: 174–5: '[*l*]*ibertas*

[. . .] *consistit in sola operandi facilitate; atque tunc liberum, et spontaneum, et voluntarium plane idem sunt'*.

20 The French version speaks less technically of '[. . .] *toutes les vérités qui ne sont rien hors de notre pensée*' (AT IXB: 45).

21 *Resp.* II ad 5, AT VII: 148: '[*i*]*am etsi fides vulgo dicatur esse de obscuris, hoc tamen intelligitur tantum de re, sive de materia circa quam versatur, non autem quod ratio formalis, propter quam rebus fidei assentiamur, sit obscura; nam contra hæc ratio formalis consistit in lumine quodam interno, quo a Deo supernaturaliter illustrati considimus ea, quæ credenda proponuntur, ap ipso esse revelata, et fieri plane nonposse ut ille mentiatur, quod omni naturæ certius est, et sæpe etiam, propter lumen gratiæ, evidentius'*.

22 C.D. Broad characterises Descartes' anthropology as picturing a 'Thomistic angel doomed for a time to haunt a penny-in-the-slot machine' (1944: 152). Despite Descartes' explicit disavowal of this view in his letter to Regius of January 1642 (CSMK: 206; AT III: 493), I take it that Broad is nearer the mark and more cutting than Ryle's attempt at 'deliberate abusiveness' with the tag 'the Ghost in the Machine' (1949: 17).

23 E.g. *Med.* IV, CSM II: 40, AT VII: 58: '[. . .] *ratio* [. . .] *impellitur*', cited above; cf. letter to Mesland, 9th February 1645, CSMK: 246; AT IV: 175: '[*a*] *rationibus impellitur*'.

24 Cf. *Med.* IV, CSM II: 41; AT VII: 58: '[. . .] *non potui quidem non judicare illud quod tam* [sc. as that I exist] *intelligebam verum esse*', which D.M. Rosenthal takes as a sample of Descartes' lack of close consideration in this department (1986: 407); but note also *Pr.* I, 43 (again) and *Resp.* II, Appendix, Axiom VII, CSM II: 117; AT VII: 166: '[*r*]*ei cogitantis voluntas fertur* [. . .] *infallibiliter, in bonum sibi clare cognitum*'.

25 *Resp.* VI, 6, CSM II: 291; AT VII: 431: [*q*]*uantum ad abitrii libertatem, longe alia ejus ratio est in Deo quam in nobis*'; CSM II: 292; AT VII: 433: '[. . .] *longe alia indifferentia humanæ libertati convenit quam divina*'.

26 For wider settings and employments of this doctrine, see Gilson (1913a: 128–56); Bréhier (1937); H.G. Frankfurt (1977); A. Funkenstein (1980); J.-L. Marion, (1981b: 264–312); E.M. Curley (1984); H. Ishiguro (1986; also in Doney (ed. 1987), along with a useful range of other articles on the topic published between 1960 and 1984); S. Gaukroger (1987: 60–71); G. Hatfield (1993); M.J. Osler (1994: 123–35); S. Menn (1998: 337–52); Devillairs (1998).

27 My own guess is that he regarded it as a rather refined doctrine that could be too easily misunderstood to be bandied about: a sort of 'unwritten doctrine' of the sort that some scholars find Plato's Theory of Principles to have been; cf. Findlay (1974); Reale (1984).

28 Moreover, there is an apparent reference to Gibieuf in the letter's second line that reprises pretty exactly the phrasing in the letter to Mersenne of 27th May 1630 (AT I: 153).

29 I.e. there is a quotation from *Med.* IV (CSM II: 40; AT VII: 58) in the text that appears, under slightly varying guises at AT III: 379 (French letter to Mersenne(?), 27th May 1641(?)): '*j'ai dit que le plus bas degré de la liberté consistait à se mouvoir aux choses auxquelles nous sommes tout à fait indifférents*', at AT III: 704 (Latin minute for letter to Mersenne(?), 27th May 1641(?)): '*dixi* infimum libertatis gradum in hoc consistere, quod possimus nosmet determinare ad res eas, ad quas sumus prorsus indifferentes' (emphasis original corresponding to a quotation from memory of what he had said/written), and at AT IV: 173 (Latin continuation of French letter to Mesland, 9th February 1645): '*scripsi infimum esse gradum libertatis, quo nos ad eas, ad quæ sumus indifferentes determinemus*'.

30 *Pr.* I, 43, which is particularly felicitous in the French, AT IXB: 43: '*nous sommes naturellement si inclins à donner notre consentement aux choses que nous appercevons manifestement, que nous n'en saurions douter pendant que nous les appercevons de la sorte*', where the *sorte* is that of keeping a steady attention on the manifestness. In this direction, Kenny (1973: 109).

31 Ibid.: '[. . .] *modo tantum cogitemus bonum libertatem arbitrii nostri per hoc testari*'.

32 A sturdy principle in *Med.* III, CSM II: 33; AT VII: 48: see also letters to Mersenne, 21st April 1641, CSMK: 180–1; AT III: 362 and for Arnauld June 1648 CSMK: 355; AT V: 193.

33 St Augustine in, especially, *De Natura et Gratia* and *De Gratia Christi et de Peccato Originali*, and St Jerome in *Dialogus adversus Pelagianos* are both elaborate in citing and commenting material for which we have no other source, notably the *Libellus Fidei*, the *Pro Libero Arbitrio* and the *Liber Testimoniorum*. Note also that Pelagius' *Commentarii in Epistolas S. Pauli*, was attributed to St Jerome until 1901 (see *PL*, XXX: 645–902). Of course, without opponents like these, Pelagius' writings would not have come in for such powerful censure, and thus have had to depend on the indirect tradition of his critics.

34 On Gibieuf's use of Pelagianism as an accusation against Molina, see Gilson, (1913a: 357–9); Arnauld sees a '*conformité*' between Semi-Pelagianism and Molinism in Bk IV of the *Apologie pour les Saints Pères de l'Eglise* (1651), in Arnauld (1775–83: XVIII 311); for a curious attribution of Molinism to Descartes, see A. Del Noce (1964: 434–49). Also, on attempts to purge Suarez of Pelagianism, Verbeek (1992: 44–5).

35 See also the parenthetic addition to the 'Synopsis' (CSM II: 11) in response to Arnauld's urgings that Descartes avoid raising sticking-points for the theologians (*Obj.* VI, CSM II: 151–2; AT VII: 215–16). All the same, even the pro-Cartesian Arnauld was later inclined, after reading the first volume of Descartes' correspondence, to think that Descartes was in odour of Pelagianism, see letter to unknown recipient of 18th October 1669, where he says '[. . .] *ses lettres sont pleines de Pélagienisme*' (Arnauld 1775–83: I, 671).

36 For instance, the general response in Italy in September 2000 to Cardinal Ratzinger's letter *Jesus Dominus*, which asserts the exclusiveness of the Roman Catholic Church, was shame or disdain for its arrogance.

37 Cf. the distinction of the adverb and adjective in discussing a case of apple-eating in *Fifth Replies* (over *Med.* IV, ad 3), CSM II: 259; AT VII: 377: '[*c*]*um autem prave judicamus, non ideo prave volumus, sed forte pravum quid*'.

6 The modes of scepticism

1 *PH*, I, 29: ἐπισχοῦσι δὲ αὐτοῖς οἷον τυχικῶς ἡ ἀταραξία παρκολούθησεν ὡς σκιὰ σώματι; also Diogenes, *Lives*, IX, 107, where the simile is attributed to Timon and Ænesidemus.

2 R. Tosi notes that the use of σκιά as a figure for aleatoriness appears in both tragic and comic writing of ancient Greece (Tosi 1991: 243).

3 Sextus seems to be trading on the sort of doxastic passivity attributed in the last two chapters to Hobbes and, at one remove, to Williams and Hampshire and, at two, to Locke, Hume, Mill and Russell.

4 I am grateful to Steve Makin for drawing my attention to uses of the 'nothing more' principle, not only in sceptical, but also in dogmatic (specifically Atomist and Aristotelian) thought.

5 This suggestion was elaborated by Doug Hutchinson in a paper to the Cambridge University 'B' Club in December 1986, 'How do the Sceptics Weigh the Balance of Reasons?', in which I recall he cited (along with the appropriate Pyrrhonist sources) *A Midsummer Night's Dream*: 'Weigh oath with oath and you will nothing weigh:/ Your vows to her and me, put in two scales,/ Will even weigh, and both as light as tales' (III, ii, 131–3).

6 As V.G. Morgan notes (1994: 39 n. 3), Descartes nowhere uses the phrase '*morale provisoire*', which is common in the secondary literature. The phrase '*par provision*' (*Dis*. III, CSM I: 122; AT VI: 22) is glossed by Alquié (Descartes 1963–73: I, 592) as '*en attendant*'. Hence my 'interim', rather than the more common 'provisional' (CSM, Anscombe and Geach, Descartes 1954: 24; Sutcliffe, Descartes 1968: 45; Cress, Descartes 1980: 12) or 'provisory' (Veitch, Descartes 1912: 19); HR offers 'for the time being' (Descartes 1911: I, 95), which seems about right.

7 *Dis*. III, CSM I: 122; AT VI: 23: '[*suivant les opinions*] *qui fussent comunément reçues en pratique par les plus sensés* [. . .] *je devais plutôt prendre garde à ce qu'ils pratiquaient qu'à ce qu'ils disaient*'.

8 *Dis*. III, CSM I: 122; AT VI: 23: '[. . .] *ce sont toujours les plus commodes pour la pratique*'.

9 *Dis*. III, CSM I: 123; AT VI: 24: '[. . .] *j'[ai] pensé commettre une grande faute contre le bon sens, si, parce que j'approuvais alors quelque chose, je me fusse obligé de la prendre pour bonne encore près, lorsqu'elle aurait peut-être cessée de l'être, ou que j'aurais cessé de l'estimer telle*'.

10 *Dis*. III, CSM I: 123; AT VI: 25: '[. . .] *nous devons néamoins nous déterminer à quelques unes* [sc. *opinions*], *et les considérer après, non plus comme douteuses, en tant qu'elles se rapportent à la pratique, mais comme très vraies et certaines*'.

11 Baillet specifies some time after Descartes' return to Paris on St Martin's day (11th November) of 1628 (1691: I, 161), and, on this evidence, Gaukroger proposes a date in December of that year (1995: 183). Gouhier notes a range of other speculations (1924: 58 and 315–16). In Rodis-Lewis (1992a: 34–5), deploying evidence of Descartes' relations with Beeckman, and in Rodis-Lewis (1995: 100–1), deploying evidence of the military history involved in Descartes' travels, G. Rodis-Lewis argues in favour of a date in November 1627, thus giving doubly powerful support to the rather tentative suggestion made by F. Alquié (1950: 64).

12 E.g., Gibson (1932: 42), Popkin (1960: 174), Williams (1978: 16), Gaukroger (1995: 183, CSMK: 32n.), Rodis-Lewis (1995: 102). Garin (1967: 79) dates the execution to 14th June 1631, though Moréri's *Grand dictionnaire historique* (reviewed, corrected and augmented by M. Drouet (1759), '*nouvelle édition*': the 1st and 2nd editions (1731 and 1746) lack any article on De Chandoux) gives that as the date on which the court of justice that condemned him was given its letters patent (Moréri III: 465, col. 2).

Gouhier (1924: 59) is among those who give his initial as 'N', following presumably Moréri, who offers no forename. My suspicion of 'Nicholas' supplies from memory from I recall not where; but I suspect that, in giving 'M.' as if it were an initial, Garber may be confusing title and name (1992a: 15); the title would be '*sieur*', which I can choose not to be '*mon*'.

13 AT (I: 217) suggest that Baillet's account here (1691: I, 162–3) is a dramatised amplification of few lines in Borel (1656), that they there cite: '*Ille* [sc. Descartes] *tunc, laudato oratoris sermone, cætum non laudavit, quod verisimili tantum contenti fuissent, et promisit se quamlibet veritatem duodecim argumentis verisimilibus falsam probaturum, et e contra*'; I may have overrendered the (too?) terse '*et e contra*'. What Baillet gives is

that Descartes undertook, '*démontrer en douze arguments les faussetés d'une proposition dont la verité était unanimement admise; et il recommença son exercice avec une proposition que tout le monde croyait fausse et dont il fit éclater la verité*'.

14 For a couple of relatively concentrated bursts, see *Fourth Replies*, CSM II: 172–7; AT VII: 248–55 (on the Eucharist); *Sixth Replies*, CSM II: 289–91; AT VII: 428–31 (on God as capable as deception).

15 *Topics*, I i, 100 a 18–20:'Η μὲν πρόθεσις τῆς πραγματείας μέθοδον εὑρεῖν, ἀφ' ἧ δυνησόμεθα συλλογίσθα περὶ παντὸς τοῦ προτεθέντος προβλήματος; a structurally similar move – though obviously in a different context – is made at *Rhetoric*, I ii, 1355 b:῎Εστω δὴ ῥητορικὴ δύναμις περὶ ἕκαστον τοῦ θεωρῆσαι τὸ ἐνδεχόμενον πιθανον.

16 *Reg.* III, AT X: 366: '[*l*]*egendi sunt Antiquorum libri, quoniam ingens beneficium est tot hominum laboribus nos uti posse*'; cf. also *Dis.* I, CSM I: 111 and 113; AT VI: 1–2 and 5. On the necessity of learning in matters of particular revelation, see *Con.*, CSMK: 350; also *Notes*, CSM I: 300 and 310; AT VIIIB and 353 and 368.

17 *Reg.* XIV, CSM I: 58; AT X: 442: '[*o*]*ptaremus hoc in loco lectorem nancisi ad Arithmeticæ et Geometriæ studia propensum, etiamsi in iisdem nondum versatum esse malim, quam vulgari more eruditum*'; also letter to Plempius, 3rd October 1637, CSMK: 61; AT I: 411: '[he wants] *lectores non modo peritos eorum quæ hactenus in Geometria et Algebra cognita fuere, sed etiam valde laboriosos, ingeniosos et attentos*'.

18 *Dis.* VI, AT VI: 77: '[. . .] *si j'écris en français, qui est la langue de mon pays, plutôt qu'en latin, qui est la langue de mes précepteurs, c'est à cause que j'éspère que ceux qui ne se servent que de leur raison naturelle toute pure jugeront mieux mes opinions que ceux qui ne croient qu'aux livres anciens*'. See also the paragraph on related issues and written in French dropped in the midst of the (Latin) letter to Regius, January 1642, CSMK: 206–7; AT III: 499. Elsewhere, however, he seems to allow that there is something that fits the bill of attending to '*quid singula verba Latine significent*' (*Reg.* III, CSM I: 14; AT X: 369).

19 *Reg.* XII, CSM I: 48; AT X: 426: '[. . .] *sæpe litterati tam ingeniosi esse solent, ut invenerit modum cæcutiendi etiam in illis quæper se evidentia sunt atque a rusticis numquam ignoratur*'. A case here might be that of the peasants who knew the circulation of the blood without Harvey in Pears (1997: 88–9).

20 *Reg.* III, AT X: 367: '[. . .] *si omnia Platonis et Aristotelis argumenta legerimus, de propositis autem rebus stabile judicium ferre nequeamus: it enim non scientias videremur didicisse, sed historias*'; also letter to Beeckman, 17th October 1630, CSMK: 26–7; AT I: 158: [*c*]*ogita imprimis qualia sint, quæ aliquis alium potest docere: nempe linguæ historiæ, experimenta, item demonstrationes certæ et manifestæ, quæque intellectum convincunt, quales sunt Geometrarum, possunt doceri. Placita autem opiniones, quales sunt Philosophorum, non docentur protinus, ex eo quod dicantur. Unum dicit Plato, aliud Aristoteles, aliud Epicurus, Telesius, Campanella, Brunus, Basso, Vaninus, novatores omnes, quisque aliud dicunt*'; cf. Montaigne (1580: 136): '[*n*]*ous savons dire "Ciceron dit ainsi; voilà les mœurs de Platon; ce sont les mots mêmes d'Aristote". Mais nous, que disons nous nous mêmes? que jugeons nous? que faisons nous? Autant en dirait bien un perroquet*'.

21 LP, AT IXB: 3: '[. . .] *il vaut beaucoup mieux se servir de ses propres yeux pour se conduire [. . .] que de les tenir fermés et suivre la conduite d'un autre*'; cf. also, *Reg.* III, CSM I: 13; AT X: 367.

22 *Dis.* I, AT VI: 5: '[. . .] *il n'y avait aucune doctrine dans le monde qui fût telle qu'on m'avait fait espérer*'; cf. Eudoxus in *Re.*, CSM II: 411; AT X: 516: '[. . .] *omne id quod me* [leg. *preceptores mei*] *docuerint adeo dubium fuit, majores, quam si magis rationi consentaneum fuisset; eo enim in casu pauxilla illa ratione, quam in eo deprehendissem, contentus fuissem forte,*

atque hoc remissionem me in inquirenda accuratius veritate reddidisset'.

23 Letter to Dinet, AT VII: 580: '[. . .] *nihilque ex iis* [sc. the ensemble of Aristotelian principles] *quod non sit controversum, et ex more scholarum a singulis Philosophis mutari possit'*.

24 Paradoxically, by refusing and recommending that others should refuse to read earlier authors as authorities, Descartes opens up the possibility of reading them historically, without, that is, commitment to thinking that what we find in books is true because written (Verbeek 1993: 180). And this is what I am aiming at here.

25 Even so, he seems to think that some sorts of revealed knowledge is of negligible importance, as when he refuses to pursue his study of the Hebrew Bible (cf. AT IV: 700–1); and, in *Dis.* I, he implies that abstruse knowledge of dogmatic formula is redundant, given '*que le chemin* [sc. to Heaven] *n'est moins ouvert aux plus ignorants qu'aux doctes, et que les vérités révélées qui y conduisent sont audessus de notre intelligence*' (CSM I: 114; AT VI: 8). Presumably, the path here is also that of *Luke* 13: 24, leading to a gate that is as strait for the learned as for the ignorant.

26 E.g. Harvey on the vascular system in *Human Body*, CSM I: 316–19 (abridged); AT X: 239–45; it is noticeable that, in *Dis.* V, Mersenne added the reference to the oblique acknowledgement (CSM I: 136; AT VI: 50): what makes it noticeable is that it is the only bit of apparatus in the whole book. Likewise, Descartes is too impatient to read up the views of Gomez Pereira on animals as machines (letter to Mersenne, 23rd June 1641, CSMK: 184 (passages omitted); AT III: 386). Also, Copernicus and Tycho on the heavens, *Pr.* III, 17–19, CSM I: 250–1; AT VIIIA: 85–6; though he treats these two with caution; compare that with his leery use of Gilbert on magnets in *Reg.* XIII (CSM I: 52; AT X: 431).

27 Such an explanation also fits the references in *Dis.* V to getting someone *else* to dissect the heart of a large animal; CSM I: 134–5; AT VI p 47: '[. . .] *faire couper devant eux* [. . .] *se fissent montrer* [. . .] *qu'on leur montrât'*; for an account of the broader sociological significance of this, see Shapin (1994) on, especially, the relative roles of Boyle and Hooke.

28 Cf. Montaigne (1580: 1045: '[i]*l y a plus affaire à interpreter les interpretations qu'à interpreter les choses, et plus livres sur les livres que sur autre sujet: nous ne faisons que nous entregloser*'). Why can't I learn from this? Why couldn't Montaigne?

29 Preamble to *Re.*, AT X: 497–8: '[. . .] *quand bien même toute la science qui se peut désirer, serait comprise dans les livres, si ce que ce qu'ils ont du bon est mêlé parmi tant de choses inutiles, et semé confusement dans un tas de si gros volumes, qu'il faudrait plus de temps pour les lire, que nous n'en avons pour demeurer en cette vie, et plus d'esprit pour choisir les choses utiles, que pour les inventer de soi même'*.

30 Cf. Eudoxus in *Re.*, CSM II: 405; AT X: 506: '[. . .] *un bon esprit, quand bien même il aurait été nourri dans un desert, et n'aurait jamais eu de la lumière que celle de la nature, ne pourrait avoir d'autres sentiments que les nôtres, s'il avait bien pesé toutes les mêmes raisons'*. This seems to encapsulate the standard of what success in argumentation has become.

31 For incorporation of these retreats into the *Ratio Studiorum* (undertaken, somewhat reluctantly in 1558, substantially composed in 1586, finally revised in 1599 and first printed in France in 1603, the year of foundation of La Flèche) see De Rochemonteix (1889: I, 50ff. and 83–4, III, 11ff. and IV, 21ff.). The plan of the retreats was based on the *Spiritual Exercises* of St Ignatius Loyola. Although Descartes may never have seen, and pretty certainly never studied, this book, I have thought it prudent to consult a fairly primitive version of it: the Spanish text of the '*Autografo*' of 1534 (or so) and the so-called '*Vulgate*', translated into Latin

(presumably mostly) by A. de Freux (1548) are printed as parallel texts in *Esercizi Spirituali*, edited P. Bondioli (Loyola 1534a). Although the Latin was certainly gone over by Aquaviva (1591) and by a 'definitive' commission of twelve Jesuits (1599), these texts seem adequate for the purpose of getting a grip on what was laid down in Descartes' day.

32 The full treatment of the *Spiritual Exercises* ought to last around thirty days; but, following each of the thirty-seven saints' days observed in Jesuit colleges, a day was set aside for recalling one's religious duties (De Rochemonteix 1889: II, 40–3; 142ff. and 215–18: '*souvenir*'). Annually, a retreat of eight days was arranged, generally in Holy Week (De Rochemonteix 1889: I, 130–1 and 140–1), in which an abridged timetable of spiritual exercises could be carried through. For the specification of, approximations to and relaxations about, thirty days, see, Loyola (1534a, *passim*, but specifically Part I, 'Annotations', para. 4 (p. 8): '*poco más o menos*'; '*circiter*'). For the eight-day abbreviation, see the appendix to Loyola (1534b: 361–3).

33 *Dis.* II, CSM I: 116; AT VI: 11: '[. . .] *je demeurais tout le jour enfermé seul dans un poêle, où j'avais tout loisir de m'entretenir de mes pensées*'; cf. *Med.* III, CSM II: 24; AT VII: 34: '[. . .] *meque solum alloquendo*'; IX A: 27: '[. . .] *m'entretenant seulement moi-même*'. While the date of 10th November 1619 was doubtless, in one way or another, a turning point for Descartes, my suspicion is that the use of the imperfect here ('*demeurais*' and '*avais*') could well mean that seclusion was the general way Descartes spent his time at Neuburg. Hence the suggestion of plural days.

34 Baillet 1691: I, 49: '*genre de vie*'; cf. Loyola 1534a (2nd Week, 'Election', para. 86): 160 and (para. 105): 172: '[. . .] *reformar la propria vida y estado*' = '[. . .] *reformatio* [. . .] *circa vitæ statum*'; also (ostensibly referring to a period before November 1619) *Dis.* I, CSM I: 116; AT VI: 10: '[. . .] *résolution d'étudier en moi-même et d'employer toutes les forces de mon esprit à choisir les chemins que je devais suivre*'.

35 *Dis.* II, CSM I: 122; AT VI: 22; also letter to Newcastle, October 1645, CSMK: 275; AT IV: 329–30; and *Conv.*, CSMK: 354; AT V: 179. Rodis-Lewis (1992b: 440) suggests that in these latter places Descartes may be (mis)remembering a (mis)quotation in Montaigne (1580: 1056) or silently correcting the thought that, by the age of 20, a man knows what's good for him. While AT (followed by CSMK: 276) trace the thought to Suetonius' account of Tiberius (*Life*, 69), all that is reported there is that the emperor had no doctor after the age of 30, which is contradicted two sections later by the naming of Charicles as Tiberius' doctor in later life. At least as likely a source for Descartes' citation (though he half-attributes it to Cato in the *Con.*, AT V: 179) is Tacitus, *Annals*, VI, 46, 5: '[. . .] *solitusque eludere medicorum artes atque eos, qui post tricesimum ætatis annum ad internoscenda corpori suo utilia vel noxia alieni consilii indigerent*', where the irony is that, at this stage, the ageing emperor is suffering ill health because of his excesses ('*libidinibus*').

36 If Eike Pies (1996) is to be believed, even staying within the confines of the French Embassy did not secure Descartes against fatal interference. I am grateful to Alberto Castoldi for bringing this booklet to my attention.

37 Compare *Dis.* III, CSM I: 125; AT VI: 31: '[. . .] *m'éloigner de tous les lieux où je pouvais avoir des connaissances*' with Loyola 1534a: 28: '[. . .] *se apartar de todos amigos y conoscidos, y de toda solicitud terrena*' = '[. . .] *a[b] amicis notisque omnibus et ab omnium rerum humanarum sollicitudine sese abduxerit*' (Bondioli prints '*ad*', a mere typographical error).

38 Loyola 1534a: 28: '[. . .] *estando ansí apartado no teniendo el entendimiento partido en muchas cosas, más poniendo todo el cuydado en sola una*' = '[. . .] *per huiusmodi secessum,*

intellectu minus quam antea distracto in diversas partes, sed collecta redactaque omni cogitatione ad rem unam'.

39 St Ignatius, too, sees that there is some difficulty in recognising that one has fallen into sin; but he takes a direct line, saying that one must *'pedir a Dios* [. . .] *gracia para acordarse cuantas vezes ha caydo in quel pecado particular o defecto'* (Loyola 1534a: 36).

40 Cf. Loyola 1534a: 38. It has been conjectured that the abbreviation used ('g') in the elaborate rigmarole of drawing up a chart of the days of the week and noting how frequently one runs into the sin one wishes to extirpate, is the initial of the sin of gluttony (Spanish *'gula'*), see Loyola 1534c: note ad loc. (p. 204).

41 A similar trope occurs in St Ignatius, who recommends that the retreatant have before his eyes, in the form of a flag or banner, a painted representation of Lucifer: Loyola 1534a: 134; other words used for the devil are (Spanish) *'demonio'*, *'adversario'*, *'espíritu malo'*, corresponding to (Latin) *'dæmon'*, *'hostis'*, *'adversarius'* and *'spiritus malus'*. Whereas Descartes' demon incarnates only the vice of scepticism – despair about our ability to acquire any belief that is immune to doubt – the Jesuit demon stands in for all declinations from a Christ-like life.

42 Cf. the third maxim of *Dis.* III (which refers to the conduct of ordinary life, but is all the more applicable to the state of seclusion): '[. . .] *tâcher toujours plutôt de vaincre moi-même que la fortune'* (CSM I: 123; AT VI: 25). Gilson (Descartes 1925: 246) properly suggests two passages (from Epictetus and Seneca) as sources which, as the maxim is spelt out, are fully integrated into what I have suggested above is a Stoic context. St Ignatius too says that what he has in hand are *'[e]xercicios espirituales para vencer a sí mismo y ordenar su vida, sin determinarse por affección alguna que desordenada sea'* = *'[e]xercitia quædam spiritualia, per quæ homo dirigitur, ut vincere seipsum possit, et vitæ suæ rationem determinatione a noxiis affectibus liber instituere'* (Loyola 1534a: 32). St Ignatius is presumably himself borrowing from the Stoics.

43 I.e. Hume 1739–40: 269: '[. . .] since reason is incapable of dispelling these clouds [sc. of his various sceptical conclusions], nature herself suffices to that purpose, and cures me of this philosophical melancholy and delirium, either by relaxing this bent of mind, or by some avocation, and lively impression of my senses, which obliterate all these chimeras. I dine, I play a game of back-gammon, I converse, and am merry with my friends; and when after three or four hour's [*sic*] amusement, I wou'd return to these speculations, they appear so cold, and strain'd, and ridiculous, that I cannot find in my heart to enter them any farther.'

44 St Ignatius offers the following intriguing sub-division of sources of mental contents in the 'General Examination': *'[p]resupongo ser tres pensamientos en mí, es a saber, uno proprio mío, el qual sale de my mera libertad y querer, y otros dos vienen de fuera, el uno que viene del buen espíritu y el otro del malo'* = *'[p]ro comperto ponitur triplex incidere homini cognitionum genus: unum ex proprio surgens moto ipsius hominis; reliqua vero duo extrinsecus advenientia, ex boni scilicet vel mali spiritus suggestione'* (Loyola 1534a: 42). In his adaptation of this scheme, Descartes' adventitious and invented ideas would all be diabolical.

7 The form of scepticism

1 Two areas where this machinery has been having a vogue are AI modellings of non-monotonic reasoning and construals of the notion of defeasible presumption in the law. The variety of ways that the terminology has been deployed allows me to feel free to make up my own version; and I thank Donald Peterson for comments on the strategy of the chapter.

312   *Notes*

2 AT VII: 19–20. The French at AT IXA: 14–16 divides the paragraphs slightly differently, starting afresh with '*Et par la même raison . . .*' (p. 15 = AT VII: 20 l. 8) and running straight on from '. . . *sont formées*' to '*De ce genre . . .*' (ibid. = AT VII: 20 ll. 14–15).

3 I set aside Norman Malcolm's much-discussed claim that what we have when sound asleep is not, properly speaking, an experience of any sort and, hence, that, if a dream is an experience, it is so only when we are awake. See his 'Dreaming and Skepticism' (1956: esp. 73–5). I set it aside because, though interesting in its own way, Malcolm's claim is set to refute, rather than understand, Descartes.

4 Several years ago, I had a dream in which I seemed to be considering whether I was thinking and, recalling that to deny it would be self-defeating, I seemed to conclude that I was. Still in the dream, I seemed to manage to persuade myself that, if that were so, then, though I might be dreaming, the *cogito* was still in great shape.

5 Compare *Med*. III, CSM II: 26; AT VII: 37–8: '[. . .] *aliæ* [sc. *ideæ*] *a me ipso factæ mihi videntur* [. . .] *Syrenes, Hyppogryphes, et similia, a me ipso finguntur*' with *Med*. I, CSM II: 13; AT VII: 20, referring to '*Sirenas et Satiricos*'.

6 *Med*. I, CSM II: 14; AT VII: 20: '[. . .] *item* [sc. as a member of the class of defeated notions] *figura rerum extensarum; item quantitas, sive earumdem magnitudo et numerus; item locus in quo existunt, tempusque per quod durent, et similia*'; the French specifies time as '*qui mesure leur durée*' (AT IXA: 15), and follows the broad sweep of the '*et similia*': '*et autres semblables*' (ibid.), where the governing noun must be '*choses*' (three lines earlier) in the sense of 'notions' or '(categories of) things', rather than '*choses*' (two lines earlier) in the sense of 'bodies'.

7 *Med*. VI, CSM II: 62; AT VII: 90: '[. . .] *necessitas rerum agendarum*'. It might be noted that this alleged necessity sits ill with the Stoic indifference to bodily suffering that the *Pass*. enjoins.

8 Descartes' exposition of this condition is complicated by the fact that he is, at first, considering, rather, the object or source of the idea – a person who pops up and then disappears as happens in dreams (AT VII: 89: '[. . .] *mihi derepente appareret, statimque postea dispareret, ut fit in somnis*') – and proceeds more vaguely by talking about 'things' – (AT VII: 90: '*res*') including, presumably, ideas.

9 *Med*. VI, AT VII: 89: '[. . .] *summa illa* [sc. *dubitatio*] *de somno, quem a vigilia non distinguebam*'; cf. also *Med*. V, CSM II: 49; AT VII: 70–1.

10 As Richard Tuck says in introducing his edition of the text, Hobbes offers 'rather low-level criteria' (p. xv). Yet, there may be something more challenging that could be developed from Hobbes' remarking that '[. . .] waking I often observe the absurdity of dreams, but never dream the absurdities of my waking'; at least that raises the question of how well joined up my waking experiences actually are.

11 Also letter to Voetius, May 1634, CSMK: 222 and to the Curators of Leiden, 4th May 1647, CSMK: 316.

12 *Med*. I, CSM II: 15; AT VII: 22: '[*s*]*upponam* [. . .] *genium aliquem malignum, eundemque summe potentem et callidum, omnem suam industriam in eo posuisse, ut me falleret*'; reprised at CSM II: 15; AT VII: 23 as '*deceptor, quantumvis potens, quantumvis callidus*'; cf. *Med*. II, CSM II: 17; AT VII: 26: '[. . .] *suppono deceptorem aliquem potentissimum, et, si fas est dicere, malignum, data opera in omnibus, quantum potuit, me deluisse*'.

13 See Curley 1978: 116–18, and Beyssade 1992: esp. 33. John Cottingham seems rather to misspeak himself in using the word 'criterion' for the general '*regula*' at AT VII: 35 (1993: 32); if this were an appropriate rendering, the so-called

problem of the so-called Circle would be real and insuperable.

14 In his translation of *PH*, II, 20, Bury (Sextus 1933) renders δὲ εἰς τὸν διάλληλον ἐμπίπτοντος τρόπον λόγου ἄπορος as 'when the argument thus reduces itself to a form of circular reasoning'. It is true that *petitio principii* is one sort of circular reasoning; but this formulation would be more appropriate for, e.g. the fifth mode of Agrippa (cf. *PH*, I, 169). What is in play here is something more etymologically aporetic: the defender of the criterion is left without resources, rather as Socrates' interlocutors are reduced to either repetition or speechlessness at the end of dialogues like the *Euth.*

15 *Reg.* VII, AT X: 388: '[*q*]*uamobrem illas continuo quodam cogitationis motu singula intuentis simul et ad alia transeuntis aliquoties percurram, ut* [. . .] *rem totam videar intueri*'. Although both manuscripts give '*imaginationis*' in place of '*cogitationis*', I follow AT's note ad loc. that '*imaginationis*' sits ill with the earlier uses of '*cogitatio*' in the same rule. For more on complexity and simplicity, see the next chapter.

16 Like many other recent commentators (including Nozick 1981: 168ff.), Putnam directs his argument against the hypothesis that we may (seem to) be brains in vats being manipulated by a Mad Scientist. This has now become a standard, perhaps even unreflective, assimilation (see, e.g. Owens 2000: 61–4). I am not concerned to consider whether it is a faithful continuation of the sort of scepticism Descartes vexes himself with; but I suspect it is not, not least because a brain is already 'external'.

17 Setting aside the English translators who follow the French (HR, Descartes 1911: I, 159; Veitch, Descartes 1912: 97; Sutcliffe, Descartes 1968: 115), I find myself in agreement with the main renderings. CSM gives 'I must examine whether there is a God, and if there is one whether he can be a deceiver' (II: 25); Anscombe and Geach stress with an upper case that it is God who is the subject of what might be a deceiver: 'I must examine whether there is a God, and, if so, whether He can be a deceiver' (1954: 78); and Cress quite properly offers 'I ought at the first opportunity to enquire if there is a God, and, if there is, whether or not he can be a deceiver' (1980: 68), but unfortunately reads '*hac re ignorata*' as if it were '*his rebus ignoratis*': 'if I am ignorant of these matters'.

18 Janowski (2000: 144–6) offers a list of seventeen points of convergence between Descartes and St Augustine, indicating that these will be fully documented in his forthcoming *Index Augustino-Cartésien* (Paris: Vrin).

19 E.g. letters to Mersenne, 25th May 1637, AT I: 376; to Colvius, 14th November 1640, CSMK: 159; AT III: 247; and perhaps to Mesland, 2nd May 1644, CSMK: 232; AT IV: 113; likewise at the beginning of the *Resp.* IV, CSM II: 154; AT VII: 219.

8 *Tota methodus*

1 '*Et parum abest ut dicam (regulas Cartesii) similes præcepto Chemici nescio cujus: "sume quod debes, et operare ut debes, et habebis quod optas"*' (Leibniz 1870–95: IV, 329); cited by Laporte (1945: 28 n. 4) and Beck (1952: 286) and with qualified approval by Williams (1978: 32) and Cottingham (1993: 123); also Keeling (1934: 63), Micheli (1990: 213–14) and Lojacono (1996: 46). Other places where Leibniz makes similar remarks can be found in Leibniz (1956: 88, 152, 433, and 655).

2 The definition he gives in *Reg.* IV is as follows: '[*p*]*er methodum autem intelligo regulas certas et faciles, quas quicumque exacte servaverit* [i.e. they are not foolproof: again the moral of '*ut recte utor*'] *nihil unquam falso pro vero supponet, et nullo mentis*

conatu inutiliter consumpto, sed gradatim semper augendo scientiam, perveniet ad veram cog-nitionem eorum omnium quorum erit capax' (AT X: 371–2).

3 *Reg.* VII, AT X: 389; CSM I: 26 gives the by now perfectly natural 'method'. see also *Resp.* II, CSM II: 111 ('analytic method'); AT VII: 156 (*'via analytica'*) IXA: 122 (*'voie analytique'*).

4 The title of the manuscript in Leibniz' possession (AT's 'H') bore a title from which the word is missing: *'Regulæ ad inquirenda veritate'*; in the inventory of Descartes' papers made soon after his death, the *Reg.* is described as *'partie d'un traité des règles utiles et claires pour la direction de l'Esprit en la recherche de la Verité'* (AT X: 9); cf. also Gouhier's *'Notice'* to Descartes (1939: xi).

5 Nevertheless, Descartes indicates in a letter to Vatier of 22nd February 1638 (CSMK: 85; AT I: 559) that the order of exposition in the publications of 1637 (referring, I suspect more to the *Essays* than to the *Dis.*) differs from the order of discovery in accordance with the method. Note also *Reg.* VII, CSM I: 27; AT X: 392, which explicitly denies that there is any obligatory order to be followed in expounding the rules.

6 *Dis.* I, AT VI: 2: '[. . .] *la puissance de bien juger, et distinguer le vrai d'avec le faux, qui est proprement ce qu'on nomme le bon sens ou la raison, est naturellement égale en tous les hommes'*. This claim does not strictly follow from the initial observations of the *Dis.* (that everyone is satisfied with the amount of good sense that she has and that, in this respect, good sense is the best distributed thing in the world (loc. cit.)), which seem to derive from Montaigne (1580: 640: '[. . .] *mais l'avantage de jugement, nous ne le cedons à personne'*). See also *Pr.* I, 50, CSM I: 209; AT VIIIA: 24. For protest against optimism about how widespread good sense is, see Arnauld (1683: 17).

7 See *Reg.* II, CSM I: 11; AT X: 362; *Dis.* III, CSM I: 126; AT VI: 30. I am indebted, here as elsewhere in this account, to the guidance given by Gilson's commentary on Descartes (1925, here: 198).

8 Also *Dis.* II, CSM I: 119; AT VI: 16–17: *'je me résolus d'aller si lentement, et d'user tant de circonspection en toutes choses, que, si j'avançais que fort peu, je me garderai bien, au moins, de tomber'*; cf. LP, CSM I: 189; AT IXB: 19: '[. . .] *il y a des esprits qui se hâtent et qui usent de si peu de circonspection* [. . . *que* . . .] *il ne sauraient rien bâtir d'assuré'*.

9 See *Dis.* IV, CSM I: 130; AT VI: 38: '[. . .] *nos idées ou notions, étant des choses réelles, et qui viennet de Dieu, en tout ce en quoi elles sont claires et distinctes, ne peuvent en cela être que vraies'*. As Alquié notes ad loc. (Descartes 1963–73: I, 611 n. 1), Descartes has no need explicitly to affirm God's veraciousness in the *Dis.*, because the hypothesis has never been raised of His being deceitful.

10 All the English translations I have consulted suppress the quasi-hypothetical structure, giving 'what was presented' or 'what presented itself' for *'qui se présenterait'*. The *'connusse'* in the first part of the precept is a subjunctive dictated by the negative form.

11 There is, when all is said and done, no translation of *'cognitio'* that could impose itself as a standardised Englishing in all the places that Descartes uses the word: anything from the blandly pseudo-technical 'cognitive state' that I suggested in Chapter 4 to the (sometimes over-) committal 'knowledge' will do; the two most widely consulted French versions (Alquié, in Descartes 1963–73: I, 80 and Le Roy, in Descartes 1953: 39), both give *'connaissance'* here; there is nothing to be said against CSM's and HR's (I: 3) 'cognition', and I throw 'awareness' in just to keep the pot boiling.

12 *Reg.* VII, CSM I: 27; AT X: 390: '[s]*i denique per enumerationem velim ostendere, circuli*

aream esse majorem omnibus areis aliarum figurarum, quarum peripheria sit æqualis, non opus est omnes figuras recensere, sed sufficit de quibusdam in particulari hoc demonstrare, ut per inductionem idem etiam de aliis omnibus concludatur'. Against CSM's note ad loc., I would suggest that Descartes' choice of the mathematical example indicates that '*inductio*' here does not have its 'standard sense of "inference from particular instances of something to all instances"', if the 'standard' sense is that which we have come to associate with the Humean problem. Rather, what Descartes must have in mind is the ἐπαγωγή Aristotle describes at *Topics*, II xii, 105 a 15–19 (also *AnPo*., II 19, 100 b 5–14) which, while it certainly does pass from particular to universal, is meant to do so because the class from which the particular is taken at random is so specified that what applies to one member will apply to all.

13 Descartes seems to be wishing on himself the predicament of the hero of Jorge Luis Borges' 'Funes the Memorious', who is gifted or afflicted with total recall of everything he perceives; he is described as the 'solitary and lucid spectator of a multiform, instantaneous and almost intolerably precise world', because, for him, the line between perception and memory is elided. This is also God's position.

14 See letter to, perhaps, Fournier of October 1637, in which he discusses the difficulty for readers in following the *Geometry*, saying '[. . .] *c'est une chose qui ne se peut faire que la plume à la main*' (AT I: 457).

9 Rectitude and science

1 Aristotle frequently appeals to the person of practical reason as a yardstick for correct action in any given situation; e.g. I viii, 1099 a 7; II vi, 1107 a 1–2; II ix, 1109 a 24–6; III iv, 1113 a 33–4; VI v, 1140 a 24. Even so, the good person may not be skilful in explaining what virtue consists in (cf. the conclusion to be drawn from X ii, 1172 b 15–17): though there is a strong intellectual element in knowing the right thing to do, it need not be discursive. Moreover, though the good man functions rather like (and is the predecessor of) the 'reasonable man' of the common law, he does not constitute the good for man, he *detects* it (cf. Gottlieb 1991: 25–45).

2 Letter of 15th April 1630, CSMK: 21; AT I: 137–8: '[. . .] *pendant que j'y travaillais j'acquérais un peu plus de connaissance que je n'en avais eu en commençant, selon laquelle me voulant accommoder, j'étais contraint de faire un nouveau projet, un peu plus grand que le premier.*'

3 I follow D. Garber (1987) in thinking that, at least on this point, there is no essential difference of doctrine between the two texts. After all, there is reason for thinking that the composition of parts of each overlapped in point of time; for one timetable of the various parts of the *Dis.* see the classic study of G. Gadoffre (1943), reprised and revised in his (1987); for the *Reg.*, see again Weber (1964).

4 For references and discussion of the function and fate of this concept over Descartes' career, see Keeling (1937); Beck (1952: 66ff.); O'Neil (1972); Schuster (1980); Schouls (1980: 32–4); J.-L. Marion (1992b).

5 The axiom is employed in *Dis.* IV (CSM I: 128; AT VI: 34), where denial of it is described as '*manifestement impossible*' and a '*répugnance*'; it gets a good airing in *Med.* III (CSM II: 28; AT VII: 40–1) and is cited as the third axiom in the appendix to *Second Replies* (CSM I: 116; AT VII: 165). It also appears as a prime example of an eternal verity in *Pr.* I, 49 (CSM I: 209; AT VIIIA: 23–4). Interestingly, it is not cited in *Reg.* XII, where we might expect it to appear alongside the other '[. . .]

notiones, quæ sunt veluti vincula quædam ad alias naturas simplices inter se conjugandas' (CSM I: 45; AT X: 419), though it is clearly at work a little later when Descartes concludes from his own existence as a contingent being the existence of a God (CSM I: 46; AT X: 421–2).

6 In discussing the relation of a prism to the colours that result from a light shone through it, he says, '[. . .] *il peut ici être changé sans qu'elles changent*': *Met.* VIII, AT VI: 330.

7 One version is to be found in de Dominis (1611), succinctly expounded by J.F. Scott (1952: 72–4). On an accusation of plagiarism against Descartes, see Beck (1952: 21–1); more generally on Descartes' unacknowledged debts to medieval optical theories, see Sabra (1981: Ch. 1).

8 It is interesting to note (what I do not pretend to explain) that, whereas in the diagram used to illustrate the rainbow proper (AT VI: 326), the sun's rays are supposed parallel, in the one that treats the prism (330 and 335), they appear to come to some sort of focus before hitting the hypotenuse of the triangle (MN); Descartes' wavering here may underlie his saying that *'les rayons du soleil ABC traversent MN à angles droits* ou presque droits' (p. 330, emphasis added).

9 E. Grosholz puts the point by speaking of 'items' in 'the linear unfolding of knowledge' forming 'a chain of reasoning that is intended to be both truth-preserving and ampliative', (Grosholz 1991: 2). Her doubts about these chains are mostly focused on whether they can provide a suitable sense of the 'unity of complex objects' (ibid.); but I take her starting place to involve the thought that the content of the principles of metaphysics has to be entirely 'transparent', which is what I do not attribute to Descartes.

10 I.e. pre-existence is a pointless and extravagant addition that simply pushes the question back one stage. For what must be one of the few jokes in AT, about Huygens' former life as an explanation of how he can understand Descartes so well, see letter to Golius, 16th April 1635, AT III: 315–16.

11 This falls somewhere between Plato's image of enquiry in accordance with the Ideas as carving nature along the joints (*Phædrus*, 265E), and Leibniz' image (e.g. in the 'Preface' to Leibniz 1982) that the soul is not a *tabula rasa* but like a block of veined marble, within which there lurks a statue just waiting to be liberated. This latter image seems to be in play also in a sonnet of Michelangelo that begins: '[*n*]*on ha l'ottimo artista alcun concetto/ Ch' un marmo solo in sé non circonscriva/ Col superchio, e solo a quello arriva/ La man che ubbidisce all'intelletto'*. Cf. the statue of Mercury referred to in *Resp.* V, CSM II: 262; AT VII: 382.

12 E.g. both CSM and Alquié cut the *Pr.* and *Lum.* at the embarrassing bits; the third edition of E. Garin's Italian translation is unblushing about the full text of each (Descartes 1986: I 125–201 and III respectively).

13 What is described corresponds neatly to the definition of matter as extension in *Med.* V and in *Pr.* I, 51–3 (CSM I: 210–1; AT VIIIA: 24–5), elegantly expounded by R. Woolhouse (1993: 18–21). Cf. Galileo, who says that he proceeds '[. . .] *astraendo tutte le imperfezioni della materia e supponendola perfettissima ed inalterabile e da ogni accidental mutazione esente'*, *Due Nuove Scienze* (Leiden 1638), in Galilei (1890–1909: VIII, 51).

14 This latter motivation, which may be related to his unwillingness to set out his doctrine of the creation of the eternal verities and to the reason Plato gives for not writing down the most important truths of metaphysics: *Phædr.*, 275 D–E; *Ep.*, VII, 344 A–D.

15 Clarke reads a slightly earlier passage from the same letter to mean that Descartes

distinguishes between a sense of 'demonstration' with the 'special connotations of deducing a conclusion rigorously from first principles' from a sense that is 'less strict in which one [. . .] argues from effects to hypothetical causes' (Clarke 1992: 264). On my account, the distinction in play is between the direction of analysis (from causes to effects) and that of synthesis (from effects to causes). The muddle may be caused by the absence, to which we have already referred, of the terminology from the *Dis.*; in the published works, he is only explicit about it in *Resp.* II, CSM II: 110–11.

10 What rectitude permits

1 On the 'teachings of nature', see Kennington (1972), but note that Descartes nowhere nominalises the 'teaching'; it is always '*natura*' that is the agent of '*docere*', whether the construction is active or passive: '[*n*]*ihil autem est quod me ista natura magis expresse doceat* [. . .]' (AT VII: 80); [*d*]*ocet etiam natura*' (81); '*doceor a natura*' (ibid.); '*a natura doctus esse*' (82); '*cum dico me aliquid doceri a natura*' (ibid.).

2 CSM I: 289; AT VIIIA: 327: '[*s*]*ufficere si de insensibilibus qualia esse possint, explicerim, etsi forte non talia sint*'; cf. AT IXB: 322, which suppresses the final clause: '[*q*]*ue touchant les choses que nos sens n'apperçoivent point, il suffit d'expliquer comment elles peuvent être*'.

3 Loc. cit., CSM I: 289; AT VIIIA: 326: '[*q*]*uamombrem, ut ii qui in considerandis automatis sunt exercitati, cum alicuius machinæ usum sciunt et nonnullas eius partes aspiciunt, facile ex istis, quo modo aliæ quas non vident sint factæ*'; which is both hedged and rein-forced in the French: AT XIB: 322: '[*u*]*n horloger* [perhaps this is Picot, because there is no classical Latin for this trade], *en voyant une montre qu'il n'a point faite* [its use is assumed], *peut ordinairement juger, de quelques-unes de ses parties qu'il regarde, quelles sont toutes les autres qu'il ne voit pas*'. This quasi-perceptual faculty of having an eye for how mechanical parts fit together is being tested, for instance, in the exam to join Lord Suffolk's bomb disposal squad in Michael Ondaatje's *The English Patient* (1992: 200–1), where the candidates have to reassemble the bits of a machine without prior knowledge of its use.

4 *Pr.* IV, 204, CSM I: 289; AT VIIIA: 327: '[. . .] *non dubium est, quin summus rerum opifex omnia illa, quæ videmus, pluribus diversis modis potuerit efficere*'; much expanded in the French, AT IXB: 322: '[. . .] *il est certain que Dieu a une infinité de divers moyens, par chacun desquels il peut avoir fait que toutes les choses de ce monde paraissent telles que main-tenant elles paraissent, sans qu'il soit possible à l'esprit humain connaître lequel de tous ces moyens il a voulu employer à les faire*'.

5 Cf. Sextus Empiricus, *Adv. Math.*, VII, 213 (Usener: 247). On the doubtfulness of Sextus' source because of the strangeness of the example, see Sedley (1982). Gassendi was certainly happy enough with it: see *Syntagma Philosophicum* in (1568: I, 192–3). For variants on related argument in the late medieval and early modern periods, see E. Grant (1981: 24–66).

6 In Diogenes Laertius, *Lives*, X 86 (Usener: 36): δῆλον ὅτι καὶ ἐκ παντὸς ἐκπίπτει φυσιολογήματος, ἐπὶ δὲ τὸν μῦθον καταρρεῖ.

7 Cf. Lucretius, *DRN*, VI, 706–7: '[. . .] *fit ut omnis dicere causas/ Conveniat leti, dicatur ut illius una*'.

8 To the end of his life, Mersenne seems to have been open to the (anti-realist) idea that there was no truth of the matter to decide between the leading astronomi-cal hypotheses of the day; cf. R. Lenoble (1943: 456–61). H. Busson gives a list of eminent doubters of geocentrism, including the Cardinal de Retz, who seems

to have thought there was nothing to choose between Tycho and Copernicus (Busson 1933: 287–9). This is a matter to which we return in our final chapter.

9 Even if this addition were Picot's work, there would remain the question of what contrast there is, in Descartes' mind, between the moral certainty of *Pr.* IV, 205 and the more than moral certainty of IV, 206 (i.e. a contrast that does not depend on the specifications of the quasi-technical terms, but is itself a load-bearing part of the argument).

10 *Pr.* IV, 206, CSM I: 291; AT VIIIA: 329: '[. . .] *vix aliter quam a me explicata sunt, intelligi posse videntur*'; in the French Descartes recalls the assumption of II, 46 about the fluidity of the heavens which he says he has used in such a way as to have '*prouvé par démonstration mathématique toutes les choses que j'ai écrites*' (AT IXB: 325).

11 A.P. Herbert 'reports' a suit for defamation centring on a crossword with two solutions, one libellous and obvious, the other neither (but claimed by the defendant to be the one intended); the case finishes with lunch, rather than a decision.

12 Flage (1999: 42) seems to think that there is some way of eliminating all the possible keys so as to leave just one. An inability even to imagine a 'library of Babel'?

13 See e.g. Epicurus, *Letter to Herodotus*, 59; Lucretius, *DRN*, I, 746ff.

14 CSM give 'boundaries'; AT VII: 381: '*ut termini*'; Descartes 1963–73: II, 829: '*comme des termes*' – improved in the note to '*comme des limites*'; presumably, a source here would be the Aristotelian notion of the mathematician's interest being the πέρας of bodies (e.g. *Phys.*, II ii, 193 b 32–3).

15 A closely related point comes out in an anecdote in which an astronomer's wife was boasting to Mrs Einstein about a big new telescope that her husband had secured; Mrs Einstein responded 'my husband does it on the back of an old envelope', cited by J.R. Lucas (1984: 2).

16 The wording is so thorough as, perhaps, to be worth quoting in full: '[*J*]*e me moque du Sieur Petit et de ses paroles, et on n'a, ce me semble, pas plus sujet de l'écouter lorsqu'il promet de réfuter mes réfractions par l'expérience, que s'il voulait faire voir, avec quelque mauvaise équerre, que les 3 angles d'un triangle ne sauraient pas égaux à 2 droits. Mais je ne saurais pas empêcher qu'il n'y ait au monde des médisants et des crédules; tout ce que je puis, c'est de les mépriser, ce que je fais de telle façon que, si vous pouvais aussi bien persuader, je m'assure que vous ne prendiez jamais plus la peine de m'ennuyer de leurs papiers ou de leurs nouvelles, ni même de les écouter*'. Compare also his dismissiveness over the Puy-de-Dôme experiment in 1649, documented by Garber (1992a: 141–2).

17 This I take it would have been Einstein's response had the observations of the eclipse of 29th May 1919 failed to fulfil expectation.

18 Cf. *Pr.* II, 53, CSM I: 245; AT VIIIA: 70; AT IXB: 93. His words for the quality that is lacking in gross bodies are '*durus*' and '*dur*'; C.D. Broad claimed to 'have worked though all the cases, and found that some of his laws hold only when bodies are perfectly elastic, others only when they are perfectly inelastic, and others under no conditions whatsoever', cited by N.K. Smith (1952: 211 n. 1).

19 Cf. also the strangely Aristotelian phrase '*phénomènes sublunaires*' in the letter to Mersenne, 8th October 1629, CSMK: 6; AT I: 23 ·

20 E.g. Anscombe and Geach edit out the five long paragraphs AT VI: 46–56 with a note saying that the passage is 'now of merely historical interest' (Descartes 1954: 41 n. 1).

21 See letter to Mersenne, 13th November 1639, AT II: 621; and, referring to an autopsy witnessed in 1637, letter to the same 1st April 1640, CSMK: 146; AT III: 49. G.A. Lindeboom suggests that Descartes may have been exaggerating about how much anatomy he had actually got himself sticky with (Lindeboom 1978:

Ch. 3); for more charitable accounts Sawday (1995: 146–58) and Barker (1984: 77, 95ff.) I am especially grateful to Alessandra Violi for these latter references (see her 1998: Ch. 1).

22 CSM give 'means' (I: 144) which seems to me an undertranslation. Sutcliffe (Descartes 1968: 81) and Cress (Descartes 1980: 34) both offer 'expedient'. Anscombe and Geach (Descartes 1954: 48) suggest 'resource'. HR (Descartes 1911: I, 121) giving 'I don't know any other plan but again to try to find experiments' and Veitch (Descartes 1912: 51) with 'out of this difficulty I cannot otherwise extricate myself than by finding certain experiments' seem to be both following De Courcelles' Latin (AT VI: 576) which reads '[*h*]*inc enim aliter me extricare non possum, si rursus aliqua experimenta quæram*', indication at least that he is in a tight spot.

23 It has been thought that this lands St Augustine with a confusion between a sign as a name and a word as a component in a sentence; see M. Sirridge (1976). All he needs is the notion that, if we understand a sentence made up of words we do know, then the novelty was implicit in what we understand and so, the novelty is not really taught.

24 These moves are reminiscent of Meno's challenges, at *Men.*, 80D: (i) how is one to look for what one does not know at all? (ii) what one is to pick on among the things one does not know to enquire further? and (iii) even if, by chance, one picks on the right thing, how is one to know that it is the very thing one did not know? They are telescoped by Socrates at 80 E into the sophism (ἐριστικός λόγος) that a man can enquire neither into what he knows (because there is in that case no need for enquiry), nor into what he does not (because he does not know the thing he is to enquire into).

25 Cf. St Augustine's own account of the *Mag.* at *Ret.*, I, 12, paraphrasing *Matthew*, 23: 10, cited by M.F. Burnyeat (1987–8: 4–5).

11 What rectitude forbids

1 This is the shortest summary of the *Meditations* I can manage: cf. I (CSM II: 12; AT VII: 17): '*a primis fundamentis* [. . .] *quid aliquando firmum et mansurum cupiam in scientiis*'; II (CSM II: 16; AT VII: 23) '[*i*]*n tantas dubitationes* [. . .] *conjectus sum*'; III (CSM II: 24; AT VII: 34) '[*c*]*laudam nunc oculos, aures obturabo, avocabo omnes sensus*'; IV CSM II: 37: AT VII: 52) '[. . .] *me his diebus assuefeci in mente a sensibus abducenda*'; V (CSM II: 44; AT VII: 63) [*m*]*ulta mihi supersunt de Dei attributis, multa de mei ipsius sive mentis meæ natura investiganda* [. . .] *considerare debeo illarum ideas, quatenus sunt in mea cogitatione, et videre quænam ex iis sint distinctæ*'; VI (CSM II: 50; AT VII: 71) '[*r*]*eliquum est ut examinem an res materiales existat*'. But I am not meaning to compete with the 'Encore' to Stoppard's *Dogg's Hamlet*: five hours' worth of drama in thiry-seven spoken lines.

2 For a range of variants on the relation between the 'fable' and *res ipsa*, see Tillmann 1976: 1230–91.

3 Again, the French is more emphatic: AT IXB: 124: '[. . .] *considérant la tout-puissance de Dieu nous devons juger que tout ce qu'il a fait a eu dès le commencement toute la perfection qu'il devait avoir*'.

4 I see no reason to think that their correspondence was being deliberately tampered with in transit or that either thought that it was.

Had Bruno had the sense to stay in Germany and not to accept Mocenigo's invitation to Venice, he would presumably not have come to his sticky end; as John

Bossy concludes, 'it served him right' (Bossy 1991: 183).

6 By May 1637, Descartes is saying that he may yet be given reason for publishing his treatise (AT I: 367). Though he writes about the book to other correspondents (e.g. Vatier (February 1638, AT I: 562) Huygens (9th March 1638, AT II: 662 and 31st January 1642, AT III: 523) and Morin (July 1638, AT II: 201)), I am uncertain whether Huygens had actually seen a copy when, on 15th May 1639, he encourages Descartes '*à mettre le Monde au monde*' (AT II: 679; cf. also letter of 28th May 1639, AT II: 680: '*mettez vous à nous entendre la Lumière*'). Likewise, it is less than certain that, among the papers that Regius had access to and that, as Descartes held, he had '*mal transcrit et changé l'ordre* (LP, AT IXB p, 19), there were drafts or parts of the *Treatise on Light*.

7 Clarke glances (1982: 84–5) at another 'option', which he calls 'L3' (ibid.: 87), namely the thesis that the conjunction of the metaphysical principles and the propositions of intellectual intuition entail the physical principles. For my money, this is precisely Descartes' position. It to his credit that Clarke mentions it; but it is a pity he gives it such short shrift.

8 AT's editorial suggestion on p. 290.

9 Galilei (1890–1909, XIX: 405), Finocchiaro (1989: 291) do not include, and CSMK (45) suppress, the apparatus of shouting: italics in AT, and presumably underlining in the manuscript.

10 I.e. the *Responsio pro Telluris quiete ad Jacobi Lansbergii Apologiam pro Telluris motu*, published at Paris after June 1634 (asterisked note to AT I: 324). This text is not discussed in Garber's engaging and informative account of Morin (Garber 1995).

11 It is worth noting that Barberini was one of the dissenting minority of three Cardinal Inquisitors who did not sign the Sentence of 1633. Descartes' intention to approach him as an authority is thus open to interpretation. Either he hoped that Barberini would give his cause a sympathetic hearing, and perhaps not reflect the view of the Church as a body, or he thought that Barberini would give a fair account of the state of play, even from the point of view of those who were losing ground in the debate.

12 I do not know whether it has been noticed that the title of *Lum.* XII ('*Du flux et du reflux de la Mer*') corresponds with uncanny accuracy to the title originally intended (but withdrawn because tendentiously Copernican) for Galileo's *Two World Systems* ('*Dialogo del flusso e reflusso del mare*', see Galilei 1890–1909: XIII, 236; also the earlier [1616] *Discorso del flusso e reflusso del mare*, in Galilei 1890–1909: V, 377–95). Cf. letter to Mersenne, November or December 1632, AT I: 281; also to the same, 14th August 1634, AT I: 304 and 6th August 1640, AT III: 144–5.

13 Descartes would thus be in the position of Milton's Adam at the beginning of *Paradise Lost* VIII, when, contemplating the heavens, he says that '[s]omething yet of doubt remains,/ Which only thy [i.e. the Archangel Raphael's] solution can resolve./ When I behold this goodly frame, this world/ Of heav'n and earth consisting, and compute/ Their magnitudes, this earth a spot, a grain,/ An atom with the firmament compared' (ll. 13–18). On which see Sawday (2000: 30), who perhaps overestimates how much closer Descartes is to the Royal Society than to Aquinas.

14 The phenomenon of stellar parallax, arising from the different positions that the Earth occupies in its annual rotation, was not observed until 1838. Until that time, it continued to be reasonable for the vulgar to maintain a sense in which the movement of the Earth is imperceptible.

15 I.e. Descartes says to Mersenne that he picked up his knowledge about t

condemnation of Galileo from an announcement printed at Liège, a city one might suppose no less demon-infested than others. See letter already amply cited of April 1634, CSMK: 43.

16 E.g., *Dis.* VI, CSM I: 141–2; AT VI: 60; *Resp.* IV, to the Theologians, CSM II: 176–7; AT VII: 254; and, more roundly, *Pr.* IV, 207, CSM I: 291; AT VIIIA: 329: '[*a*]*t nihilominus, memor meæ tenuitatis, nihil affirmo: sed hæc omnia, tum Ecclesiæ Catholicæ auctoritati; tum prudentiorum judiciis submitto*'.

17 See letter to Mersenne, 31st March 1641, CSMK 177; AT III: 350: '[. . .] *je me fais fort de montrer qu'il n'y a aucune opinon, en leur* [sc. the Thomists'] *philosophie, qui s'accorde si bien avec la foi que les miennes*'; and, on the exquisitely theological question of the Eucharist, *Resp.* IV, CSM II: 173–8; AT VII: 248–56.

18 '*Debemos siempre tener para en todo acertar, que lo blanco que yo veo, creer que es negro, si la Yglesia hierárchica assí lo determina*' = '[*d*]*enique ut ipsi Ecclesiæ catholicæ omnino unanimes conformesque simus, si quid quod nigra illa oculis nostris apparet album, nigra illa esse definieret, debemus itidem, quod nigrum sit pronuntiare*'.

Bibliography

Abbagnano, N. (1946) *Storia della filosofia* (7 vols), 3rd edition, 1975, reprinted Turin: UTET, 1993.

Abercrombie, N. (1938) *Augustine and French Classical Thought*, Oxford: Oxford University Press.

Allan, D.J. (1953) 'Aristotle's Account of the Origin of Moral Principles', reprinted in Barnes (ed. 1975): II, 72–8.

Alquié, F. (1950) *La découverte métaphysique de l'homme chez Descartes*, Paris: Presses Universitaires de France, 3rd edition 1987.

— see also Descartes (1963–73).

Annas J. (1985) *The Modes of Scepticism*, with J. Barnes, Cambridge: Cambridge University Press.

— (1994) *The Morality of Happiness*, Oxford: Oxford University Press.

Anscombe, G.E.M. (1965) 'The Intentionality of Sensation: a Grammatical Feature', reprinted in her *Philosophical Papers* (3 vols), Oxford: Basil Blackwell 1981: II, 1–20.

— see also Descartes (1954).

Anselm, St (see Index of primary texts).

— (1938–61) *Opera Omnia* (6 vols), edited by F.S. Schmitt, anastatic reprint in 2 vols, Stuttgart-Bad Canstatt: Fromann Verlag, 1968.

— (1992) *De Libertate Arbitrii*, Italian translation by I. Sciuto, Florence: Nardini.

— (1995) *Monologion*, edited with Italian translation by I. Sciuto, Milan: Rusconi.

Aquinas, St Thomas (see Index of primary texts).

— (1934) *Summa Contra Gentiles*, vols 13–15 of *Opera Omnia* (Leonine ed. 1882ff), Vatican: Polyglot Press.

— (1962) *Summa Theologiæ*, Milan: Editiones Paulinæ, 2nd edition, 1988.

— (1989) *Summa Theologiæ, a Concise Translation*, selected and translated by T. McDermott, London: Methuen.

Ariew, R. (ed. 1995) *Descartes and his Contemporaries: Meditations, Objections and Replies*, edited by R. Ariew and M. Grene, Chicago: Chicago University Press.

— (ed. 1998) *Descartes' Meditations, Background Source Materials*, edited and translated by R. Ariew, J. Cottingham and T. Sorell, Cambridge, Cambridge University Press.

— (1999) *Descartes and the Last Scholastics*, with M. Grene, Ithaca N.Y.: Cornell University Press.

Aristotle (see Index of primary texts).

— (1915) *Nicomachean Ethics*, translated by W.D. Ross, in *The Works of Aristotle* (11 vols), edited by W.D. Ross, vol. IX, Oxford: Oxford University Press, revised 1925.

— (1926) *Nicomachean Ethics*, edited and translated by H. Rackham in *Aristotle* (23 vols), vol. XIX, Loeb Classical Library, Cambridge, Mass. and London: Harvard University Press and Heinemann, revised 1934.

— (1938) *Categories, On Interpretation* and *Prior Analytics*, translated by H.P. Cook (*Cat., DI*) and H. Tredennick (*An.Pr.*) in *Aristotle* (23 vols), vol. I, Loeb Classical Library, Cambridge, Massachusetts and London: Harvard University Press and Heinemann.

— (1953) *Nicomachean Ethics*, translated by J.A.K. Thomson, revised by H. Tredennick with introduction and bibliography by J. Barnes, Harmondsworth: Penguin, 1976.

— (1963) *Categories, On Interpretation*, translated with notes and glossary by J.L. Ackrill, Oxford: Clarendon Press.

— (1972) *Parts of Animals*, translated with commentary by D. Balme, Oxford: Clarendon Press.

Armogathe J.-R. (1977) *Theologia Cartesiana*, The Hague: Martinus Nijhoff.

— (ed. 1999) *La Biografia Intellettuale di René Descartes attraverso la* Correspondance, edited by J.R. Armogathe, G. Belgioioso and C. Vinti, Naples: Vivarium.

Armstrong, D.M. (1973) *Belief, Truth and Knowledge*, Cambridge: Cambridge University Press.

Arnauld A. (see Index of primary texts)

— (1683) *La Logique ou l'Art de Penser*, with P. Nicole, ed. by L. Marin, Paris: Flammarion, 1970.

— (1775–83) *Œuvres de M. Arnauld* (43 volumes), anonymously edited by G. du Parc de Bellegarde, Paris: S. D'Arnay.

Aubrey, J. (1975) *Brief Lives*, selected and edited by R. Barber, London: Folio Society.

Audi, R. (1995) 'Acting from Virtue', *Mind*, 150, 415: 449–71.

Augustine, St (see Index of primary texts)

— (1970) *Nuova Biblioteca Agostiniana* (34 vols still in progress), founding series editor A. Trapè, Vatican City nr. Rome: Città Nuova Editrice.

— (1993) *La Parola e il Maestro*, edited with introduction, facing Italian translation of *De Magistro* and *De Grammatica*, bibliography and notes by M. Bettetini, Milan: Rusconi.

— (1997) *Confessioni*, edited with facing Italian translation by C. Vitali, reprinted Milan: Rizzoli, 1999.

Austin, J.L. (1962) *Sense and Sensibilia*, edited by G.J. Warnock, Oxford: Oxford University Press.

Ayer, A.J. (1936) *Language, Truth and Logic*, 2nd edition, 1946, Harmondsworth: Penguin, 1971.

— (1973) *The Central Questions of Philosophy*, London: Weidenfeld & Nicholson.

Ayers, M., see D. Garber.

Bacon, Francis (1620) *Novum Organum* in *The Philosophical Works of Francis Bacon*, edited by R.L. Ellis and J. Spedding (1857), revised and condensed by J.M. Robertson, London: Routledge, 1905: 256–387.

— (1625a) *Essays* in *The Philosophical Works of Francis Bacon*, edited by R.L. Ellis and

J. Spedding (1857), revised and condensed by J.M. Robertson, London: Routledge, 1905: 735–807.

— (1625b) *Gli 'Essayes' di Francis Bacon: Studio Introduttivo, Testo Critico e Commento*, edited by M. Melchionda, Florence: Leo Olschki Editore, 1979.

Baillet, A. (see Index of primary texts).

— (1691) *Vie de M. Des Cartes* (2 vols), Paris: Horthemels.

Bannan, J.F. (1960) 'Contemporary French Readings of Descartes', *Review of Metaphysics*, XIII, 3: 412–38.

Barker, F. (1984) *The Tremulous Private Body*, London: Methuen.

Barnes, J. (1969) 'Aristotle's Theory of Demonstration', in Barnes (ed. 1975): I, 65–87.

— (1972) *The Ontological Argument*, London: St Martin's Press.

— (ed. 1975) *Articles on Aristotle* (4 vols, 1975–9) edited by J. Barnes, M. Schofield and R. Sorabji, London: Duckworth.

— (1982) 'The Beliefs of a Pyrrhonist', reprinted in *Elenchos*, 4 (1983): 5–43.

— (1989) 'The Size of the Sun in Antiquity', *Acta Classica Scientiarum Debrecensis*, 25: 29–41.

— (1990) *The Toils of Scepticism*, Cambridge: Cambridge University Press.

— see also J. Annas (1985).

Beck, L.J. (1952) *The Method of Descartes*, Oxford: Oxford University Press, revised 1964.

— (1965) *The Metaphysics of Descartes*, Oxford: Oxford University Press.

Belgioioso G. (1990) *Descartes: il metodo e i saggi* (2 vols), edited by G. Belgioioso, G. Cimino, P. Costabel and G. Papuli, Florence: Æ, Istituto dell'Enciclopedia Italiana Treccani.

— (ed. 1999) 'Cartesio e gli artigiani', in Armogathe (ed. 1999): 113–65.

— see also J.R. Armogathe (ed. 1999).

Ben-Zeev, A. (1984) 'Aristotle on Perceptual Truth and Falsity', *Apeiron*, 18: 118–25.

Bettetini, M. (1997) 'Die Wahl der Engel, Übel, Materie und Willensfreiheit (Buch XI–XII)' in *Augustinus 'De Civitate Dei'*, edited by C. Horn, Berlin: Akademie Verlag, 131–53.

Beyssade, J.-M. (1990) 'Sur les "trois ou quatre maximes" de la morale par provision', in Belgioioso (ed. 1990): I, 139–53.

— (ed. 1994) *Descartes: Objecter et Répondre*, edited by J.-M. Beyssade and J.-L. Marion, Paris: Presses Universitaires de France.

Beyssade, M. (1992) 'The Cogito: Privileged Truth or Exemplary Truth', in Voss (ed. 1992): 31–9.

— (1999) 'La règle de la vérité: une règle d'abord provisionelle', *Acta Philosophica Fennica*, 64: 71–86.

Blaise, A. (1975) *Lexicon Latinitatis Medii Ævi*, Turnhout: Brepols.

Bolton, M. (1986) 'Confused and Obscure Ideas of Sense', in A.O. Rorty (ed. 1986): 389–404.

Bonnen, C.A., see D.E. Flage.

Bordas-Desmoulins, J.-B. (1853) *Le Cartésienisme, ou la Véritable Rénovation des Science* Paris: Hetzel.

Borel, P. (1656) *Vitæ Renati Cartesii Compendium*, Paris: Billaine et Dupuis.

— (1657) *Discours nouveau prouvant la pluralité des mondes*, Geneva, anastatic reprint edited by A. del Prete, Lecce: Conte Editore, 1998.

Bortolotti, A. (1983) *Saggi sulla formazione del pensiero di Descartes*, Florence: Leo Olschki.

Bossy, J. (1991) *Giordano Bruno and the Embassy Affair*, New Haven, Conn.: Yale University Press.

Bouillier, F. (1842) *Histoire et Critique de la Révolution Cartésienne*, Lyon: Boitel.

Boyer, C.B. (1959) *The Rainbow: From Myth to Mathematics*, New York: Thomas Josehoff.

Bréhier, É. (1937) 'The Creation of the Eternal Truths in Descartes's System', translated in W. Doney (ed. 1968): 192–208.

Broad, C.D. (1944) 'The New Philosophy from Bruno to Descartes', reprinted in his *Ethics and the History of Philosophy*, London: Routledge & Kegan Paul, 1952: 144–67.

Broadic, see S. Waterlow Broadie.

Brochard, V. (1954) 'Descartes stoïcien', in his *Études de philosophie moderne et de philosophie ancienne*, Paris: Vrin: 320–6.

Browne, T. (1642/3) *Religio Medici*, edited by C.H. Herford, London: J.M. Dent & Sons, 1906.

Burnyeat, M.F. (1980a) 'Aristotle on Learning to Be Good', in A.O. Rorty (ed. 1980): 69–92.

— (1980b) 'Can the sceptic live his scepticism?', in *Doubt and Dogmatism*, edited by M. Schofield, M.F. Burnyeat and J. Barnes, Oxford: Clarendon Press: 20–53 (reprinted in M.F. Burnyeat (ed. 1983): 117–48).

— (1982) 'Idealism and Greek Philosophy', in *Idealism: Past and Present*, Cambridge: edited by G. Vesey, Cambridge University Press, 1982: 19–50.

— (ed. 1983) *Skeptical Tradition*, edited by M.F. Burnyeat, Berkeley: University of California Press.

— (1984) 'The Sceptic in his Time and Place', in R. Rorty (ed. 1984): 225–54.

— (1987–8) 'Wittgenstein and Augustine: *De Magistro*', *Proceedings of the Aristotelian Society Supplementary Volume*, 88: 1–24.

— (1998) 'Art and Mimesis in Plato's *Republic*', *London Review of Books*, 20, 10: 3–9.

— (2000) 'Plato on why Mathematics is Good for the Soul', in *Mathematics and Necessity: Essays in the History of Philosophy*, edited by T.J. Smiley, *Proceedings of the British Academy*, 103, 1–81.

Buroker, J.V. (1996) 'Arnauld on Judging and the Will', in *Interpreting Arnauld*, edited by E.J. Kremer, Toronto: University of Toronto Press: 3–12.

Burton, R. (1621) *The Anatomy of Melancholy* [. . .], London: William Tegg & Co., 1849.

Busson, H. (1933) *La Pensée Religieuse Française de Charron à Pascal*, Paris: Vrin.

Butler, R.J. (ed. 1972) *Cartesian Studies*, Oxford: Basil Blackwell.

Cahne, P.A. (1984) *Un autre Descartes*, Paris: Vrin.

Callinescu, M. (1987) *Five Faces of Modernity*, Durham, N.C.: Duke University Press.

Calvert, B. (1972) 'Descartes and the Problem of Evil', reprinted in J.D.G. Moyal (ed. 1991): IV, 396–405.

Calvino, I. (1979) *Se una notte d'inverno un viaggiatore*, Turin: Einaudi.

Campbell, C.A. (1957) *On Selfhood and Godhood*, London: Allen & Unwin.

Campbell, L. (1883) *Sophocles: The Seven Plays in English Verse*, Oxford: Oxford University Press.

Cantin, S. (1946) 'L'âme et ses puissances selon Aristote', *Laval Théologique et Philosophique*, 2: 184–205.

Carroll, L. (pseud. C.L. Dodgson) (1871, but dated 1872) *Alice Through the Looking-Glass*, edited by R.L. Green, Oxford: Oxford University Press, 1982.

Caton, H.D. (1971) 'The Problem of Descartes' Sincerity', *Philosophical Forum*, 2: 355–69.

—— (1973) 'Will and Reason in Descartes's Theory of Error', *Journal of Philosophy*, XXII, 4: 87–104.

Cavaillé, J.-P. (1994) '"Le Plus Éloquent Philosophe des Derniers Temps": Les stratégies d'auteur de René Descartes', *Annales, Histoire, Sciences Sociales*, 49e année, 2: 349–67.

Cicero, M.T. (see Index of primary texts).

—— (1876) *De Finibus bonorum et malorum*, edited D.I. Madvig, anastatic reprint, Hildesheim: Georg Olms, 1963.

—— (1885) *Academica*, edited and explained by J.A. Reid, anastatic reprint, Hildesheim: Georg Olms, 1966.

—— (1933) *Traité du Destin*, edited with French translation by A. Yon, Paris: Budé 2nd edition, 1950.

—— (1996) *Tusculane*, edited with facing Italian translation by L.Z. Clerici, Milan: Rizzoli.

Clark, S.R.L. (1992) 'Descartes' Debt to Augustine', *Philosophy*, 32: 73–88.

Clarke, D. (1982) *Descartes' Philosophy of Science*, Manchester: Manchester University Press.

—— (1989) *Occult Powers and Hypotheses*, Oxford: Oxford University Press.

—— (1992) 'Descartes' Philosophy of Science and the Scientific Revolution', in Cottingham (ed. 1992): 258–85.

Code, L. (1987) *Epistemic Responsibility*, Hanover, Pa.: Brown University Press.

Collegium Conimbricense (see Index of primary texts).

—— (1593) *In Libros Ethicorum Aristotelis ad Nicomachum: Aliquot Conimbricensis cursus disputationes in quibus præcipua Ethicæ disciplinæ capitæ continentur*, reprinted Venice: I. Vincenzi & R. Amadini, 1606.

—— (1598) *In Libros tres De Anima Aristotelis Stagiritæ* [. . .], corrected reprint, Venice: I. Vincenzi & R. Amadini, 1606.

—— (1606) *Commentarius in Universam Dialecticam*, corrected by Attilio Brunacci, reprinted Venice: Andrea Baba, 1616.

Cooper, N. (1994) 'Intellectual Virtues', *Philosophy*, 69, 270: 459–69.

Copenhaver B. (1992) *Renaissance Philosophy*, completing text by C.B. Schmitt, Oxford: Oxford University Press.

Cottingham, J. (1978) 'A Brute to the Brutes? Descartes' Treatment of Animals', reprinted under the title 'Descartes' Treatment of Animals', in Cottingham (ed. 1998): 225–33.

—— (1986) *Descartes*, Oxford: Basil Blackwell.

—— (1988) *The Rationalists*, Oxford: Oxford University Press.

—— (ed. 1992) *Cambridge Companion to Descartes*, Cambridge: Cambridge University Press.

—— (1993) *A Descartes Dictionary*, Oxford: Basil Blackwell.

— (ed. 1994) *Reason, Will and Sensation: Studies in Descartes's Metaphysics*, Oxford: Clarendon Press.

— (ed. 1998), *Descartes*, Oxford: Oxford University Press.

— see also R. Ariew (ed. 1998).

Courcelles, P. (1968) *Late Latin Writers and their Greek Sources*, Cambridge Mass.: Harvard University Press.

Cousin, V. (1845) *Fragments de Philosophie Moderne*, Paris: Charpentier.

Craig, E.J. (1987) *The Mind of God and the Works of Man*, Oxford: Oxford University Press.

Crapulli, G. (1969) '"*Mathesis universalis*": *genesi di una idea nel XVI secolo*', Rome: Ateneo.

— (1988) *Introduzione a Cartesio*, Bari-Rome, Laterza.

Cress, D.A. (1994) 'Truth, Error and the Order of Reasons: Descartes's Puzzling Synopsis of the Fourth Meditation', in Cottingham (ed. 1994): 141–55.

— see also Descartes (1980).

Crisp, R. (ed. 1997) *Virtue Ethics*, edited by R. Crisp and M. Slote, Oxford: Oxford University Press.

Curley, E.M. (1972) 'Locke, Boyle and the Distinction between Primary and Secondary Qualities', *Philosophical Review*, 81, 4: 438–64.

— (1975) 'Descartes, Spinoza and the Ethics of Belief', in *Spinoza: Essays in Interpretation*, edited by M. Mandelbaum and E. Freeman, Lasalle, Ill.: Open Court Press: 159–89.

— (1978) *Descartes against the Skeptics*, Oxford: Basil Blackwell.

— (1984) 'Descartes on the Creation of the Eternal Truths', *Philosophical Review*, 93: 569–97.

— (ed. 1987) *Eternal Truths and the Cartesian Circle*, New York: Garland.

D'Auger, J.-E. (1954) 'Sénèque, Epictète et le stoïcisme dans l'œuvre de René Descartes', *Revue de théologie et de philosophie*, III: 169–96.

Davies, R. (1998a) 'L'ora di filosofare', appendix to M. Nussbaum, *La Terapia del Desiderio*, Milan: Vita e Pensiero: 617–53.

— (1998b) 'Some Quodlibets on the Virtues', *The Modern Schoolman*: 43–60.

— (forthcoming) 'Descartes' Letters', *Archiv für Geschichte der Philosophie*.

de Dominis, A. (1611) *De Radiis Visus et Lucis*, Venice.

De Lacey, P. (1958) 'οὐ μᾶλλον and the Antecedents of Ancient Scepticism', *Phronesis*, III: 57–71.

De Plinval, G. (1943) *Pélage: ses ecrits, sa vie et sa réforme*, Lausanne: Librairie Payot.

De Rochemonteix, C. (1889) *Un Collège de Jésuites, L'Histoire du Collège de la Flèche* (4 vols), Le Mans: Leguicheux.

De Sacy, S. (1956) *Descartes*, Paris: Seuil.

Dear, P. (1998) 'Method and the Study of Nature', in Garber (ed. 1998): 147–77.

Del Noce, A. (1964) 'Il problema Pascal e l'ateismo contemporaneo', in his *Il problema del ateismo*, Bologna: Il Mulino, 4th edition, 1990: 377–511.

Delhez, J. (1970) 'Descartes lecteur de Sénèque', *Revue des études latines*: 392–401.

Dennett, D. (1976) 'Are Dreams Experiences?', reprinted in his (1979): 129–48.

— (1978) 'Artificial Intelligence as Philosophy and as Psychology', reprinted in Dennett (1979): 109–26.

— (1979) *Brainstorms*, Brighton: Harvester Press.

328   *Bibliography*

— (1993) *Consciousness Explained*, Harmondsworth: Penguin.

Dent, N.J.H. (1981) 'The Value of Courage', *Philosophy*, 56: 574–7.

Descartes, R. (various editions and translations, for standard references see Index of primary texts).

— (1657–67 Clerselier) *Lettres de M. Descartes* (3 vols), edited by C. Clerselier, Paris: Angot-Le Gras.

— (1824–6 Cousin) *Œuvres Complètes* (12 vols) edited by V. Cousin, Paris and Strasbourg: F.G. Levrault, 4th edition, Paris, 1847.

— (1911 Haldane, Ross) *The Philosophical Works of Descartes* (2 vols), translated by E.S. Haldane and G.R.T. Ross, Cambridge: Cambridge University Press, corrected 1931.

— (1912 Veitch) *A Discourse on Method Etc.*, translated by J. Veitch and introduced by A.D. Lindsay, London: J.M. Dent & Sons.

— (1925 Gilson) *Discours de la Méthode, texte et commentaire*, edited with commentary by É. Gilson, Paris: Vrin (4th edition), 1967.

— (1925 Smith) *The Geometry of René Descartes*, facsimile of 1637 edition with facing English translation by D.E. Smith and M.L. Latham, New York: Dover, reprinted 1954.

— (1939 Gouhier) *Regulæ ad Directionem Ingenii*, edited with introduction by H. Gouhier, Paris: Vrin.

— (1953 Bridoux) *Œuvres et Lettres*, Pléiade, edited and translated by A. Bridoux and others, Paris: Gallimard.

— (1954 Anscombe, Geach) *Descartes: Philosophical Writings*, selected and translated by G.E.M. Anscombe and P.T. Geach, London: Nelson, revised 1970.

— (1963–73 Alquié) *Œuvres philosophiques de Descartes* (3 vols), edited and translated by F. Alquié, Paris: Garnier.

— (1968 Sutcliffe) *Discourse on Method and the Meditations*, translated with introduction by F.E. Sutcliffe, Harmondsworth: Penguin.

— (1976 Cottingham) *Conversation with Burman*, translated with introduction and notes by J. Cottingham, Oxford: Oxford University Press.

— (1977 Marion) *Règles Utiles et Claires pour la Direction de l'Esprit et la Recherche de la Verité*, French translation by J.-L. Marion, with notes on the mathematics by P. Costabel, The Hague: Martinus Nijhoff.

— (1980 Cress) *Discourse on Method and the Meditations on First Philosophy*, translated by D.A. Cress, Indianapolis: Hackett.

— (1986 Garin) *Opere filosofiche di Cartesio* (4 vols), Italian translation by E. Garin and others, directed by E. Garin, Bari-Rome: Laterza.

— (1989 Voss) *The Passions of the Soul*, translated by S.H. Voss with an introduction by G. Rodis-Lewis, Indianapolis: Hackett.

— (1998 Gaukroger) *The World and Other Writings*, translated with an introduction by S. Gaukroger, Cambridge: Cambridge University Press.

Devereux, D.T. (1992) 'The Unity of the Virtues in Plato's *Protagoras* and *Laches*', *Philosophical Review*, 101, 4: 765–89.

Devillairs, L. (1998) *Descartes, Leibniz: les vérités éternelles*, Paris: Presses Universitaires de France.

Dicker, G. (1993) *Descartes: An Analytical and Historical Introduction*, Oxford: Oxford University Press.

Dijksterhuis, E.J. (1961) *The Mechanisation of the World Picture*, translated by C. Dikshoorn, Oxford: Oxford University Press.

Diogenes of Œnoanda (1971) *The Fragments*, translated with a commentary by C.W. Chilton, Oxford: Oxford University Press.

Diogenes Laertius (see Index of primary texts).

— (1925) *Lives of the Eminent Philosophers* (2 vols), edited and translated by R.D. Hicks Loeb Classical Library, Cambridge, Mass. and London: Harvard University Press and Heinemann.

Doignon, J. (1986) 'La praxis de l'*admonitio* dans les dialogues de Cassiciacum de Saint Augustin', *Vetera Christianorum*, 23: 21–37.

Doney W. (ed. 1968) *Descartes, A Collection of Critical Essays*, London: Macmillan.

— (ed. 1987) *Eternal Truths and the Cartesian Circle*, New York: Garland.

Dretske, F. (1981) *Knowledge and the Flow of Information*, Cambridge Mass.: MIT Press.

Dummett, M. (1973) *Frege: Philosophy of Language*, London: Duckworth, 2nd edition, 1981.

Eldridge, R. (1989) *On Moral Personhood*, Chicago: Chicago University Press.

Epicurus of Samos (see Index of primary texts).

— (1887) *Epicurea*, edited by H. Usener, Leipzig: Teubner, anastatic reprint, Stuttgart: Fromann Verlag, 1966.

— (1993) *Opere*, Italian translation by M. Isnardi Parenti, Milan: Eitri Associati.

Eustace of St Paul (1609) *Summa Philosophiæ quadripartita*, reprinted Cologne 1629.

Findlay, J.N. (1974) *Plato: The Written and Unwritten Doctrines*, London: Routledge.

Finocchiaro, M.A. (1989) *The Galileo Affair*, Berkeley: California University Press.

Firth, R. (1981) 'Epistemic Merit, Intrinsic and Instrumental', *Proceedings of the American Philosophical Association*, 55: 149–56.

Fisher, P. (1999) *Wonder, the Rainbow and the Aesthetics of Rare Experiences*, Cambridge Mass.: Harvard University Press.

Flage, D.E. (1999) *Descartes and Method*, with C.A. Bonnen, London and New York: Routledge.

Fogelin, R.J. (1990) 'What Hume Actually Said About Miracles', reprinted in his *Philosophical Interpretations*, Oxford: Oxford University Press, 1992: 95–101.

Frankfurt, H.G. (1970) *Demons, Dreamers and Madmen*, Indianapolis: Bobbs-Merrill.

— (1977) 'Descartes on the Creation of the Eternal Truths', *Philosophical Review*, 86: 36–67.

— (1978) 'Descartes on the Consistency of Reason', in Hooker (ed. 1978): 26–39.

Frede, M. (1979) 'The Skeptic's Beliefs' reprinted in his (1987): 179–200.

— (1983) 'The Method of the So-Called Methodical School of Medicine', reprinted in his (1987): 261–78.

— (1984) 'The Skeptic's Two Kinds of Assent and the Question of the Possibility of Knowledge', reprinted in his (1987), 201–24.

— (1987) *Essays in Ancient Philosophy*, Oxford: Oxford University Press.

Freeland, C. (1986) 'Aristotle on Possibilities and Capacities', *Ancient Philosophy*, 6: 69–89.

Frege, G. (1923) 'Compound Thoughts', in *Logical Investigations*, edited and translated by P.T. Geach and translated by R. Stoothoff, Oxford: Basil Blackwell, 1977, 55–77.

330   Bibliography

Funkenstein, A. (1980) 'Descartes, Eternal Truth and the Divine Omnipotence', in Gaukroger (ed. 1980): 181–95.

Gadoffre, G. (1943) 'Sur la Chronologie du "Discours de la Méthode"', *Revue d'Histoire de la Philosophie et de Civilisation*, 2: 45–70.

— (1987) 'La Chronolgie des six parties', in Grimaldi (ed. 1987): 19–40.

Galilei, G. (1890–1909) *Opere di Galileo Galilei* (Edizione Nazionale, 20 vols), edited by I. de Lungo and A. Favaro, Florence: Barbera.

Gallagher, D.M. (1994) 'Free Choice and Free Judgment in Thomas Aquinas', *Archiv für Geschichte der Philosophie*, 76, 3: 247–77.

Garber, D. (1978) 'Science and Certainty in Descartes', in Hooker (ed. 1978): 114–51.

— (1986) '*Semel in vita*: the Scientific Background to Descartes' *Meditations*', in A.O. Rorty (ed. 1986): 81–116.

— (1987) 'Descartes et la Méthode en 1637', in Grimaldi (ed. 1987): 65–87.

— (1992a) *Descartes' Metaphysical Physics*, Chicago: Chicago University Press.

— (1992b) 'Descartes and Experiment in the *Discourse* and *Essays*', in Voss (ed. 1992): 288–310.

— (1995) 'J.-B. Morin and the *Second Objections*', in Ariew (ed. 1995): 63–82.

— (ed. 1998) *The Cambridge History of Seventeenth Century Philosophy* (2 vols), edited by D. Garber and M. Ayers, Cambridge: Cambridge Unversity Press.

Garin, E. (1967) *Vita e Opere di Cartesio*, Bari-Rome: Laterza, revised 2nd edition, 1986.

— see also Descartes (1986).

Gassendi, P. (1658) *Opera Omnia*, edited by H.L. Habert de Montmor, Lyons: Annisson & Devenet.

Gaukroger, S. (1980) 'Descartes' Project for Mathematical Physics', in his (ed. 1980): 97–140.

— (ed. 1980) *Descartes: Philosophy, Mathematics and Physics*, Brighton: Harvester.

— (1987) *Cartesian Logic*, Oxford: Oxford University Press.

— (1994) 'The Sources of Descartes's Procedure of Deductive Demonstration in Metaphysics and Natural Science', in Cottingham (ed. 1994): 47– 60.

— (1995) *Descartes, An Intellectual Biography*, Oxford: Oxford University Press.

Gibson, A.B. (1932) *The Philosophy of Descartes*, London: Methuen.

Gilbert, N.W. (1960) *Renaissance Concepts of Method*, New York: Columbia University Press.

Gilson, É. (1913a) *La Liberté chez Descartes et la Théologie*, presented by J.-L. Marion, Paris: Vrin, 1982.

— (1913b) *Index Scolastico-Cartésien*, Paris: Vrin, 2nd expanded edition, 1979.

— (1924) *The Philosophy of St Thomas Aquinas*, translated by E. Bullough, New York: Dorset Press, 2nd edition, 1929.

— see also Descartes (1925).

Glanvill, J. (1665) *Scepsis Scientifica*, in *Collected Works of Joseph Glanvill* (6 vols), Hildesheim: George Olms, 1970–85: III, 1–184.

Goad, C. (1993) 'Descartes and Leibniz on Innateness', *SouthWestern Philosophical Review*, 9: 77–89.

Gottlieb, P. (1991) 'Aristotle and Protagoras: the Good Human Being as the Measure of Goods', *Apeiron*, XXIV, 1: 25–45.

— (1994) 'Aristotle on Dividing the Soul and Uniting the Virtues', *Phronesis*, XXXIX, 3: 275–90.

Gouhier, H. (1924) *La Pensée Religieuse de Descartes*, Paris: Vrin, 2nd edition, 1972.

— (1962) *La Penséee Métaphysique de Descartes*, Paris: Vrin, 3rd edition, 1978.

— (1978) *Cartésienisme et Augustinisme au XVIIème siècle*, Paris: Vrin.

— see also Descartes (1939).

Grafton, A. (1990) *Forgers and Critics: Creativity and Duplicity in Western Scholarship*, Princeton N.J.: Princeton, University Press.

— (1997) *The Footnote: a Curious History*, London, Faber & Faber.

Grant, E. (1974) 'The Condemnation of 1277, God's Absolute Power and Physical Thought in the Later Middle Ages', *Viator*, 10: 211–44.

— (1981) *Much Ado About Nothing: Theories of Space and the Vacuum from the Middle Ages to the Scientific Revolution*, Cambridge: Cambridge University Press.

Greco, J. (1993) 'Virtues and Vices of Virtue Epistemology', *Canadian Journal of Philosophy*, XXIII, 3: 413–32.

Grene, M. (1985) *Descartes*, Brighton: Harvester Press.

— see also R. Ariew.

Grimaldi N. (ed. 1987) *Le Discours et sa Méthode*, edited by Grimaldi N., and J.-L. Marion, Paris: Presses Universitaires de France.

Grosholz, E.R. (1991) *Cartesian Method and the Problem of Reduction*, Oxford: Oxford University Press.

Grossi, V. (1969) 'Il Battesimo e la polemica pelagiana negli anni 411/413', *Augustinianum*, 9: 30–61.

Guenancia, P. (1998) *L'Intelligence du Sensible*, Paris: Gallimard.

Gueroult, M. (1953) *Descartes selon l'ordre des raisons* (2 vols), Paris: Aubier-Montaigne, 2nd edition, 1968.

— (1954) 'Métaphysique et physique de force chez Descartes et chez Malebranche', reprinted in his *Études sur Descartes, Spinoza, Malebranche et Leibniz*, Hildesheim: Georg Olms, 1970 (part translated in Gaukroger (ed. 1980): 196–229).

Guthrie, W.K.C. (1961–81) *A History of Greek Philosophy* (6 vols), Cambridge: Cambridge University Press.

Hackett, J. (1997) 'Roger Bacon, Aristotle, and the Parisian Condemnations of 1270, 1277', *Vivarium*, 35: 283–314.

Hacking, I. (1973) 'Proof and Eternal Truths: Descartes and Leibniz', *Proceedings of the British Academy*, LIX: 1–16, and reprinted in Gaukroger (ed. 1980): 169–80, and elsewhere.

— (1975) *The Emergence of Probability*, Cambridge: Cambridge University Press.

Hamelin, O. (1910) *Le Système de Descartes*, edited by L. Robin, Paris: Alcan, 2nd edition, 1921.

Hampshire, S. (1959) *Thought and Action*, London: Chatto & Windus.

Hankinson, R.J. (1995) *The Sceptics*, London: Routledge & Kegan Paul.

Hatfield, G. (1986) 'The Senses and the Fleshless Eye: the *Meditations* as Cognitive Exercises', in A.O. Rorty (ed. 1986): 45–79.

— (1993) 'Reason, Nature and God in Descartes', in Voss (ed. 1993): 259–87.

Heil, J. (1983) 'Believing What one Ought', *Journal of Philosophy*, 80: 752–65.

Hobbes, T. (see Index of primary texts).

— (1651) *Leviathan*, edited by R. Tuck, Cambridge: Cambridge University Press, 1991.

Hooker, M. (ed. 1978) *Descartes: Critical and Interpretive Essays*, Baltimore: Johns Hopkins University Press.

Hookway, C. (1990) *Scepticism*, London: Routledge and Kegan Paul.

Huguet, J. (1925) *Grand Dictionnaire de la Langue Française au XVIème siècle*, Paris: Champion.

Hume, D. (1739–40) *A Treatise of Human Nature*, edited by L.A. Selby Bigge (1888) revised by P.H. Nidditch, Oxford: Oxford University Press, 1978.

— (1748) *Enquiry concerning Human Understanding*, reprinted from the edition of 1777 by L.A. Selby-Bigge, 3rd edition, revised by P.A. Nidditch, Oxford: Clarendon Press, 1975.

— (1776) *Dialogues concerning Natural Religion*, edited with introduction by N. Kemp Smith, Indianapolis: Bobbs-Merrill, 1947.

Husserl, E. (1913) *Ideas* (*Ideen zu einer reinen Phänomenologie und phänomenologischen Philosophie*), translated by W.R. Boyce Gibson, London: George Allen & Unwin, 1931.

Ishiguro, H. (1986) 'The Status of Necessity and Impossibility in Descartes', in A.O. Rorty (ed. 1986): 459–71.

Isnardi Parente, M. (1993) *Lo Stoicismo Ellenistico*, Bari-Rome: Laterza.

Israel, G. (1990) 'Dalle *Regulae* alla *Géométrie*', in Belgioioso (ed. 1990): II, 441–74.

Jackson, H. (1920) 'Aristotle's Lecture-room and Lectures', *Journal of Philology*, 35: 191–200.

Jaeger, W. (1934) *Paideia* (*Formung des griechischen Menschen*) (3 vols), translated by R. Highet (2 vols), Oxford: Basil Blackwell, 1957.

James, S. (1997) *Passion and Action*, Oxford: Clarendon.

— (1998) 'Reason, the Passions and the Good Life', in Garber (ed. 1998): 1358–96.

James, W. (1907) *Pragmatism*, reprinted in *Pragmatism and the Meaning of Truth*, edited by F.T. Bowers with introduction by A.J. Ayer, Cambridge, Mass.: Harvard University Press, 1975.

Janowski, Z. (2000) *Cartesian Theodicy: Descartes' Quest for Certitude*, Dordrecht: Kluwer Academic.

Jardine, L. (1988) 'Humanistic Logic', in Schmitt (ed. 1988): 173–98.

Joachim, H.H. (1957) *Descartes's Rules for the Direction of the Mind*, edited by E.E. Harris, anastatic reprint, Bristol: Thoemmes, 1997.

Johnson, S. (1984) *The Oxford Authors: Samuel Johnson*, edited by D. Greene, Oxford: Oxford University Press.

Jolley, N. (1990) *The Light of the Soul: Theories of Ideas in Leibniz, Malebranche and Descartes*, Oxford: Oxford University Press.

Jones, H. (1989) *The Epicurean Tradition*, London: Routledge & Kegan Paul.

Joy, L.S. (1978) *Gassendi the Atomist: Advocate of History in an Age of Science*, Cambridge: Cambridge University Press.

Kambouchner, D. (1999) 'Morale des lettres et morale des *Passions*', in Armogathe (ed. 1999): 541–57.

Kant, I. (1781) *Critique of Pure Reason* (*Kritik der Reinen Vernunft*), 2nd edition (Riga: Hartnock, 1787) translated by N. Kemp Smith, London: Macmillan, 1929, corrected 1933.

Keefe, T. (1972) '*Morale Définitive* and the Autonomy of Ethics', *Romanic Review*, 26: 85–98.

Keeling, S.V. (1934) *Descartes*, Oxford: Oxford University Press, 2nd edition, 1968.

— (1937) 'Le Réalisme de Descartes et le rôle des natures simples', *Revue de Métaphysique et de Morale*: 63–99.

Kemp Smith, see Smith, N.K.

Kennington, R. (1972) 'The "Teaching of Nature" in Descartes' Soul Doctrine', *Review of Metaphysics*, XXVI: 86–117.

Kenny, A.J.P. (1968) *Descartes: a Study of his Philosophy*, New York: Random House.

— (1972) 'Descartes on the Will', in Butler (ed. 1972): 1–31, reprinted in Cottingham (ed. 1998): 132–59.

— (1973) *The Anatomy of the Soul*, Oxford: Basil Blackwell.

— see also N. Kretzmann (ed. 1982).

Kidd, I.G. (1971) 'Stoic Intermediates and the End for Man', in *Problems in Stoicism*, edited by A.A. Long, London: Athlone Press: 150–70.

Kilcullen, J. (1988) *Sincerity and Truth, Essays on Arnauld, Bayle and Toleration*, Oxford: Clarendon Press.

King, R. (1998) 'Making Things Better: the Art of Changing Things (Aristotle *Metaphysics*, Θ 2)', *Phronesis*, XLIII, 1: 63–83.

Kornblith, H. (1983) 'Justified Belief and Epistemically Responsible Action', *Philosophical Review*, 92: 33–48.

— (1985) 'Ever Since Descartes', *The Monist*, 68: 264–76.

Korolec, J.B. (1982) 'Free Will and Free Choice', in Kretzmann (ed. 1982): 629–41.

Kosman, L.A. (1986) 'The Naïve Narrator: Meditation in Descartes' *Meditations*' in A.O. Rorty (ed. 1986): 21–44.

Kraut, R. (1989) *Aristotle on the Human Good*, Princeton, N.J.: Princeton University Press.

Kretzmann N. (ed. 1982) *Cambridge History of Later Medieval Philosophy*, edited by N. Kretzmann, A.J.P. Kenny and J. Pinborg, Cambridge: Cambridge University Press.

— (1993) 'Philosophy of Mind', in Kretzmann (ed. 1993): 128–59.

— (ed. 1993), *The Cambridge Companion to Aquinas*, edited by N. Kretzmann and E. Stump, Cambridge: Cambridge University Press.

Kvanvig, J.L. (1986) 'How to be a Reliabilist', *American Philosophical Quarterly*, 23: 189–97.

— (1992) *The Intellectual Virtues and the Life of the Mind*, Lanham, Maryland: Rowman & Littlefield.

LaCroix, L.R.R. (1984) 'Descartes on God's Ability to do the Logically Impossible', *Canadian Journal of Philosophy*, 14: 455–75.

Laplace, P.-S. (1795) *Essaie philosophique des probabilités*, in *Œuvres complètes* (14 vols), Paris, 1878–1912: VII (1886).

Laporte, J. (1945) *Le Rationalisme de Descartes*, Paris: Presses Universitaires de France.

Latham, R. (1965) *Revised Medieval Latin Word-List*, Oxford: Oxford University Press.

Lear, J. (1988) *Aristotle: the Desire to Understand*, Cambridge: Cambridge University Press.

Leibniz, G.W. (1870–95) *Philosophische Schriften* (7 vols), edited by C.I. Gerhardt, Berlin.

— (1956) *Philosophical Papers and Letters*, edited and translated by L.E. Loemker Reidel, Dordrecht, 2nd edition, 1969.

— (1982) *New Essays on Human Understanding*, translated by P. Remnant and J. Bennett, Cambridge: Cambridge University Press.

Lennon, T.M. (1993) *The Battle of the Gods and the Giants*, Princeton, N.J.: Princeton University Press.

Lenoble, R. (1943) *Mersenne ou la Naissance du Méchanisme*, Paris: Vrin.

Leroy, M. (1929) *Descartes, le philosophe au masque*, Paris: Rider.

Lesses, G. (1989) 'Virtue and the Goods of Fortune in Stoic Moral Theory', *Oxford Studies in Ancient Philosophy*, VII: 95–127.

Lewis, C. (1879) *A Latin Dictionary*, edited by C. Short, Oxford: Oxford University Press, 1980.

Lewis, D.K. (1973) *Counterfactuals*, Oxford: Basil Blackwell.

Liard, L. (1882) *Descartes*, Paris: Baillière.

Lindeboom, G.A. (1978) *Descartes and Medicine*, Amsterdam: Rodopi.

Lloyd, G.E.R. (1983) *Science, Folklore and Ideology*, Cambridge: Cambridge University Press.

— (1992) 'The *Meno* and the Mysteries of Mathematics', *Phronesis*, XXXVII: 116–83.

— (1996) 'Theories and Practices of Demonstration', in his *Aristotelian Explorations*, Cambridge: Cambridge University Press: 7–37.

Locke, J. (1689) *Essay Concerning Human Understanding*, edited with an introduction by P.H. Nidditch, Oxford: Oxford University Press, 1975.

Loeb, L.E. (1981) *From Descartes to Hume*, Ithaca, N.Y.: Cornell University Press.

— (1986) 'Is there Radical Dissimulation in Descartes' *Meditations*?' in A.O. Rorty (ed. 1986): 243–70.

— (1988) 'Was Descartes Sincere in his Appeal to the Natural Light?', *Journal of the History of Philosophy*, 26: 377–406.

Lojacono, E. (1996) 'Epistémologie, méthode et procédées méthodiques dans la pensée de R. Descartes', *Nouvelles de la République des Lettres*, I: 39–106.

Long, A.A. (ed. 1987) *The Hellenistic Philosophers* (2 vols), edited, translated with commentary by A.A. Long and D.N. Sedley, Cambridge: Cambridge University Press.

Lottin, O. (1942) *Psychologie et morale aux XIIe et XIIIe siècles* (2 vols), Louvain: Abbaye du Mont César.

Loyola, St Ignatius (1534a) *Esercizi Spirituali*, edited by P. Bondioli, Spanish and Latin, with facing Italian, Milan: Vita e Pensiero, 1929.

— (1534b) *Spiritual Exercises*, translated with commentary by G.A. Longridge, London: Robert Scott, 3rd edition, 1930.

— (1534c) *Exercicios Espirituales*, edited by I. Iparraguirre, Madrid: La Editorial Católica, 1963.

Lucas, J.R. (1984) *Space, Time and Causality*, Oxford: Oxford University Press.

Lucretius (see Index of primary texts).

— (1924) *De Rerum Natura*, edited and translated by W.H.D. Rouse, revised by M.F. Smith (1975), 2nd edition, Loeb Classical Library, Cambridge, Mass. and London: Harvard University Press and Heinemann, 1982.

McClaughlin, T. (1979) 'Censorship and Defenders of the Cartesian Faith in Mid-Seventeenth France', *Journal of the History of Ideas*, 40: 563–81.

McDowell, J. (1979) 'Virtue and Reason', reprinted in Crisp (ed. 1997): 141–62.

McInerney, R. (1993) 'Ethics', in Kretzmann (ed. 1993): 196–217.

MacIntyre, A. (1981) *After Virtue*, London: Duckworth.

MacKenzie, A.W. (1994) 'The Reconfiguration of Sensory Experience', in Cottingham (ed. 1994): 251–74.

Mackie, J.L. (1977) *Ethics, Inventing Right and Wrong*, Harmondsworth: Penguin.

— (1982) *The Miracle of Theism*, Oxford: Oxford University Press.

M'Taggart, J. (1930) *Some Dogmas of Religion*, introduced by C.D. Broad, London: Edward Arnold & Co.

Madec, G. (1975) 'Analyse du *De magistro*', *Revue des études augustiniennes*, 21: 63–71.

Malcolm, N. (1956) 'Dreaming and Skepticism', reprinted in Doney (ed. 1968): 54–79.

Malebranche, N. (1680) *Traité de la Nature et de la Grâce*, in Pléiade, *Œuvres* (2 vols), edited by G. Rodis-Lewis, Paris: Gallimard, 1979: II, 3–189.

Marion, J.-L. (1974) 'Ordre et Rélation', *Archives de Philosophie*, 37: 243–74.

— (ed. 1977) *Règles Utiles et Claires pour la Direction de l'Esprit et la Recherche de la Verité* with notes on the mathematics by P. Costabel, The Hague: Martinus Nijhoff.

— (1981a) *L'Ontologie Grise de Descartes*, Paris: Vrin.

— (1981b) *Sur la Théologie Blanche de Descartes*, Paris: Presses Universitaires de France.

— (1992a) 'Generosity and Phenomenology: Remarks on Michel Henry's Interpretation of the Cartesian *Cogito*', in Voss (ed., and in this case tr., 1992): 52–74.

— (1992b) 'Cartesian Metaphysics and the Role of the Simple Natures', in Cottingham (ed. 1992): 115–39.

— (1994a) 'Le statut originairement résponsorial des *Meditationes*', in Beyssade (ed. 1994): 3–20.

— (1994b) 'Entre analogie et principe de raison: la *causa sui*', in Beyssade (ed. 1994): 305–34.

— (1995) 'The Place of the *Objections* in the Development of Cartesian Metaphysics', in Ariew (ed. 1995): 7–20 (English version of Marion (1994a).

— (1999) 'La création des vérités éternelles – le réseau d'une "question"', in Armogathe (ed. 1999): 387–407.

— see also Descartes (1977), Grimaldi (ed. 1987) and J.-M. Beyssade (ed. 1994).

Marlies, M. (1978) 'Doubt, Reason and Cartesian Therapy', in Hooker (ed. 1978): 89–113.

Marrou, H. (1938) *Saint Augustin et la fin de la culture antique*, consulted in Italian translation of 2nd edition, 1949, *S. Agostino e la fine della cultura antica*, Milan: Feltrinelli, 1987.

Maund, B. (1995) *Colours: their Nature and Representation*, Cambridge: Cambridge University Press.

Menn, S. (1998) *Descartes and Augustine*, Cambridge: Cambridge University Press.

Mersenne, M. (1932–72) *Correspondance du P. Marin Mersenne* (13 vols), edited by P. Tannery and C. de Waard, Paris: CNRS.

Micheli, G. (1990) 'Il metodo nel *Discours* e negli *Essais*', in G. Belgioioso (ed. 1990): I, 211–22.

Midgley, M. (1979) *Beast and Man*, London: Methuen.

Mill, J.S. (1843) *System of Logic*, London: Longman, 8th edition, 1911.

Montaigne, M. (see Index of primary texts).

— (1580) *Essais*, in Pléiade, *Œuvres complètes*, edited by A. Thibaudet and M. Rat, Paris: Gallimard, 1962.

Montmarquet, J.A. (1987) 'Epistemic Virtue', *Mind*, 96: 482–97.

— (1992a) 'Epistemic Virtue and Doxastic Responsibility', *American Philosophical Quarterly*, 29, 4: 331–41.

— (1992b) *Epistemic Virtue and Doxastic Responsibility*, Lanham, Mass.: Rowman & Littlefield.

Moore, G.E. (1925) 'A Defence of Common Sense', reprinted in his *Philosophical Papers*, London: Allen & Unwin, 1959: 32–59.

— (1962) *Commonplace Books 1919–1953*, edited by C. Lewy, London: Allen & Unwin.

Morgan, V.G. (1994) *Foundations of Cartesian Ethics*, Atlantic Highlands, N.J.: Humanities Press.

Moser, P.K. (1989) *Knowledge and Evidence*, Cambridge: Cambridge University Press.

Moyal, J.D.G. (ed. 1991) *Descartes: Critical Assessments* (4 vols), London: Routledge & Kegan Paul.

Newman, J.H. (1870) *Essay in Aid of a Grammar of Assent*, edited by N. Lash, Notre Dame, Indiana: University of Notre Dame Press, 1979.

Newman, L. (1999) 'The Fourth Meditation', *Philosophy and Phenomenological Research*, LIX: 559–91.

Nicole, P., see A. Arnauld.

Niemeyer, J. (1976)'s *Mediæ Latinitatis Lexicon*, with B. van de Kieft, Leiden: Brill.

Niziolius, M. (1588) *Thesaurus Ciceronianus*, Venice.

Nock, A.D. (1933) *Conversion*, Oxford: Oxford University Press.

Normore, C. (1982) 'Future Contingents', in Kretzmann (ed. 1982): 358–81.

Nozick R. (1981) *Philosophical Explanations*, Oxford: Oxford University Press.

Nussbaum, M.C. (1986) *The Fragility of Goodness*, Cambridge: Cambridge University Press.

— (1987) 'The Stoics on the Extirpation of the Passions', *Apeiron*, 20: 129–77.

— (1994) *Therapy of Desire*, Princeton, N.J.: Princeton University Press.

Ockham, see William of Ockham.

O'Connor, D.J. (1964) 'Aristotle' in his *Critical History of Western Philosophy*, edited by D.J. O'Connor, New York: Free Press: 36–61.

Ondaatje, M. (1992) *The English Patient*, London: Bloomsbury.

O'Neil, B.E. (1972) 'Cartesian Simple Natures', *Journal of the History of Philosophy*, 10: 161–79.

On-Van-Cung, K.S. (ed. 1999) *Descartes et la question du sujet*, Paris: Presses Universitaires de France.

Osler, M.J. (1993) 'Ancients, Moderns, and the History of Philosophy', in *The Rise of Modern Philosophy*, edited by T. Sorell: Oxford: Clarendon: 129–43.

— (1994) *Divine Will and the Mechanical Philosophy*, Cambridge: Cambridge University Press.

Oswald, I. (1987) 'Dreaming', in *The Oxford Companion to the Mind*, edited by R.L. Gregory, Oxford: Oxford University Press: 201–3.

Owens, D. (2000) *Reason without Freedom*, London: Routledge.

Pagès, F. (1996) *Descartes et le cannabis: pourquoi partir en Hollande*, Paris: Mille et une nuits.

Park, K. (1988) 'Organic Soul', in Schmitt (ed. 1988): 464–84.

Pascal, B. (1656) *Lettres Provinciales*, edited with introduction and notes by H.F. Stewart, Manchester: Manchester University Press, 1920.

— (1670) *Pensées*, edited L. Lafuma, Paris: Seuil, 1962.

Pears, I. (1997) *An Instance of the Fingerpost*, London: Jonathan Cape.

Peirce, C.S. (1868) 'Some Consequences of Four Incapacities', in *The Collected Papers of Charles Sanders Peirce* (6 vols), edited by C. Hartshorne and P. Weiss, Cambridge Mass.: Harvard University Press, 1931–5: V, §§ 264–317.

— (1903) *Principles of Philosophy*, in *The Collected Papers of Charles Sanders Peirce* (6 vols) edited by C. Hartshorne and P. Weiss, Cambridge Mass.: Harvard University Press, 1931–5: I, §§ 15–677.

Penelhum, T. (1983) 'Skepticism and Fideism', in Burnyeat (ed. 1983): 287–318.

Pépin, J. (1964) 'Une nouvelle source de Saint Augustine: le ζήτημα de Porphyre sur l'union de l'âme et du corps', *Revue des Études Anciennes*, 66: 53–107.

Petrik, J.M. (1992) *Descartes' Theory of the Will*, Durango, Colo.: Hollowbrooke Publishing.

Pies, E. (1996) *Il delitto Cartesio*, Italian translation of *Der Mordfall Descartes*, by M. Rubino, Palermo: Sellerio, 1999.

Plantinga, A. (1993) *Warrant and Proper Function*, Oxford: Oxford University Press.

Plato (see Index of primary texts).

Plinval, G., see G. De Plinval.

Plutarch of Chæronea (see Index of primary texts).

— (1927) *Moralia* (17 vols), Loeb Classical Library, Cambridge, Mass. and London: Harvard University Press and Heinemann.

Pohle, J. (1913) 'Pelagius', in *The Catholic Encyclopedia*, electronic English translation (1996) at http://www.csn.net/advent/cathen/11604a.htm.

Pollock, J. (1974) *Knowledge and Justification*, Princeton: Princeton University Press.

— (1987) 'Defeasible Reasoning', *Cognitive Science*, 11: 481–518.

Pope, A. (1711) *An Essay on Criticism*, in *Poems, Epistles and Satires*, introduced by E. Rhys, London: Everyman, 1924.

Popkin, R.H. (1960) *History of Scepticism* (1st edition, *From Erasmus to Descartes*, revised 1964 and 1968) expanded as *From Erasmus to Spinoza*, Berkeley: University of California Press, 1979.

Pouchet, R. (1964) *La rectitudo chez saint Anselme: un itinéraire augustinien de l'âme à Dieu*, Paris: Presses Universitaires de France.

Prior, A.N. (1965) 'The *Cogito* of Descartes and the Concept of Self-Confirmation', in his posthumous *Papers in Logic and Ethics*, edited by P.T. Geach and A.J.P. Kenny, London: Duckworth, 1976: 165–75.

Prichard, H.A. (1932) 'Duty and Ignorance of Fact', reprinted in his *Moral Obligation*, Oxford: Clarendon Press, 1949: 18–39.

Putnam, H. (1975) 'The Meaning of "Meaning"', reprinted in his *Mind, Language and Reality: Philosophical Papers*, Cambridge: Cambridge University Press, 1975: II, 215–71.

— (1977) 'Realism and Reason', *Proceedings of the American Philosophical Association*, 50: 483–98.

— (1981) *Reason, Truth and History*, Cambridge: Cambridge University Press.

Quine, W.v.O. (1936) 'Truth by convention', reprinted in *Philosophy of Mathematics:*

Selected Readings, edited by P. Benacerraf and H. Putnam, Cambridge: Cambridge University Press, 1964, 2nd edition, 1983: 329–54.

— (1951) 'Two Dogmas of Empiricism', reprinted in his *From a Logical Point of View*, Cambridge, Mass.: Harvard University Press, 1953: 20–46.

Radice, R. (1995) *Aristotle's* Metaphysics: *Annotated Bibliography of the Twentieth Century Literature*, re-elaborated and translated by R. Davies, Leiden: Brill, 1997.

Ramsey, F.P. (1926) 'Truth and Probability', reprinted in his *Foundations*, edited by D.H. Mellor, London: Routledge & Kegan Paul, 1978: 58–100.

Reale, G. (1984) *Per una nuova interpretazione di Platone*, Milan: Vita e Pensiero, 20th edition, 1997.

Rée, J. (1987) *Philosophical Tales*, London: Methuen.

Regius, H. (1646) *Fundamenta Physices*, Amsterdam: Elzevier.

Reid, T. (1785) *Essays on the Intellectual Powers of Man*, reprinted in *The Works of Thomas Reid DD*, edited by W. Hamilton, 1863, anastatic reprint, Hildesheim: Georg Olms, 1967.

Renouvier C. (1842) *Manuel de philosophie moderne*, Paris: Paulin.

Rochemonteix, C., see C. De Rochemonteix.

Rodis-Lewis, G. (1950) *Le problème de l'inconscient et le cartésianisme*, Paris: Presses Universitaires de France.

— (1951) 'Innéité cartésienne et sa critique par Lelarge de Lignac', in her (1985): 51–62.

— (1975) 'Maitrise des Passions et Sagesse chez Descartes', in *Cahiers de Royaumont*, edited by M. Gueroult and H. Goutier, *Philosophie* 11, Paris: Editions de Minuit: 208–36.

— (1982) 'Création des vérités éternelles, doute suprême et les limites de l'impossible chez Descartes', in her (1985): 119–38.

— (1985) *Idées et Vérités Éternelles chez Descartes et ses Successeurs*, Paris: Vrin.

— (1987) 'Le dernier fruit de la métaphysique cartésienne: La générosité', *Les études philosophiques*, 1: 42–4.

— (1989) 'Introduction', to *The Passions of the Soul*, edited and translated by S.H. Voss, 1989.

— (1992a) 'Descartes' Life and the Development of his Philosophy', in Cottingham (ed. 1992): 21–57.

— (1992b) 'Doute pratique, doute spéculatif chez Montaigne et Descartes', *Revue philosophique*, 1107, 117, 4: 439–49.

— (1992c) 'From Metaphysics to Physics', in Voss (ed. 1992): 242–58.

— (1995) *Descartes: biographie*, Paris: Calmann-Lévy.

Rorty, A.O. (ed. 1980) *Essays on Aristotle's Ethics*, Berkeley: University of California Press.

— (1986) 'The Structure of Descartes' *Meditations*', in her (ed. 1986): 1–20.

— (ed. 1986) *Essays on Descartes' 'Meditations'*, Berkeley: University of California Press.

Rorty, R. (1980) *Philosophy and the Mirror of Nature*, Oxford: Basil Blackwell.

— (ed. 1984) *Philosophy in History*, edited by R. Rorty, J.B. Schneewind and Q. Skinner, Cambridge: Cambridge University Press.

Rosenthal, D.M. (1986) 'Will and the Theory of Judgment', in A.O. Rorty (ed. 1986): 405–34.

Roth, L. (1937) *Descartes' 'Discourse on Method'*, Oxford: Oxford University Press.

Rovane, C. (1994) 'God without Cause', in Cottingham (ed. 1994): 89–109.

Rubidge, B. (1990) 'Descartes's *Meditations* and Devotional Meditations', *Journal of the History of Ideas*, 51: 27–49.

Ryle, G. (1949) *The Concept of Mind*, London: Hutchinson.

Sabra, A.I. (1981) *Theories of Light from Descartes to Newton*, Cambridge: Cambridge University Press.

Sawday, J. (1995) *The Body Emblazoned*, London: Routledge & Kegan Paul.

— (2000) 'Towards the Renaissance Computer', in *The Renaissance Computer*, edited by N. Rhodes, J. Sawday, London: Routledge: 29–44.

Schmaltz, T. (1991) 'Platonism and Descartes' View of Immutable Essences', *Archiv für Geschichte der Philosophie*, 73, 129–70.

Schmitt, C.B. (ed. 1988) *Cambridge History of Renaissance Philosophy*, edited by C.B. Schmitt and Q.R.D. Skinner, Cambridge: Cambridge University Press, 1988.

— see also B. Copenhaver (1992).

Schneewind, J.B. (1980) 'The Misfortunes of Virtue', reprinted in Crisp (ed. 1997): 178–200.

— see also R. Rorty (ed. 1984).

Schoockius, M. (1643) *Admiranda methodus novæ philosophiæ Renati Descartes*, edited with French translation and commentary in Verbeek (1988): 153–320.

Schouls, P. (1980) *The Imposition of Method*, Oxford: Oxford University Press.

— (1986) 'Descartes: The Primacy of Freewill', reprinted in Moyal (ed. 1991): I, 292–300.

— (1989) *Descartes and the Enlightenment*, Edinburgh: Edinburgh University Press.

Schuster, J.A. (1980) 'Descartes' *Mathesis Universalis* 1619–28', in S. Gaukroger (ed. 1980): 41–96.

Sciuto, I. (1992) *Libertà e arbitrio: Anselmo d'Aosta, De Libertate Arbitrii*, Florence: Nardini.

Scott, D. (1995) *Recollection and Experience: Plato's Theory of Learning and its Successors*, Cambridge: Cambridge University Press.

Scott, J.F. (1952) *The Scientific Work of Descartes*, London: Taylor & Francis.

Scribano, M.E. (1997) *Guida alla lettura delle* Meditazioni Metafisiche *di Descartes*, Bari-Rome: Laterza.

— (1998) *Da Descartes a Spinoza, Percorsi della teologia razionale nel Seicento*, Milan: Franco Angeli.

Sedley, D.N. (1980) 'The Protagonists', in *Doubt and Dogmatism*, edited by M. Schofield, M.F. Burnyeat and J. Barnes, Oxford: Clarendon Press, 1980, 1–19.

— (1982) 'On Signs', in *Science and Speculation*, edited by J. Barnes (et al.) Cambridge: Cambridge University Press: 239–72.

— (1983) 'The Motivation of Greek Skepticism', in Burnyeat (ed. 1983): 9–29.

— see also A.A. Long (ed. 1987).

Sellars, W. (1963) *Science, Perception and Reality*, London: Routledge & Kegan Paul.

Seneca, Lucius Annaeus. (see Index of primary texts).

— (1917–25) *Ad Lucilium epistulæ morales* (3 vols), edited and translated by R.M. Gummere, Loeb Classical Library, Cambridge, Mass. and London: Harvard University Press and Heinemann.

— (1922–7) *De la vie heureuse*, edited with French translation by A. Bourgery in *Dialogues* (4 vols), under the direction of A. Bourgery and R. Waltz, vol. II, reprinted in Paris: Collection Guillaume Budé, 1955.

— (1994) *Tutti gli scritti*, introduced by G. Reale, Italian translation and notes by A. Marastoni and M. Natali, Milan: Rusconi.

Sextus Empiricus (see Index of primary texts).

— (1933) *Works* (4 vols), edited and translated by R.G. Bury, Loeb Classical Library, Cambridge, Mass. and London: Harvard University Press and Heinemann.

— (1994) *Outlines of Pyrrhonism*, translated by J. Annas and J. Barnes, Cambridge: Cambridge University Press.

Shapin, S. (1994) *Social History of Truth: Civility and Science in 17th Century England*, Chicago: Chicago University Press.

Shea, W.R. (1991) *The Magic of Numbers and Motion: The Scientific Career of René Descartes*, Nantucket, Mass.: Watson International; edition consulted: *La magia dei numeri e del moto*, Turin: Bollati Boringhieri, 1994.

Shoemaker, S. (1970) 'Persons and their Pasts', reprinted in his *Identity, Cause and Mind*, Cambridge: Cambridge University Press, 1984: 19–48.

Sirridge, M. (1976) 'Augustine: Every Word is a Name', *The New Scholasticism*, 50: 183–92.

Sirven, J. (1930) *Les années d'apprentissage de Descartes (1596–1628)*, Paris: Vrin.

Skinner, Q.R.D., see R. Rorty (ed. 1984) and C.B. Schmitt (ed. 1988).

Smith, A.D. (1996) 'Character and Intellect in Aristotle's Ethics', *Phronesis*, XLI: 56–74.

Smith, H. (1983) 'Culpable Ignorance', *Philosophical Review*, 92: 543–71.

Smith, N.K. (1952) *New Studies in the Philosophy of Descartes*, London: Macmillan.

Sorabji, R. (1980) 'Aristotle on the Role of Intellect in Virtue', in A.O. Rorty (ed. 1980): 201–19.

— (1996) *Animal Minds and Human Morality*, London: Duckworth.

Sorell, T. (1987) *Descartes*, Oxford: Oxford University Press.

— (ed. 1993) *The Rise of Modern Philosophy*, Oxford: Clarendon Press.

— see also R. Ariew (ed. 1998).

Sosa, E. (1991) *Knowledge in Perspective: Collected Essays in Epistemology*, Cambridge: Cambridge University Press.

— (1993) 'Proper Functionalism and Virtue Epistemology', *Noûs*, 27, 1: 51–65.

Spade, P.V. (1982) 'The Semantics of Terms', in Kretzmann (ed. 1982): 182–96.

Spallanzani, M. (1990) *Immagini di Descartes nell'Encyclopédie*, Bologna: Il Mulino.

— (1999) '"La vita ritirata"del filosofo: Le lettere di Descartes a Guez de Balzac e a Elisabetta di Boemia', in Armogathe (ed. 1999): 457–92.

Spinoza, B. (1663) *Renati des Cartes principiorum philosophiæ*, Amsterdam.

— (1926) *Tractatus de Intellectus Emendatione*, in *Opera* (4 vols), edited by C. Gebhart, Heidelberg: Winter.

Stephens, J. (1975) *Francis Bacon and the Style of Science*, Chicago: Chicago University Press.

Stevenson, J.T. (1975) 'On Doxastic Responsibility', in Lehrer (ed.) *Analysis and Metaphysics*, Dordrecht: Reidel, 1975: 229–53.

Stone, J. (1993) 'Cogito ergo Sum', *Journal of Philosophy*, XC: 462–8.

Striker, G. (1980) 'Sceptical Strategies', reprinted in her (1996): 92–115.

— (1983) 'The ten tropes of Ænesidemus', reprinted in her (1996): 116–34.

— (1990) 'Ataraxia: Happiness as Tranquillity', reprinted in her (1996): 183–95.

— (1996) *Essays on Hellenistic Epistemology and Ethics*, Cambridge: Cambridge University Press.

Stroud, B. (1984) *The Significance of Philosophical Scepticism*, Oxford: Oxford University Press.

Stump, E., see N. Kretzmann (ed. 1993).

Taylor, C. (1981) *The Ethics of Responsibility*, Cambridge, Mass.: Harvard University Press.

Tempier, É. (1277a) '*Opiniones ducentæ undeviginti* [. . .] *condemnatæ*', in *Chartularium Univesitatis Parisiensis* (4 vols), edited by H. Denifle and A. Chatelain, Paris: Delalain, 1889–97: I, 543–61.

— (1277b) '*Condemnatio*', in P. Mandonnet, *Siger de Brabant et l'averroïsme latin au XIIIe siècle*, Louvain, 1908: 175–91.

— (1277c) 'Condemnation of 219 Propositions', translated in A. Hyman and J.J. Walsh, *Philosophy in the Middle Ages*, Indianapolis: Hackett, 2nd edition, 1983: 584–91.

Thomson, A. (1972) 'Ignace de Loyola et Descartes', *Archives de Philosophie*, XXXV: 61–84.

Tierno, J.T. (1997) *Descartes on God and Human Error*, Atlantic Heights, N.J.: Humanities Press International.

Tillmann, A. (1976) *L'Itinéraire du jeune Descartes*, Paris: Honoré Champion.

Tosi, R. (1991) *Dizionario delle sentenze greche e latine*, Milan: Rizzoli.

Trianosky, G. (1987) 'Virtue, Action and the Good Life: Towards a Theory of the Virtues', *Pacific Philosophical Quarterly*, 68: 127–47.

Unger P. (1975) *Ignorance: a Case for Scepticism*, Oxford: Oxford University Press.

Van Cleve, J. (1979) 'Foundationalism and Epistemic Principles and the Cartesian Circle', reprinted in Cottingham (ed. 1998): 101–31.

Verbeek, T. (1988) *La Querelle d'Utrecht*, Paris: Vrin.

— (1992) *Descartes and the Dutch: Early Reactions to Cartesian Philosophy, 1637–1650*, Carbondale, Ill.: Southern Illinois University Press.

— (1993) 'Tradition and Novelty: Descartes and some Cartesians', in Sorell (ed. 1993): 167–96.

Vernier, P. (1976) 'Thomas Reid on the Foundations of Knowledge and his Answer to Skepticism', in *Thomas Reid: Critical Interpretations*, edited by S. Barker and T. Beauchamp, Philadelphia: Philosophical Monographs: 14–24.

Vickers, B. (1968) *Francis Bacon and Renaissance Prose*, Cambridge: Cambridge University Press.

Vieillard-Baron, J.-L. (1992) 'L'image de l'Homme chez Descartes et chez le Cardinal de Bérulle', *Revue Philosophique*, 1107, 117, 4: 403–19.

Violi, A. (1998) *Le cicatrici del testo*, Bergamo: Bergamo University Press.

Von Wright, G.H. (1963) *The Varieties of Goodness*, anastatic reprint, Bristol: Thoemmes, 1998.

Voss, S. (ed. 1992) *Essays on the Philosophy and Science of René Descartes*, Oxford: Oxford University Press.

— see also Descartes (1989).

Vossius, G.J. (1618) *Historiæ de Controversiis quas Pelagius ejusque reliquiæ moverunt*, expanded 1655, in *Opera* (6 vols), Amsterdam: P. and J. Blaeu, 1701: VI, 541–830.

Wallace, J.D. (1978) *Virtues and Vices*, Ithaca, N.Y.: Cornell University Press.

Waterlow Broadie, S. (1982) *Nature, Change and Agency in Aristotle's* Physics, Oxford: Clarendon Press.

— (1991) *Ethics with Aristotle*, Oxford: Oxford University Press.

Watson, G. (1990) 'The Primacy of Character', reprinted in D. Statman (ed.), *Virtue Ethics*, Edinburgh: Edinburgh University Press, 1997: 56–81.

Weber, J.-P. (1964) *La Constitution du Texte des 'Regulae'*, Paris: Sedes.

White, N.P. (1990) 'Stoic Values', *The Monist*, 73, 1: 42–58.

Wieland, W. (1962) 'The Problem of Teleology', translated in Barnes (ed. 1975): I, 141–60.

William of Ockham (1957) *Philosophical Writings*, selected and translated by P. Boehner, Indianapolis: Bobbs-Merrill.

Williams, B. (1955) 'Tertullian's Paradox', in *New Essays in Philosophical Theology*, edited by A. Flew and A. MacIntyre, London: SCM Press: 187–211.

— (1970) 'Deciding to Believe', reprinted in his *Problems of the Self*, Cambridge: Cambridge University Press, 1973: 136–50.

— (1978) *Descartes: The Project of Pure Enquiry*, Harmondsworth: Penguin.

— (1983) 'Descartes's Use of Skepticism', in Burnyeat (ed. 1983): 337–53.

Williams, M. (1986) 'Descartes and the Metaphysics of Doubt', in A.O. Rorty (ed. 1986): 117–39.

Wilson, M.D. (1978) *Descartes*, London: Routledge & Kegan Paul.

— (1993) 'Descartes on the Perception of Primary Qualities', in S. Voss (ed. 1993), 162–76.

Wippel, J. (1977) 'The Condemnations of 1270 and 1277 at Paris', *Journal of Medieval and Renaissance Studies*, 7: 160–201.

Woerther, B. (1847) 'Pélagienisme', in *Dictionnaire Encyclopédique de la Théologie Catholique*, originally edited as *Kirchen Lexicon* by Wetzer and Welte, French translation by I. Goschler, Paris, 1863: XVII, 508–23.

Woodruff, P. (1988) 'Aporetic Pyrrhonism', *Oxford Studies in Ancient Philosophy*: VI, 139–68.

Woolhouse, R. (1993) *Descartes, Spinoza, Leibniz: The Concept of Substance in Seventeenth Century Metaphysics*, London: Routledge.

Yolton, J.W. (1956) *Locke and the Way of Ideas*, Oxford: Oxford University Press.

Zagzebski, L.T. (1996) *Virtues of the Mind*, Cambridge: Cambridge University Press.

Index of primary texts

for publication details see Bibliography

General Index

for Descartes and his correspondents, see Index of primary texts